The Tarzan Novels of Edgar Rice Burroughs

The Tarzan Novels of Edgar Rice Burroughs

An Illustrated Reader's Guide

by

DAVID A. ULLERY

McFarland & Company, Inc., Publishers
Jefferson, North Carolina, and London

Acknowledgments. This book would not have been possible without the help and support of Danton Burroughs and Sandra Galfas of Edgar Rice Burroughs, Inc. To them I give my utmost thanks. I would also like to thank George T. McWhorter for his advice and a listening ear — he might never know how much our short and infrequent conversations helped. Also, thanks go out to Orson Scott Card and his wife Kristine for helping me keep things in perspective.

Without the support of my wife, Margie, however, this guide book could never have been finished.

But, most of all, I have my parents to blame for encouraging me to read in the first place. Thank you.

FIRST EDITION, *first printing*

Library of Congress Cataloguing-in-Publication Data
Ullery, David A., 1964–
    The Tarzan novels of Edgar Rice Burroughs : an illustrated reader's guide / by David A. Ullery.
        p.   cm.
    Includes index.
    ISBN 0-7864-0825-1 (softcover : 50# alkaline paper) ∞
    1. Burroughs, Edgar Rice, 1875–1950 — Characters — Tarzan.
    2. Burroughs, Edgar Rice, 1875–1950 — Handbooks, manuals, etc.
    3. Adventure stories, American — History and criticism.   4. Tarzan (Fictitious character)   5. Africa — In literature.   I. Title.
    PS3503.U687Z93   2001   813'.52 — dc21   00-49554

British Library cataloguing data are available

Manufactured in the United States of America

McFarland & Company, Inc., Publishers
  Box 611, Jefferson, North Carolina 28640
  www.mcfarlandpub.com

Table of Contents

Abbreviations Used

Introduction

"I'm bored," I whined in my eleven-year-old voice. "There's nothing to do here at Grandma's."

"Well, we're not going home just yet," my mother returned, "so why don't you get a book to read from one of Grandma's bookcases."

"Those are all adult books without pictures."

"They are still good books," she replied, slightly irritated. "I've read many of them myself."

We'd had this discussion before, and not wanting to go through it again I dragged myself over to the bookshelves, making sure my reluctance showed. Lazily I began looking over the many titles of the old red, green, blue and beige hardbound books. I did this mainly to appease my mother so she would stop suggesting reading when I was bored at my grandmother's. I knew it was just a way for her to get me to do something educational during summer vacation. Reading during the summer — of all the ideas! Summer was for playing outside. But today it was raining, and what was a boy to do? At least the next time we had this argument I would be able to say that I had looked for a book but did not find any to my liking. That would give me the edge over my mother.

As I continued scanning titles I found mostly westerns, and even though I liked cowboy movies I was not in the mood to read about the West that day. Besides, how could a book be as good as a TV show or movie? My adolescent mind demanded instant stimulation. I needed pictures to spur my imagination into action. But the books I skimmed through had nary a one. Absently, I continued my search.

Then a name I recognized flashed before my eye and I came to an immediate halt. What was that? I looked again and there on the slightly weathered

Roy G. Krenkel illustration from *Tarzan and the Tarzan Twins* (© 1963 Edgar Rice Burroughs, Inc.).

spine of a pale khaki green hardback I read the title *Tarzan of the Apes*. I stared in disbelief.

Tarzan? Not *the* Tarzan. No. Tarzan is not a book. It could not be the same Tarzan I had watched swinging almost naked through the trees on television every week. Nor could it be the same monkey-loving ape-man I watched at the Saturday matinees with my dad, fighting evil men and savage animals with only his cunning and Herculean strength. Neither could it be the Tarzan who leaped out of the comic books my dad brought home to me. No, it just wasn't possible. My frail old grandmother did not read Tarzan books. This had to be some other character named Tarzan that was not like the Tarzan I knew and loved. Still... Just to be certain I decided to check it out.

Removing the slightly soiled tome from the shelf, I opened the cover and flipped through the pages. Aha! I knew it. I didn't see a picture anywhere. It couldn't be Tarzan, because he would need the visual medium of drawings to make his story complete and do it justice, and thereby render it worth reading. But, wait... What was that near the beginning? Okay, so there was a picture — a simple black silhouette of a man in a tree who... No. It couldn't be. The image looked Tarzan-esque. But why weren't there more pictures? How could Tarzan, a man of action, be properly represented in mere words? Okay, maybe it was Tarzan, but just a weak imitation, and not the real Tarzan of the movies and comics. How adults could enjoy black print on white paper was beyond me. I felt sorry for them — I really did. I hoped I never lost my ability to enjoy the visual arts when I got older.

I looked down again at the book in my hand. It just had to be about a different character named Tarzan. It had to. But, still, I needed to find out for sure. So I asked my mom.

"Is this book about the same Tarzan from the movies and comics?"

"Yes, it is."

"I mean the Tarzan with the leather swimsuit-thing who kills lions?"

"Yes, dear."

"Are you sure?"

"As a matter of fact that book is where they got the ideas for the movies and comics."

What! No. I stared skeptically at the book before me, and I knew I was down to my last test of authenticity: reading.

Apprehensively I opened to the chapter titles and scanned down the list. "The White Ape." That looked promising. Turning to that chapter, I tentatively began to read.

Immediately images began forming in my brain. I saw the great apes. I smelled the jungle. I felt the heat. And then I saw Tarzan. He looked better than he did in the movies and comics or on the television. He actually became more real. Unbelievable! What was happening to me? How was this possible? These were only black words on a dull page. Incredible. How long were adults going to keep this beautiful secret from children like me? Scandalized, I read on. And shortly, through the magical medium of print, I no longer was a spectator. I was taken in. I *became* Tarzan.

From that moment on I was a Tarzan connoisseur. This naturally led me through the Earth's crust to Pellucidar; then across the cold abyss of space to Barsoom; and on to Amtor and all points in between. In other words, I became an Edgar Rice Burroughs fanatic. Yet Tarzan was always my favorite hero. And having blazed through every Burroughs book I could get my hands on, I forgot specific characters and story lines as they got mixed in and confused with each other. How I longed for a Tarzan reference or guide book to quickly bring things back to my remembrance and help sort things out. At last it is finally here.

As my title says, this is a reader's guide to the Tarzan novels. All references and interpretations of Tarzan from movies, television, comics, radio and so on have been left out. Instead I have attempted to give a thorough yet concise description of all the characters, languages, peoples, and places in the Tarzan series as close to Burroughs' own as possible without interpolating my (or others') opinions. A good example is Section One which deals with a sensitive issue — a description of Tarzan. Every person who knows of Tarzan has created in his or her own mind an image of the Jungle Lord. Understanding this, I made every effort to present only Burroughs' description of the Apeman as found in his own works. Consequently, most of Section One consists of quotes taken directly from the books. The only possible outside influence in this guide is from author Joe R. Lansdale, who completed and fleshed out Burroughs' unfinished work, *Tarzan: The Lost Adventure*.

The illustrations were also taken from the various printings of the Tarzan books to keep things in a historical setting.

Besides the 24 standard books in the Tarzan series and Mr. Lansdale's completed *Tarzan: The Lost Adventure*, I have also included *The Eternal Savage (Lover)*. Even though this book is not a Tarzan novel per se it does have John Clayton (Tarzan), Jane, Esmeralda, and Jack. It was written between *The Return of Tarzan* and *The Beasts of Tarzan* and presented a very nonaggressive Tarzan in an almost cameo appearance that was at best frustrating, for this reader at least. Regardless, I still enjoyed the story and felt it was important to include it in this guide.

I have also included the out of print *Tarzan and the Tarzan Twins* which contains two sequential Tarzan stories written for adolescents. This again I felt necessary to include because they were stories written by Edgar Rice Burroughs about Tarzan.

There is also a quote taken from the *Tarzan Clans of America* as well as the Dictionary of the Ape Language that Edgar Rice Burroughs compiled. This aided me in weeding out terms that are not found in the original works — terms which have come from other sources.

A word about names and how they are listed in this guide: In Section Four, "Cast of Characters," I list the entire roster of Tarzan characters (human and otherwise) alphabetically by last name, if a last name is available — "Porter, Jane" under P, for example. I realize, however, that this could present problems if a reader cannot remember a character's last name (often mentioned only once in a story) or if the reader remembers nothing except what book the character appeared in.

To help readers in such circumstances, Section Five, "Book Summaries," includes a cast list for each book. In these lists the characters are alphabetized by *first* name, uninverted ("Jane Porter" under J). That way, anyone who remembers only a first name or a book title can locate the character in the cast list (Section Five), then turn to Section Four for a complete character description.

Each reference in Section Four begins with the name in boldfaced type. Next, a translation of the name (if possible) is placed in quotes. Then a brief description of the character is given or a list of some events that took place involving the character. At the end, the titles of the books the character was in are listed. For example:

> **Go-lat:** "Black-nose." An older king of a tribe of Mangani that Tarzan wished to gain peaceful acceptance into. At first Go-lat attacked the Ape-man, but Tarzan forced the old king to say "kagoda" by tossing him to the ground several times. Afterwards Tarzan was accepted into the tribe. *Tarzan the Untamed*

Enjoy!

A Brief Biography of Edgar Rice Burroughs

September 1, 1875, was the day Edgar Rice Burroughs was born into the world in Chicago, Illinois. He grew up the youngest child with three brothers and no sisters. From the first he was creative with a quick sense of humor that he put onto paper as soon as he learned how. Whether it was writing poetry or fiction or drawing illustrations and cartoons Ed had an insatiable desire to express his imagination.

Leaving the dreary life of public and private education at the age of fifteen Ed was sent to Idaho by his father to help at a ranch with two of his brothers. There he was able to experience rugged country life and see real cowboys and miners. After a year of this his father called him back to schooling. Ed eventually entered Michigan Military Academy, but finding the regimented life there much against his liking, he deserted. After a little consideration, however, he returned and became an excellent horseman in the cavalry and also made the football team. He then became an editor for an academy newsletter and his grades improved. While there Ed rose to the rank of a cadet officer and looked forward to a career as a commissioned officer in the regular army. When he entered the army he was assigned to Fort Grant in Arizona.

A miserable experience in Arizona caused Ed to go back to Chicago to be with his family. While contemplating another career choice he became dissatisfied and restless again. Wishing to express his creativity and fulfill his lust for adventure he headed back to Idaho where he bought a store. But the store venture turned out to be unprofitable and he returned to Chicago where he married his childhood sweetheart Emma Hulbert on January 31, 1900.

He also began working for his father. But the ever restless Edgar Burroughs soon left to work with his brothers in Idaho. This time at gold mining. After their company went bankrupt Ed took a job as a low paid railroad policeman in Salt Lake City, Utah. Unable to make ends meet there, he returned to Chicago to be with his family. After numerous small jobs that dissatisfied him or were failures, his creative restlessness finally erupted and Ed wrote *Under the Moons of Mars* (*A Princess of Mars*) in 1911 on the backs of old letterheads. It sold, and Edgar Rice Burroughs decided to make writing his career.

His third book was *Tarzan of the Apes* and it was an instant success. Ed then gave his imagination free reign and turned out stories at an amazing rate. While continuing his Mars series, his mind took him into still other worlds and lands, spinning tales of fantastic adventure. These included inside the Earth to the primeval savage land of Pellucidar, then Venus, the Moon, and beyond. Ed also returned to the Tarzan story with the idea of only one sequel. But the public demanded more, and Ed delivered. Tarzan became his most successful character, spawning movies, comics, radio shows, and imitators. The stories were published in several languages, including braille, and received worldwide recognition. Tarzan became a household name.

Ed and his family moved to California and bought 550 acres of land outside Los Angeles which they dubbed Tarzana. He later sold some of the land for development, and Tarzana ultimately received its own zip code and city status. With the success of the Tarzan movies Ed created his own movie production company to obtain more creative control of his main character on the silver screen. He even started his own book publishing company. After having three children Ed divorced Emma and remarried. In the 1940's he became a war correspondent and lived in Hawaii. At the end of the war he moved back to California to relax and be with friends and family. He died there in 1950.

After the passing of Edgar Rice Burroughs several unpublished manuscripts were found in his safe by family members. These have been published, to the glee of Burroughs enthusiasts worldwide. And his following of fans continues to grow from generation to generation.

SECTION ONE

Portrait of Tarzan

Anyone who has ever read a book about a specific hero or heroine creates in their mind's eye what they think the character looks like, as they do with the supporting characters. Often the reader imagines that they are the hero, or they give the character a bit of themselves. Either way the reader is usually affected in an emotional and personal way. At least that is the hope of the author. With Tarzan it is no different. Readers create an image of the Jungle Lord that is an interpretation of the words used to describe the Apeman by the author. The author in this case is Edgar Rice Burroughs. Book cover paintings, interior illustrations, comic book and comic strip renditions, movie actors, and cartoon versions of Tarzan are all other people's interpretations. Some of these the reader may agree with more than others. Yet, these renditions often add to the image of Tarzan the reader creates for themselves. They may even compose an amalgam of their favorite versions coupled with their own interpretation. Regardless, their image would still be unique.

In other words, for every reader there is a different image of Tarzan.

With this in mind, Section One will not attempt to present any facts or information about Tarzan other than that which Burroughs had a hand in writing himself. Therefore much of this section will be in the form of direct quotes taken from the Tarzan series.

Tarzan: The Man, the Myth, the Legend

Tarzan was born in his marooned parents' cabin somewhere in the coastal jungles of West Africa and named John Clayton after his father. He was an

Charles Vess illustration from *Tarzan: The Lost Adventure* (© 1995 Edgar Rice Burroughs, Inc.).

English lord by birthright and heir to the Greystoke estate. At the age of one, immediately after both parents had died, he was taken by a female great ape named Kala and raised as one of the tribe. There he was given the name of Tarzan which means "white skin" in the ape language. Young Tarzan grew in strength and stature and achieved supremacy in the jungle and over all animals including his original tribe of apes.

Physically, Tarzan had a deep dark bronzed tan that often made him appear Negroid in coloration. He was almost perfectly built with extremely handsome features and great musculature. His muscles were often compared to steel cords, but "not as the muscles of the blacksmith or the professional strong man were the muscles of Tarzan of the Apes, but rather as those of Mercury or Apollo, so symmetrically balanced were their proportions, suggesting only the great strength that lay in them. Trained to speed and agility were they as well as to strength, and thus, clothing as they did his giant frame, they imparted ... the appearance of a demi-god" (TGL). Tarzan had steel gray eyes and a "mass of black hair falling to his shoulders behind and cut with his hunting knife to a rude bang upon his forehead, that it might not fall before his eyes.... A personification, was Tarzan of the Apes, of the primitive man, the hunter, the warrior. With the noble poise of his handsome head upon those broad shoulders, and the fire of life and intelligence in those fine, clear eyes" (TA).

His bearing is often compared to that of a lion in majesty, power, and grace. When Prince Alexis Sborov witnessed Tarzan confronting a lion he noted that the Jungle Lord "was really not of gigantic proportions, yet he conveyed the impression of great size. Perhaps it was the suggestion of power and majesty in his mien that gave him the appearance of towering over other creatures. He stood, perhaps, a couple of inches over six feet; rounded muscles flowed smoothly beneath clear, bronzed skin; his proportions were as perfect for his kind as were those of the great lion he faced. It occurred to Sborov that these two were very much alike, and he began to be as afraid of the man as of the other beast" (TQ).

Tarzan's agility and quickness were legendary, because "from earliest childhood his muscles had been trained by the fierce exigencies of his existence to act with the rapidity of thought" (RT). In comparison, "quick was Sabor, the lioness, and quick were Numa and Sheeta, but Tarzan of the Apes was lightning" (TA). And "when he did move his quickness would have put Ara, the lightning, to shame" (TU). With all this going for him it is easy to understand why "it is no disgrace to fall beneath the superhuman strength of Tarzan of the Apes" (RT).

Although a swift and tireless runner the ground was not the only place that the Ape-man could travel quickly. Through the branches of the trees, whether the higher, lower, or middle terraces, Tarzan could travel even faster than on the ground. "From early childhood he had used his hands to swing from branch to branch after the manner of his giant mother, and as he grew older he spent hour upon hour daily speeding through the tree tops with his brothers and sisters.... He could spring twenty feet across space at the dizzy heights of the forest top, and grasp with unerring precision, and without apparent jar, a limb waving wildly in the path of an approaching tornado.... He could drop twenty feet at a stretch from limb to limb in rapid descent to the ground, or he could gain the utmost pinnacle of the loftiest tropical giant with the ease and swiftness of a squirrel" (TA). The trees were Tarzan's home and it was there that he usually slept for the night. Whether he were fitted snugly in the crotch of a jungle giant or curled up on a handmade platform, the Lord of the Jungle preferred to sleep amid the safety of the trees rather than the risks of the ground.

The Ape-man's only physical flaw was the battle scar across his forehead which "starting above his left eye ran across the top of his head, ending at the right ear. It was the mark left by Terkoz when he had torn the scalp away" (TA). This scar is the only telltale physical distinguishing mark that helps determine Tarzan's identity from an impostor. It is usually only visible when the Jungle Lord is angry: the blood rushes to his head causing the scar to stand out in a crimson or scarlet band. As Flora Hawkes, a former maid of the Greystokes, fearfully observed, "I have heard the story of that scar, and I have seen it burn scarlet when he was aroused to anger. It is scarlet now, and Tarzan of the Apes is angry" (TGL).

For apparel Tarzan usually wore a G-string made of doe or leopard skin, because "clothes he abhorred — uncomfortable, hideous, confining things that reminded him somehow of bonds securing him to the life he had seen the poor creatures of London and Paris living. Clothes were the emblems of that hypocrisy for which civilization stood — a pretense that the wearers were ashamed of what the clothes covered, of the human form made in the semblance of God" (TU). Occasionally, Tarzan also wore a leopard skin over his shoulder, and a head band.

As for his other accouterments, "the hunting knife of his father hung at his left hip, his bow and his quiver of arrows were slung across his shoulders, while around his chest over one shoulder and beneath the opposite arm was coiled the long grass rope without which Tarzan would have felt quite as naked as would you should you be suddenly thrust upon a busy highway clad only in a union suit. A heavy war spear which he sometimes carried in one hand and again slung by a thong about his neck so that it hung down his back completed his armament and his apparel" (TU). Tarzan often also wore the diamond studded locket of his long dead mother, Lady Alice. After giving it to Jane as a token of affection the locket was taken from her by the Germans and used as a sign to get information for the spy Bertha Kircher. Tarzan recovered the locket and began wearing it again even after being reunited with Jane. It is another way to identify the real Tarzan.

When hunting no one could hear, see, and smell as well as the Ape-man or move as silently, because "he moved ... with the stealth and quietness of a panther. Apparently he took no cognizance of where he stepped, yet never a loose stone was disturbed nor a twig broken — it was as though his feet saw" (TU). This is only possible because "Tarzan of the Apes had been forced in childhood to develop senses that an ordinary mortal scarce ever uses.... Nor was Tarzan dependent alone upon his sense of smell. Vision and hearing had been brought to a marvelous state of development by the necessities of his early life, where survival itself depended almost daily upon the exercise of the keenest vigilance and the constant use of all his faculties"

(TJO). And when Tarzan awoke or was awakened he was in full possession of all these senses.

Though he was raised by animals Tarzan had human intelligence; an attribute that placed him above his brother animals and gave him the advantage over them that saved his life on more than one occasion. He was self educated in reading and writing English from the school primers that his parents had in their cabin. Growing up Tarzan never knew of his origin or of the fact that he was of another species, but after reading the primers and other books he began to learn the truth. Then the Ape-man desired the companionship of his own kind and wanted to learn more about them and himself. He did not see another human being, however, until his teenage years, and these were African natives. A few years after that, Tarzan finally met members of his own race. He fell in love with Jane Porter who was part of the first group of white people he had encountered and the first white woman he had ever seen.

Once Tarzan began learning to speak English and French through his new and rescued friend, Lt. Paul d'Arnot, he left the jungle and went with d'Arnot into society and civilization. While in Europe the Jungle Lord took every opportunity to read, study and learn as much as he could. "In the daytime he haunted the libraries and picture galleries. He had become an omnivorous reader, and the world of possibilities that were opened to him in this seat of culture and learning fairly appalled him when he contemplated the very infinitesimal crumb of the sum total of human knowledge that a single individual might hope to acquire even after a lifetime of research; but he learned what he could by day and threw himself into a search for relaxation and amusement at night" (RT). The Lord of the Jungle also became well versed in the art of sword play which he was again taught by d'Arnot who himself was "recognized as one of the cleverest swordsmen in the service and to his friend Greystoke he had imparted a great measure of his skill during the many hours that the two had whiled away with foils ... and to [Tarzan's] skill was added his great strength and his agility" (TAM). Despite all this education and civilizing, Tarzan states, "Let me see red in anger but for a moment, and all the instincts of the savage beast that I really am, submerge what little I possess of the milder ways of culture and refinement" (RT).

One of the things Tarzan, unfortunately, also learned was that men were worse than the beasts of the jungle; "civilized man is more brutal than the brutes" (RT), and "in the bottom of his savage heart he held in contempt both civilization and its representatives — the men and women of the civilized countries of the world. Always was he comparing their weaknesses, their vices, their hypocrisies, and their little vanities with the open, primitive ways of his ferocious jungle mates, and all the while there battled in that same big heart with these forces another mighty force — Tarzan's love and loyalty for his friends of the civilized world" (TU). Because "gratitude and loyalty were marked characteristics of the ape-man" (TGL). Therefore, "no one who is honorable need ever be afraid of Tarzan" (TFC). Because "inherent in his English brain and heart was the spirit of fair play, which prompted him to spontaneous espousal of the cause of the weak" (TGL).

The conflict within him between the freedom of the jungle and civilization was constant, for Tarzan's "civilization was at best but an outward veneer which he gladly peeled off with his uncomfortable European clothes whenever any reasonable pretext presented itself. It was a woman's love which kept Tarzan even to the semblance of civilization — a condition for which familiarity had bred contempt. He hated the shams and the hypocrisies of it and with the clear vision of an unspoiled mind he had penetrated to the rotten core of the heart of the thing — the cowardly greed for peace and ease and the safeguarding of property rights. That the fine things of life — art, music and literature — had thriven upon such enervating ideals he strenuously denied, insisting, rather, that they had endured in spite of civilization" (TJO). And "civilization meant to Tarzan of the Apes a curtailment of freedom in all its aspects — freedom of action, freedom of thought, freedom of love, freedom of hate" (TU). And he notes, "It is a silly world, an idiotic world, and Tarzan of the Apes was a fool to renounce the freedom and the happiness of his jungle to come into it" (RT).

When Tarzan first came in contact with civilization and its many vices, however, he partook; and "if he smoked too many cigarettes and drank too much absinthe it was because he took civilization as he found it, and did the things that he found his civilized brothers doing" (RT). The Lord of the Jungle later gave up smoking as he proclaimed, "I do not smoke" (TLM), because he lacked one of the excuses that civilized people often give for smoking: "My nerves are never tired," he said (TLM). Tarzan also despised cooked meat — feeling that it ruined the taste. Instead the Ape-man preferred eating his meat fresh and raw. When he did so "he squatted on his haunches and tore at his portion with his strong, white teeth" (LM). Incidentally, Bara, the deer, and Pacco, the zebra, are the two meats Tarzan loves the most. However, "if Tarzan of the Apes had any weakness whatsoever it was for an occasional cup of black coffee late at night" (TGL). This supposed weakness became his undoing when he was given a drugged cup of coffee by his former maid, Flora Hawkes, in *Tarzan and the Golden Lion*. On a moral and mental note, "among the numerous refinements of civilization that Tarzan had failed to acquire was that of profanity" (TTT).

Tarzan also learned of the power of money in the civilized world. But material wealth never meant much to the Jungle Lord who had all that he needed in his well-trained physical body that responded to his every wish along with his instincts and highly developed senses. In the jungle that is all that is required. Even though the Ape-man, himself, did not need money in the wild he did need it to survive in society and to provide for his wife and family the comforts they desired. Luckily, for him wealth was just a lost city away in the forgotten treasure vaults of mysterious Opar.

When Tarzan traveled through the jungle he preferred to do so alone and enjoyed being by himself, because, as he explained, "That is always my way. Alone I may travel much more rapidly and when I am alone the jungle holds no secrets from me — I ... obtain more information along the way than would be possible were I accompanied by others.... [The] jungle people consider me as one of themselves. They do not run away from me as they would from ... any other man" (TLE). Tarzan enjoyed being alone, or at least apart from humans, because he "thought of many animals as friends, but few men" (TM). This loner attitude came because "the ape-man, reared as he had been by savage beasts amid savage beasts, was slow to make friends. Acquaintances he numbered by the hundreds; but of friends he had few. These few he would have died for as, doubtless, they would have died for him" (TU).

One of Tarzan's oldest and greatest friends was Tantor, the elephant. Even strange elephants Tarzan considered friends, because "almost as old as Tarzan was the friendship of Tarzan and Tantor. Perhaps he had never seen ... [a particular] elephant before; but still, to Tarzan, he would be Tantor — the name and the friendship belonged to all elephants" (TM). Tarzan often tried to make friends with different tribes of Mangani during his travels. Unfortunately, this meant that he had to fight the king or other bulls of the tribe to prove himself worthy and be accepted. When he did fight he usually attempted to do so without having to kill the challenger. To achieve this Tarzan fought until he gained an advantage and asked if the challenging ape would surrender by saying "Kagoda" in the ape language. If the challenger surrendered and no others opposed him then the Ape-man was accepted into the tribe. Tarzan's other more frequent animal friends included the boastful cowardly monkey named Nkima, and Jad-bal-ja, the Golden Lion.

Nkima often accompanied Tarzan on his journeys perched safely upon his great master's shoulder, and, if necessary, would scamper away to get the Waziri to come help Tarzan. Jad-bal-ja usually roamed about the jungle alone, but often came to Tarzan's rescue. Besides these and the various Mangani Tarzan's other animal friends were Sheeta, the Terrible, from Jungle Island in *The Beasts of Tarzan*, and the great black lion named Numa of the Pit from *Tarzan the Untamed*. There was also a monkey named Keta that Tarzan made friends with in Japanese-held Sumatra in the Dutch East Indies in the book *Tarzan and the Foreign Legion*. Then in *The Eternal Savage (Lover)* it was revealed that Tarzan had a wolfhound named Terkoz. Otherwise, "toward all other animals, the crocodile alone excepted, Tarzan could have respect — but for Dango, the Hyena, he could have only contempt" (TC). Yet, "nothing in the jungle inspired within the breast of Tarzan so near a semblance to fear as did the hideous Histah" (JTT).

In the jungle they "kill for food and for self-preservation, or in the winning of mates and the protection of the young" (RT), or "when there is no other way to thwart an enemy" (TI). "Tarzan had never killed for 'pleasure,' nor to him was there pleasure in killing. It was the joy of righteous battle that he loved — the ecstasy of victory. And the keen and successful hunt for food in which he pitted his skill and craftiness against the skill and craftiness of another" (RT). Yet, "Tarzan had learned from experience that there is no surer way of reducing a man to subservience than by shaking him. Perhaps he knew nothing of the psychology of the truth, but he knew the truth" (TC). And "when Tarzan killed he more often smiled than scowled, and smiles are the foundation of beauty" (TA).

The Lord of the Jungle "seldom if ever laughed aloud," (TAM) but "Tarzan of the Apes enjoyed a joke" (TA), and he did have "his own grim and grisly sense of humor" (TLJ). This sense of humor the Ape-man developed as a youth "for Tarzan was a man-thing and sought amusement and adventure and such humor as the grim and terrible jungle offers to those who know it and do not fear it — a weird humor shot with blazing eyes and dappled with the crimson of lifeblood. While others sought only food and love, Tarzan of the Apes sought food and joy" (JTT).

As a youth Tarzan often pondered religion and deity while studying in his biological parents' cabin, because it was there that he was first introduced to the concept of God. The story *The God of Tarzan*, the fourth in *Jungle Tales of Tarzan*, takes on the young Ape-man's personal search for the Supreme Being. *Bulamutumumo* is how the young Tarzan pronounced the English written word God in the language of the Mangani, and as an inquisitive youth Tarzan attempted to understand what, or who, this god was that he read about. At one point he was told by an old Mangani in his tribe that Goro, the moon, was God, and Tarzan went to investigate. He called aloud to Goro, but received no reply. He then challenged Goro, and again, there was no response. Disappointed, but not discouraged, his investigation led to the native village of Mbonga where he confronted their witch doctor. This attempt also failed to give a satisfying answer, but by the end of the story and after what seemed to be a fruitless search, Tarzan found God even though he did not learn what God was or what He looked like. However,

Tarzan was "sure that everything that was good came from God ... and he spent the whole day in attributing to Him all of the good and beautiful things of nature" (JTT).

Joined closely with religious belief is the power of life and death that constantly surrounded Tarzan his entire existence. Yet, Tarzan did not fear death, because he knew it was inevitable and he believed that "we must die sometime. What difference whether it be tonight, tomorrow night, or a year hence, just so that we have lived — and I have lived!" (TU). And "we can die but once ... and that once we must die. To be always fearing, then, would not avert it, and would make life miserable" (TGL). But he never gave up his fight for survival. His attitude always was, "While there is life, ... there is hope" (TU).

In *Tarzan at the Earth's Core* when the Jungle Lord was literally face to face with death at the fangs and talons of a *tarag,* "he felt no fear, but a certain sense of anticipation of what would follow after death. The Lord of the Jungle subscribed to no creed. Tarzan of the Apes was not a church man; yet like the majority of those who have always lived close to nature he was, in a sense, intensely religious. His intimate knowledge of the stupendous forces of nature, of her wonders and her miracles had impressed him with the fact that their ultimate origin lay far beyond the conception of the finite mind of man, and thus incalculably remote from the farthest bounds of science. When

Hanlon illustration for *Jungle Tales of Tarzan* (© 1919 Edgar Reese Burroughs, Inc.).

he thought of God he liked to think of Him primitively, as a personal God. And while he realized that he knew nothing of such matters, he liked to believe that after death he would live again" (TEC). Despite this belief in God and the hereafter Tarzan believed firmly in self and individual prowess that came from training and experience. Divine intervention was not something to count on in the jungle, especially if it is based on false gods. This caused Tarzan to declare, "I need no gods" (TFC).

Hand in hand with this association of religion and life and death was the search for perpetual youth in the Tarzan books — the opportunity to cheat death. This theme is used several times in the series and adds to the mythic life of Tarzan of the Apes who acquired this status. Obtaining or creating this power of immortality, however, usually meant the death of someone or some animal. In *Tarzan and the Lion Man* a lost civilization was discovered in the Valley of Diamonds whose citizens were English speaking gorillas. Their leader, God, was a physically transformed human scientist who had discovered how to live forever by taking certain cells from the bodies of humans and gorillas and implanting them in his own body. The method of doing this involved eating the donor's flesh and glands. Tarzan, however, did not partake.

In *Tarzan's Quest* the Kavuru warriors discovered the secret of never aging and of maintaining their youth and put it in an elixir pill. Their leader, Kavandavanda, who was the high priest of the priests of the Kavuru, as well as their god, was the scientific inventor of this eternal youth elixir pill. In the end Tarzan and Jane, along with a few others including Nkima, were able to obtain a supply of these pills. Then, in *Tarzan and the Foreign Legion*, the Ape-man related a separate experience that happened to him when he was younger. The Jungle Lord explained that he had saved the life of a witch doctor who had discovered the secret of perpetual youth. In gratitude the witch doctor offered Tarzan this same ability. The Ape-man accepted and went through the lengthy treatment that included, among other things, a blood transfusion. These two things gave Tarzan an immortal quality that only adds to his myth and legend and to his demi-god status.

By living as long as he did, Tarzan became known throughout the jungles and deserts of Africa by most tribes of natives and among almost all tribes of Mangani. The Jungle Lord also made his presence known on two islands (Uxmal and Jungle Island) as well as Sumatra, and somewhat in Europe and America. He also went inside the Earth to the primal, savage land of Pellucidar. All this traveling about naturally led Tarzan to learn many languages. Some are currently known to modern man, but others are only native to the lost lands and civilizations that Tarzan came across. These include the languages of Pal-ul-don, the Minuni, Cathne and Athne, Pellucidar, the Alalus body language, as well as the dead language of Latin.

The Mangani tongue was the first language that he learned to speak which "all creatures of the jungle understand to a greater or lesser extent" (TI). This caused people to believe that he could talk to all animals much like Dr. Doolittle. This is simply not true (see Section Two: Languages of Tarzan for more information), but this false perception adds to Tarzan's mythic abilities. Yet, despite knowing all these languages, Tarzan "spoke only when conversation seemed necessary, and that, in reality was seldom" (TEC), because "all his life [he] had been accounted taciturn" (TLE). When Tarzan did speak and ask questions his "voice was low and deep. It questioned, but it also commanded…. It was the well-modulated assured voice of a man who was always obeyed" (TM).

Natives, as well as any poacher, slave raider, or despoiler of the jungle, knew of Tarzan and feared him and his wrath, because "all who know the jungle, know Tarzan," and "the word of Tarzan is the law of the jungle" (TLJ). Many of the natives feared him because of their superstitious belief that Tarzan was a demon, devil, evil spirit or some other being with supernatural powers, and "he has the same hold upon their imaginations and superstitions as any of their demons, and they are even more fearful of incurring his displeasure" (TLJ). All wrong-doers feared the punishment the Ape-man's far reaching arm would inflict upon them in retribution for any wrong that they did to blacks, whites, or animals not killed for food, because, as Tarzan told some Arab slavers, "the arms of the ape-man are long — they may reach out even in death and their fingers encircle your throat" (TLJ).

Others looked to Tarzan to assist them in some way to solve some problem or find a missing person. People simply felt safe with Tarzan in their company and on their side, because he instilled trust and confidence in others. Jane felt this upon their first meeting: "With him near, who could entertain fear? She wondered if there was another man on earth with whom a girl could feel so safe in the heart of this savage African jungle. Even the lions and panthers had no fears for her…" (TA). And Stanley Wood, a rare friend of Tarzan's, observed when he was with the Ape-man, "I had no sense of responsibility at all, not even for my own welfare. I just took it for granted that he'd look after everything" (TM).

Tarzan eventually married Jane Porter and together they had a son named Jack. The couple spent most of the next several years in Europe trying to put the jungle and Tarzan's primitive past behind them. Jane also attempted to keep their son from the knowledge of her husband's birth and childhood, but to no avail. Jack ended up having a jungle experience of his own and became known as Korak, the Killer, in the language of the Mangani. Korak married the French Princess, Jeanne Jacot, who he at first only knew as Merriem, the abused Arab girl. Together they had at least one son which they also named Jack. This would make Tarzan a grandfather, but because of his and Jane's longevity and eternal youth from the Kavuru elixir pills, and Tarzan's blood transfusion from the witch doctor, neither of them appeared physically aged. As mentioned earlier Tarzan did not care for civilization, and so he and Jane eventually began splitting their time between Europe and their African estate, which they did for many years.

At the end of *Tarzan: The Lost Adventure* the Ape-man is trapped in the underground tunnels of the lost city of Ur. Unable to return to the surface world he turned his feet, without a backward glance, down a tunnel that he believed led to the prehistoric, untamed inner world of Pellucidar. Because of his feelings about civilization and the encroaching and industrious humans that were destroying and taking over the last of his jungles, Pellucidar may have been a fitting place for the Jungle Lord to live out the remainder of his days. It was probably the only place left in the world — literally, *in* the world — where Tarzan could live the life he loved. "This looks like heaven to me" (TEC), he stated as his eyes first took in the primeval and lush land at the Earth's core. Because "Tarzan had thought that there was no world like his own world and no jungle like his own, but the more deeply he dipped into the wonders of Pellucidar the more enamored he became of this savage, primitive world, teeming with the wild life he loved best. That there were few men was Pellucidar's chiefest recommendation. Had there been none the ape-man might have considered this the land of ultimate perfection, for who is there more conversant with the cruelty and inconsideration of man than the savage beasts of the jungle?" (TEC)

To think that Tarzan would be gone from the surface world forever is a sad ending indeed. What about his wife, Jane? What about Korak and Tarzan's grandson Jackie? What about all his human friends from both civilized lands and lost lands? What about his animal friends? What will society do without such a man as Tarzan who has so many desirable qualities and attributes people can pattern their lives after? Is all hope lost? No. Emphatically, no. Pellucidar has polar openings that may be accessed, and there is the iron mole that can breach the Earth's crust and return Tarzan to the surface. With the help of David Innes, Emperor I of Pellucidar, perhaps an excavating committee might be organized that could clear the tunnels below Ur and make a permanent hidden passageway between the two worlds. Then Tarzan could always have access to both. The Gridley Wave is also available and could be used to contact the surface and ask for a return flight of the O-220 dirigible or some other craft. So it may still be possible to meet the legendary Tarzan of the Apes, Lord of the Jungle.

Yet, if Tarzan be indeed gone from the surface in physical form, he is not gone in the minds and imagination of all those who have read about

Gary Gianni illustration for *Tarzan: the Lost Adventure* (© 1995 Edgar Rice Burroughs, Inc.).

him through Edgar Rice Burroughs' pen or seen his image on movie and television screens, book covers, and within the pages of the comics. With all these, Tarzan will truly live forever.

Tarzan by Any Other Name

The Lord of the Jungle was raised with an identity crisis. At birth, he was John Clayton by name; an English viscount, Lord Greystoke, by title. At the age of one he was taken and raised by apes and given the descriptive name of Tarzan which is interpreted as "white skin." While growing up young Tarzan discovered that he was not an ape, but something more. Upon encountering other humans such as natives Tarzan was unable to speak to them so they gave him names of their own making such as River Devil or Munan-go-Keewati. After finally meeting members of his own race Tarzan was faced again with a language barrier — he could only communicate with them in written messages. This only muddled things more and caused the Porter party to think that they were involved with two different people: one named Tarzan, and another they believed to be a savage mute. In civilization things got worse. After rejecting his birthright and title Tarzan needed a name to get along in society that was more than just Tarzan. Thus he became Jean C. Tarzan. Then, in his first job, he became an agent for the Ministry of War — an occupation which throve upon aliases and secret identities. With the beginning he had, coupled with all his traveling and discovering of lost societies and riches, Tarzan's life was destined to be full of mistaken identities, impersonators, multiple titles and various names. Listed here are the known majority.

Alalus: The Minuni of both Veltopismaskus and Trohanadalmakus at first mistook Tarzan for one of the large barbaric female-dominated Alalus humans found within the valley who they call Zertalacolols. *Tarzan and the Ant Men*

Aopontando: The Minuni (Ant Men) word for the number 800^3+21. Which was the slave number given to Tarzan after he was captured by the warriors of the city Veltopismakus and shrunken to their size by the walmak (wizard), Zoanthrohago. The num-
eral was placed on the shoulder of the standard issue tunic worn by all first generation slaves. Tarzan was then sent to work in the quarries where he at first pretended not to speak their language. Out of necessity he was called by this number or by the term Zuanthrol, which interpreted means giant. In the Minunian hieroglyphics, Zuanthrol is written as shown at the right. *Tarzan and the Ant Men*

Ape-man: Since Tarzan was raised by apes and talked and occasionally acted like one around other humans he was often referred to as an ape-man.

Big Bwana: (Big Lord) Used by the Waziri and most natives that knew of Tarzan.

bumude-mutomuro: See **he-boy.**

Brian Gregory: Tarzan was mistaken for this missing brother of Helen Gregory by Magra, a beautiful consort of Atan Thome, who thought that she loved Brian. When she saw how strong, brave, and fearless the Ape-man was she realized that he was not Brian Gregory, and fell in love with Tarzan. *Tarzan and the Forbidden City*

Bwana: (Swahili for Lord) A common title given to Tarzan by most natives. It was also used by Meriem after overhearing the Waziri address him thus when she was first rescued by the Jungle Lord.

Che, Lord Forest: When Tarzan was shipwrecked upon the lost Mayan island of Uxmal he saved a hunter, Thak Chan, from a lion. The man had never seen a lion before. And he had never seen a man like Tarzan either, and naturally thought the Jungle Lord was one of his gods known as Che, Lord Forest. Thak Chan's faith that Tarzan was this god was strengthened after he saw him talking and associating with orangutans who Thak Chan took to be other gods. Later, when Tarzan was captured by the Mayans while attempting to rescue Patricia Leigh-Burdon, he was put through a water test that consisted of having to stay afloat in a pool of water in a volcano crater for a whole morning without drowning. The Lord of the Jungle passed the test and proved to the people that he was a god. To further impress them with his godliness Tarzan called Tantor, the elephant, to him for a ride back to his camp. The Mayan people were indeed impressed for they had never seen an elephant before. *Tarzan and the Castaways*

Clayton: The name Tarzan gave for himself to the American travel writer, Stanley Wood, in order to keep his anonymity. Wood remarked, however, that the man Clayton reminded him of the character Tarzan. The truth was later revealed to Wood. *Tarzan the Magnificent*

Colonel John Clayton of the Royal Air Force: What Tarzan was called aboard an American B-24 bomber named *Lovely Lady* during a reconnaissance mission to photograph Japanese-held Sumatra of Netherland East Indies. The crew finally figured out that he was Tarzan after witnessing his wood craft and prowess while traveling through the jungle. *Tarzan and the Foreign Legion*

Daimon: The name of a bad spirit that Tarzan pretended to be while searching around Athne, the City of Ivory. Daimon was believed to roam around at night looking for someone to kill. The people of Athne attribute all unexplained deaths to Daimon, especially those that occurred at night. When Tarzan was seen sneaking around at night by a citizen of Athne he claimed to be Daimon so the person would leave him alone and not raise an alarm. The ruse worked. *Tarzan the Magnificent*

Deliverer of the Son of Adendrohahkis: One of the many titles and names the grateful Minuni of Trohanadalmakus gave to Tarzan for rescuing their prince, Komodoflorensal, from an Alalus woman. *Tarzan and the Ant Men*

Demi-god: A common description people gave to Tarzan when they saw this naked Apollonian bronzed giant come out of the jungle.

Devil-god: The name affixed to him by several tribes including the Bantango cannibals in *Tarzan the Magnificent*. It was first attached to him by the village of Mbonga and the witch doctor Bukawai.

Dor-ul-Otho: Means "Son of god" in the language of Pal-ul-don. Pretending to be this deity Tarzan used the name to gain entrance to the city of A-lur while searching for Jane. The fanatically religious Pal-ul-donians believed him to be the Dor-ul-Otho because he fit many of the descriptions of their god Jad-ben-Otho. The primary physical characteristic being that Tarzan was tailless. *Tarzan the Terrible*

Eight Hundred Cubed Plus Twenty-one: See **Aopontando**

Esteban Miranda: The most successful Tarzan look-a-like. Miranda was a very well built Spanish actor who stood six feet three inches tall and looked remarkably like Tarzan. Esteban was recruited by Flora Hawkes to impersonate Tarzan, and help her and some henchmen steal gold from the lost city of Opar. Esteban got into his role, and all who encountered him believed him to be the real Tarzan (both humans and animals alike), but were surprised by his unusual cruelty. Esteban even fooled the Waziri and Jane, and eventually started to believe that he really was the Jungle Lord. *Tarzan and the Golden Lion* and *Tarzan and the Ant Men*

Forest God: The tribe of Mbonga called Tarzan the Munan-go-Keewati, or forest god. *Tarzan of the Apes*

Forest Man: This is what Jane dubbed Tarzan after first meeting him, and before she learned what his name was. *Tarzan of the Apes*

The Giant: In the language of the Minuni the term for giant is Zuanthrol. This name was given to Tarzan by the warriors of Veltopismakus after he fought against them on the side of the Trohanadalmakus warriors. The Ape-man was known by this name even after he was shrunken to a quarter of his size, which is the normal size of the Minunians, by Zoanthrohago, the walmak of Veltopismakus. *Tarzan and the Ant Men*

Giant of the Forest: One of the many names the grateful Minuni people of Trohanadalmakus gave to Tarzan after he was accepted into their society for rescuing their prince, Komodoflorensal, from an Alalus woman. *Tarzan and the Ant Men*

God: Tarzan was never called God. But in one instance, that name was given to a man who thought he was Tarzan — Colin T. Randolph, Jr., of West Virginia. In *Tarzan and the Madman*, King Cristoforo da Gamma of the lost city of Alemtejo, and his high priest, Pedro Ruiz, claimed Randolph as their people's deity, and called him God. When the real Tarzan finally arrived in Alemtejo, he took Randolf's place and pretended to be God. For more information see "2. God" in Section Four. *Tarzan and the Madman*

Gomangani with his skin off: A description given by Gozan, a fellow bull-Mangani in the tribe of Kerchak. Gozan wanted Tarzan killed and tried to turn others against him with this sarcastic and descriptive appellation. *Jungle Tales of Tarzan*

Great Sheykh of the Jungle: Name given to Tarzan by the young Arab Zeyd. *Tarzan, Lord of the Jungle*.

Greater than Walumbe: Walumbe is the term for god, or god of death, in a native dialect. In *Tarzan and the Lion Man*, Tarzan proclaimed himself greater than Walumbe to Rungula the chief of the Bansuto as they prepared to torture the Tarzan look-alike actor Stanley Obroski. Rungula believed Walumbe could duplicate himself in Tarzan and Obroski, and in fear promised to do whatever Tarzan asked. *Tarzan and the Lion Man*

Guest of the King: One of the many titles and names the grateful Minuni people of Trohanadalmakus gave to Tarzan for rescuing their prince, Komodoflorensal, from an Alalus female. *Tarzan and the Ant Men*

he-boy: After learning to read English from the books in his parents' cabin the young Tarzan put together the English words that he felt best described himself. The result was *he-boy*. Tarzan then translated this into the Mangani language and came up with the word bumude-mutomuro. *Jungle Tales of Tarzan*

Jad-guru-don: "The-terrible-man" in the language of Pal-ul-don. The Wazdon in the city of Kor-ul-ja called Tarzan this after he cut off the tail of one of their warriors in a fight. Once they learned his name they called him Tarzan-jad-guru or Tarzan-the-terrible. *Tarzan the Terrible*

Jean C. Tarzan: The French name Tarzan used while traveling in civilization before he acknowledged his birthright as John Clayton, Lord Greystoke. *The Return of Tarzan*

John Caldwell, London: An alias Tarzan used when he left Algiers to go back to Europe while working for the Ministry of War. He was using this name when he met Jane's best friend Hazel Strong. *The Return of Tarzan*

Jungle Lord: See **Lord of the Jungle**

Kavuru: The Kavuru were white men who dressed somewhat like native African warriors. When Tarzan entered the Bukena village that was near the Kavuru country the villagers mistook him for a Kavuru warrior. *Tarzan's Quest*

King of all the apes: Tarzan declared himself king of all the apes after besting Mal-gash, the king of the apes of Ho-den, near Alemtejo while Ungo and his tribe of apes looked on. *Tarzan and the Madman*

King of the apes: After Tarzan killed Kerchak he became the king of his home tribe. He also became the king of other Mangani tribes. *Tarzan of the Apes*

Lion-Man: Although often compared to a lion in bearing, majesty, strength, bravery, growling, and eating in *Tarzan the Invincible* Zora Drinov, not knowing Tarzan's name, called him her "Lion-Man" to herself. In *Tarzan and the Lion Man* the Jungle Lord pretended to be the slain actor Stanley Obroski who looked like Tarzan, and who up until his death, was playing the Tarzanesque role in the *Lion Man* motion picture being filmed on location in Africa. The cast was fooled and believed him to be the late Stanley Obroski. *Tarzan and the Lion Man*

Lord Greystoke: The title Tarzan was born with as an English viscount.

Lord of the Jungle: He earned this title through his intelligence, prowess, and cunning, but the irony of it is that he was an English lord who reigned supreme in the jungle. Also the title of Lord Tarzan was given to him in the Valley of the Sepulcher in *Tarzan, Lord of the Jungle.*

Lord Passmore: An alias taken by Tarzan when he and his Waziri fronted as a big game hunter and his safari, while the Jungle Lord really investigated rumors of a cruel band of *shiftas* led by a white man. *Tarzan Triumphant*

Lord Tarzan: The Ape-man's title in the lost medieval Valley of the Holy Sepulcher when they learned that he was an English viscount. *Tarzan, Lord of the Jungle*

The Man: Numa, the lion, used this term to distinguish Tarzan of the

Roy G. Krenkel iillustration from *Tarzan and the Tarzan Twins* (© 1963 Edgar Rice Burroughs, Inc.).

Apes from other humans. *Tarzan and the Tarzan Twins*

Monkey man: Tarzan was called this by many people either in jest or insult, but especially by the hired guide and hunter named Wolff of the Gregory safari. Wolff used this derogatorily because he had a personal grudge against Tarzan. *Tarzan and the Forbidden City*

Munan-go-Keewati: The name given to Tarzan by the cannibal tribe of Mbonga. It primarily means forest god, but also devil, demon, and river god. *Tarzan of the Apes*

Muzimo: The name and title given to an amnesiac Tarzan by Orando, the son of Lobongo, the chief of the Tumbai. *Muzimo* is Swahili for a protecting guardian spirit of a deceased ancestor, and Orando thought that Tarzan was the spirit of the dead

ancestor who he was named after. Having lost his memory Tarzan accepted and believed that he was Orando's *muzimo* and played out the role until his memory returned. *Tarzan and the Leopard Men*

River Devil: The Obebe natives thought Tarzan was a river devil who could change from a man to a crocodile. *Tarzan and the Ant Men*

Savior of the Prince: One of the many titles and names the grateful Minuni people of Trohanadalmakus gave to Tarzan for rescuing their prince, Komodoflorensal, from an Alalus female. *Tarzan and the Ant Men*

Stanley Obroski: The name of the leading man in the *Lion Man* motion picture that was to be shot on location in Africa. Obroski was a muscular world champion marathoner who looked very much like Tarzan, and when the other members of the cast and crew saw the real Tarzan they mistook him for Obroski. Tarzan rescued Obroski from some cannibals, but eventually Obroski contracted a fever and died. Tarzan then went to the filmmakers, and, not revealing his true identity to them, finished shooting the picture as Stanley Obroski. *Tarzan and the Lion Man*

Tarzan-jad-guru: "Tarzan the terrible" in the language of Pal-ul-don. Given to Tarzan when he cut off the tail of one of the attacking Waz-don warriors of Kor-ul-ja. The name stuck when the people saw what a fierce fighter he was. *Tarzan the Terrible*

Tarzan of the Apes: The name Tarzan means "white-skin" in the language of the Mangani. It was given to the one-year-old Tarmangani Balu (white-great ape-baby), John Clayton, by Kala, the bereaved she-ape of the Mangani tribe of Kerchak, after she took him from his deceased parents' cabin to raise as her own. *Tarzan of the Apes*

Tarzan, son of Kala: The name Tarzan used to introduce himself to Tibo, the black native boy, who he had kidnapped from the village of Mbonga to raise as his own. *Jungle Tales of Tarzan*

The True God: In the lost Portuguese city of Alemtejo Tarzan helped overthrow the throne by claiming to be the true god after a man who thought he was Tarzan was accepted as their god. The Jungle Lord proved the veracity of his claim by already having single-handedly subdued a maddened water buffalo in front of several citizens and the Captain-General, Osorio da Serra. Da Serra encouraged the Jungle Lord to continue his charade and assist him in the usurpation. Tarzan did so. *Tarzan and the Madman*

Viscount: As Lord Greystoke, Tarzan's rank in the English peerage. He re-

vealed this to the questioning sentries at the giant cross before the tunnel entrance into the Valley of the Sepulcher. Thereafter they called him Lord Tarzan. *Tarzan, Lord of the Jungle*

War Chief of the Waziri: When Tarzan was unanimously made the chief of the Waziri after their old chief, Waziri, died the Jungle Lord accepted. He later opted to only be their war chief and have Muviro, who was the hereditary chief, run things while he was away. *The Return of Tarzan*

Waziri: Tradition mandated that Tarzan take on this name when he first became the chief of the Waziri after the death of the elder Chief Waziri. *The Return of Tarzan*

White god of the jungle: Given to Tarzan by the tribe of Mbonga. To scare their children into obedience, native parents said he ate little boys. They also thought he was a shapechanger because of a trick he pulled on the village with a lion skin. Many natives felt that his medicine and magic were stronger than their witch doctors. *Jungle Tales of Tarzan*

Wild man: A descriptive label used by many people who encountered this almost naked individual who armed himself like a native man, but acted like an anthropoid ape.

Zertalacolol: The Minuni of both Veltopismaskus and Trohanadalmakus at first mistook Tarzan for one of the large barbaric female-dominated Alalus humans found within the valley who they called Zertalacolols. *Tarzan and the Ant Men*

Zertol: This is the term for prince in the language of the Minuni. Adendrohahkis, the King of the city Trohanadalmakus, made Tarzan a Zertol for saving his son, Komodoflorensal, the blood prince. *Tarzan and the Ant Men*

Zuanthrol: Means "the giant" in the

language of the Minuni. When Tarzan was overcome and captured by the warriors of the city of Veltopismakus he was shrunken to a quarter of his size (which is the size of the Minuni) by the wizard, Zoanthrohago. Thereafter Tarzan pretended not to speak and the people gave him the name of Zuanthrol even though he was now their size. *Tarzan and the Ant Men*

Tarzan's Many Lovers

The Jungle Lord made it easy for women to admire him and be attracted to him. His strength and confidence alone drew people to trust him without question. But those qualities coupled with his intellect and perfectly sculpted physique make quite a package. On top of that, Tarzan was endowed with godlike good looks and a primitive savage nature that only added to his allure. With the fact that he was English nobility and wealthy thrown in, it would be hard to visualize a more perfect catch. He even had a sense of humor. With all this it is no wonder that women found him fascinating. And, as can be imagined, Tarzan easily made men jealous.

While Tarzan attracted many women, not all desired him for a mate. Some admired him simply for the fine specimen of a man that he was. But those who did want the Lord of the Jungle for a mate or lover, especially those Tarzan was attracted to in return, are the women talked about here.

Balza: Means Golden Girl in the Mangani language. In the English-speaking gorilla lost city of London, on the Thames, Balza was born of genetically altered gorillas as a beautiful blonde human with some tendencies toward gorilla behavior. Because of her human appearance she was an outcast and had to join the tribe of half-breeds that lived in the jungles outside the city. There she became the mate of their king, Malb'yat, who was a human male on the outside, but was completely gorilla mentally and instinctually on the inside. When Tarzan arrived and bested Malb'yat Balza felt that she belonged to the Jungle Lord. Fortunately, Tarzan was able to leave her with the motion picture company that was filming a Tarzanesque movie nearby. Balza went back to Hollywood with them and became a star. *Tarzan and the Lion Man*

Bertha Kircher: Tarzan admired this beautiful German spy for her courage, prowess, and intellect even though he despised her for her heritage. Tarzan constantly struggled with his feelings for Bertha and saved her on different occasions. Fräulein Kircher herself became very attracted to Tarzan, but felt a relationship between them was hopeless because of what she knew he thought of her. Bertha even helped save Tarzan's life. At one point while traveling together the Jungle Lord could not deny his protective feelings for Bertha, and went so far as to hold her hand as they escaped the maniac city Xuja. Bertha hoped Tarzan would change his feelings for her, but he could not. After they were safe and Fräulein Kircher was sent away on a plane Tarzan found out that she was a double agent working for the English against the Germans. It was also then that he found out that Jane might still be alive. *Tarzan the Untamed*

Hazel Strong: The best friend of Jane Porter. When Tarzan first saw Jane in his cabin he took and read a note that she had written to Hazel. Later, after Jane left to marry Tarzan's cousin, William Cecil Clayton, Tarzan worked for the Ministry of War and took a boat to Cape Town under the name of John Caldwell of London. He met Hazel Strong on the voyage, and she developed a fond admiration for Mr. Caldwell. Tarzan was later thrown overboard by Alexis Paulvitch and Nikolas Rokoff. Hazel then fell in love with Lord Tennington who took her on a cruise in his yacht. Tennington and Hazel were married with Tarzan and Jane in a double ceremony performed by Jane's father next to Tarzan's parents' cabin. *The Return of Tarzan*

Itzl Cha: A young virgin maiden who was to be sacrificed in the Mayan city of Chichen Itza on the lost island of Uxmal. Tarzan saved Itzl Cha from this religious death at the hands of her high priest and took her on an elephant back to his camp of shipwrecked castaways. In camp, Itzl Cha was put under Patricia Leigh-Burden's care. She taught Tarzan and Patricia the Mayan language, and in turn learned to speak English. The young maiden's association with Tarzan caused her to fall in love with the Jungle Lord, and when she realized that Patricia was also in love

with him, Itzl Cha became jealous. This jealousy caused her to run away from camp and return to Chichen Itza to warn the high priest that Tarzan was coming to rescue Patricia who had earlier been taken prisoner. *Tarzan and the Castaways*

Jane Porter: Named after her mother, Jane was the beautiful daughter of Professor Archimedes Q. Porter of Maryland. She was the first white female ever seen by the Jungle Lord, and he immediately had a "strange longing [for her] which he scarcely understood" (TA). After the Apeman rescued Jane from a lioness and then a bull-mangani, they fell in love with each other. Tarzan eventually followed Jane to America to claim her as his own. But he decided that their union would be hopeless, did not press his suit, and left her.

Fate brought them together again near Tarzan's cabin some time later, when she was finally honest with herself and proclaimed her love for Tarzan to her fiancé William Cecil Clayton, Tarzan's cousin, and broke off their engagement. After so doing she was immediately taken captive to Opar to be offered as a sacrifice to the Flaming God. Tarzan arrived in time to save her from the sacrificial knife of La, High Priestess of Opar, who also desired him. Free and with Jane once again in the jungle Tarzan "took the girl he loved in his strong arms, and kissed her not once but a hundred times, until she lay there panting for breath; yet when he stopped she put her arms about his neck and drew his lips down to hers once more" (RT). The Ape-man and Jane were married by her father next to Tarzan's parents' cabin and graves. It was Tarzan's love for Jane that kept any semblance of civilization in him. Jane's beauty caused her to be

Roy G. Krenkel illustration from *Tarzan and the Tarzan Twins* (©1963 Edgar Rice Burroughs, Inc.).

abducted and desired by many men, but she remained faithful to Tarzan. Together they had a son named Jack, who later became Korak, the Killer. *Tarzan of the Apes*

Janzara: The beautiful, yet spoiled, daughter of King Elkomoelhago of the Minuni city Veltopismakus. Janzara was attracted to Tarzan, and as was the custom of the Minuni, she chose him to be her mate and become a prince even though he was a slave. She then tried to seduce him in her apartments, but Tarzan spurned her. In her rage she tried to kill him. He survived and in a turn of events she helped him escape with the aid of Zoanthrohago, a prince that loved Janzara. She ended up returning Zoanthrohago's love. *Tarzan and the Ant Men*

La of Opar: The beautiful High Priestess of Opar who spoke the language of the Mangani. La fell hopelessly in love with Tarzan. He was the most beautiful and worthy man she had ever seen, especially compared to the half-breed brutes who were the males and priests of her society and who she was supposed to mate with. Tarzan defiled the temple and the altar of the Flaming God several times by not only escaping on his own, but by taking other sacrifices away as well. This made him worthy of death without question, and La struggled within herself about Tarzan because of her religious duties. She was willing to forsake all, however, and run off with him if he would return her love. She did eventually give up her throne and all that she knew in *Tarzan and the Golden Lion*. Together they escaped Opar and went through a back pass that led to the Valley of the Palace of Diamonds. There, Tarzan called her his mate, to make the Gomangani in the

valley understand that she was under his protection and care and not to be harmed, under threat of his punishment.

Tarzan wrestled with his feelings for La. Not only was she beautiful but she was more on his savage level than Jane, who he loved.

> Tarzan extended a bronzed hand and laid it upon her slender, tapering fingers. "You have always possessed my heart, La," he said, "up to the point of love. If my affection goes no further than this, it is through no fault of mine nor yours."
>
> La laughed. "It is certainly through no fault of mine, Tarzan," she said, "but I know that such things are not ordered by ourselves. Love is a gift of the gods. Sometimes it is awarded as a recompense; sometimes as a punishment. For me it has been a punishment, perhaps, but I would not have it otherwise. I had nurtured it in my breast since first I met you; and without that love, no matter how hopeless it may be, I should not care to live." (TI)

Tarzan always supported La and returned her to Opar and reinstated her to her throne when necessary. *The Return of Tarzan, Tarzan and the Jewels of Opar, Tarzan and the Golden Lion, Tarzan the Invincible*

Magra: The beautiful consort of Atan Thome. Magra at first mistook Tarzan for Brian Gregory who she thought she loved. Magra did not believe Tarzan was not Gregory until the Jungle Lord saved her from a lion. Then she fell in love with Tarzan. Magra later betrayed Atan Thome and willingly aided and accompanied Tarzan and the Gregory safari to the lost land of Tuen-Baka. When Magra professed her love for Tarzan he gently rebuked her. *Tarzan and the Forbidden City*

Mentheb: The queen of Thobos, a rival city across the lake from Ashair, the Forbidden City, in the lost crater world of Tuen-Baka. When Tarzan was taken a willing prisoner in Thobos, Queen Mentheb admired the Ape-man's physique and courage in the arena. Both Mentheb and her husband had extramarital affairs, and on this occasion the queen desired Tarzan. The king, however, became jealous and sentenced Tarzan to fight two lions simultaneously in the arena. During the contest Mentheb leaned forward in an attempt to gain a better view of the action and fell into the arena. Tarzan caught her and defended her against the one remaining lion. The Jungle Lord left Thobos before any further designs were made upon him. *Tarzan and the Forbidden City*

Nemone: The insanely jealous and vain queen of Cathne, the City of Gold. Nemone had all women considered prettier than her killed or disfigured. When Tarzan arrived as a prisoner she took a strong liking to this insubordinate Ape-man, and tried to seduce him several times. She even went to the point of begging for his love. Tarzan had difficulty resisting her allure and beauty, and it took great control on his part to walk away:

> The Lord of the jungle looked down at her, at a queen groveling at his feet, and the spell that had held him vanished; beneath the beautiful exterior he saw the crazed mind of a mad woman; he saw the creature that cast defenseless men to wild beasts, that

disfigured or destroyed women who might be more beautiful than she; and all that was fine in him revolted. (TCG)

For refusing her love Nemone tried to have Tarzan killed by her lion, Belthar, who she felt a bond with. When Jad-bal-ja slew Belthar in defense of Tarzan, Nemone took her own life. *Tarzan and the City of Gold*

Olga de Coude: A young and beautiful Russian woman who was attracted to the handsome and athletic Tarzan even though she was faithfully married, albeit by her father's arrangement, to a count 20 years her senior. Tarzan befriended both the Count and Countess de Coude after foiling a blackmail attempt by Nikolas Rokoff, who happened to be Olga's brother, and Alexis Paulvitch. Rokoff and Paulvitch became Tarzan's enemies and manipulated the Jungle Lord into a supposed liaison with Olga while her husband was away. Alone together, the still single Tarzan and the sad and lonely Olga had a weak moment. They embraced and kissed, because, "Olga de Coude was a very beautiful woman, and Tarzan of the Apes a very lonely young man, with a heart in him that was in need of the doctoring that only a woman may provide." (RT) It was then that her husband returned and caught them. The count attacked Tarzan, who returned the fight, and Olga had to stop the younger and stronger Ape-man from killing her husband. For honor's sake a duel was set, and Tarzan offered his life in forfeiture to win back Olga's honor and atone for the affront to them both. This sacrifice and acknowledgment of his dishonorable wrongdoing won the respect of the count, and all was forgiven. The Count and Countess de Coude remained Tarzan's friends. *The Return of Tarzan*

Ouled-nail: The beautiful captive dancing girl of Sisi Aissa who was the daughter of Sheik Kadour ben Saden. Tarzan was kind to her and she repaid him by warning him of an ambush in the club she danced at. During the attack she led him into an upper room where they both escaped onto the roof. From there they traveled together through the desert to her father's camp. Ouled-nail fell in love with Tarzan, and he admired her courage and found her a fit companion to travel with, and thought of her as a sister. Tarzan was well accepted by her father who approved of and hoped for a possible relationship between the two youths. Tarzan very much enjoyed the Arab lifestyle and desired to live with these nomads of the desert. It was difficult for him to leave them. *The Return of Tarzan*

Patricia Leigh-Burden: A physically fit young woman from the yacht *Naiad* that was pirated by the cargo ship *Saigon* on which Tarzan was being held captive in a cage. Patricia admired Tarzan's bravery and prowess and developed strong feelings for him, but the Jungle Lord downplayed them. After the *Saigon* was shipwrecked upon the lost Mayan island of Uxmal Tarzan left to search the jungle. Patricia stubbornly tried to follow and was promptly taken captive by Mayan warriors. In the city she tried to fool the king and high priest into thinking that she was a goddess and Tarzan's mate, because many of the Mayans already thought Tarzan was their god called Che, Lord Forest. When Tarzan went to rescue Patricia he was taken prisoner, but won his freedom by

proving by their standards that he was God. Not knowing that Tarzan was already married Patricia voiced her love for him. When his status was revealed it did not change her feelings for him, and the Lord of the Jungle had to gently rebuke Patricia and deny her love. *Tarzan and the Castaways*

Talaskar: A second generation slave princess in the quarries of the Minuni city Veltopismakus where Tarzan was shrunken and assigned work. Talaskar cooked for Tarzan and the captive prince of Trohanadalmakus, Komodoflorensal. Although Tarzan never loved Talaskar as a man loves a mate he became her friend, admired her, and desired to protect her. On her part Talaskar returned his friendship and admired him for his bravery and prowess. Komodoflorensal, who had fallen in love with Talaskar, misread their feelings and thought that they loved each other enough to become mates. The Minuni prince became jealous, but because of his friendship with Tarzan, he controlled himself. Janzara, the jealous princess of Veltopismakus who desired Tarzan, also misunderstood the relationship between Tarzan and Talaskar, and tried to have both of them killed. Once all was explained Talaskar and Komodoflorensal were married. *Tarzan and the Ant Men*

Teeka: A beautiful she–Mangani who was a childhood playmate of Tarzan in the tribe of Kerchak. Due to the maturity of both she became attractive to Tarzan and consequently his first love. A love triangle was formed, however, with Taug, a giant bull–Mangani who was another of Tarzan's former playfellows. Teeka at first chose Tarzan, but being fickle quickly changed her mind and mated with Taug. Teeka and Taug gave birth to Gazan. *Jungle Tales of Tarzan*

Woman Number One: The giant and brutish Alalus female who found the downed and unconscious Tarzan in the wreckage of Korak's airplane in the basin beyond the Great Thorn Barrier. Placing Tarzan over her shoulder, Woman Number One carried the Jungle Lord back to her village, where he would be her mate for the season then released, as was their custom. There she successfully defended her right to have him, against the other females. Woman Number One then stripped the still unconscious Tarzan of his clothes and placed him in her stone nursery corral where her children were kept. She challenged a returning female for food and was killed by her. Tarzan later escaped the nursery with one of Woman Number One's sons. *Tarzan and the Ant Men*

The Languages of Tarzan

Raised speaking the language of the Great Apes, which is believed to be the basic foundation of all languages, Tarzan was destined to be multilingual. After discovering that he was not an ape but a M-A-N, the inquisitive young Jungle Lord taught himself to read and write English to become more of the M-A-N he was born than the ape he was raised. To make matters worse (or better) Paul d'Arnot taught Tarzan his mother tongue of French despite the fact that Tarzan wrote to him in English. This forced the Lord of the Jungle to learn yet another spoken language (English) under the tutelage of d'Arnot. While in Europe the knowledge hungry Tarzan pored over every book he could find to add to his understanding and mastery of English and French and human society. During his first job with the Ministry of War the Jungle Lord learned Arabic, and over the years German. The ever curious Tarzan desired to learn the culture and language of each lost society and civilization he came across. Below is a list of the languages he was known to have acquired in his life.

Alalus: The female-dominated race of the Alali in the land of the Minuni spoke a sign and body language. Tarzan learned it from the Son of the First Woman who he helped escape the Alali village. *Tarzan and the Ant Men*

Arabic: Tarzan learned to speak the Arabic language while he was work-ing as a special agent of the French Ministry of War in Algeria. *The Return of Tarzan*

Athne and Cathne: After rescuing Valthor, Tarzan desired to visit his land. Along the way Valthor taught him to speak the language of the cities of gold and ivory. This helped Tarzan immensely after he was taken

Gary Gianni illustration from _Tarzan: The Lost Adventure_ (© 1995 Edgar Rice Burroughs, Inc.).

prisoner by the people of Athne. He later returned to the cities in a second book. _Tarzan and the City of Gold_ and _Tarzan the Magnificent_

Dutch: Tarzan revealed that he spoke the Dutch language in _Tarzan and the Foreign Legion._

English: The young Jungle Lord taught himself to read and write English from primer books and a dictionary in his parent's cabin. He was later taught to speak it by Lt. Paul d'Arnot. _Tarzan of the Apes_

French: The first spoken civilized human language Tarzan learned. French,

not English, was taught to him by Lt. Paul d'Arnot because that was d'Arnot's mother tongue. And this happened despite the fact that Tarzan wrote his original messages to d'Arnot in English. _Tarzan of the Apes_

German: Tarzan picked up German while living with civilized people. It helped him during the world wars. _Tarzan the Untamed_

Latin: The Lord of the Jungle recognized the language of the Lost Empire from his studies in Europe. He then had Festivitas, the mother of Maximus Praeclarus, teach it to him while he was staying in their home in seclusion. *Tarzan and the Lost Empire*

Mangani: Tarzan's mother tongue, so to speak. Called the language of the "first man" by the Oparians it was theorized by Tarzan to be the basic foundation language of all creatures. Kala, Tarzan's foster ape mother, raised and protected Tarzan, and taught him everything he needed to know to survive in the jungle, including her language. (For a collection of known terms, see The Ape Language that follows in this section.) *Tarzan of the Apes*

Mayan: While marooned upon the lost Mayan island of Uxmal, the Lord of the Jungle learned to speak their forgotten tongue from the rescued sacrificial maiden, Itzl Cha. *Tarzan and the Castaways*

Minuni: After Tarzan saved the Minuni prince, Komodoflorensal, from a giant Alalus female he was welcomed as a friend into their city even though he was four times their height. Upon discovering that Tarzan desired to learn their language and culture every citizen took it upon themselves to teach him all they could at every opportunity. (For a collection of known terms, see The Language of the Ant Men that follows in this section.) *Tarzan and the Ant Men*

Pal-ul-don: While searching for Jane, Tarzan entered the lost and primitive land of Pal-ul-don. Once there he made friends with a member of the Ho-don race and with a member of the Waz-don race. They taught Tarzan their language and culture. (For a collection of known terms, see The Language of Pal-ul-don that follows in this section.) *Tarzan the Terrible*

Pellucidar: At the Earth's core, several languages were spoken. The Sagoths spoke the Mangani language, but some terms were new to Tarzan. This can possibly be explained by the fact that some animals which they had names for were no longer in existence on the outer crust. Yet, they used other terms for still existing species, such as gilak instead of Tarmangani. Gilak was the term used by the humans at the Earth's core and mixed in their own language. Perhaps a crossover occurred among the languages during the different levels of man's evolution. The Gilaks or humans of Pellucidar also understood and spoke enough of the Mangani language to get by. Once Tarzan met up with the Gilak, Thoar, he was able to learn from him the tongue of the human Pellucidarians. *Tarzan at the Earth's Core*

Swahili and other native dialects: Tarzan easily learned to speak Swahili along with various dialects of the native tribes he encountered.

The Ape Language

The language of the great apes is not like our language. It sounds to man like growling and barking and grunting, punctuated at times by shrill screams, and it is practically untranslatable to any tongue known to man.... It is a means of communicating thought and there its similarity to the languages of men ceases. — Tarzan at the Earth's Core

Mangani, the language of the great apes, was called the language of the first man by the Oparians. Tarzan theorized that it was the basic foundation language for all creatures, because all creatures of the jungle understood it to a greater or lesser extent. The Oparians spoke the language of the Mangani along with their native Atlantian. The Sagoths of Pellucidar spoke it, but with Inner Earth terms mixed in and a few other differences (i.e. Gilak instead of Tarmangani, Sagoth instead of Mangani or Bolgani). Most of the unfamiliar terms used by the Sagoths of Pellucidar were for animals and things that no longer existed on the outer crust, due to extinction. Therefore, their names, in the surface world, had become extinct along with them. The separate language of the Gilaks, or Homo sapiens, in Pellucidar contained many of these same unfamiliar terms as well. Also, the Gilaks understood much of the Mangani language. The similarities between these two languages in Pellucidar could indicate that the language of the Gilaks was one of the first offshoots of Mangani. This possibility supports Tarzan's theory that the Mangani language was the first basic foundation of all language. Additional proof to support this theory is the fact that the troglodyte Nu, the son of Nu, from the Niocene period of Earth's history, spoke Mangani in the crossover story *The Eternal Savage (Lover)*.

Bolgani, the gorilla, Manu, the monkey, Tongani, the baboon, and all other primates spoke the Mangani language. Tarzan called the orangutans in *Tarzan and the Foreign Legion* and in *Tarzan and the Castaways* Mangani, and they also spoke the ape language. Tarzan spoke it to Tantor, the elephant, and "through it Tarzan could convey his feelings more than his wishes to the great beasts" (TC). Numa, the lion, and other nonprimate animals were said to comprehend some of the Mangani language even though it may have been just the tone of the growling that they understood: "Perhaps Numa does not understand the words that I use but I believe that my tones and my manner carry the impression that I wish them to convey." (TU)

In learning the ape language it is important to remember that all large things are considered male and smaller things female. And, as for Bara, the deer:

> ... the scent of which was always translated to the nostrils of the foster son of Kala the she-ape as Bara the deer, though in fact, as practically always, the animal was an antelope. But strong are the impressions of childhood and ... that long-gone day upon which he had pored over the colored alphabet primer in the far-off cabin of his dead father beside the landlocked harbor on the West Coast, and learned that "D stands for Deer," and had admired the picture of the pretty animal. The thing that most closely resembled it, with which he was

familiar in his daily life, the antelope, became for him then and always remained, Bara the deer. (TAM)

Editor's note: Upon studying the Tarzan novels, some additions and corrections were necessary to Burroughs' own "Dictionary of the Ape Language" in *Tarzan Clans of America*. These have been marked with the typographical symbol ‡.

Dictionary of the Ape Language

In compiling this dictionary of the ape language, with the assistance of Tarzan of the Apes, the author has been greatly handicapped by the fact that the apes have no words to describe many things that are common to us and that their language consists mostly of nouns and verbs, having almost no auxiliary parts of speech.

They have no word for village and none for house; so the word for nest must stand for house, and the word for village would be a compound of the word for many and the word for nest.

Doubtless many words of their simple, yet strange language have been omitted; but enough are given to ... carry on a conversation or a correspondence in the language of the Mangani, or Great Apes, just as Tarzan talked with the apes of the tribe of Kerchak. — Tarzan Clans of America

Ape-English Dictionary

ä: light
ab: boy
abalu: brother
abu: knee
ala: rise
amba: fall
ara: lightning
arad: spear
argo: fire
argo-ved‡: fire-mountain; volcano
aro: shoot; throw; cast
at: tail
atan: male
bal‡: golden (*Prefix: i.e.,* **bal-za:** golden girl)
balu: baby; small
balu-den: small-tree; stick; branch; limb
band: elbow

bar: battle
bara‡: deer; antelope (*see* **wappi**)
ben: great
bo: flat
bolgani: gorilla
bu: 1. he. 2. (*A masculine prefix, i.e.* **bu-balu:** boy baby)
bulamutumumo‡: God. (*How the young Tarzan vocalized the English written word God in the language of the Mangani. The masculine prefix* **bu** *is placed before* **la** *which is the word Tarzan gave the letter* **g**. *A masculine prefix is used because the* **g** *in* **God** *is capitalized and all things that are large are considered male by the Mangani. Hence, the feminine prefix* **mu** *is used for the lower case letters* **o** *and* **d** *to which Tarzan*

assigned the words **tu** *and* **mo** *respectively. Or, seeing the word written thus* **Bula**[G]**mutu**[o]**mumo**[d] *may help a better understanding of Tarzan's vocalization of the English written word* God. *See* "The God of Tarzan" *in* Jungle Tales of Tarzan.)

bund: dead
bundolo: to kill; to fight; "I kill"
bur: cold
busso: fly
buto: rhinoceros
b'wang: hand
b'yat: head
b'zan: hair
b'zee: foot
dak: fat
dak-lul: lake
dako: thick
dako-zan: thick-skin; meat; flesh
dan: rock; stone
dan-do: stop
dango: hyena
dan-lul: ice
dano: bone
dan-sopu: nut
den: tree
do‡: (*The sound assigned by the young Tarzan to the written English letter of the alphabet* b *in* Jungle Tales of Tarzan)
dotoro‡: (*The word that the young Tarzan invented for the written English word* boy: **do**[b]**to**[o]**ro**[y].)
dum-dum: 1. tom-tom; drum. 2. *The Mangani's ceremonial dance and feast.* (*For more information, see Mangani in Section Three.*)
duro: hippopotamus
eho: much
eho-dan: hard
eho-kut: hollow
eho-lul: wet
eho-nala: top
es: rough
eta: little
eta-gogo: whisper
eta-koho: warm

Roy G. Krenkel illustration from *Tarzan and the Tarzan Twins* (© 1963 Edgar Rice Burroughs, Inc.).

eta-nala: low
etarad: arrow
ga: 1. red. 2. (*Prefix: i.e.,* **ga-zan**: *red skin.*)
galul: blood
gando: win
gash: tooth; fang
gimla: crocodile; alligator
go: 1. black. 2. (*Prefix: i.e.,* go-zan: *black skin.*)
gogo: talk
gom: run
gomangani: great black ape (*usually means* a Negro)
gom-lul: river
gor: growl
gorgo: buffalo; (*sometimes*) moon
goro: moon
gree-ah: like; love
gu: stomach; belly
gumado: sick
gund: chief
histah: snake
ho: many
hoden *or* **Ho-den**: forest
hohotan: tribe
horta: boar; pig
hotan: clan
ho-wala: village
ho-wa-usha: leaves (*see* wa-usha)

huh‡ : yes; I agree; I understand; okay (*see also* **rak**)

hul: star

jabo: shield

jar: strange

kagoda *or* **ka-goda**: surrender (*i.e.* Do you surrender? *or* Have you had enough? *or* I do surrender, *depending on the circumstance and inflection*.)

kal: milk

kalan: female

kalo: cow

kalu: mother

kambo: jungle

kando: ant

karpo: middle; center

kas: jump

klu: hen

klu-kal: egg

ko: mighty

kob: hit, strike

koho: hot

kor: walk

kordo: to dance (*see* **voo-dum**)

kota: tortoise or turtle

kreeg-ah *or* **kree-gah**: danger; beware (*either, depending on the circumstance*)

kree-gor: scream

kudu: sun

kut: hole

la‡: (*The sound assigned by the young Tarzan to the written English letter of the alphabet* g *in* Jungle Tales of Tarzan.)

lan: right

lana: sting

lano: mosquito

lat: nose

litu: sharp

lob: kick

lot: face

lu: fierce

lufo: side

lul: water

lul-kor: swim

lus: tongue

Roy G. Krenkel illustration from *Tarzan and the Tarzan Twins* (© 1963 Edgar Rice Burroughs, Inc.).

mado: lame

mal: 1. yellow 2. (*Prefix: i.e.* **mal-zan**: yellow skin)

mangani: 1. (*The great anthropoid apes of the Tarzan stories that are more human than any other primate.*) 2. orangutan. (*For further information see* Mangani *in Section Three.*)

manu: monkey

meeta: rain

mo: 1. short. 2. ‡ (*The sound assigned by Tarzan to the written English letter of the alphabet* d *in* Jungle Tales of Tarzan.)

mu: 1. she 2. (*A feminine prefix, i.e.* **mu-Balu**: female baby.)

m'wa: blue

nala: up

neeta: bird

nene: beetle

nesen: grasshopper

no: brook

numa: lion

nur: lie (*an untruth*)

olo: wrestle

om: long
omtag: giraffe
pacco: zebra
pal: country; place; land (*tribe's hunting ground*)
pamba: rat
pan: soft
pand: thunder
panda: noise
pandar: loud
pand-balu-den: gun; rifle; revolver
pan-lul: weep
pan-vo: weak
pastar: father
pele: valley
pisa or **Pisah**: fish (*noun*)
po: hungry
popo: eat
por: mate
por-atan: husband
por-kalan: wife
rak: yes (*see also* **huh**)
rala: snare
ramba: lie down
rand: back
rea: word
rem: catch
rep: truth; true
ro: 1. flower. 2. ‡ (*The sound assigned by the young Tarzan to the written English letter of the alphabet y in* Jungle Tales of Tarzan.)
rota: laugh
ry: crooked
ry-balu-den: bow (*archery*)
sabor: lioness
sato: kind
sheeta: leopard; panther; black panther
ska: vulture; buzzard
skree: wildcat
so: eat
sopu: fruit
sord: bad
ta: high; tall
tag: neck
tan: warrior
tand: no; not (*a prefix used to make things their opposite*)

tandak: thin
tand-ho: few
tandlan: left
tand-litu: dull; blunt
tand-lul: dry
tand-nala: down
tand-panda: silent; silence
tand-popo: starve
tand-ramba: get up
tand-unk: stay
tand-utor: brave
tand-vulp: empty
tan-klu: rooster
tantor: elephant (*African or Indian*)
ta-pal: hill
tar: 1. white 2. (*Prefix i.e.* **tar-zan**: white skin)
tar-bur: snow
tarmangani: great white ape (*usually means a Caucasian human*)
tho: mouth
thub: heart
tongani: baboon
tor: beast
tro: straight
tu: 1. bright. 2. ‡ (*The sound assigned by the young Tarzan to the written English letter of the alphabet o in* Jungle Tales of Tarzan.)

Roy G. Krenkel illustration from *Tarzan and the Tarzan Twins* (© 1963 Edgar Rice Burroughs, Inc.).

tub: broken
ubor: thirsty
ud: drink
ug: bottom
ugla: hate
ungo or unga: jackal
unk: go
unk-nala: climb
usha: the wind
ut: corn
utor: fear; afraid
van: well
vando: good
ved: mountain
vo: muscle
voo-dum: dance (*noun*) (*see* kordo)
voo-voo: sing
vulp: full
wa: green
wala: nest; hut; home; house
wang: arm
wappi: antelope
wa-usha: leaf
whuff: smoke

wo: this
wob: that
yad: ear
yang: swing
yat: eye
yato: look
yel: here
yeland: there
yo: friend
yud: come
yut: stab; gore
yuto: cut
za: girl
za-balu: sister
zan: 1. skin 2. (*Suffix: i.e.* ga-zan: red-skin)
zee: leg
zor: in
zu: big
zu-dak-lul: ocean
zugor: roar
zu-kut: cave
zut: out
zu-vo: strong

English-Ape Dictionary

afraid: utor
agree: rak; (*or sometimes*) huh ‡
alligator: gimla
ant: kando
antelope: wappi; (or sometimes) bara ‡
apes (*great*): mangani
arm: wang
arrow: etarad
b (*the written English letter*): do ‡
baboon: tongani
baby: balu
back: rand
bad: sord
battle: bar
beast: tor
beetle: nene
belly: gu
beware: kreeg-ah
big: zu

bird: neeta
black: go
black panther: sheeta
blood: galul
blue: m'wa
blunt: tand-litu
boar: horta
bone: dano
bottom: ug
bow (*archery*): ry-balu-den
boy: ab
boy (*the written English word*): dotoro
    ‡
branch: balu-den
brave: tand-utor
bright: tu
broken: tub
brook: no
brother: abalu

Roy G. Krenkel illustration from *Tarzan and the Tarzan Twins* (© 1963 Edgar Rice Burroughs, Inc.).

buffalo: gorgo
buzzard: ska
cast: aro
catch: rem
Caucasian human: tarmangani (*great white ape*)
cave: zu-kut
center: karpo
chief: gund
clan: hotan
climb: unk-nala
cold: bur
come: yud
corn: ut
country: pal
cow: kalo
crocodile: gimla
crooked: ry
cut: yuto
d (*written English letter*): mo ‡
dance (*verb*): kordo
dance (*noun*): voo-dum
danger: kreeg-ah
dead: bund
deer: bara ‡
down: tand-nala
drink: ud
drum: dum-dum
dry: tand-lul
dull: tand-litu

ear: yad
eat: popo; (or sometimes) so
egg: klu-kal
elbow: band
elephant: tantor
empty: tand-vulp
eye: yat
face: lot
fall: amba
fang: gash
fat: dak
father: pastar
fear: utor
female: kalan
few: tand-ho
fierce: lu
fight: bundolo
fire: argo
fish (*noun*): pisa; pisah
flat: bo
flesh: dako-zan
flower: ro
fly: busso
foot: b'zee
forest: hoden; ho-den
friend: yo
fruit: sopu
full: vulp
g (*the written English letter*): la ‡
get up: tand-ramba
giraffe: omtag
girl: za
go: unk
god (*the written English word*): bula-mutumumo ‡
golden: bal
good: vando
gore (*verb*): yut
gorilla: bolgani
grasshopper: nesen
great: ben
great ape: mangani
green: wa
growl: gor
gun: pand-balu-den
hair: b'zan
hand: b'wang
hard: eho-dan

hate: ugla
he: bu
head: b'yat
heart: thub
hen: klu
here: yel
high: ta
hill: ta-pal
hippopotamus: duro
hit: kob
hole: kut
hollow: eho-kut
home: wala
hot: koho
house: wala
hungry: po
hunting ground: pal
husband: por-atan
hut: wala
hyena: dango
I kill: bundolo
ice: dan-lul
in: zor
jackal: ungo, or unga
jump: kas
jungle: kambo
kick: lob
kill: bundolo
kind: sato
knee: abu
lake: dak-lul
lame: mado
land: pal
laugh: rota
leaf: wa-usha
leaves: ho-wa-usha
left: tandlan
leg: zee
leopard: sheeta
lie (*an untruth*): nur
lie down: ramba
light: ä
lightning: ara
like (*verb*): gree-ah
limb: balu-den
lion: numa
lioness: sabor
little: eta

long: om
look: yato
loud: pandar
love: gree-ah
low: eta-nala
male: atan
many: ho
mate: por
meat: dako-zan
middle: karpo
mighty: ko
milk: kal
monkey: manu
moon: goro; gorgo
mosquito: lano
mother: kalu
mountain: ved
mouth: tho
much: eho
muscle: vo
neck: tag
Negro: gomangani (*great black ape*)
nest: wala
no: tand
noise: panda
nose: lat
not: tand
nut: dan-sopu
o (*the written English letter*): tu ‡
ocean: zu-dak-lul
okay: huh ‡ ; (*or sometimes*) rak
orangutan: mangani
out: zut
panther: sheeta
place: pal
pig: horta
rain: meeta
rat: pamba
red: ga
revolver: pand-balu-den
rhinoceros: buto
rifle: pand-balu-den
right: lan
rise: ala
river: gom-lul
roar: zugor
rock: dan
rooster: tan-klu

Roy G. Krenkel illustration from *Tarzan and the Tarzan Twins* (© 1963 Edgar Rice Burroughs, Inc.).

rough: es
run: gom
scream: kree-gor
sharp: litu
she: mu
shield: jabo
shoot: aro
short: mo
sick: gumado
side: lufo
silent *or* **silence**: tand-panda
sing: voo-voo
sister: za-balu
skin: zan
small: balu
smoke: whuff
snake: histah
snare: rala
snow: tar-bur
soft: pan
spear: arad
stab: yut
star: hul
starve: tand-popo
stay: tand-unk
stick: balu-den
sting: lana
stomach: gu
stone: dan
stop: dan-do
straight: tro
strange: jar
strike: kob
strong: zu-vo
sun: kudu
surrender: kagoda; (*or sometimes*) ka-goda

swim: lul-kor
tail: at
talk: gogo
tall: ta
that: wob
there: yeland
thick: dako
thin: tandak
thirsty: ubor
this: wo
throw: aro
thunder: pand
tom-tom: dum-dum
tongue: lus
tooth: gash
top: eho-nala
tortoise: kota
tree: den
tribe: hohotan
true *or* **truth**: rep
turtle: kota
up: nala
valley: pele
village: ho-wala
volcano: argo-ved ‡
vulture: ska
walk: kor
warm: eta-koho
warrior: tan
water: lul
weak: pan-vo
weep: pan-lul
well: van
wet: eho-lul
whisper: eta-gogo
white: tar
wife: por-kalan
wildcat: skree
win: gando
wind (*noun*): usha
word: rea
wrestle: olo
y (*the written English letter*): ro ‡
yellow: mal
yes: rak; (*or sometimes*) huh ‡
zebra: pacco

The Language of Pal-ul-don

When Tarzan first heard and learned the language of Pal-ul-don he claimed that it was "entirely unrelated to any with which he was familiar." (TTT) Nonetheless, there are similarities between Pal-ul-don and Mangani, and terms common to both. Perhaps pronunciation and accent made words sound different. Some had the exact spelling and definition, while others which were spelled the same had different meanings. The Pal-ul-don terms that are identical in Mangani have been marked with an asterisk (*) But here is Burroughs' introduction to the language of Pal-ul-don.

> From conversations with Lord Greystoke and from his notes, there have been gleaned a number of interesting items relative to the language and customs of the inhabitants of Pal-ul-don that are not brought out in the story. For the benefit of those who may care to delve into the derivation of the proper names used in the text, and thus obtain some slight insight into the language of the race, there is appended an incomplete glossary taken from some of Lord Greystoke's notes.
>
> A point of particular interest hinges upon the fact that the names of all male hairless pithecanthropi, or Ho-don, begin with a consonant, have an even number of syllables, and end with a consonant, while the names of the females of the same species begin with a vowel, have an odd number of syllables, and end with a vowel. On the contrary, the names of the male hairy black pithecanthropi, or Waz-don, have an even number of syllables, but begin with a vowel and end with a consonant. The female Waz-don have an odd number of syllables in their names which begin always with a consonant and end with a vowel. [Glossary in *Tarzan the Terrible*.]

> I have used the Pal-ul-don word for *gorge* [kor] with the English plural [*kors*], which is not the correct native plural form. The latter, it seems to me, is awkward for us and so I have generally ignored it throughout my manuscript, permitting, for example, Kor-ul-ja to answer for both singular and plural. However, for the benefit of those who may be interested in such things I may say that the plurals are formed simply for all words in the Pal-ul-don language by doubling the initial letter of the word, as *k'kor, gorges*, pronounced as though written *kakor*, the *a* having the sound of *a* in *sofa*. *Lions*, then, would be *j'ja*, or *men d'don*. (TTT)

a*: light
ab*: boy
Ab-on: acting *gund* of Kor-ul-ja
ad: three
adad: six
adadad: nine
adaden: seven
aden: four
adenaden: five
A-lur: City of Light
an: spear
An-un: father of Pan-at-lee
as: sun
at*: tail
bal*: gold; golden
bar*: battle
ben*: great
bu*: moon
Bu-lot: (moon face) son of Chief Mo-sar
Bu-lur: (moon city) the city of the Waz-ho-don
dak*: fat
Dak-at: (fat tail) chief of a Hodon village
Dak-lot: (fat face) one of Ko-tan's palace warriors
dan*: rock
den*: tree
don: man
dor: son
Dor-ul-Otho: (Son of God) Tarzan
e: where
ed: seventy
el: grace; graceful
en: one
enen: two
es*: rough
Es-sat: (rough skin) chief of Om-at's tribe of hairy black Waz-don
et: eighty
fur: thirty
ged: forty
go*: clear
gryf: "'Triceratops. A genus of huge herbivorous dinosaurs of the group Ceratopsia. The skull had two large horns above the eyes, a median horn

on the nose, a horny beak, and a great bony hood or transverse crest over the neck. Their toes, five in front and three behind, were provided with hoofs, and the tail was large and strong.' Webster's Dict. The *gryf* of Pal-ul-don is similar except that it is omnivorous, has strong, powerfully armed jaws and talons instead of hoofs. Coloration: face yellow with blue bands encircling the eyes; hood red on top, yellow underneath; belly yellow: body a dirty, slate blue; legs same. Bony protuberances yellow except along the spine — these are red. Tail conforms with body and belly. Horns, ivory." [Glossary in *Tarzan the Terrible*.] The *gryf* has almost no odor, and is very silent and quick despite its great bulk. Its hood can be erected for protection or flattened. It is a determined and patient hunter. When prey is treed the *gryf* will wait tirelessly below the tree or follow if it travels through the trees. It does not even appear to sleep at such times; it merely waits for its cornered victim to fall to the ground.
gund*: chief
gund-bar: chief battle. (*A fight between two opponents to determine which should be the chief, using only nature's weapons.*)
guru: terrible
het: fifty
ho: white
Ho-don: the hairless white men of Pal-ul-don
id: silver
Id-an: one of Pan-at-lee's two brothers
in: dark
In-sad: (Dark-forest) Kor-ul-ja warrior accompanying Tarzan, Om-at, and Ta-den in search of Pan-at-lee
In-tan: (Dark-warrior) Kor-ul-lul left to guard Tarzan
ja: lion

jad: the
Jad-bal-ja: the golden lion
jad-bal-lul: the golden lake
jad-ben-lul: the big lake
Jad-ben-Otho: the Great God
Jad-guru-don: (the terrible man) Tarzan
jad-in-lul: the dark lake
Ja-don: (lion man) chief of the Ho-don village Ja-lur and father of Ta-den
Jad Pele ul Jad-ben-Otho: the valley of the Great God
Ja-lur: (lion city) Ja-don's capital
jar*: strange
Jar-don: (stranger) name given Korak by Om-at
jato: smaller, striped saber-toothed hybrid with a disposition like a devil
ko*: mighty
kor*: gorge
Kor-ul-gryf: gorge-of-the *gryf*
Kor-ul-ja: (gorge of lion) name of Essat's gorge and tribe
Kor-ul-lul: (gorge of water) name of another Waz-don gorge and tribe
Ko-tan: (mighty warrior) king of the Ho-don
lav: run or running
lee: doe
lo: star
lot*: face
lu*: fierce
Lu-don: (fierce man) high priest of A-lur
lul*: water
lur: city
ma: child
mo*: short
Mo-sar: (short nose) chief of Tu-lur and a pretender
mu*: strong
no*: brook
o: like; similar
od: ninety
O-dan: (like a rock) Kor-ul-ja warrior accompanying Tarzan, Om-at, and Ta-den in search of Pan-at-lee
og: sixty

O-lo-a: (like starlight) Ko-tan's daughter
om*: long
Om-at: (long tail) a black Waz-don who became chief of Kor-ul-ja
on: ten
otho: god
pal*: place; land; country
pal-e-don-so: place where men eat; banquet hall
Pal-ul-don: (land of men) name of the country
pal-ul-ja: place of lions
Pan*: soft
Pan-at-lee: (soft-tailed doe) Om-at's sweetheart
Pan-sat: (soft skin) a priest
pastar*: father
Pastar-ul-ved: Father of Mountains
pele*: valley
ro: flower
sad: forest
san: one hundred
sar: nose
sat: skin
so: eat
sod: eaten
sog: eating
son: ate
ta*: tall
Ta-den: (tall tree) a white hairless Hodon and the first Pal-ul-donian Tarzan met in the country
tan*: warrior
Tarzan-jad-guru: Tarzan the Terrible
to: purple
ton: twenty
tor*: beast
tor-o-don: beast-like man
tu*: bright
Tu-lur: (bright city) Mo-sar's city
ul: of
un: eye
ut*: corn
ved*: mountain
waz: black
Waz-don: (black-man) the hairy black men of Pal-ul-don

Waz-ho-don: (black-white-men) a mixed race

xot: one thousand

xot tor!: a thousand beasts (*an oath*)

yo*: friend

za*: girl

The Language of the Ant Men

Not much information is given about the Minuni language, but there is sufficient to warrant a list of terms.

amak: a military unit of 1000 men, commanded by a Kamak

Aoponato: "800^3 + 19" the slave number for the Trohanadalmakus prince Komodoflorensal while he was a prisoner and slave of Veltopismakus. See Komodoflorensal in Section Four.

Aopontando: "800^3+21" which was the slave number given to Tarzan after he was captured by the warriors of the city Veltopismakus and shrunken to a quarter of his size by the Walmak (wizard), Zoanthrohago. This quarter size was the normal size of size of the Minunians.

cambon: a ratel; the African member of the badger family

Diadet: the Royal Antelope that the Minunians used for riding

Diadetax: cavalry of *diadet* (Royal Antelope) riding warriors

ee-ah-ee-ah!: one form of cheering or applause

ental: a military unit of ten men, commanded by a vental

entex: a military unit of 50 men, commanded by a ventex

hual: the basic unit of measurement equal to about one foot to the Minuni; about three inches to humans

jetak: a piece of money

kamak: a commander of an Amak, a unit of 1000 men

novand: 1. A military unit of 250 men. 2. The commander of 250 men

Minuni: the race of the 18-inch tall Ant Men

Thagosto: chief royal; king

tuano: good night

vental: commander of an ental, a unit of ten men

ventex: commander of an entex, a unit of 50 men

walmak: wizard; scientist who works miracles

Zertalacolol: the term used for the giant barbaric female-dominated Alalus people

zertol: prince; chief; noble

zertolosto: prince royal; the prince in direct bloodline to the throne

Zuanthrol: (the giant) When Tarzan was overcome and captured by the warriors of the city of Veltopismakus and shrunken to a quarter of his size, he pretended to to be unable to speak. Not knowing his name, therefore, the Minuni called him Zuanthrol, the Giant.

Ant Men Sayings

May your candles burn long and brilliantly: A toast, blessing, or expression of good fortune usually given at parting, similar to "live long and prosper." The saying had its origins in the fact that the candles the Minuni used in their large and partially subterranean dwellings produced oxygen for them to breathe.

Trust not too far the loyalty of even the stones of your chamber: The walls have ears.

May the shadow of disaster never fall upon you: May you always have good luck.

SECTION THREE

Lost Cities, Civilizations, Tribes, Peoples, and Religions

In many of the Tarzan novels there was a lost society found and explored by Tarzan or some other outside character. A typical scenario had two rival lost cities that had been hidden from modern civilization for years. Tarzan started out in one city but eventually got to the other. While there he often offended the city's leader and had a queen fall in love with him. The religious rites of most of these lost societies involved human sacrifice in one form or another. There was also often an arena where battles took place between contestants, and Tarzan usually became one. Once in the society, he did not mind disrupting the established traditional flow of things, and often overthrew the evil governing body or unmasked the false religion's teachings and leader.

Following is a compendium of the lost societies, lands and peoples in the Tarzan novels with a description of the city and way of life of each. Whether Christian, heathen, or something else, the religious convictions of Burroughs' characters and societies were major motivating forces for actions in his stories, so each society's religious practices and teachings are written in as much detail as was obtainable.

Alalus or Alali: see **Minuni and Alalus**
ALEMTEJO: *Tarzan and the Madman.* Beyond the Great Thorn Forest in the high cliffs of (perhaps) the

Maginot Line in the Ruturi Mountains was a lost civilization established some four hundred years before by Portuguese Christians. There they built a castle and a city. Alemtejo had a king and a high priest with his priests who wore long gowns with cowls. Gold was plentiful in this lost Portuguese city with royalty using much of it in their ornaments. Male servants wore leather jerkins and broad brimmed hats, while the women servants went topless and wore only a sarong about their waist. Swords and battle-axes were the primary weapons of the people of Alemtejo. They also carried ancient muskets that they no longer knew how to use since there had not been ammunition for almost the full four hundred years of their existence in the land. They still maintained these muskets purely for decorative purposes. The Alemtejo's skin was darker than normal because of interracial mating. And they spoke a cross between Portuguese and Bantu. Water buffalo were bred and trained for war in the community.

The Alemtejos still believed they were fighting the Muslims as their forefathers had four hundred years earlier. These Muslims were really a village of Galla natives ruled by a sultan that lived across the valley from the castle city of Alemtejo. The Muslims mined gold they traded with the Alemtejos at certain times. The Gallas' only enemy were the people of Alemtejo whose method of war had remained the same over the intervening four centuries. It began by the Alemtejos sounding trumpets and giving war cries. They then rushed across the fields with their water buffaloes. The Gallas meet their charge, and after a brief skirmish with few casualties and the capturing of prisoners on both sides, the armies returned to their respective cities.

There were two entrances into the mountain land of Alemtejo. One was relatively easy but went through the territory of the Alemtejos' enemies, the Muslims. The other was extremely treacherous and difficult. It ran through a narrow gorge that had a large palisade across its entrance with a small stream running underneath it. In this gorge were kept the guardians of Alemtejo: Lions — lots of lions. Human captives were often used to feed them. To get past the lions it was necessary to take a narrow and steep trail along the side of the gorge. The trail ended at the base of vertical cliffs two to three thousand feet high. Over the top of these cliffs, a beautiful waterfall cascaded down, feeding the stream. The sheer cliff face must be scaled very carefully, because there was almost no hand or foot hold, and waiting below for anyone who fell were the lions. The strong and agile servants of god — the Mangani, who the people of Alemtejo trained and taught their language — were some of the few who could ascend the cliffs. And the servants of god helped humans ascend the cliffs. At one point of the climb, there was a natural chimney that had to be wormed through. The whole ascent took almost three hours.

Atop the cliffs was a level mesa. A forest lay in the distance with a stream coming from it which fed the waterfall. After a half mile of forest, the trees gave way to a plain where stood the castle of Alemtejo. A wall encircled the city and built into it were gates which were guarded. Inside the walls were gardens.

The religion of Alemtejo was originally Christian based, but over the years the people had allowed heathen practices to creep into their

J. Allen St. John illustration from *The Beasts of Tarzan* (© 1916 Edgar Rice Burroughs, Inc.).

rites and beliefs. Some of these heathen practices involved human blood sacrifices and voodoo. The sacrificial ceremony consisted of the high priest (who, at the time Tarzan arrived, was Ruiz) burning incense upon an altar which, by the smell, may have been made mostly of hair. The assembly in the altar room would intone a chant accompanied by tom-toms. The names of Kibuka, the war god, and Walumbe, the god of death, were often supplicated, while *muzimo* (departed spirits) were also mentioned during the chant and prayers. Throughout, Ruiz would occasionally make the sign of the cross. Dancing girls would then enter and a wild writhing dance would take place around the altar to the beat of the tom-toms. Then a chained living human would be forcibly brought and placed face up on the altar. The high priest would pass his hands over the victim several times while muttering gibberish. At this juncture a deathly silence would come over the crowd, and the high priest would take a knife from his robes and raise it overhead. The knife would then be plunged into the heart of the victim, and immediately after this the victim's throat would be cut. The high priest would then place his hands into the blood of the victim and sprinkle it over the waiting crowd which surged forward to receive it.

When the American Colin T. Randolph, Jr., who looked and acted like Tarzan, accidentally parachuted into Alemtejo, he was struck unconscious and awoke with amnesia. The people of Alemtejo felt his descent was miraculous and claimed Randolph was their god. Not knowing otherwise Randolph accepted his godhood although personally he believed he was Tarzan of the Apes. In his presence the people knelt and crossed themselves. When the real Tarzan arrived the Jungle Lord pretended to be the true god to get the information he desired.

Ant Men: see **Minuni and Alalus**
Ashair: see **Tuen-Baka**

Athne: see **Cathne and Athne**
Cannibals: see **Natives**
Castra Sanguinarius: see **Lost Empire**
Castrum Mare: see **Lost Empire**
CATHNE and ATHNE: *Tarzan and the City of Gold* and *Tarzan the Magnificent*. In the mountains of Kaffa lay the Valley of Onthar, and in that valley was Cathne, the City of Gold. A paved rode followed the valley, but branched off in two directions. One branch went east while the other followed a river. The eastern road led through the Pass of the Warriors and into the Valley of Thenar. Several miles below Cathne, the river flowed into a gorge where, at the far end, it became a great waterfall. At the north end of Onthar was the volcano named Xarator. In the Valley of Thenar, east of Xarator, was Athne, the City of Ivory—Cathne's rival. Athne was located just northeast of the center of the valley.

Both cities had a monarchical form of government. The common people and warriors of each were regularly proportioned men and women, although they looked somewhat ignorant and brutal. The royalty and nobles were better looking and more intelligent. There were also slaves and servants in both cities. In Athne the lower class of people were called the *Erythra*— they overthrew the government during Tarzan's first visit to the city in *Tarzan the Magnificent*. The warriors of Cathne and Athne enjoyed raiding each other, so peace between the two cities was seldom possible. To them, war was a thrilling game fraught with peril; and peace could be considered boring.

When attacking, the Cathneans came with their lions and hunted the goats, sheep, elephants and people of Athne. The Cathneans took heads as trophies, and relished the heads of humans the most. These they used to adorn and decorate their rooms. The more important the person killed, the more valuable their head and the more prestige and honor to the obtainer. The Athneans raided for sport and the joy of killing and capturing slaves. To capture a slave just sold to a Cathnean was especially satisfying. However, once each year there was a truce between Athne and Cathne. Then the Cathneans traded gold, food, and hay for the steel, salt, and women that the Athneans had bought from *shiftas* of the outside world. The hay was more valuable to the people of Athne than the gold, because they needed it for their elephants.

As a token of greeting, friendship, and loyalty it was customary in both cities to place a hand upon the shoulder of the other person instead of giving a handshake like in the outside world.

CATHNE: The City of Gold was the rich walled city that lay at the bend of the river near the end of the forest. Its buildings were predominantly white, with many having domes of gold layered up to an inch thick. Outside the city, and spanning the river which ran the length of the valley, was a bridge made out of solid gold blocks: the Bridge of Gold. It was the gateway into the city of Cathne. Slaves worked in the gold mines located in the hills south of the city. Cathneans also raised fruits, vegetables, cereal, and hay. Their craftsmen worked in gold and some ivory. The names of some of their currency were *obol* and *drachma*. In Cathne, the customary way to assassinate someone was to poison their wine.

When Tarzan arrived in Cathne,

the people were ruled by an unmarried, vain and jealous queen named Nemone. She had underofficers and officials to do her bidding. Nobles were usually called lion-men, which meant that they owned and used lions. The common soldier wore helmets, habergeons, anklets and wristlets made of elephant hide heavily embossed with gold studs. Lion hair was used to trim the tops of their anklets and wristlets as well as along the outside of some helmets, shields and weapons. In the center of their shields was a boss of gold. The elephant hide that made up their habergeons was cut up into discs that overlaid one another. Officers wore similar trappings except that theirs were made of solid gold down to, and including, the hilts and scabbards of their dagger-like swords. The people had never seen a bow and arrow before Tarzan arrived and were impressed by the capability of the arrow which at first seemed like a puny weapon to them.

Cathne had a coliseum-like arena where combatants were pitted against each other. Whether man against man, animal against animal, or a combination of both. Often it was prisoner against prisoner with the winner earning his or her freedom. Tarzan broke tradition by not killing his adversary in the arena. During these gladiator-like battles heavy betting took place in the stands. A smaller arena, or court, also existed in the palace. Here private battles and wagers were offered. These contests usually consisted of a human against a lion and were purposely one-sided, because they were, in reality, just a more entertaining way of execution. The lion was often young and strong and the human not given any weapons to injure it, because the beast was considered more valuable than the human. As a rule, a champion could volunteer to take the place of a victim in the pit against the lion. If the champion won (which never happened until Tarzan arrived) both were set free.

The great plain across the river from Cathne was called the Field of the Lions. There wild lions roamed free. Cathneans raised and bred lions to be used for sport and war. Hunting lions were those with speed and endurance; others were used to draw the royal chariots. One of the sports the lions were used for was called the Grand Hunt, where the great carnivore hunted man. During the Grand Hunt one or more lions wearing a collar and chain were led by slaves out into the Field of Lions. If it was a royal event the human quarry was chained to the chariot of the king or queen and escorted out onto the field. If not, the victim was merely escorted under guard. The quarry was then given a long enough head start to reach the edge of the forest, then the lions were released to pursue them. If the human prey took to the trees he was forced to come down by thrown sticks and stones. Then he was given another head start, and the lions were again released to track him. The keepers of the lions liked to be there at the kill, for the sheer thrill and excitement of witnessing lions slaying a man.

Lions were allowed to roam the streets free and untethered in Cathne. Through training they killed very few, if any, of the citizens. Often, dead humans who were not diseased were purposely thrown into the streets to help feed the lions if no one would pay for a proper funeral. In such a case, the human was first stripped of his or her clothing which signified to the populace that they were already dead. It was considered an honor to be eaten by a lion, because their god was a lion. If any lions acquired a taste for human flesh and killed citizens, they were exterminated. The beasts were usually fed on goats, sheep, and elephants.

The lion god of Cathne was named Thoos and was an actual living lion. Verbal oaths from the people included: "by Thoos"; "by the claws of the all-high"; "by the great fangs of Thoos"; and "by the teeth of the great one." The temple of Thoos was a great three-storied building with a large dome. Before the temple was a square and a broad staircase leading to an elaborate entrance. The interior of the dome was gold, and around and inside it were galleries on the second and third levels supported by pillars. The walls of the room were covered in mosaics, and on the floor below the dome was a large cage in a niche. On either side of the cage was an altar that supported a lion of solid gold. Facing the cage were a throne and a row of benches with a stone railing behind them. During ceremonies, Thoos, an old mangy lion, entered the cage and the queen, or whoever presided, could then pray to him. With Thoos present the priests began chanting in a gibberish that even they did not understand, and the people joined in. If a human gift offering, or sacrifice, was to be given, a priest would lead the victim away in chains. Then an opening was uncovered over Thoos in the cage, and the living sacrifice was thrown down to be killed or eaten.

The active volcano, Xarator, was used for proper funerals and as another method of sacrificing humans.

Xarator had been active for as long as the cities had been in existence, and because of this, and the fact that it sent people into eternity, the saying, "the eternal fires of frowning Xarator" had a double meaning. Xarator was considered a holy mountain created by Thoos to consume the enemies of the kings and queens of Cathne. When a living sacrificial ceremony was to take place it became a grand daylong event, because of the length of the journey from the city to the brim of the frowning volcano. Many people including families with children accompanied the procession and brought food to eat along the way. Warriors also accompanied the sacrificial or funeral party to protect it from any roaming wild lions or an attack from Athne. Before leaving the city, however, the sacrifice was tied into a skin sack and not seen again. At the crater's edge the sack containing the sacrifice was placed at the feet of the queen. The priests chanted and played instruments (drums and pipes). At the appropriate time, two priests lifted the sacrifice in the sack and tossed it into the molten crater.

ATHNE: The main gate of the walled City of Ivory looked south upon the trail that led to Cathne. This gate was well guarded and had two towers that contained sentries 24 hours a day. A large dusty plain stretched before the gates. Nothing really grew on it because the elephants of Cathne were constantly trained there. The farming fields of the Athneans lay to the north of the city where the slaves labored growing fruit, vegetables and hay. The city was not very well guarded on the north side. Athneans also raised goats, sheep, and elephants. Their craftsmen made leather goods and used wool and goat hair for cloth, while their carvers worked in wood and ivory. The armor and trappings of Athneans were made predominantly from ivory. The people did trade a little with the outside world, using gold and ivory as their medium of exchange. The palace was located in the center of the city, and close by there was an arena for contests.

The soldiers of Athne wore accessories of ivory, mainly. Their garb, which was more armorlike than ornamental, was similar to the Cathneans' except everything was made with ivory including their habergeon. The warriors also wore a headband with an ivory ornament in the center shaped like a concave trowel that pointed up and forward. From this headband, and covering each ear, was a large ivory disc suspended from a smaller disc. Other ivory discs with designs on them were worn below each shoulder. The habergeon was supported by leather suspenders and a piece of leather that hung from an elaborately carved ivory disc necklace. These suspender straps also held in place the large wedge shaped pieces of ivory that covered and protected the shoulders. Their sandals were of elephant hide. For weapons they used stout spears, short swords and daggers.

The Athneans raised elephants for war and sport much like the Cathneans raised lions. The men who rode and owned elephants were nobles, called elephant-men. To capture the wild beasts they use trained elephants. If it was a male elephant they wanted to capture, they rode close to it with female elephants to gently work and lead the bull into a big corral inside the city. To help calm all the elephants involved, the elephant-men employed a low sing-song wordless monotone.

Dyaus was the elephant god of Athne and was an actual living elephant. "Mother of Dyaus" was a common oath. Athneans believed in a bad spirit named Daimon that roamed around at night looking for anyone to kill. The people of Athne attributed all unexplained deaths to Daimon, especially those that occurred at night. In *Tarzan the Magnificent*, after Tarzan was seen sneaking around at night by a citizen of Athne, the Jungle Lord claimed to be Daimon so the person would leave him alone and not raise an alarm. The ruse worked.

Chichen Itza: see **Uxmal**

Forbidden City: see **Tuen-Baka**

Gomangani from the Valley of the Palace of Diamonds: see **Valley of the Palace of Diamonds**

Ho-don: see **Pal-ul-don**

KAJI and ZULI: *Tarzan the Magnificent*. The Kaji and the Zuli were two rival tribes of female Amazon-like warriors in which the men were subservient and used as slaves. In both tribes the people (citizen and slave alike) were controlled mentally through a large jewel that had hypnotic powers. The jewel used by the Kaji was a nearly 6000-carat diamond named Gonfal. The one used by the Zuli was approximately the same size and called The Great Emerald of the Zuli. These jewels must be touched by a strong-willed person in order to work. The diamond and the emerald together made for supreme power; separated, the power was greatly reduced.

The rulers of the two villages, who touched the stones and controlled the people through them, were two old and shriveled male twins from Columbia named Mafka and Woora, who were believed to be immortal. Mafka was the magician–witch doctor dictator of the Kaji, and Woora was the same for the Zuli. The brothers used to live and work together in the same village, but after becoming jealous and angry with each other, they fought and divided. Woora left and took the Great Emerald with him, and formed his own village and following of women warriors and slaves. The twins then became greatly opposed to one another.

The power of the diamond Gonfal and the Great Emerald of the Zuli was a hypnotic homing influence that attracted people, especially men, and caused them to be drawn inexplicably against their will into the Kaji country. Once there they were unable to leave of their own free will. If they attempted to escape they were helplessly drawn back to either Mafka in the City of the Kaji, or to Woora in the City of Zuli. With these jewels the twin brothers controlled all the people in the vicinity, and were known to be able to strike a man dead at a certain distance. The influence of the Gonfal and the Great Emerald of the Zuli was like feeling a presence watching from very close by, and hearing strange sounds. Neither jewel had any effect upon Tarzan, however. But when the Jungle Lord wrapped up the Great Emerald of the Zuli and took it with him, he did *feel* a presence very near him. His senses told him that there was nothing around, but he *felt* something or someone very close. When Tarzan actually held the emerald in his hand he experienced a tingling sensation similar to a small current of electricity coming from it; then he felt as if he became one with the jewel. Tarzan was the only one besides Mafka and Woora who was able to bend the will of others with the jewels. The jewels were also known to control animals, to a greater extent than humans.

The rough and secluded country of the Kaji and Zuli was north of Lake Rudolph up an affluent of the Neubari River called Mafa. The only feasible entrance or exit to the country was along the river. All else was mountainous and too treacherous and difficult to cross. Natives feared the land and avoided it because of their superstitions concerning the Kaji and the Zuli.

KAJI: The land of the Kaji was upon a high plateau above the falls of the Mafa river. It was almost inaccessible except for a trail in the gorge of the Mafa from the Neubari. Kaji was a walled city of limestone blocks. The buildings were one or two stories tall and also built of limestone. Mafka lived in a castle that appeared to be of Portuguese construction and design. It was four stories high and appeared ancient. Its only entrance was constantly guarded by his women warriors. The interior of the palace had many skins and weapons hanging upon the walls which may have been stolen from captured safaris. Hidden passages honeycombed the castle, some not entirely known even to Mafka. His private quarters in the palace was a multiroomed suite which included a lab where he dabbled in regular chemistry as well as the black arts. With one of his experiments he developed a phony duplicate of the Gonfal to allow others to handle while believing it to be the real thing. The actual diamond he kept with him at all times unless it was locked and guarded. Since the Gonfal must be touched by him to be effective, Mafka rested it on a pedestal next to him in the throne room for easy access.

The Kaji were all warrior women. Their skin colors ranged from brown to white, but years before they had all been black. Their desire to be white caused them to keep only the white men that were lured into the land by the Gonfal diamond. The blacks they either killed or chased away. After several generations, they were almost exclusively white skinned, but occasionally a throwback Negroid baby was born. These black newborns were destroyed. So were all male babies, because the Kaji felt that skin color was inherited from the father, and a male child born to them who survived would have some Negroid blood to pass on to future generations. But there was a scarcity of white men, which necessitated them being married to more than one Kaji woman. This polygamy was legal according to Kaji law, with the marriage ceremonies being performed by Mafka in the presence of the Gonfal diamond.

Gonfala was the name of the queen of the Kaji. She was the daughter of the lost, and dead, explorers Lord and Lady Mountford. Because they believed she was the Gonfal diamond personified, the Kaji revered Gonfala and drew her name from the jewel. They considered her their goddess as well as their queen, and consequently Gonfala wore a lot of gold and a crown. Nonetheless, she was just a figurehead: Mafka, wielding the Gonfal diamond, held the real power in Kaji.

In her palace Gonfala had the mummified heads of dead Zuli

women warriors hanging by their hair as trophies of war.

ZULI: East of the city of Kaji, over treacherous mountains, deep gorges, and precipitous cliffs, and at a point near the headwaters of the Mafa river, lay the large village of the Zuli. Here, as in Kaji, the women were the true citizens and the main warriors while the men were slaves. These male slaves comprised of bearded whites as well as blacks who wore well-worn loincloths of wild animal skins, barbaric ornaments such as necklaces of animal teeth, anklets and armlets. Some men, though, were permitted to bear weapons and be warriors along with the women. They all wielded bows and arrows, short heavy spears, and small shields of buffalo hide which they carried upon their backs. Their tongue was a haphazard mix of several African dialects and European languages. In Zuli the men were more valuable because there were so few of them. Each white man there was married to anywhere from seven to twelve women who each had to fight for the right to have him. The men remained in Zuli for two main reasons. One, because they were compelled to by the power and influence of the Great Emerald of the Zuli wielded by Woora. The other was that the only accessible way out of the land of the Zuli was through Kaji country, where they knew they would be killed, or enslaved again, but without weapons.

The Zuli village was stockaded and consisted of stone huts thatched with grass. At night a large bonfire was lit in the center of the main street. The palace of Woora was a larger two-story stone affair guarded by a dozen warrior women. Its interior was lit by oil crescent lamps. In the palace was a guard room decorated with weapons, shields, and animal skins hanging from the wall. The throne room was spacious and more elaborately decorated than the others with skins and weapons. The most outstanding decorations in the room were the hundreds of mummified heads of women which hung by their long hair around the walls and ceiling. At one end of the room, standing on a dais, stood the large throne Woora sat upon. And on a table in front of Woora rested the Great Emerald of the Zuli, close enough so that he could readily place his hand upon it. With this jewel, through fear and compulsion, he maintained dictatorial control over his warrior women and the men who were their slaves.

Prisoners were kept in a small cell room on the second floor of the palace building directly above Woora's three-room suite which adjoined the throne room. There were heavy wooden bars in its single window. Below the window was a walled compound that contained a panther used to guard Woora and help deter prisoners from escaping. If Woora found something that a prisoner or slave excelled in, he would eat the relevant part of that person's body. This practice was based upon the belief that those attributes of the person would be passed on to Woora. Those he did not approve of were either fed alive to the lions for sport and entertainment, or tortured. Woora usually did not have intelligent looking white male captives killed, but gave them to his warrior women to fight for as husbands to propagate the race.

Rarely was anyone permitted to enter Woora's suite. He took his morning meals there after they were passed to him through an opening near the floor. Occasionally a warrior woman was taken in, but out of terror she never revealed what she saw or experienced. In one of his rooms he had all the items of a medieval alchemist: vials, test tubes, lamps, a crystal ball, and books on the occult and voodooism. Also in his suite could be found mummified heads of women suspended from the ceiling by their long hair.

As with the Kaji, Woora was trying to create a white bloodline in Zuli. When Tarzan entered the land of the Zuli, it was almost exclusively white babies that were born. But occasionally there were Negroids. These were always killed. But white babies fared little better. The village had only a finite population it could support because, although meat was plentiful, fruits and vegetables were not. Therefore, almost all newborns were killed, regardless of color, as were most new captives, unless a need had been created due to someone's death or capture from a raid by the Kaji.

KAVURU: *Tarzan's Quest*. The Kavuru people were a race of strong, young, good looking, white male warriors who spoke a Bantu dialect. Their arms, wrists and ankles were loaded with jewelry, and hanging prominently around their necks were necklaces of human teeth. Their loincloths were made of gorilla hide and held up with a thin fiber rope looped around the waist several times. From this rope was suspended a multipurpose pouch. Transversely through the septum of their nose was a bone or ivory tube six to eight inches long. They also wore many earrings. Their hair was cut in a Mohawk style from the forehead to the nape of the neck. In their hair they

had many brilliant feathers, and their faces were hideously painted. For weapons they used a knife and heavy spear. All the Kavuru were priests who had taken a vow of celibacy, because they believed that if they succumbed to the wiles of women they would become contaminated and live in torment after their death and not obtain godhood. The Kavuru also had a superstitious fear of airplanes.

The land of the Kavuru was far to the east of the Waziri country, and no one was allowed to escape from it. The terrain before their village was open and beautiful with many park-like areas. Tarzan found it a country he would like to explore. At the edge of a forest was a large rolling boulder-strewn plain. Across the plain stood a mountain range. The Kavuru village lay at the base of a perpendicular cliff of this range and had a large three-sided palisade made of stone with the fourth side being the cliff face. A small river ran beneath the palisade wall and into the plain. A large main gate opened into a narrow street. The buildings in the village were small and made of stone and adobe, with flat roofs which indicated little rain. The Kavuru cooked in exterior ovens out in the street near their homes. Prisoners were kept in a circular building that must be entered by ascending a ladder to the roof and then climbing down through an opening via another ladder. Behind the village proper, a large gate enclosed a box canyon where the farming took place. For servants the Kavuru employed only human males who had mental disorders, because they thought that these men had a demon in their head, and calculated that if they somehow escaped no one would believe a word they said, thereby protecting the location of the Kavuru village. Captive women were kept in the temple where eunuchs were used as servants and guards.

The Kavuru had perpetual youth and beauty. To maintain their immortality they made an elixir pill that had to be taken every month. This pill was made from, among other things, the blood and glands of young girls and the spinal fluid of leopards. Consequently there were no women citizens among the Kavuru except those held captive for the sole use of making the elixir pills. As a result of this, the Kavuru had no children. Eighty years before Tarzan arrived, the last true Kavuru woman died giving her life so that the men might have their perpetual youth. After that the Kavuru began abducting girls of all races from the outside world.

To achieve this, they approached their intended victim through the trees, which they could travel through fairly well, although not as easily as Tarzan. The Kavuru called to the unwary girl in a low monotonous droning chant that hypnotized her and gave her a compelling urge to obey that she could not deny. Her senses became numbed and she felt neither fear nor happiness. The victim then walked in a trance toward the Kavuru who, while still in the trees, retreated further into the jungle, leading the girl away from any possible observers. Once at a safe location the Kavuru warrior took the rope from around his waist and lassoed the hapless female. While still chanting he pulled her up into the trees and carried her off into the jungle for several hours before returning to the ground. The effect of the hypnosis went away an hour

or so after this. When evening came the Kavuru securely tied the girl's arms and legs so she could not escape. Back in the village, the girl was killed in the making of the elixir pills and her teeth were given to her captor for a necklace as a symbol of his prowess and skill. Among the Kavuru the necklaces were a sign of importance and prestige — the more necklaces the greater the prominence.

The inventor of the elixir pill was Kavandavanda, the king, witch doctor, high priest of the priests of Kavuru, and their god. Kavandavanda was very young and good looking with perfect proportions and blonde hair. He was the most handsome man Jane had ever seen. Kavandavanda's only drawback physically was his cruel mouth. For adornment he wore only a loincloth and ornaments similar to the other Kavuru. He had many necklaces of human teeth that hung very low down his front. Kavandavanda kept a large supply of his elixir pills locked in an elaborately carved and decorated cabinet in his personal chambers. Although he and the Kavuru believed that they could not obtain godliness with women, Kavandavanda was willing to break his vow of celibacy with Jane, who he felt had cast a spell over him with her beauty, and take her as his mate. He said he would make her his goddess and give her the elixir pills so she too could live forever.

Kavandavanda lived in a castle-like palace near the cliff face that also housed the rooms for the temple. The throne room of the temple was circular with wooden columns made of tree trunks darkened by antiquity. Upon the capitals of the columns were the toothless skulls of numerous victims. The dais of the throne was covered with leopard skins. The rooms of the temple were named and marked with images and carvings of animals placed above the doorways. A secret tunnel led from the palace to the jungle. Only Kavandavanda and six others knew of its existence. Many leopards ran loose in the outer courtyard as guardians of the palace and temple. These well-fed beasts left the people alone during the day, but at night made terrible and relentless watchdogs. Besides this and being used for the elixir pills, the leopards served the purpose of taking care of any dead or living humans thrown to them. When ever their diet was about to be augmented in this fashion, they were called to the feast by a strange and unclean yell given by one of the eunuchs.

LEOPARD MEN: *Tarzan and the Leopard Men.* The Secret Order of the Leopard Men was first mentioned in *Tarzan and the Lost Empire*, but a complete narrative and description appeared in *Tarzan and the Leopard Men.* The Leopard Men were a secret society of men from any and all tribes. Not even their own wives knew they were members of this feared clan. If their wives found out, they would reveal it to the village and their husbands would be killed. The Leopard Men met in the village of their chief, Gato Mgungu. Entry to it was obtained only after giving the secret signs of the clan. From the village they took canoes downriver for a mile or two. Then they turned up a small stream with thick foliage on either side and hanging down from above. After another few miles they came to shore near a large grass thatched building that was 200 feet long and 50 wide

and 50 high. This was the temple of the Leopard God.

For costume the Leopard Men wore leopard headdresses. As weapons, they had poison tipped steel leopard claws on their hands. They only used spears and arrows as a last resort or against superior numbers. The Leopard Men had filed teeth and were considered cannibals, even though they ate only certain parts of the human body. In accordance with the unholy rites of their cannibal religious rituals, before they could eat human flesh, they must have killed their victims with their steel leopard claws.

In the religion of the Leopard Men there was a high priest with his priests and priestesses. Within the temple were carved idols of human bodies with animal heads. Upon the walls and pillars hung skulls, masks and gaudy shields. A large raised dais covered with clay stood at one end of the main temple room, and upon it a smaller dais covered with animal skins sat. A long post with a human skull on it had been placed in the center of the smaller dais and near its rear. Chained to a post close to the daises was a giant devil-faced leopard, the god of the Leopard Men. During ceremonies the high priest, wearing a hideous mask as were his priests, petitioned the Leopard God in a high pitched voice and asked it questions. The Leopard God answered his high priest in the same tongue, but with a voice that was low and husky and intermixed with growls and snarls. This was a trick of the high priest, and he accomplished it through ventriloquism. Other portions of the temple ceremony consisted of dancing and beer drinking along with the eating of the human body parts that had been collected.

Another rite performed by the Leopard Men in their temple was human sacrifice. If a living prisoner was to be sacrificed and eaten, the priests holding the sacrifice threw the victim on the floor and pinion him or her. Then club wielding priestesses danced around the victim to the beat of a drum, and every now and then one would rush in with her club in a mock attempt to hit the sacrifice. At this juncture a priest would fend off this false attack. As the dance continued the more frenzied the priestesses became and the more difficult it was to hold them off. At the climax of the dance the high priest gave a signal that caused the dancing to stop and the onlookers to fall silent. Then the priestesses crept forward and broke the bones of the living victim with their clubs in preparation for cooking and eating.

The high priest in *Tarzan and the Leopard Men* was named Imigeg. He was old and beginning to lose his memory. Lulimi, an upstart younger man high in the priesthood who hoped to be high priest after Imigeg's death, manipulated the old man into having a captured white girl, referred to as Kali Bwana, made high priestess to the Leopard God. In preparation to becoming high priestess, Kali Bwana was given over to the priestesses of the Leopard God. Naked but for a G-string, the priestesses tore off Kali's clothes, threw her on the ground, and covered her all over with a rancid oil which they rubbed into her skin. Then they anointed her with a greenish liquid that burned, rubbing it all over her body until it evaporated. Then they dressed her. For raiment she wore about her slim waist a loincloth made out of the skins of unborn leopard cubs. Over

a shoulder was draped a brilliant black speckled hide of leopard fur. This was tied loosely about her waist by a rope of leopard tails. A bracelet of human teeth circled her neck, along with necklaces of other items. Bracelets, armlets and anklets — many of them gold — adorned her wrists, arms and ankles. Upon her head, the priestesses placed a circular diadem of leopard skin with various feathers and plumes. Lastly, she wore upon her fingers and thumbs long golden curved talons. Fortunately for Kali Bwana she was rescued from the temple during her introductory ceremony.

Tarzan, with natives from various villages, took over Gato Mgungu's village and helped break up the Secret Order of the Leopard Men.

London on the Thames: see **Valley of Diamonds**

LOST EMPIRE: *Tarzan and the Lost Empire*. In the Wiramwazi Mountains lay a plateau which ended at a sheer canyon 25 to 30 miles long (east to west), 15 to 20 miles wide (north to south), and one mile deep. This canyon contained the rival Roman cities of Castra Sanguinarius on the west end, and the island city of Castra Mare on the east. The people of both these cities together made up the legendary Lost Tribe of the Wiramwazi Mountains, spoken of by natives in the vicinity. The two Roman cities had existed in the canyon for over 1800 years, and the citizens spoke Latin and believed that ancient Rome still existed.

In A.D. 90 the land's founder, Marcus Crispis Sanguinarius, was accused by Nerva, the newly appointed Caesar of Rome, of treason and ordered to place himself under arrest. Instead, Sanguinarius fled with his army. During their flight they captured a caravan of goods and treasures along with slaves of various sexes and skin colors who had been taken from several countries. The majority of the lighter skinned slaves were young girls. After attempting to settle in different areas, Sanguinarius finally found, and settled permanently in, the large, lost and hidden canyon of the Wiramwazi Mountains. Here he built and named a city after himself and declared himself Caesar. He then had his own calendar made and coins stamped with his image upon them.

A large swamp-like lake they named Mare Orientis took up the majority of the eastern half of the canyon. The western side had a forest of mainly oak trees where several unfamiliar types of birds nested. Although the dangerous descent of the sheer rock wall could feasibly be made as a way of entering the canyon, there was really only one way in: through a narrow gorge that entered the canyon from the west near Castra Sanguinarius. A man-made wall 100 feet high separated the gorge from the canyon. At the base of the wall was an arched doorway made with heavy timbers where guards continually stood watch. This narrow gorge could only be reached after first passing through the country of the Bagegos natives.

The Romans considered the Bagegos barbarians and enemies of the people of the Lost Tribe. Nevertheless, once a year they had a truce and traded with each other out of necessity. At all other times, though, the Romans regularly came out and raided the Bagegos' village, for prisoners to use as slaves, and for other items. Many of the Bagegos believed that the members of the Lost Tribe

were the ghosts of their departed ancestors.

Slaves of the Lost Tribe were black and spoke a mixture of Latin and a Bantu dialect. For weapons these slaves used pikes and broad double-edged short swords hung over the right shoulder in a scabbard. The shopkeepers and soldiers of the Lost Tribe were higher on the social scale and were a tan color with more Caucasian features. They wore Roman cloaks, tunics, and sandals. They also had a helmet and a leather cuirass, and bore an ancient shield with a pike, and a Spanish sword. The military was equipped with heavy artillery including small ballistae, catapults, testudines, battering rams, and devices to loft large fireballs at an enemy. The officers, aristocrats, and official citizens of both cities were Caucasian and wore finer apparel that comprised of colored cloaks and tunics as well as simple togas. Centurions had been admitted into the patrician class.

Traveling about as a member of the ruling class was done in wheelless litters carried by slaves. Throughout the cities grew many private gardens with trees and winding gravel walkways. The people wrote upon rolled parchment with a reed pen and used an inkstand. These Romans still believed in the mythological god Jupiter and the half-breed Hercules, and had a temple. A high priest officiated in Castra Sanguinarius, and vestal virgins tended the temple's sacred fires.

In *Tarzan at the Earth's Core* it was revealed that a very light and durable metal was discovered in the valley of the Lost Empire. It was dubbed harbenite after Eric von Harben who determined its value. The harbenite was used to make the dirigible

O-220 that took Tarzan to Pelluci-dar.

CASTRA SANGUINARIUS: First of the two cities built and constructed entirely upon land, Castra Sanguinarius lay west of Mare Orientis. Its ruler was Sublatus Imperator, the Imperial Caesar and Emperor of the West. His palace, a large building, had a select division of the military always guarding it. The accouterments of the guards were more elaborate than those of the common soldiers: their armor was made out of what appeared to be gold, and their weapons were inlaid with jewels. They also wore scarlet cloaks. Inside the palace were many chambers and columns. The throne room was oblong and decorated with things of war including shields, banners, and crude murals. Sublatus sat upon a large carved chair upon a raised dais. He wore an abundance of gold and a royal purple robe hung over his shoulders. A fillet of embroidered linen adorned his brow.

Gold was one of Castra Sanguinarius' main trade goods because the city controlled the only gold mine in the valley. This precious metal they traded with Castra Mare in exchange for their goods and wares. The other important commodity Castra Sanguinarius had was slaves. Since the only entrance into the valley was through Sanguinarius, slaves who were not taken by force during a war between the two cities, had to come through Sanguinarius to be traded. Any new breeding stock for herds from the outside world also came by way of Castra Sanguinarius.

Inside the valley near the canyon entrance were native villages made up of conical beehive huts.

The city itself was surrounded by a lofty rampart surmounted by palisades and battlements. A moat ran around the foot of the rampart, and a bridge crossed it to the main gate which was guarded by twin towers. The nearer buildings within the city wall were single storied, and made of stucco and built around a courtyard. These were the dwelling places. There was a central area for the shops. Having been constructed amidst the forest Sanguinarius had many groves of trees within its walls. Trees also overhung the avenues, the streets and the houses.

Castra Sanguinarius had a large Colosseum similar to Rome's made of hewn granite blocks. Beneath the Colosseum lay dungeons where the prisoners and wild animals were kept for the tournament. Usually whites and blacks were not held together in the same cell unless there was an overcrowding problem.

Before each tournament there was a parade of prisoners called the triumph of Caesar. The people began lining the streets for it a day before, spending the night outside to save their chosen space. The parade was mainly a military show, with Sublatus riding in a lion-drawn chariot with gold leashes. Prestigious prisoners were collared and chained with gold, attached to Caesar's chariot, and forced to walk behind. Military floats depicted wars, and litters carried other dignitaries. Flocks and herds stolen from the Bagegos brought up the rear of the parade.

The tournament lasted about a week, and to keep the people entertained that long, Sublatus kept the greatest exhibitions for the end. The thumbs up or down sign from the crowd indicated whether or not they wanted a fight to end with the death of one of the combatants. In the arena, various supplied weapons could be used, including a hempen net. The victor won a laurel wreath and their freedom, whether man, woman or beast.

CASTRA MARE: This city was located on an island in the lake Mare Orientis in the eastern half of the valley. Its ruler and Caesar was Validus Augustus, Emperor of the East. Castra Mare's population, a little over 22,000, comprised 3000 whites and 19,000 of mixed blood.

Outside the city and all along the eastern shore of the lake lived 26,000 lake-dwelling natives. These indentured servants (barbarians) were scattered about the waterways and lived in beehive huts built upon the roots of papyrus plants. These native slaves used dugout canoes to travel through the marshy areas and along the channels cut through the tall papyrus plants. Near the raised land of the city's entrance, the papyrus had been completely cleared out. Upon this land rose an earthen rampart topped by a sturdy stockade. Two lofty towers mark the entrance over the rampart. The waterfront of Castra Mare was poorly guarded because the crocodile-infested lake formed an effective barrier.

When water travelers came in sight, guards sounded a trumpet from the towers. The approaching canoes were required to stop about a hundred yards away until proper identification was made. Then one canoe was permitted to approach at a time. An officer had to grant permission for any barbarians to enter the city, and they had to carry passes with them.

The only road to Castra Mare from Castra Sanguinarius had a fort built over it which was virtually impregnable by anything other than heavy artillery. This fort had a moat, embankments, palisade and towers. A pontoon bridge gave access to the island from the land.

Castra Mare itself had stone and stucco buildings. The streets were dirt and enclosed either side in an unbroken run by the facades of buildings and by walls built between them. This, along with heavily barred doors and windows, were not to protect the citizens from crime, but from slave uprisings.

Crime was rare in Castra Mare, so the people left their doors unlocked at night. This custom began after Castra Mare's founder, Honus Hasta, revolted from Castra Sanguinarius about a hundred years after the valley was discovered and inhabited. At that time, Castra Sanguinarius was overrun with criminals. Disgusted, Honus took a hundred families with him and built his island city, and made very stringent rules dealing with crime that were strictly enforced. The result was a veritable crime free environment that still existed in Castra Mare when Eric von Harben arrived. The two cities, however, were constantly at war, and there was little commerce between them. Their mutual animosity was propagated by the two rulers who both feared that if the people became too friendly they would band together and usurp their separate rulers in favor of one. Otherwise, Castra Mare had had good and fair leadership over the centuries and was richer and more cultured than Castra Sanguinarius.

Communal baths for men and women, popular among the ruling class of Castra Mare, were held in a large building amidst exclusive shops. The men and women's dressing rooms were separate, though. After a bather had removed their clothes, his or her body was anointed with oils in a warm room. From there they entered a hot room that led to the main bathing area and a large pool-sized bath. Diving was an unknown art in the valley until Eric von Harben arrived.

The palace of Validus had a vault-like library with many parchment rolls of written documents. The parchment was made from the papyrus that grew in Mare Orientis. Papyrus was one of the few things that Castra Mare traded with Castra Sanguinarius. Other items of trade included ink, snails, fish and jewels. Castra Mare also had the only iron mine in the valley which provided another item of trade between the two cities.

The city did have a Colosseum and its own tournament, although neither was as grand as Castra Sanguinarius'. This was due to a lack of participants, since criminals were almost nonexistent and slaves too valuable to waste in the games. The majority of the participants in Castra Mare's games were political prisoners, professional gladiators and animals.

Lost Tribe of the Wiramwazi Mountains: see **Lost Empire**

MANGANI: (See also the Ape Language in Section Two) The great anthropoid apes of Tarzan were called the first men by the people of Opar and the great man-apes of Africa by Eugene Hanson in *Tarzan: The Lost Adventure*. Mangani were not quite gorillas or chimpanzees. Nor were they orangutan, although the orangutan were also considered Mangani. Tarzan's great apes were more hominoid than other anthropoids and thought to be the possible missing link between man and ape. Mangani were hairy and tailless with broad flat noses, beetling brows, and low receding foreheads. Older apes had gray in their hair and whiskers. Their intellect was superior to that of all other anthropoids and primates except man. They also had highly developed senses of smell and hearing. Superbly muscled, the great apes possessed superhuman strength, and they had sharp pointed fangs which they used for battle and for eating. The males could exceed seven feet in height when fully erect, and their arms were longer than their legs. The Mangani were capable of bipedal locomotion, but often used their arms and knuckles to walk upon all fours. Despite the fact that they were able to travel through the trees as easily as upon the ground, the great apes were usually territorial and not very ambitious, and enjoyed spending their time idly searching for food. As the Mangani were carnivorous as well as herbivorous, their diet normally consisted of insects, fruits, nuts, small rodents and tubers. They used tools such as a twig for assistance in digging for food or gathering bugs. Occasionally they ate the flesh of large animals killed for the ceremonial dum-dum gathering. As youths the Mangani were playful, but as they matured they became indolent, and, especially among the males, more surly. The Mangani loathed to submerge themselves in water, but they did drink it. Their way of transporting water was to carry it in their mouths.

The great apes lived in tribes with a dominant ruling king. Kingship was earned by challenging and then besting (usually by killing) the existing king in battle. None of the other apes interfered when a kingship battle took place, and the mates of the vanquished customarily became the possessions of the victor.

The Mangani avoided other tribes of apes, and if they encountered any a battle could break out. When a bull approached a strange or challenging male both walked stiff legged and sniffed about each other with much boasting and bragging. Their hair bristled as they appeared to be trying to work themselves into a fighting rage, but more often than not it was just a ruse to scare the other away. Bulls were known, however, to throw temper tantrums and go into berserk rages without warning. When such a rage gripped a bull, there was tremendous danger for whoever or whatever got in his way: and they were wont to attack anyone or anything they could get their hands on. Otherwise the Mangani avoided encounters, preferring to relax and search for grubs.

Not known for their long attention span, the Mangani lost interest quickly or were easily distracted unless constantly reminded. Tarzan tried many times to teach the tribe of Kerchak and other Mangani new ways and ideas. The Ape-man showed the tribe of Kerchak how to post sentries in *Jungle Tales of Tarzan* to help protect them from Numa, Sabor, and Sheeta. This they began doing even though it almost led to Tarzan's death. In *The Beasts of Tarzan* the Jungle Lord got the tribe of Akut to paddle a canoe. In *Tarzan and the Jewels of Opar* Tarzan convinced a few Mangani to wear clothes and sneak into an Arab camp. The Mangani who became the servants of god in *Tarzan and the Madman* not only spoke the ape language, but learned a language taught them by the people of Alemtejo.

The language spoken by the great apes was common among all anthropoids including Bolgani, the gorilla, Manu, the monkey, Tongani, the baboon, and the orangutans (also known as Mangani). Most other jungle animals understood the Mangani language to a greater or lesser extent (for more information see the Ape Language in Section Two).

Another form of communication was the victory cry of the bull ape. It was given after vanquishing a foe. Usually the champion placed his foot on the throat of the deceased enemy and, after throwing his head back, let loose this weird and terrifying bawl. The sound of the victory cry sent shivers down human spines and caused all animals to grow silent in fear. Often it was taken as a challenge by other large animals like Numa, the lion, Sheeta, the panther, and even Tantor, the elephant, and an answering roar or trumpet was sounded in return. Tarzan used the victory cry or a similar cry to call the Mangani, Tantor, and his Beasts (from *The Beasts of Tarzan*) to his assistance. He also used it to strike fear in the hearts of his enemies. Most natives knew it for what it was: the victory cry of a great ape who had just made a kill.

The Mangani did consider humans a form of themselves, and called the white man the white great apes or Tarmangani, and the black man the black great apes or Gomangani. Consequently, the Mangani males were not loath to take a white woman as a slave or mate. An example of this was when the recently exiled Terkoz first saw Jane Porter in *Tarzan of the Apes* he decided to make her "the first of his new household." (TA) Then Toyat,

J. Allen St. John illustration from *The Beasts of Tarzan* (© 1916 Edgar Rice Burroughs, Inc.).

the king ape, in *Tarzan, Lord of the Jungle* saw Princess Guinalda, and having "once seen another Tarmangani she ... [he] decided that he would like to have one as a wife." (TLJ) In *Tarzan: The Lost Adventure*, Go-lot, an upstart young bull in the

tribe of Zu-yad, saw Jean Hanson and desired her for a slave, because "it was a great prize and status symbol to have a Tarmangani slave. It had only been thus a few times— Zu-yad had owned two—and of course the slaves did not last long—

but it was still prestigious." (TLA) This gives credibility to the notion of a female Mangani taking a human infant to raise as her own, as in the case of the infant Tarzan when the bereft she-ape, Kala, took him to her bosom.

The people of the lost city of Opar, the last bastion of Atlantis, actually mated with the Mangani and spawned half-blooded offspring. The males of such unholy unions became the priests of Opar. On the other hand, all female Oparians born with ape-like attributes were killed, in order to keep the blood of the priestesses as pure as possible. Other half-blooded creations of the Oparian and apes mating were the intelligent great apes in the nearby Valley of the Palace of Diamonds, who were the hereditary enemies of the Oparians. These Bolgani had the intellect and cunning of humans, but the bodies of apes. Called great apes by La, High Priestess of Opar, the Bolgani were larger than gorillas.

DUM-DUM: Like the Mangani language the Dum-Dum was a rite perhaps older than the human race, and from it all religions may have sprung. The Mangani's ceremonial sacrificial dance and feast was usually held to celebrate an important event in the life of the tribe — the ascension of a king, a victory, the capture of a prisoner, the killing of certain large enemies of the great apes such as Bolgani and Numa or a Mangani from a rival tribe. The Dum-Dum was expected to occur upon a regular basis, and usually at every full moon if not earlier for some reason. For these regular celebrations, a sacrifice often had to be found, although it was not uncommon for a Dum-Dum to be performed without one.

If a sacrifice was acquired, two bulls took the body, alive or dead, to the secluded area of the jungle only accessible from the trees where the tribe always held its Dum-Dum ceremonies. Here, in the center of this natural arena, the Mangani had a raised and rounded mound of dirt. The two bulls deposited the sacrifice, then remained as guards, or the female apes assumed that duty. The rest of the tribe waited or slept until the moon was seen at night. At the appropriate time several old females (usually about three), and often young apes, sat in a circle around this natural earthen drum and beat upon it with sticks about 18 inches long. There was also an outer circle of young, old, and female apes. The bulls were ranged in between.

At first the beating upon the drum was slow and soft as the moon continued rising overhead and its rays filtered through the branches of the trees. As more light flooded into the arena the drummers increased their beating. Then the king ape leaped between the males and the drummers and, while beating upon his chest, threw his head back and gave forth a challenging cry to the moon. He then approached and passed by the sacrifice that had been placed before the altar-drum, always keeping his eyes upon the victim. The Dum-Dum was a representation of the hunt. Other males joined the king ape, and beat upon their chests and screamed at the moon. A dance of sorts began, as the apes leapt around the drumming circle and the body of their quarry while working themselves into a frenzy, all to the primal beat. After every male had joined in this "Dance of Death" and the moon was at its zenith signifying the moment for the kill, the king would grab a club from a nearby pile built there for the purpose (if he did not already have one) and began beating the sacrifice. The other males followed his lead and did the same. This continued for about a half hour until the body was a bloody pulp. When the victim was dead — if not dead to begin with — at another signal from the king the drumming stopped and the males fell upon the corpse of their enemy, tore it apart, and ate it. Naturally the best or biggest portions went to the stronger and craftier participants. The women and children were last to partake, if there was anything left.

MIDIAN: *Tarzan Triumphant.* High in the Ghenzi Mountain range was a crater that contained a lake. This was where the people of Midian dwell. The only feasible way into the crater other than parachuting was through a natural vertical narrow cleft in the mountainside. As the cleft progressed, upward at first, it became wider and was several hundred yards long, with many rock fragments upon its floor. The fissure then curved downward and became steeper and narrower, with the floor clearer because the upper walls had closed together. This closing of the walls at the top reduced the light in the fissure. The exit from it, and the threshold to the crater valley, was a small aperture just big enough for a human body to worm through at the base of the inner cliff. It was hidden and had been forgotten over the centuries since the crater had first become inhabited by the Midians.

The people of Midian were fanatically religious and had biblical names, but they possessed only a basic Christian belief mixed with Judaism. There was no written language among the Midians, so their histories and customs had been handed down orally, and consequently over time their beliefs had become twisted and changed. Their history began, though, immediately after the time of Christ when Paul of Tarsus was martyred in Rome. Augustus the Ephesian, who was a homely, unintelligent epileptic and a fanatic follower of Paul, fled possible persecution after this and headed south. During his journey Augustus stopped at the Island of Rhodus where he acquired a young and pretty slave girl with fair hair. After much more traveling the two ended up in the isolated crater in the Ghenzi Mountains where they began propagating.

From these humble beginnings in the crater sprang two rival villages that contained separate and distinctly different looking people. In the beginning, however, they were united, living in the same village. The reason for the division was prejudice and persecution caused by some of the children being born with Augustus' sub-normal physical and intellectual attributes while others were born with the more appealing slave girl's. But since Augustus was the original leader, those that looked like him thought themselves superior and persecuted the fairer. After several generations of this prejudicial abuse, the better looking, fair-haired people banded together and moved away from the original village to the other side of the lake near a small forest, and became the North Midians. The ones left in the original village with the characteristics of Augustus were known as the South Midians.

SOUTH MIDIANS: Most of the people of South Midian bore the genes of Augustus and were, therefore, dark haired, unintelligent, epileptic, and homely, with extremely large noses and receding chins. South Midians did not comb or trim their beards and hair; nor did they appear to bathe themselves regularly. When they walked, they leaned forward as if about to fall over. Their garments, made of plant fiber, were scant and ill kept. They lived in caves dug out of the softer volcanic walls of the crater with loose grass as floor coverings and bedding. A zig-zag path led from the base of the cliff up to the caves. There were also a few huts at the base of the cliff.

The South Midians felt they were the chosen people of god. Therefore, if a child was born with the genetics of the fair haired, beautiful, and intelligent slave girl taken by Augustus at the Island of Rhodus, they were either killed or, if allowed to live, considered more inclined to evil. They were persecuted and abused their whole life until they died of natural causes, were killed, or ran away to live with the North Midians. The South Midians had a religious leader who they considered to be the Prophet of Paul the Apostle, the son of Jehovah. They also believed that Paul had been dark haired, and if anyone believed otherwise (as did the North Midians) they were a sinner and a heretic. Their prophet leader had apostles who were the subordinate leaders of the people.

All the villagers were epileptic. When they succumbed to a seizure they claimed that they were walking and talking with God during that time, and often that they had received revelation. Seizures frequently overtook them, especially when they were excited. When praying (but not in the grip of a seizure) the prophet spoke in gibberish that was not language, although it was claimed to be. Only the prophet and his apostles were allowed to use this unintelligible holy language. But no one, including the prophet and apostles themselves, really understood it.

Human sacrifices were a part of the religion of the South Midians and were performed by the prophet. One form of sacrifice took place at dusk and began with a man leaving his cave chanting and bearing a torch. Others would join him, and the chant would increase in volume. Then a child would be dragged out of a cave screaming, and taken along with the torch-bearing marchers. Once they reached a boulder in the bottom of the crater, they would circle it and continue chanting. The prophet would then raise his hand and the chanting would cease. With eyes cast towards the heavens he would then begin a monotonous prayer. At this juncture the sacrificial child would be placed upon the waist high boulder, usually crying and screaming the whole way. The prophet would then simply raise a crude knife above his head and kill the child.

The other modes of religious ceremony and sacrifice included a drowning judgment and a fire punishment. In drowning, a supposed sinner would be placed in a net with a rock tied to it, and lowered three times into the crater lake named Chinnereth. If she survived her sins were washed clean and forgiven. If she perished then, according to the prophet, her sins were too great to be forgiven. The fire punishment simply consisted of the victim being burned alive upon a cross.

Anything that gave pleasure was considered a lure of the devil among the South Midians. Consequently they considered the act of procreation a sin, and in shame for having succumbed to its temptation the women often killed their first born. They also deemed smiling a sin, because it led to laughter and laughter was believed by them to be carnal. A person caught smiling would be punished by being either burned on a cross or dipped into the crater lake Chinnereth.

NORTH MIDIANS: The more intelligent, better looking, blond haired and blue eyed descendants of the slave girl taken from the island Rhondus: these were the North Midians. Due to persecution, they split off from the South Midians and fled to the northern end of the crater near a small forest, and created their own village and society that was larger and cleaner and considered more pretentious than the South Midians'. North Midians were short and stocky, wore a single goat skin garment, and had better hygiene than the South Midians. They were very talkative and given to long narratives and discussions. They lived in grass or stone huts, raised goats, and carried clubs which they could throw very accurately. They also used sharpened sticks and instruments of stone and bone as tools.

In contrast to the beliefs of the South Midians, the men of North Midian desired women for mating, and laughter was commonplace among all the villagers. If North Midians caught any South Midians they killed the men and made the women slaves. If those captured had the same genetics as themselves, they were accepted into the society and the women taken for wives. If a child was born to the North Midians with Augustus' looks or epilepsy, it was

killed, because they felt that any person with epilepsy had a demon inside them.

The North Midians were fanatically religious too. They believed that they were the real chosen people and that their leader was the true Prophet of Paul, the son of Jehovah. They believed the Apostle Paul had blond hair and that believing it to be a different color was heresy. Most of the North Midians were superstitious: some felt the world outside the crater was inhabited by demons; others that it was inhabited by angels. Part of their religion involved a sacrificial form of judgment where the accused was buried alive. The judgment pit was dug before the prophet's hut, and to begin the ceremony, the prophet uttered a long prayer while all the people gathered around, knelt, and gave voice to hallelujahs and amens. If the sacrifice survived, it meant that the person had spoken the truth, was considered clean, had been forgiven, or had been accepted.

MINUNI and ALALUS: *Tarzan and the Ant Men* (see also the Language of the Ant Men in Section Two). Beyond a great thorn forest barrier lay a vast basin where two isolated and distinct races dwelt. One was the primitive and giant female-dominated Alalus; the other, the tiny Minuni, or Ant Men.

MINUNI: Physically the Minuni were not pygmies, but normally proportioned and tan Caucasian human beings, on average about 18 inches tall. On the whole they were good looking and smooth faced. The Minuni were highly civilized and advanced, although their society most closely resembled that of Europe in its medieval period. When they saw Tarzan eat his meat raw the Minuni were repulsed and concerned, because in their experience the only creatures that ate raw meat also ate the Minuni. They believed that the thorn forest surrounding their land went on till it reached the wall of the blue dome (sky) under which they dwelt, and that the only life and world that existed were theirs inside the thorn forest basin. The Minuni had their own distinct spoken and written language, and numbers, mathematics, and measurements. Among them, a person's name was sacred and could only be used by permission. Using it meant a deep friendship and was therefore usually restricted to close friends and family members. When applauding, the Minuni rubbed their palms together in a rapid circular motion or exclaimed, "Ee-ah-ee-ah!" in a shrill voice.

There were two Minuni cities that Tarzan came in contact with. The first was Trohanadalmakus and the second was Veltopismakus. The two were rivals. There were other cities in the land, but only one was specifically mentioned (but not visited), and that was Mandalamakus.

Minuni cities were made up of several large domed buildings that housed thousands of people. Each city had a monarchy for government, with a king and a royal family. The king and his family had their own royal dome which was usually larger than all others. A group of administrators called the Royal Council oversaw agriculture, building construction, maintenance and so on. They also had wizards or scientists called *walmaks*. Their money was made from gold, iron, lead and wood. Human slaves were also a form of currency. Despite their great luxury, the Minunians

slept on very thin mats or thick fabric. What the mat lay upon indicated status. This base of the bed could be wood, metal or marble, depending on the owner's caste or wealth.

Minunians had a great military discipline and organization. Their warriors were very brave and efficient, doing things with little lost motion. They wore a harness and used a hood and cloak when necessary. For weapons they had a straight rapier sword, a lance, javelin, and a two-edged dagger. They knew nothing of the bow and arrow or fist fighting until Tarzan came. However, the Minuni warriors loved to fight and had to rotate assignments so all could get a chance in the advance cavalry which saw the most action in their battles. During combat there was no need for songs, horns or other encouragements for the troops: they were prepared and eager enough without them.

For beasts of burden and riding, especially in war, the Minuni used a slightly larger version of the tiny Royal Antelope of the West Coast which they called a *diadet*. The upper class and warriors broke and trained these naturally timid animals themselves, and saddled and rode them like horses. The men loved their mounts and treated them kindly, and the faithful animals loved and trusted their masters. The *diadets* were even ridden within the domes. When mounting an antelope the warrior held the bridle and at a signal the *diadet* took off with a leap forward. The rider mounted the antelope using its motion and momentum. When battling other Minuni the cavalry attempted to jump over their opponents and strike down on them with their rapiers.

When attacking the giant Alalus they attempted to overwhelm the larger human by sheer numbers of personnel and spearpoints, or hamstring them with their swords, or knock them over by charging their mounts headfirst into the Alalus' midsection.

After a battle if a wounded mount or warrior was too severely injured, others would quickly put them out of their misery in the field. For battlefield burials, the Minuni always carried a shovel blade on their saddle, which could be easily attached to a lance butt. If many were killed, they dug a trench in which the dead were laid next to each other like sardines, and two layers high. They piled earth in between bodies and rows, then placed a layer of stones over the top. They topped off the mass grave with the remaining dirt. Any warrior or noble who died but not in the field was cremated.

As mentioned above, the Minuni cities comprised several beehive-like domed buildings, constructed from mounds of stacked boulders. The diameter of the buildings was 150 to 200 feet, by our equivalent measure. There were four entrances, one at each point of the compass. The ground floor did not have windows, but all the floors above had many narrow slit windows. The corridors were the equivalent of 12 feet wide. In the center of the building, from top to bottom, was a ten foot circular shaft that let in air and light. Ramps and ladders were used to get from level to level. The insides of the domes were framed with wood and finished with boulders. Doweling was used to fasten the wood together and an asphaltum to help fill the ceilings and seal the roof.

In order to breathe in these large dwellings, and beneath the surface in their quarries, the Minuni used a large, slow-burning, smokeless candle of their own invention, which turned noxious gases in the air into oxygen. For cooking, they used a hard, clean charcoal that gave off very little smoke.

In the royal dome, the warriors dwelt in the west side, called the Warriors' Corridor, while the white tuniced slaves had the north side, called the Slaves' Corridor. The King's Corridor lay on the south side of the royal dome, and the Women's Corridor on the east.

The buildings were constructed by slaves, who were prisoners of war or descendants of prisoners of war. These particular slaves lived in the quarries they usually worked in. Their underground chambers were extremely large and had low entrances that could only be passed through upon hands and knees. They were sealed for the night with a guard placed outside the door. During a war the quarries were guarded to prevent the slaves escaping or being captured. First generation slaves were worked very hard. But second generation were treated better and were allowed to have their children educated. If slaves showed aptitude in a trade or skill they were transferred out of the mines and quarries and placed in the domes to work in a middle-class environment. Although not a very common practice, a slave might even be set free.

Any slave could be *chosen* for marriage by a ruling class noble or warrior. If this happened the slave would be elevated out of the quarries regardless of skill achievement, and be advanced and accepted in the ruling class they married into. This process was started generations before by the Trohanadalmaskusians to help bring new blood into the ruling class of nobles and warriors. The idea worked, and the first generation of mixed-class citizens showed a marked improvement in stamina and vitality. Other cities saw the wisdom and advantages of this social cross-breeding, and adopted and practiced it themselves in order to survive. It then became illegal for a noble to marry anyone other than a slave. Through this custom, princes were required to marry princesses captured from other cities. In none of these marriages was love necessary. At the time of Tarzan this practice had advanced to such a degree that the goal was to capture the most beautiful women from other cities to make as slaves, so they could be raised to the ruling class through marriage to a noble. To help facilitate this cross-breeding and avoid inbreeding, the cities kept genealogical records for themselves as well as many of the nearby cities.

All slaves wore sandals, but slaves of the first and second generation wore green knee-length tunics to distinguish them from the others. These tunics had written on them which city the person had been taken from and which individual they currently belonged to. The advanced upper-class slaves wore tunics of white with red writing on them, as well as a mark to indicate their trade. The white-tunics helped to oversee the work of the green-tunics. Even though a slave did all the work, the money and praise went to their master. Women slaves could be asked, or could volunteer, to cook for the male slaves. All slaves were loyal to each other, and any betrayer was destroyed by the others. If a fight broke out between two slaves they had to fight fairly. Slaves who died in the cities were taken to the edge of the jungle and fed to wild beasts. Some of these beasts were old toothless lions which had grown accustomed to the feedings and often met the approaching party and waited to be fed. The slaves did everything but break the antelopes. This was considered an honorable activity — a task for warriors and nobles only.

TROHANADALMAKUS: There were no trees or shrubbery in Trohanadalmakus to allow an enemy to enter and hide unseen. The beehive-like domed palace of the king had 36 floors and could house 80,000 people. The rest of the city consisted of ten more similar, although slightly smaller, domes. The total population was 500,000 with two-thirds being slaves. In addition, 500,000 unskilled laborer slaves dwelt in the underground mines or quarries where they also worked.

VELTOPISMAKUS: The rival of Trohanadalmakus. When Tarzan arrived Veltopismakus consisted of eight finished domes with a ninth under construction. Its surface population was 480,000 souls. Veltopismakus had beautiful gardens with flowers and shrubbery crisscrossed with gravel sidewalks. The military were more showy, and constantly paraded and practiced maneuvers and formations in the city, but they lacked practical field experience. When women went abroad in Veltopismakus their faces were painted a deep vermilion, their ears blue, and their garments were so arranged that their left legs and arms were bare. If their right ankles or wrists became exposed, they would embarrassedly hurry to cover them back up.

The king on Tarzan's arrival was

J. Allen St. John illustration from the *Tarzan and the Jewels of Opa* newspaper serialization (© 1918 Edgar Rice Burroughs, Inc.).

Elkomoelhago, a self-indulgent dictator who heavily taxed the wealthy in his city, but not the poor. He had also outlawed the drinking of wine. Regardless, all were lazy from prosperity. Elkomoelhago's palace was gorgeously painted and decorated with different colored candles and murals upon the walls. He had a throne room with a raised dais and throne. Throughout the royal dome were hidden corridors and passageways, many long forgotten or unused. When presented before King Elkomoelhago, a person was required to go down on one knee and raise their arms as high as possible with the palms forward. While leaning back as far as they could, they were then required to give their salutation in a dead level monotonous voice.

In Veltopismakus lived the greatest scientist, or *walmak*, in all of Minuni. His name was Zoanthrohago, and while attempting to make an enlarging machine he accidentally invented the size-reducing machine that was used to shrink Tarzan. The machine worked with disks that caused a vibration which affected the hypophysis gland at the base of the skull. The effects of the shrinkage lasted from a few moments to over three years, but ordinarily at least a few months. A positive side effect of the shrinkage for Tarzan was that he was able to keep his original strength and not lose it proportionately with his size.

ALALUS (*Alali*; plural): These were a race of giant barbaric female-dominated people who also dwelt within the land of the Minuni, beyond the great thorn forest. The Alalus were the hereditary enemies of the Minuni who called these giants *Zertalacolols*. The Alalus were a contrasting race of humans to the Minuni, even though they were both Caucasian. The Alali were very barbaric and had no spoken language, although they did communicate with hand signs and body language. They did not have names to distinguish one from another, even with their sign language.

The Alali females were the larger dominating sex in the society, and they averaged about six feet in height. They had a large face with a broad nose and a wide, full-lipped mouth. Their eyes were normal sized, but set beneath bushy beetling brows which were topped by a wide and low forehead covered with long unkempt hair. These females were well muscled and hulking, especially around the back, shoulders, and arms. They had big feet, and large ears they could flap. They also had hairy chests, arms and legs. A unique feature of the Alalus was their ability to twitch their skin like a horse to dislodge flies or dust. For clothing they wore a single G-string garment about their waist supported by a belt of hide. As weapons they used a club, a rude stone knife, and a type of sling made from strips of hide about 18 inches long. They carried this sling on their leather belt, together with its projectiles spaced about two inches apart and suspended in netted leather string. Close to each of these stones, or its string, were attached small brilliant feathers. The whole arrangement of sling and stones formed a skeleton-like knee-length skirt around their waist.

The males of the race were much shorter than the women: on average about five feet tall. They were also of a much lighter build and had longer legs. Their forehead was lower than the females', and they had closer set eyes. The men had merely a trace of beard, and kept their hair in a ball above their forehead, held in place with 12-inch-long wooden skewers. In contrast to the women, who wore no ornamentation, the men sported bracelets, anklets, and necklaces of teeth and pebbles. The males lived solitary lives in the wilderness and woods. They avoided and feared each other, but more importantly, they avoided and feared capture by the women.

The women were basically loners too. This was especially so when they hunted, although occasionally, when the need was great, they hunted in small groups. When hunting they used their enhanced sense of sight, smell, and hearing to their advantage. Each season the females went out to hunt down one of the smaller males as a mate. If they found and captured one, they would bring him back alive by force, conscious or not. They took him then to their cave village, where all the females resided, but in separate caves. Once in the vicinity of the other females the successful huntress must be prepared to defend her *prize* from the other women. If she did, the submissive man was forced to cook and mate with her for the entire season or until he was either killed or could escape. These temporary mates were set loose after the mating season, because it was easier to hunt for a new mate later than feed the same one year round.

Until mature enough to leave, children were kept in the center of the village in an oval corral, the walls and roof of which were made of large stone slabs. Each female had a corral for her own children, and she provided food for them on a regular basis. Even in these nursery corrals the girls dominated the boys and were permitted to treat them brutally. The boys were kept in the corrals until they were between the ages of 15 and 17; then they were chased into the forest. Thereafter, their mothers could not tell them from the other males already in the woods. At about the same age, the girls were brought out to live and train with their mothers until they could capture their first mates. Once this happened, the tie between mother and daughter was cut completely and the girl had to find her own cave to live in.

When Tarzan arrived he escaped from the corral of the Alalus woman who had captured him, and out of loyalty took a teenage male youth with him. Tarzan taught this boy how to fight and stand up for himself. He also trained him in the making of the bow and arrow and the spear which were weapons previously unknown in their society. This too gave the youth courage. The overall result was that the other formerly solitary men rallied around this boy, and he taught and trained them. After this the men began to dominate the larger women.

MUSLIM or MOSLEM: Arabs appeared in many of the Tarzan books. Their religion was normally Muslim and their supreme being Allah. All non–Muslims were considered unbelievers. In *Tarzan, Lord of the Jungle* the knights in the Valley of the Sepulcher believed that they were still at war with the Saracens, another name for Muslims. Later, in *Tarzan and the Madman*, a similar situation existed for the lost Portuguese castle city of Alemtejo. There the Alemtejos believed they were at war with Muslims who were in reality Galla natives who had a sultan.

NATIVES: Many native tribes were mentioned in the Tarzan series. Some were friendly like the Gallas, Utengas, and the Waziri. Others were unfriendly, even cannibals. The first humans Tarzan encountered in his life were native cannibals from the recently relocated tribe of Mbonga. In the Tarzan series natives were used as porters and askari in safaris. For a native it was considered a great offense to disobey or abandon a white person. Nonetheless, because of their superstitions or their employers' cruelty, they might desert a safari by running off in the night.

All villages had access to a witch doctor, although one witch doctor might practice in several. Often these magic men held more power than the village chief. The witch doctors preyed on the superstitious fears of their villagers. Most of the natives believed in gods, demons, and *muzimos*, the spirits of deceased ancestors which either inhabited the bodies of animals or had taken on some other physical form such as another human's. On several occasions Tarzan and Nkima, his monkey companion, were thought to be the *muzimos* of departed native ancestors. Tarzan also became known and feared as *Munan-go-Keewati*, the river or forest god or devil. This was because of his seemingly mysterious ability to consort with and talk to the animals, fly through the air (swing through the trees), kill from above, sneak into and out of villages and huts unseen and unheard, and defy witch doctors' magic. In addition, they believed he had superhuman strength and that he could transform himself into any animal he chose. Tarzan played on this su-

perstitious portrayal of himself by constantly terrorizing the villages he did not care for and which were unfriendly or cannibalistic. He even went so far as to eat the food laid out for him as offerings. This practice completely unnerved the villagers of Mbonga, because never had they known a god or demon to actually partake of their pittance.

Most natives ornamented themselves with armlets and anklets and necklaces. Some painted, tattooed, even scarred their face and bodies. Almost all native villages were palisaded, with grass thatched beehive huts inside. Natives tilled the ground and planted crops; they had dogs as pets; and they raised goats and chickens. They also dug pits to capture elephants or larger beasts such as lions. Baited cages and snares were sometimes used to capture animals. When mustering courage to fight or when working themselves up to do something else they were afraid of, some natives repeatedly jumped as high as they could and yelled and screamed. Native beer was another source of courage: it strengthened and facilitated celebration.

CANNIBALS: The sacrificial cannibal rites of the tribe of Mbonga were similar to those of other tribes. After capturing a victim alive, they marched him through the village street where he was beaten, scratched and spat upon by the women and children. Usually during this, all of the prisoner's clothing was torn from him. Before they could kill the victim, however, the women and children were driven back by the warriors. All the onlookers could do then to continue their torment of a prisoner was throw insults and spit at him. If it was not yet night or the selected day to eat, the prisoner was placed under guard in a hut. If desired, other tribes might be invited to the feast, and it could take days for all of them to arrive.

When it was time to be eaten, the prisoner was taken at dusk to the center of the village and tied to a large post. The women gathered their cooking pots and utensils, and began preparations for feasting by boiling water and cutting vegetables. The cooking fires dispelled the darkness as the ceremony got under way, and the warriors began circling and dancing about the victim at the stake while brandishing their spears. Slowly the circle of dancing warriors tightened around the helpless victim. Finally, a spear point reached out and pricked the victim's flesh, drawing blood. This was the signal for the others. As the dance and blood frenzy increased more spears struck out cutting the flesh of the still living and tortured sacrifice, yet no death blow was delivered. Then, Mbonga, or the chief, would sever the victim's ear with his knife. This heralded the beginning of a fast end to the life of the prisoner. Afterwards, all that remained upon the post would be a bloody mass of flesh.

Most cannibal tribes had filed teeth. But some, like the good-looking Babangos, did not file their teeth at all. The Babangos had an unusual way of preparing their sacrifices — a method used by only a few other tribes. They held their live victim down and broke all the main bones in their body several times with a club. They then placed the still living unfortunate in mud up to his neck, and kept them alive until they softened up, which could take days. Other tribes like the Secret Order of Leopard Men only ate specific parts of the human body.

WAZIRI: These intellectually and physically superior natives were tall and handsome and possessed legendary bravery and prowess. After Tarzan joined the Waziri and impressed them with his courage and doughtiness and led them to victorious battle against some Arab slave and ivory raiders (which battle took the life of Chief Waziri) the tribe made Tarzan their new leader. Tarzan accepted and took for himself the old chief's name. He later relinquished the role of chief, but remained their warchief. He gave the actual everyday running of the Waziri over to Muviro.

Besides their strong and clean looks, the Waziri were recognizable by the white plumes they wore upon their heads. They were proficient in the use of firearms and other modern devices, and many of them spoke English. The Waziri were mentioned, and members of the tribe appeared, in several of the Tarzan books. Nkima the monkey often fetched the Waziri to Tarzan's rescue, and they always seemed to arrive just in time to help turn the tide of a battle in favor of the Ape-man. Ten of them even went with Tarzan to the Earth's core aboard the O-220 dirigible to help save David Innes, Emperor of Pellucidar, from the Korsars.

Over the years the Waziri became Tarzan and Jane's personal friends, family, and body guards. The Waziri loved and worshipped Tarzan and Jane, their master and mistress. There was nothing that the Waziri would not do or sacrifice for them. From Tarzan they learned to rely upon their own prowess instead of the assistance of gods or demons they could not see.

As to an emperor or god they went upon their knees before him, and those that were nearest him touched his hands and his feet in reverence; for to the Waziri Tarzan of the Apes, who was their king, was yet something more and of their own volition they worshipped him as their living god. (TI)

The Waziri's hereditary enemies were the Bantangos, a warlike tribe of cannibals.

NIOCENE: *The Eternal Savage (Lover).* The Niocene was a period of time in Earth's history and not a geographical location. Nevertheless, it contained several groups of people from man's early existence and took place in Tarzan's Africa 100,000 years before the existence of the Jungle Lord.

During the Niocene period the area of Tarzan's jungle and African estate were mostly covered by the Restless Sea and the land was volcanic and experienced frequent earthquake activity. So much so that the cave dwelling people of Nu, the son of Nu, decided to leave the locale in search of a more stable country. The people of the Niocene had their own spoken language that they used to the accompaniment of many hand signs and pantomime. They could also speak the language of the apes which was considered the basic foundation of all modern languages. The constant nearness of and occasional intercourse between these two similar creatures had also given their languages many of the same terms. There was also an unspoken truce between them, maintained for the good of both.

The men of the Niocene were called *Pah* and they were normally proportioned Homo sapiens and had beards. There were, however, various stages of anthropoid development existing at the same time. One more savage than the others had reddish brown fur, piglike eyes, wolfish tusks and short stocky legs. When cut open these beasts had one less rib then the regular apes. On the ground they walked erect, but could also travel through the trees very quickly.

In the Niocene the air was humid and the sun a swollen red orb. The land and forests teemed with life. Not only were the plants larger and different than in the time of Tarzan, many of the denizens of the Niocene woods and plains were bigger and more ferocious than their modern counterparts. Others were extinct. These include:

- *Gluh*: the mammoth.
- *Oo*: the saber tooth tiger and hunter of men.
- *Ta*: the large and woolly rhinoceros.
- *Ur*: the cave-bear.
- *Zor*: the large lion.

There were also many strange winged birds and reptiles of various sizes, and a myriad of large finned and scaled creatures swimming in the Restless Sea.

Religion was not yet a concept of the men of the Niocene. However, a slight fear of natural phenomena, such as earthquakes and storms and the movements of the sun, moon, and stars, might have constituted the early makings of a future religion.

THE CAVE DWELLERS: These men and women lived in caves along a cliff face which they could scale as readily as they traveled through the trees. The women wore a single animal skin garment usually of doe hide. The men wore a loincloth with a furry pelt across their shoulders. They all wore laced sandals made from the thick hide of Ta, the woolly rhino. The hair of the people was usually unkempt, but they often used a leather fillet to hold it away from their face. Men and women alike occasionally put feathers in their fillet for decoration and ornamentation. They also wore necklaces of claws and talons.

For bedding they used soft pelts and furs. Their weapons were a stone-tipped spear, hatchet and knife. The spear usually hung down a man's back by a leather thong around his neck, while the stone hatchet and knife hung from his G-string. This helped free his hands for other things. For tools they had a wedge and hammer for cutting and splitting the logs to be made into spear shafts. They used a bladder to fetch, carry and store the water the family needed in the cave. They made their own fire by rapidly spinning a fire stick against another piece of hard wood. The friction of the wood rubbing together created heat which ultimately caused the tinder to ignite. When cooking, water was put in a small hollow on the cave floor, and after pieces of food were dropped in it, heated rocks and pebbles from the fire were added until the water boiled and the food cooked.

A man's ability to hunt and fight won prestige and prominence in the village. To obtain a mate the men usually had to prove themselves worthy by killing some great predator of the land. The ultimate prize was Oo, the saber-toothed tiger. If successful the hunter presented the head of the beast to his future mate, then hung the fangs of the vanquished beast from his loincloth. It was a belief among the people that women who mated willingly had braver, happier, and better looking children. Therefore, the primitive custom of dragging a mate away to a cave to dwell in captivity was frowned upon and no longer practiced. To become a man a youth must go through ordeals.

When the men hunted they used all their senses including smell. If the hunt was successful, a man might give a victory dance around his dead prey while brandishing his weapons and voicing shrieks and growls that were sometimes in imitation of the sound of the fallen beast. These then turned to deep-toned roars — the victory call of the triumphant cave man. If a woman was present she might accompany the man during his dance by clapping her hands.

At the base of the cliff that contained the caves in which they dwelt, the villagers had cleared away an area in the shape of a rectangle. Here feasts were held, and meetings among the men of the tribe, and other functions involving the presence of many people. The person delivering an address stepped to the center of a circle of older men. Beyond this circle were more men, and beyond them, the young men.

To the cave dwellers, boats were entirely unknown.

THE BOAT BUILDERS: They were ground dwellers and did not climb cliffs and trees very easily. Boat Builders wore the skins of herbivorous animals and headdresses with the antlers and horns of these same animals. This made them appear somewhat fearsome. Often they wore the skull of an animal such as a bison as a helmet and a large hide as a cape or robe. Their weapons were shaped differently than the cave dwellers'. Most notable in this regard was their spear which was more like a harpoon with a short haft and a barbed point. It also had a rope tied to its end with the rest coiled by the warrior's side. They used clay pots for cooking, and flint to skin and work leather.

Boat Builders made teepee-like dwelling places with poles made out of saplings that they leaned inward against each other in a circle and then covered with skins, brush, and large leafed plants. At night they encircled their camp with fires to keep out beasts of prey. Young girls were required to stay awake through the night and keep the fires burning, as they were the most expendable people in the camp. Among the Boat Builders, it was also not unusual for a woman to be beaten by a man.

Boat Builders earned their name from the canoes they made. They felled trees, cut them down to 15 or 20 feet, then burned them out hollow. Their paddles were wooden poles flattened at one end. When the Boat Builders fished, they put many boats into the water, spread out. They stood and speared fish, then reeled them back into the boats. Once a canoe was full, its crew headed back to shore, put their catch into a leather sewn bag, and dragged it to camp.

Prisoners might be tortured by being tied to a stake, then slowly roasted after some ceremonial dancing and chanting.

THE LAKE DWELLERS: These people lived on a large island that had an inland lake upon it. They also used stone-tipped knives, spears and axes. Lake Dwellers herded aurochs from which they took the hides they used to cover their bodies. Their village was constructed on the surface of the

lake, and wooden causeways led from it to the shore. The huts, platforms and causeways were held above the surface by piles and poles. Each hut had a platform around it and often a window. A hearth was built in front of the hut and a fire set in it for cooking. The hearth was made of clay so as not to burn the platform. The platforms had railings to help keep people from falling into the lake. The larger platforms of the village had enough area to keep the herds of aurochs safely corralled and isolated from any land predators. At night, guards stood watch on the causeways leading to the shore, and there was a single fire lit at the end of each causeway, near the shore.

Prisoners were always kept in the farthest and last hut of the village.

OPAR: *The Return of Tarzan, Tarzan and the Jewels of Opar, Tarzan and the Golden Lion, Tarzan the Invincible* and *Tarzan and the Tarzan Twins.* This lost city of Atlantis was a 25-day march southeast of the land of the Waziri. It was accidentally discovered by the Waziri while searching for a new land to inhabit when Chief Waziri was a young man. After Tarzan joined them old Chief Waziri told the Jungle Lord about Opar, which was where the tribe obtained all its gold ornaments.

After following three rivers and crossing a low divide, a traveler came to the last natural barrier that kept Opar hidden and safe from the rest of the world. It was a mountain with perpendicular faces, capped by a flat tableland. Even higher sheer cliffs surrounded the top plateau. At one end of the plateau was a shallow narrow valley with stunted trees and many boulders. The city of Opar lay on the far side of this valley at the end of a field. During the day and from a distance Opar looked wonderful with its great inner and outer walls and many golden towers and minarets, but up close the decay was evident. In front of the rugged peaks and south of the city stood a forest, and through it wound a trail that led into a gorge through the mountains. Beyond the mountains lay the Valley of the Palace of Diamonds where the intelligent Bolgani lived. They were the rivals of the people of Opar.

Opar tradition dictated that a guard always be placed on the outer wall. When someone was seen attempting to enter the city or coming near to the walls, the sentry gave a high-pitched scream that slowly lowered into moaning sounds. Besides being a warning signal to those within, it usually effectively scared any intruders or trespassers. This outer stone wall stood 50 feet high, although parts of it had fallen in ruin, reducing it there to 30 feet above the ground. There was a 20-inch-wide cleft in the wall, however, with a worn stone staircase on its inside that led upwards until it made a sharp turn. It then became a level path that snaked along to a sharp angle at which it emptied into a narrow court. Across this court was an inner wall equally as tall as the outer, but better preserved with little rounded towers along its top that were capped with pointed monoliths. Another narrow passage led through this wall and onto a broad avenue with large crumbling edifices of hewn granite. These vacant decaying stone buildings were overgrown with vines and creepers and other plant life. Apes and monkeys lived in the tangled courts and the abandoned gardens. At the end of the avenue stood an enormous and better kept domed building. On either side of its entrance were pillars with statues of strange birds upon them. This was the Temple of the Flaming God, or of the Sun.

The temple had a large rotunda under its massive dome with many branching chambers and wings. Its outer rooms were dark and usually uninhabited. The citizens of Opar lived nearer the heart of it, are revealed after passing through a heavy wooden door. The floors of the temple were concrete and the walls granite with carvings in them. Set in the walls were also tablets of gold covered with hieroglyphics. One temple room had seven pillars of solid gold while another's entire floor was of the same precious metal. Old Chief Waziri said that the Oparians even had gold tipped spears and arrows. The platters and goblets they used for dining were also made of gold. But gold was not the only commodity of Opar — there were precious stones and jewels in abundance as well.

Through the degenerating generations, much of the wealth had been lost; even the location of several treasure rooms had been forgotten. Tarzan, however, accidentally discovered a vast storeroom of gold after breaking through a false wall in a dungeon cell where he was being held captive. The tunnel leading to this treasure room also ran under the city and ended at a forgotten exit at the top of a large granite kopje a mile beyond the city walls. Tarzan later found a long forgotten jewel room after falling into a well in the same tunnel. This jewel room contained many copper studded chests filled to capacity with diamonds and other precious stones. The passageway to the jewel room continued on, up into the main altar room inside the Temple of the Flaming God. And the well shaft came out in one of the courts near the altar room. Many of the tunnels under the temple had remained unexplored because of the fear and superstitions of the Oparians, or they had simply been forgotten with the passage of time.

Opar was the last bastion of lost Atlantis. It was built some 10,000 years before Tarzan, along with several other cities throughout Africa, by Atlantians searching for gold. Originally thousands of the citizens of Atlantis lived in the city of Opar, but only for a few months out of the year. They spent the remainder of their time in Atlantis to the north. During these periods, only enough people were left in Opar to maintain the work of the mining and to control the black slaves who performed the labor. Ships were used to transport the people, gold, and other treasures back and forth.

It was in one of these periods of reduced population in Opar that Atlantis sank into the sea, taking with it the majority of the Atlantians. The unknowing Oparians waited for the regular return of their people. When no one came they sent a ship back searching, but found nothing. That was the beginning of the end for those in the abandoned outposts of Atlantis. Black hordes from the north and south attacked and scattered the people from the various cities. Finally those who remained retreated into the mountain city and formidable fortress of Opar, and held the invaders back in a last defense.

They lived on in Opar, their wealth, power, culture, and intellect slowly degenerating. This degradation was a direct result of their in-dulging in the forbidden practice of breeding with apes. Few women were left — and they were mainly high priestesses, considered sacred and practically untouchable — so in desperation the males mated with the apes. This unholy union of man and ape spawned half-bloods. Despite this, the bloodline of the priestesses of the temple remained mostly pure. For mating, they selected the best men, mentally and physically. Eventually, though, all became tainted. At the time of Tarzan the men were mostly brutes, while the females were still completely normal looking. This was due largely to the fact that all female babies that showed any physical ape characteristics were killed, as were males that were too human looking.

The apes, or Mangani, were called the first men by the Oparians. The males of Opar looked upon the bulls of the Mangani as equals. The people of Opar learned to speak the language of the apes as proficiently as Tarzan, and it became their common day-to-day language with an occasional word of their original Atlantian thrown in. Only during the sacrificial ceremonies and other religious rites and ordinances did they use their ancient mother tongue. And the Oparian males also learned to climb trees almost as well as the Mangani.

Opar's religious hierarchy consisted of a single ruling high priestess. She was considered a goddess, and was also queen. There were also lesser priests, priestesses, and votaries. The office of high priestess was a matriarchal order descending from mother to daughter, and the high priestess must take a subordinate high priest as a mate within a certain number of years after her consecration. As mentioned above, only the most physically and mentally worthy priests could mate with the priestesses, and only the best of these with the high priestess.

The palace of the high priestess adjoined the temple. It had a throne room with a great ornate chair for a throne upon a raised dais. It also had a large banquet hall where special events were catered. At such events, ancient wine was always served.

The contemporary men and priests of Opar were short and stocky with thick matted hair over their body and especially along their shoulders and back. They were Caucasian and bearded, with heavy brows over tiny close-set bloodshot eyes. They had yellowing fangs and low foreheads. Their legs were thick, short and crooked while their arms were long and muscular. They wore the skins of leopards and lions about their loins and had necklaces made from the claws of these animals about their necks. They also had large circlets of virgin gold on their arms and legs. The priests carried heavy gnarled bludgeons and wore wicked looking knives thrust in their belts. When the priests fought within the dark of their temple, they did so in silence. But when working they were wont to sing strange hymns and chants in the language of

J. Allen St. John illustration from the *Tarzan and the Jewels of Opar* newspaper serialization (© 1918 Edgar Rice Burroughs, Inc.).

Atlantis. The priestesses were almost entirely naked too, and dressed similarly to the men, but with more jewelry on their bodies and in their hair.

The Oparians were sun worshipers, calling the great star of the solar system their Flaming God. They had no love for night, and were particularly superstitious about the darkness in the world outside their city. During the morning, the Oparians knelt and chanted for the sunrise. In the late afternoon, another religious rite took place in the throne room. In it, the people gathered to help speed the Flaming God to its rest in the evening. At one point of the ceremony, all the people prostrated themselves on the ground with their faces upon the floor. Upon their main altar in the Temple of the Sun they offered blood sacrifices (human or anthropoid ape) to their Flaming God. The priests and priestesses drank the blood of the victim while their soul was offered as a gift to the Flaming God. If a chosen victim was not healthy enough to be sacrificed, he, she or it was nursed until fit enough. With the victim ready, a religious ordinance was read, and the victim was taken from their cell and led to the altar room where they were bound hand and foot. If the victim needed no further nourishment or treatment, the sacrificial ceremony could begin as soon as the sun had risen to the appropriate position. These sacrifices could only be performed by the high priestess with her slim and wicked looking sacrificial knife. The knife was considered sacred and the people feared it.

There was one other room in which sacrifices could be made by the high priestess. The Oparians called it the Chamber of the Dead, and it was the first room Tarzan hid in after he escaped the altar and saved La from an attacking high priest. On the altar in this chamber, live victims were placed to be sacrificed by the dead. Only the high priestess could enter the chamber with the victims to be sacrificed. For that reason it was left unsearched by the priests of the temple when they looked for Tarzan. Burnt sacrifices might be offered in Opar as well. A victim could also be immolated on a pyre of wood, but this was usually done outside the temple.

Those to be sacrificed upon the main altar were bound and left in a courtroom near the altar room. The ceremony started as the rays of the sun entered the courtroom through an opening to the sky. If it was a cloudy day the sacrifice was postponed until it appeared certain that the sun could shine unobstructed into the altar room and onto the victim upon the altar. Then the people converged in the altar room and along its galleries and began a low weird chant, with their eyes toward the sun. The priests gathered about the bound victim lying upon the floor and began to dance and circle them while still looking up into the sun. After about ten minutes, they turned in unison and leapt as if to attack their victim with their bludgeons and cudgels, while emitting howls and with hideously distorted features. At this juncture a single priestess rushed into the bloodthirsty horde and laid into them with a golden club. The priests fell back and the priestess addressed them with a memorized dialogue. She then took a knife and cut the leg bindings of the sacrifice. After placing a rope about the neck of the victim, she led them farther into the temple, to the altar room, with the priests following in twos. This was all mimicry, a reenactment of a ceremony in which the victim, chosen by the sun god, was saved from the unclean hands of the worldly by a worthy priestess.

The main altar room was large and had a circular opening in the center of the ceiling that was slightly overgrown with vines but still admitted the rays of the sun. The altar itself was bloodstained and had been built with grooves for the blood of the victims to flow easily along. After the victim was placed standing in the right location in the room, a long procession of priestesses entered bearing two golden cups or goblets each. One of these she kept for herself and the other she gave to the priest lined up in a row opposite. They all took up the chant again, and then, across the room, the high priestess entered. More elaborately ornamented, she carried a golden wand instead of a club, and had the long, slender and cruel sacrificial knife. She went to the opposite side of the altar from the others, and stopped. The priests and priestesses knelt before her and, with the wand held above them, she recited a lengthy, tedious prayer. After this, the high priestess addressed the victim. If not given a satisfactory response, she motioned for the same circling dance performed in the outer chambers by the priests and priestesses to begin again around the victim and the altar. At another signal from her, the priests rushed upon the victim, lifted him bodily, and placed him on his back upon the altar, with his head hanging over one end and legs over the other. The priests and priestesses then formed

two lines with their little golden cups in readiness to catch some of the blood of the sacrifice. The high priestess continued the ceremony by reciting a long sing-song prayer in the ancient Atlantian language, and slowly raised the sacrificial knife aloft. After it reached its zenith, she began lowering it, slowly at first, while continuing to chant. Then she thrust the knife faster toward the upraised breast of the victim, and if no interruption occurred, she completed the ceremony by killing the sacrifice.

Victims could only be lawfully sacrificed by the high priestess. But in *Tarzan and the Golden Lion* when Tarzan was found unconscious outside the walls of Opar by the high priest and jealous usurper, Cadj, he attempted to sacrifice Tarzan to the Flaming God in an arrogating fit of rage, without an altar, and by himself, a male. Cadj also blasphemously asserted that the Flaming God spoke to him, even though their god was only supposed to speak through the high priestess. His sacrificial ceremony was held up, however, because the sun became obscured by a cloud. This should have been taken as a disapproving sign from the Flaming God, but Cadj nervously and patiently waited. Then it became too late. La, the high priestess, showed up, stopped the ceremony and saved Tarzan. Cadj later plotted to dispose of La and make himself the king and ruler of Opar, despite the fact that only a high priestess could be considered the supreme ruler of the people under the direction of the Flaming God. This blasphemous usurpation turned out successful, and did not necessitate the killing of La. Cadj made Oah, a coconspiring priestess, his puppet high priestess in place of La. Eventually, Cadj was killed and La returned to the throne.

In *The Return of Tarzan* the Lord of the Jungle desecrated the temple several times by being the first sacrifice ever to escape in the history of Opar. Tarzan then rescued Jane from the altar, and in *Tarzan and the Jewels of Opar* the Jungle Lord rescued the traitorous Albert Werper from the altar too. For these blasphemous offenses Tarzan was pursued and hunted by the priests of Opar under the orders of La, despite her love for him.

Another first took place in *Tarzan and the Golden Lion* when, through Tarzan's intervention and assistance, a truce and collaboration was established between Opar and their ancient rivals, the Bolgani and Gomangani of the Valley of the Palace of Diamonds.

The Lord of the Jungle was always fascinated by Opar, with its mysterious past and forgotten wealth, and it was the only lost city he visited more than twice. There was also a place in his heart for the beautiful and untamed La, the High Priestess of the Flaming God. "Opar, the enchanted city of a dead and forgotten past," Tarzan mused reminiscently. "The city of the beauties and the beasts. City of horrors and death; but — city of fabulous riches." (RT)

PAL-UL-DON (Land-of-Men): *Tarzan the Terrible.* Across a waterless steppe covered mostly with dense thorns stood a range of precipitous mountains, well watered plateaus, wide plains and swampy areas. Access to this country by land was only possible during a few days or weeks at the end of the dry season or after a drought. Even then it was dangerous because of the many large and venomous snakes and other reptilian creatures there. But on the other side of the formidable mountains lay the pristine Pal-ul-don. This land was rich in game and plant life, although some of the animals had evolved somewhat differently in this isolated microcosm than those of the outer world. One was *ja*, the lion of Pal-ul-don, which kept as an adult the spots all lions have as cubs. Other animals were slightly altered prehistoric types that never became extinct in Pal-ul-don. Two of these were the triceratops-like *gryf*, and the smaller, striped saber-toothed tiger hybrid called a *jato*. This country was also where the tailed human pithecanthropus, Ho-don, and their rival the hairy, black Waz-don lived. Besides these two distinct races there was a tribe of mixed-bloods in the valley called the Waz-Ho-don. There was as well a similar species known as Tor-o-don, which could have been a version of the Waz-don, but was more bestial and lower on the evolutionary scale.

Pal-ul-donians were brave and strong, and they had an arboreal tail that was easily used as another hand or foot. When walking they often carried the end of their tail in one hand. Their hands and feet were like those of an anthropoid ape, with the thumb extending to the first knuckle of the index finger and their big toe coming out at a right angle from the foot. These features made it possible for them to climb trees and cliffs as easily as monkeys. Otherwise, they were shaped like normal well proportioned human beings. Pal-ul-donians were farmers as well as hunters, and like Tarzan they did not mind eating their meat raw. For drink they brewed an alcoholic beverage out of corn. Pal-ul-donians had a written and spoken language common among all their races and tribes. The written language was based on hieroglyphics. In token of greeting and friendship, they placed their left hand over their own heart, and their right over the heart of their companion. When making a pact, they raised their knife overhead and verbally committed themselves. Enemies were buried with their weapons because the living feared that if they weren't, the spirit of a dead warrior might haunt them until he found his weapons and when he did, that he would kill the person who killed him. This superstitious belief was mentioned in relation to the Waz-don, but not the Ho-don.

For apparel Pal-ul-donians wore a fur skin about their loins. They also wore a transverse belt with a pouch hanging from it over the right hip. This pouch contained, among other things, healing medicines for wounds. A wide gold encrusted girdle supported the loincloth and the belt, and it was fastened with a large jeweled buckle. For weapons they carried a stout club and a sheathed knife which hung from a shoulder strap on their left side. The clubs were very effective weapons which the Pal-ul-donians worked like fencing swords. They had also become very proficient at hurling them at their enemies. In close quarters a few men were often sent to retrieve thrown clubs and return them to the fighters. They could also throw their knives very accurately.

The Pal-ul-donians had a definite religious organization and were somewhat fanatic about their beliefs. Both the Waz-dons and the Ho-dons believed that their Great God, Jad-ben-Otho, was white and hairless, yet unlike them in other ways. The main disagreement between these two dominant races concerning Jad-ben-Otho was that the Waz-don believed their Great God had a tail, and the Ho-don believed he was tailless.

HO-DON: The "White-men" or Ho-don had many cities, each with its separate monarchy, a temple, and a high priest, but they were united as one against the Waz-don. The cities were carved out of chalk-like limestone hills and hillocks of various sizes. Because of the light rock it was carved out of, A-lur shone in the sun, which is how it earned its name, the City of Light. These cities all had great chambers carved out of the limestone, and in the larger there were stairways between levels. Almost all of the buildings in a city had ledges, balconies and terraces, and several had walls around them including the king's building and the temple. There were also gardens in some of the larger buildings. The rooms and apartments were not just above the ground; they went deep into the earth as well. The excavated limestone was used for paving streets, filling in gaps between buildings, and repairing irregularities. The interior of the homes and buildings had many carvings and hieroglyphics upon the walls. Vases and other artifacts were also carved out of the marble-like, finely grained limestone. Some pieces were even gilded. There were skins of animals about, but no evidence of woven fabric. The Ho-don beds consisted of a raised dais with many skins upon it. In the king's throne room was a high pyramid with steps leading up it. At the top was the throne of the king.

Many of the Ho-don cities stood upon rivers or lakes. They traveled across the water in dugout canoes with sterns grotesquely carved and painted and bows in the form of the heads of wild birds and beasts.

The Temple of the Gryf was in the Ho-don capital city of A-lur. It was part of the same excavated hill that the palace was carved from. The high priest of Jad-ben-Otho and his priests lived in the temple. The high priest held almost as much power as the king, and in some instances more. Tradition dictated that the king did not interfere with matters of the church, and in the throne room only the king's judgments counted. The high priest could marry, but his priests could not, and were made eunuchs. Only the high priest could perform the ceremony of a king's marriage. As part of their religion the priests wore grotesque headdresses with hideous masks. Some of these masks were carved of wood, while others were made from the actual heads of wild beasts and fit snugly over the wearer's head. Either completely concealed the priest's face. The high priest, however, did not wear such masks. The temple had secret subterranean tunnels that only the members of the priesthood bearers knew of. It also had a garden where a live *gryf* was kept captive and used as a religious symbol of power. In comparison, the temple in the Ho-don city of Tu-lur had a lion pit. When showing obeisance to religious leaders, Ho-don prostrated themselves and placed their foreheads upon the ground.

Some of the religious rites that took place in the Temple of the Gryf involved sacrifice and offerings. The temple had many chambers that contained the votive offerings of worshipers. These ranged from food to gold and jewelry in quantities that rivaled Opar's. There were many oval altars throughout the temple, but they were only in the eastern and western sides of rooms and their longer axis always ran east-west. Every day at sunset and sunrise, the Ho-don sacrificed their own people and Waz-don upon the altars to appease the Great God, Jad-ben-Otho. In the morning, as the sun's first rays touched the western altars, a newborn was sacrificed. It was drowned in a hollow basin of water at the top of the altar because they believed its spirit would accompany the sun — which had just left Jad-ben-Otho's presence — in its journeys across the sky. As the last rays of the setting sun fell upon the eastern altars, an adult was sacrificed so that his spirit could be buried with the sun as it returned to the Great God for the night. Often the scalps of the sacrifices were taken and worn as decorations on the masks of the priests.

Tarzan, impersonating Dor-ul-Otho, the Son of God, in the capital city of A-lur, tried to put a stop to these heathen practices by freeing the prisoners waiting to be sacrificed. He then attempted to change the morning and evening blood sacrifices to offerings of food and clothing. These new ceremonies, he explained, were more pleasing in the sight of his father, Jad-ben-Otho. Afterwards these offered items were to be distributed to needy citizens. Lu-don, the high priest of A-lur, did not believe that Tarzan was the Dor-ul-Otho. Fearing that if many others did he would lose his power and authority, therefore, he made every effort to unmask Tarzan as an impostor and blasphemer. This Lu-don succeeded in doing.

Later, when the insane and naked German outsider, Lt. Erich Obergatz, arrived and claimed to be

Jad-ben-Otho, Lu-don saw him as an impostor too. But he also saw the power he would have as high priest if he used this new impersonator of the deity to his advantage. After capturing Tarzan, Lu-don and Obergatz were on the verge of sacrificing the Ape-man alive on an altar when Tarzan's son, Korak, arrived just in time with his Enfield rifle, and put a miraculous stop to the attempted sacrifice and to the lives of the two conspirators. Because of the sound and power of the rifle, and his resemblance to the one-time Dor-ul-Otho upon the altar, Korak was heralded by the religious people as both the Messenger of Death and the Messenger of God.

With the high priest, Lu-don, dead and faith in their ancient religion wavering, Tarzan took advantage of the opportunity and succeeded in ending the morning and evening human sacrifices and reinstituted his charitable distribution program of the votive offerings. Also under his direction, the male priesthood was disbanded and female priestesses put in their place to administer the sacrificial goods. Tarzan also helped make a pact of peace between the Ho-don and Waz-don.

WAZ-DON: The "Black-men" or Waz-don were covered with a shaggy growth of dark fur that almost completely obscured their features. The women's apparel differed from the males, only in that they wore gold plates over their breasts. They groomed themselves with a brush and a gold comb-like device. For eating they used stoneware utensils.

The Waz-don lived in a number of separate villages built in trees or caves carved out of the chalk-like cliffs that surrounded the land of Pal-ul-don. They preferred the freedom of living out in nature and felt that the permanent cities of the Ho-don, such as A-lur, the City of Light, were confining. Families passed caves down from generation to generation. Each individual cave had a verandah-like opening, carved out of the cliff and was anywhere from eight to twenty feet wide and eight feet tall and four to six feet deep. In the back of it was the exterior doorway, three feet wide and six feet high. It was covered with an animal skin and led into a large front room. There were a few windows in the exterior wall between the apartment and the verandah. Other between verandahs suggested that the entire cliff was honeycombed with apartments. Each apartment had more rooms and connecting hallways deeper into the cliff. Permanent furniture was usually chiseled out of the stone when a room was originally being excavated. A dais was carved in the sleeping chambers, and fur skins and pelts laid on it for bedding.

To scale the often sheer cliffs that the cave apartments were carved in, the Waz-don used removable stout pegs in the rock. These pegs were as thick around as a man's wrist. To prevent access to the caves by intruders, the pegs were usually removed. Only if someone had a set of pegs that they could place in the empty peg-holes, could they ascend or descend. To help slow and confuse an attacking enemy who had pegs of their own, shallow unusable holes had been placed among the deep usable holes.

When Tarzan came to the land of Pal-ul-don, the Waz-don were constantly at war with their hereditary enemies, the hairless Ho-dons. But because the Waz-don were so warlike, they also raided and did battle with neighboring tribes of other Waz-don. The Ho-don saw this internecine fighting as the main reason why the Waz-don would never win a major battle against them. When hunting other men, the Waz-don used a specific war cry.

Traditionally, no strangers were welcomed in their villages. But through Tarzan's intervention, this rule was changed in Om-at's Wazdon village in Kor-ul-ja, the Gorge-of-the Lions.

Leadership in a Waz-don village could be overthrown by a fight called a *gund-bar* or battle of the chief. If the challenger defeated the existing chief without assistance (meaning with no weapons other than nature's: hands, feet, tail, teeth, and so on) he would become chief until another challenger fought and defeated him. A substitute *gund* or chief could be appointed by the reigning *gund* while he was traveling away from the village.

As a way for all young Waz-don warriors to prove their courage, they had to climb a treacherous mountain called Pastar-ul-ved, the Father of Mountains. If they survived, they were considered worthy and accepted as adults.

WAZ-HO-DON: These "Black-whitemen" were a cross between Pal-ul-don's two dominant tribes: the hairless Ho-don and the black-furred Waz-don. They were considered outcasts and lived in a city called Bu-lor which lay near the mouth of the primary river that emptied into the morasses of Pal-ul-don. The city was made partially from a cliff of caves and partially from excavated hills at the base of the cliff. The Waz-ho-dons were not very intelligent and were superstitious and fear-

ful, but they did have their own religious leader or medicine man. When Lt. Erich Obergatz abducted Jane and later lost her in Pal-ul-don, he found this misfit tribe and lived with them for a while and learned their language.

TOR-O-DON: These "Beastlike men," few in number, were slow moving but as strong and large as a fully grown gorilla. They were hairy like the Waz-don and had an arboreal tail as well. Their faces were bestial and they had fangs. The Tor-o-don apparently had no language other than growls and snarls, although they were known to have the cunning of a man and the ferocity of a beast. Between rutting seasons, the bulls of the Tor-o-don roamed the valley and would abduct females of the Waz-don.

The Tor-o-don was the only creature unafraid of the terrible triceratops-like *gryf*. When approached and handled the right way, the *gryf* was easily broken. The Tor-o-don rode it like an elephant. After being treed by a *gryf*, Tarzan observed a Tor-o-don tame one for riding. To do so, a Tor-o-don, carrying a stick, approached a *gryf* loudly calling "whee-oo!" several times. When the reluctant *gryf* responded and rumbled over to the Tor-o-don, he struck it on the horns and snout until it acquiesced. The *gryf* then allowed the Tor-o-don to climb upon its back behind its hood, but only after taking a passing snap at the beastlike man. The *gryf* was controlled and directed by hitting its horns and beak with the stick, and prodding it with the stick's pointed end.

PELLUCIDAR: *Tarzan at the Earth's Core.* There is a lush prehistoric world in the center of the Earth where dinosaurs and the various evolutionary stages of mankind still exist. It is called Pellucidar and was discovered accidentally by David Innes and the elder scientist Abner Perry. (Their exploits and adventures along with those of others are contained in the separate Pellucidar series by Burroughs which began with the book *At the Earth's Core*.) They got there by way of an iron mole that Innes and Perry had created which they traveled in as it burrowed its way through the Earth's surface. The purpose of the mole was to locate and mine Antarctic coal deposits. After 500 miles of burrowing the iron mole broke through the surface of that world within our world. It was later learned that access to Pellucidar could be gained through polar openings in the Earth's crust.

Since Pellucidar is within the shell-like sphere of our Earth, its horizon slope up rather than down. Another peculiar and unique feature of Pellucidar is that it has more land area than the outside of the Earth. This apparent paradox is due to the fact that the land and mountains of Pellucidar are created as the reverse form of the oceans and seas that cover the surface of the outer world. Conversely, the continents of the outer world create the concave areas of the inner world in which its bodies of water lay.

Pellucidar is lit by a single centralized sun-like orb that remains stationary. This gives Pellucidar its most unique feature: it is always day there, never night. The eternal noonday sun creates many interesting time lapse peculiarities and effects. Time really has no meaning in the inner world, although it could be measured to a degree by how often a person slept, ate, or marched. But this system is highly inaccurate, and can hardly apply to two people in the same way.

With a sun always at its zenith, and with no moon, stars or other moving heavenly bodies, it could be expected that Pellucidarians have directional problems. This is not the case, however, because every Pellucidarian has an inborn homing instinct. A Pellucidarian could be put anywhere, even in unfamiliar territory at the far reaches of their world, and he would be able to make his way back to the village of his birth instinctively without err. And if it was physically possible, they would do it in an unwavering straight line.

There is actually one other celestial body in the so-called heavens of Pellucidar. It is a single unmoving moon-like orb near and below the central sun. And because it has no orbit, the land that is constantly in its shadow is void of all plant life because, as in the outer world, plants require the rays of the sun for photosynthesis to take place. This area is called the Land of Awful Shadow.

In Pellucidar several levels of human development and evolution coexist. On the low end are the tree-swinging missing link–like Sagoths who speak the language of the Mangani. They appear to fit between the surface world's anthropoid apes and modern Homo sapiens in development. There are also the Homo sapiens called Gilaks who live in the mountains and caves, and on the plains and islands. They are hunters, gatherers, farmers, and harvesters. All Gilaks speak a universal language, wear the skins of animals, and use crude weapons such as knives, spears, and clubs. They could speak

J. Allen St. John illustration from *The Son of Tarzan* (© 1915 Edgar Rice Burroughs, Inc.).

enough of the Mangani language to get by. Those upon the islands used dugout canoes. Then there was the lost race of pirates called Korsars who had sailed through the polar openings a few centuries ago in their galleons and became trapped in Pellucidar and were forced to build their own cities. As for intelligent nonhuman life, there were the Mahars, a race of large winged reptiles which had advanced mental powers and could psychically control the minds of humans and other intelligent creatures. The Mahars used the Sagoths as warriors, and the more advanced humans as slaves and food.

These four groups will not be discussed at length in this book, because they figured more prominently in the Pellucidar series of novels by Edgar Rice Burroughs, and this is a guide to the Tarzan series. There was one Pellucidarian race unique to the Tarzan books, however: the Horibs. And these are fully described below.

While in Pellucidar Abner Perry and David Innes successfully helped advance the human race by building and introducing modern conveniences. These included the development of gunpowder, and the firearms that it was used in, which were made from the metals abundant in the rich ground of the inner world. Another advancement was the building and use of large ships for sailing. Inventor Abner Perry was also able to establish radio communication between the outer and inner worlds, with Jason Gridley of Tarzana, California.

When Gridley intercepted a cry for assistance from Pellucidar he determined to make an attempt to send aid. His idea was to make a dirigible to fly through one of the polar openings and into the inner world. The first person he thought of who might well be able to successfully overcome the inherent challenges and perils of the inner world was Tarzan of the Apes. With this in mind Gridley set off to Africa and approached the Jungle Lord. Tarzan agreed to go along, and the two set about building an advanced dirigible out of a very hard yet light metal discovered in the Lost Empire by Erich von Harben and dubbed Harbenite. For the trip to Pellucidar Tarzan took along Muviro and nine other Waziri warriors.

Tarzan loved the life of Pellucidar. It was the one last place that had not felt the effects and taint of modern man (except for the advancements Perry and Innes had introduced). The Lord of the Jungle was always adverse to civilization, and Pellucidar was still relatively pristine, savage, and untamed. In the Joe R. Lansdale finished book *The Lost Adventure* Tarzan believed that the giant praying mantis god, Ebopa, of the lost city of Ur, was from Pellucidar. And at the end of the book the Ape-man became trapped in the underground tunnels beneath the city where Ebopa lived. With no other way out he took the tunnel that led down to Pellucidar. He planned to live there indefinitely, because he believed that Pellucidar was where he could have the kind of life he enjoyed and always wanted.

HORIBS: These were the Snake People of Pellucidar. Horibs were built similarly to humans as far as torso and extremities were concerned. Their arms were better muscled and proportioned than their shapeless legs, and they had three toes and five fingers which were very reptilian. Their head was that of a snake, and they had pointed ears and small horns that made them grotesque in appearance. Horibs had lidless eyes that could see in the dark to an extent beyond human ability. Their entire body was scaled, and the scales upon their face and hands were minute. These parts of their body were also lighter in color, almost white, while the rest of their body was bluish. When angry they turned bluer, and when killed, gray. Horibs were on average about six feet tall, but were considered mature when much shorter. Some grew to more than nine feet, and had rougher scales. This was due to the fact that, much like the reptiles of the outer world, Horibs never stopped growing with age, and continued to grow until killed. They spoke the language universal throughout Pellucidar. They used a shrill hissing scream as a war cry when fighting Gilaks.

Horibs wore a single apron of thick hide which was more armor than clothing, to protect their soft bellies. The breast of each apron bore a single eight pronged cross with a circle in the center. Around their waist they had a wide belt with a bone knife in a scabbard hanging from it. They also had a bone-tipped lance for a weapon which they were most adept at using. The Horibs also used rope for various purposes including the binding of prisoners. On each wrist and upon each arm above the elbow, they wore a band or bracelet. The females differed from the males only slightly. While the males had an apron and arm bands, the females went about completely naked and did not have horns. Females laid their eggs in the soft warm mud of the shore of the lake where they lived, then covered their nest with more mud, and marked it with a

wooden stake. When the eggs hatched, the young wriggled out of the mud and stumbled and rolled around or walked upon all fours, trying to become accustomed to using their limbs. These hatchlings were forever ignored by the adults.

The humans, or Gilaks, of Pellucidar feared the homosaurian Horibs and believed that they were cold blooded and without hearts. They believed this because Horibs did not possess the finer traits of the human race such as sympathy, friendship and love. They also knew that the Horibs ate human flesh. When eating anything, Horibs gorged themselves until they could barely move, and their stomachs became distended like a snake's. And while eating their color changed from the normal bluish to a reddish; for some, their normally lighter colored lower extremities became almost crimson. During digestion, their color changed again, to a dirt brown.

Human prisoners kept for feeding the females and the young were placed in a mud cave dug out of the shore below the surface of their lakeside village. Much like a crocodile's lair, these prisons were only accessible from the water. But they were extremely large, being up to 50 feet long and 20 feet wide. While in these underground chambers, the humans were fed eggs to help fatten them until they themselves were ready to be eaten. To get a human into one of these mud caves, the Horibs quickly clamped the palm of a hand over the person's mouth, while pinching his nose closed with the digits of the same hand. Then, with the human held close to their body, the Horibs dove into the lake with their other arm and deposited the captive in the lightless chamber.

The Horibs rode a swift lizard called a gorobor: the pareiasuri of the Triassic Period on the outer crust. They were considered the fastest animals in Pellucidar and could also travel well through water. Many of these gorobors were ten feet in length, but stood low on short powerful legs. To summon their mounts, the Horibs gave voice to a high pitched whistling hiss. When riding, they locked their toes behind the gorobors' shoulders.

Horibs were the only natural enemies of the triceratops (gyor) that lived in a vast plain of Pellucidar called the Gyor Cors. They hunted the gyor for its hide and flesh. When pursuing it, or anything else, the Horibs formed a single line with their mounts, and circled their prey. A trapped and enraged triceratops would always charge an individual Gorobor in the circle, but because of the Gorobor's swiftness, the gyor could never make contact and soon tired of rushing about. The Horibs then tightened their circle. At this point, one Horib rushed in and the triceratops turned to meet him. With its attention on this first Horib, three others attacked the gyor from behind and stabbed the giant triceratops with their lances. With these tactics, the gyor's heart was soon pierced.

Saracen: see **Muslim**

The Forbidden City: see **Tuen-Baka**

Thobos: see **Tuen-Baka**

Tor-o-don: see **Pal-ul-don**

Tuen-Baka: *Tarzan and the Forbidden City*. In an extinct crater named Tuen-Baka were two rival cities that had existed there for perhaps 3000 years. One was Thobos; the other Ashair, the Forbidden city. Time had passed Tuen-Baka by. There were giant lizards, or rather, minia-ture dinosaurs along the outer slopes of the crater. And Tarzan killed a bull-sized version of a Tyrannosaurus Rex in order to save Thetan, the nephew of Herat, king of Thobos.

The crater of Tuen-Baka was accessible in two ways. One was by a trail known only to the people of Thobos. The other, and more common way, was up a river which flowed from a lake called Holy Horus within the crater, and through a cavern tunnel to the outside world. This tunnel led into a ravine, which offered a steep rocky barren climb down to the jungle. The lake itself was unique. In it were sea serpents of great size, man-sized unicorn-like sea horses, sharks and other interesting and curious denizens of the deep. The nature of the lake's water was not given. But based on modern information about the Dead Sea and the Great Salt Lake in the state of Utah in the United States, Holy Horus must have been fresh water, because the river that ran from the lake would have taken the salt out of it. The lake was also said to have had clear water, making the bottom easily visible.

The warriors of Thobos wore black plumes and their armorial insignia, a bull, was embroidered upon the front and back of their tunic. Contrastingly, the warriors of Ashair wore white plumes and had a bird as their symbol. The people of both cities were Caucasian, and each had a monarchy as its form of government. By law, in both cities all strangers from the outside world were considered enemies and were to be killed unless held as slaves. In that way, no one could leave the land of Tuen-Baka and inform others of its location and the wealth of its cities.

The two cities shared a single religion based on an oversized precious stone called the Father of Diamonds. This huge gem was apparently kept in a casket upon an altar in front of the throne of god in the temple of Ashair located at the bottom of sacred Horus. The religion may have had Egyptian roots, because several people — including the man they claimed was their True God — cursed by using the name of Isis. This theory of an Egyptian heritage has some support in the fact that the founders of Ashair and Thobos came from the north as two factions with great mechanical and engineering knowledge. One faction settled Ashair, the Forbidden City, and the other Thobos.

ASHAIR: The Forbidden City was a small walled place with domes and towers. It lay on the shore of the eel and serpent infested lake, Holy Horus. To reach the outside world the Ashairians used oared galleys powered by slave oarsmen. These slaves were chained to their vessel, so if it sank, they went down with it and drowned. To obtain more slaves the Ashairians often went on slave raiding parties in the outside world. These raids usually took place at night so they could wear phosphorescent skull masks to frighten the people they sought. The masks appeared to be heads that glowed and floated in the air. To help frighten their victims even more, the Ashairians called out of the darkness in a sepulchral voice.

At the bottom of the clear water of Lake Horus lay the temple of the Father of Diamonds. Light from the windows of the submerged temple could be seen from the surface of the placid lake. Along the sides of the temple throne room were cages where prisoners were kept and often starved. To reach the temple from the city, visitors passed through a series of hallways and tunnels to a deep shaft which they were lowered down by rope. The priests did know, however, of a secret way out in case of emergency. Access to the temple could also be obtained from the water.

The priests frequently traversed the bottom of the lake in skin tight scuba suits with tanks strapped to their backs and helmets over their heads. These helmets and tanks extracted small amounts of oxygen from the water and could keep a person alive underwater indefinitely. An Ashairian scientist accidentally invented the oxygen helmet centuries before while attempting to create gold from common substances. The divers wore metal shoes to keep them on the bottom of the lake, and they bore tridents as weapons. The floor of the lake could also be reached from the temple. After divers had donned their suits, they entered a small room, and gears and levers were manipulated to fill it with water. The submerged priests then left through another door and passed out onto the lake bottom. During reentry the opposite happened — the room was emptied of water and refilled with air.

The temple itself was built over an air geyser that shot water into the air from the lake bottom. After discovering that the air was breathable the people of Ashair decided to build their temple over the spot. It took a thousand years and many lives, but finally they capped the geyser with a valve and built the temple out of lava rocks. This valve not only allowed the water to be forced from the temple, it facilitated the provision of oxygen for breathing. It also harnessed the force and energy used to control the gears and pumps of the airlocks.

Brulor, styled also the Father of Diamonds and the God of Ashair, was an old man who sat upon a throne in the temple watching over and protecting what was thought to be the actual Father of Diamonds. As mentioned above the actual Father of Diamonds was an oversized diamond that must remain in a jeweled casket upon an altar before the throne of the temple. The people of Ashair believed that all outsiders sought this diamond for worldly gain. And because of their ostensible relation to each other, Brulor and the diamond both bore the same name. Brulor had the authority to unceremoniously marry slave women to his priests with a few waves of his hands over the casket accompanied by some mumbled unintelligible words. Brulor was a false god, however, and was only permitted to retain his godhood on sufferance of the queen. As part of the religion Brulor had priests, handmaids, and *ptomes*. Regular periods of meditation — in reality only naps — were also part of the religion. When Brulor returned to the throne room after a session of meditation, the people in attendance knelt and beat their heads upon the floor. Then the handmaids danced seductively while priests joined in spontaneously.

Sacrifices in Ashair took place in another building along the lake bottom away from the temple. These began after all participants, including the victim, entered the lake in water suits through the airlock room in the temple. From there, they swam to a small tower where the person to be sacrificed was divested of their water suit and placed in a smaller chamber alone with the door sealed. The room was then filled slowly with water until the sacrifice drowned.

THOBOS: Thobos, the rival city of Ashair, was located at the upper end of the sacred Lake Horus. The city had an arena where gladiator-like battles and contests took place. Originally Thobos was the center of religion in Tuen-Baka and there was a temple there to Chon, the True God and Father of Diamonds.

Chon was an old man who tended to curse a lot. He and his priests wore white robes and hoods with slits for their eyes. Chon was thought drowned in Holy Horus along with his priests in a jealousy-provoked military attack by Queen Atka of Ashair as he performed his annual tour of the lake. The True God did not drown, though, but donned his water suit and escaped to a cave near Ashair. There he made a temple out of the cave and remained in hiding. Chon then began to capture *ptomes* swimming in the lake from the temple of Brulor. If they were still faithful to him he would add them to his entourage in his makeshift temple; otherwise he killed them. In their cave temple, Chon and his priests had built an altar which stood before a throne raised upon a dais. As part of their religious practices, they placed living humans upon the altar to be judged. After sprinkling a liquid over a potential sacrifice and chanting, Chon would raise and lower his sacrificial knife three times. Then he would ceremoniously cut open the person's entrails and read the oracle in them to determine if the person spoke the truth. If they did, they would not die. However, if the person died from this religious operation, it proved that they were a liar and deserved their fate.

The real Father of Diamonds, the precious stone, which was considered a god or the emblem of godhood, was lost to the lake bottom during this same attack upon Chon, the True God. It rightfully belonged in Thobos with Chon. It certainly did not belong in Ashair with Brulor. Yet he pretended that it was in his possession, in a casket upon the altar in front of his throne. What he actually had in the casket was a worthless piece of coal. The real Father of Diamonds was later found by Herkuf, a former priest of Brulor and Chon, in the wreckage of the galley at the bottom of Horus.

UR: *Tarzan: the Lost Adventure.* Ur was a city of Negroes with a long and rich history that stretched back before King Solomon's time. Urians were intelligent and had their own written and spoken language. They had broken and domesticated the wild zebra and used them to draw their chariots.

The roads of Ur were made with dark blocks which had been cut out of a quarry and laid in concrete by slaves. The road leading to the city was 12 feet wide and cleanly hedged upon both sides. The city itself was circled by a high and thick wall that had many sentries constantly patrolling along its top, and other sentinels did duty in small grass huts at the base of the walls. These walls were made of clay, thatch, and stone that gave them an artful look. There was a large drawbridge made of dark wood that, when lowered by chains, extended over a 30 foot polluted and crocodile infested moat which encompassed the city. Only after a horn was blown was the drawbridge raised or lowered. The crocodiles in the moat were of a sacred and a rare white breed and they fed them regularly.

The buildings within the city beyond the walls were beehive thatched huts. Farther in the buildings became more sophisticated and larger. The walls of these buildings were covered with murals of everyday activities as well as battle scenes. Many of the murals depicted a man battling a giant praying mantis-like insect. Inside this outer city lay another walled city. Its walls had a double sliding giant door that worked with pulleys and chains operated by shackled slaves. Protruding from the walls, a short distance from the doors were metal rods from which cages of human prisoners were hung. Many of the cages had living humans in them, but others had only skeletons or rotting corpses. Some of these were riddled with arrows. There was also an arena in the city for tournaments and sacrifices to their god.

Inside this inner city stood the palace of the king. The exterior palace walls were made of, among other things, gold, jewelry, and human skulls. The interior walls were lined with gold, silver, and tapestries. The throne room had purple carpet and yellow curtains, and the throne itself was encrusted with jewels. The king at the time of Tarzan had two unusually large jet black lions chained to either side of the throne. Torches and candles were used for interior lighting.

The living god of Ur was named Ebopa: the Stick That Walks, or the Undying God of Ur. Ebopa was a giant praying mantis bigger than a man that was purposefully trapped in the caves and tunnels beneath the lost city of Ur. It stayed there until summoned by a great gong to the city's arena to fight sacrificial prisoners. After the gong was sounded, Ebopa took about 20 minutes to appear. Once in the arena, Ebopa stalked its victim and fought using different posturing movements unique to a praying mantis. These movements were copied and drawn as decorations on walls and in murals as well as mimicked by the warriors of Ur. Tarzan recognized them as being similar to an oriental style of martial arts called the Seven Star Praying Mantis System. With them Ebopa never lost.

Ebopa, the Undying God of Ur, had been around for generations. Tarzan proved, however, that Ebopa was neither omnipotent nor immortal when he defeated and mortally wounded it in the arena. The Jungle Lord also discovered that instead of it being the same original mantis living forever, Ebopa was really different creatures which generation after generation had reproduced through self-impregnation. Unbeknownst to the Urians, one solitary Ebopa would replace its predecessor, thereby giving the people the impression that the Stick That Walks could not die.

Legend had it that Ebopa had come from the center of the Earth through catacombs beneath the city, and Tarzan theorized that it came from Pellucidar. The people of Ur trapped Ebopa in these tunnels in the belief that as long as it could not return to the center of the Earth its powers would bring the city great fortune. This belief seemed to hold true for decades, but in the previous 30 years or so their luck had begun to run out. Crops and meat had become scarce and children had been

born with defects. The Urians felt that Ebopa was angry and was demanding more human sacrifices. They therefore went out to seek more and more sacrifices to be offered to it, or to be sacrificed in its name and with its movements.

Some captives were immediately sacrificed by decapitation over a chopping block by an executioner with a large sword. The executioner had comrades who watched and cheered him on while a line of condemned wailed and moaned in fear and misery. Other prisoners were kept in dungeons outside the palace. Another form of sacrificing was to feed prisoners to the sacred white crocodiles in the moat around the city. In preparation, these prisoners were held down and had their arm and leg bones broken several times with a club. They were then buried alive in mud up to their chins. After the mud had softened the flesh but before the prisoner had died, they were taken out and lowered from the drawbridge with a rope. After the crocodiles had congregated below, the victims were dropped into the polluted water.

Women could be warriors and guards in Ur. Regardless of gender, though, all warriors were well built and tall and had faces ritualistically scarred with a hot bladed knife. Some warriors also had a white band painted on their foreheads and cheeks that was made from a mixture of white clay and egg whites. Some wore plumes of feathers in their hair while others let their hair grow long and had it well oiled. When hunting, they attached foliage to their bodies, and when tracking a victim, they moved very slowly. These two stratagems combined made them almost undetectable to the naked eye. They also concealed their passage from any potential followers. For weapons they used spears of varying lengths, clubs, and large sword-like knives worn either in loops at their waist or in a scabbard over their shoulder. As mentioned above, the Urians learned hand-to-hand combat by watching Ebopa and mimicking the movements of the giant mantis.

On a regular basis, small groups of these warriors set out along the jungle trails in search of food and, most importantly, humans. If they captured a human, they bound his wrists behind him and put a rope leash around his neck. Prisoners were used as slaves, gladiators in their arena games, or as sacrifices to, or for, their God, Ebopa. Pretty female prisoners were often made a part of the harem of the then king, Kurvandi.

Due to generations of inbreeding, the blood of the royal family had become tainted and the heirs insane. They had mistakenly believed that outside blood was impure. So royalty had married only royalty until, ironically, after generations their blood had become impure. King Kurvandi was insane and knew it, which was why he was looking for an influx of blood from the outside. He was hoping this would purify his bloodline. His concerns also explained why he was constantly adding women to his harem. Kurvandi believed that imitating their god, Ebopa, was a good thing, and not just in the way it fought. He felt that if Ebopa enjoyed killing human sacrifices, then he should too. To that end Kurvandi offered humans as sacrifices in the name of Ebopa and bathed in their still warm blood in the belief that by so doing he

would absorb part of their soul. He also believed that if blood was spilled on the ground it pleased Ebopa. His wise men and scholars, however, disagreed with him.

Another entrance into the city of Ur was through a cavern where they placed the bones of some of their dead. A number of the skulls in this cavern tomb were primitive, but all were stacked, and many had drawings of Ebopa in fighting postures drawn on them in charcoal and red and yellow ocher. The bones of the legs, arms, and rib cage were stacked separately. Most of the bones glowed phosphorescently. Nearby the weapons of the deceased were piled. Farther into the cavern were drawings on the walls of primitive man battling normal wild beasts as well as giant praying mantis creatures like Ebopa. The drawings also depicted praying mantises striking various fighting poses. Eventually the cavern branched off and led to the tunnels where Ebopa lived, but could not get out of. Ebopa's tunnels had gutters along them filled with oil for lighting.

UXMAL: *Tarzan and the Castaways.* Uxmal was the name of a lost island in the South Pacific hundreds of miles from land. It had no large animals upon it. Uxmal's founder was a Mayan named Chac Tutul Xiu who left the large Mayan community of Yucatan with his family and a few other followers and headed for the west coast in 1452 or 1453. At the coast they built large double dugout canoes and sailed into the Pacific Ocean never to be seen again. The dormant volcano island they landed on they named Uxmal after the city of Chac Tutul Xiu's birth. Here they built a city and community which they named Chichen

Virgil Finlay illustration for *Tarzan and the Castaways* (© 1941 Edgar Rice Burroughs, Inc.).

Itza. Over the intervening centuries these lost Mayans kept themselves untainted from outside influences and advances, which resulted in their ancient Mayan culture remaining intact.

Centrally located, the city of Chichen Itza was built upon and around a hill. On its summit stood a pyramid with stairs leading up to a temple atop it. A row of columns ran across the front of the temple. Surrounding the pyramid in Chichen Itza were other buildings, but none as large as the temple. All the buildings, including the pyramid and temple, were made from lava blocks. The city itself was encompassed by a wall with several gates in it where guards kept watch. Outside the wall were huts of grass and thatch where poorer citizens dwelt. Farther out were gardens and farms where

maize, beans, and tubers grew. The seeds for these plants had been brought along through the wisdom of Chac Tutul Xiu.

The people of Chichen Itza were short in stature. The warriors wore waist girdles which went between their legs and were elaborately embroidered with colored threads or feather work. They wore a square mantle over their shoulders, and on their feet sandals of hide. Warriors' headdresses were made of feathers while those of the noble class were made of a feather mosaic. Nobles also had lots of jade in their clothing and jewelry, which included a set of ear plugs and a carved ornament that passed through their septum. On the whole, the nobles were more gorgeously attired than the common warriors and the people. Everyone was tattooed and, of course, the nobles were more elaborately so. Warriors used a bow, two quivers of arrows, a spear, and a sling to project stones. They also used a wooden sword that had, at intervals in the sides of its blade, pieces of obsidian, partially set in, partially projecting. For protection they carried wooden shields covered with the skins of animals. When traveling through the jungle they walked erratically, without trails, and never in a consistently straight line. This threw off any would-be followers. If they traveled as a group, they spread out and adhered to the same procedure individually.

The religion of the people of Chichen Itza involved a high priest and lesser priests. These were the wealthiest in the society. There was also a high priestess who was in charge of the 50 or so volunteer female virgins who labored in the temple. These virgins stayed in the ornately carved temple atop the pyramid which was appropriately called the Temple of the Virgins. There they kept the sacred fires lit and swept the floors. They were of the noble class and could retire at any time. Those who did not retire were sought after for marriage by warriors and nobles.

Some of the gods of their religion were Che, Lord Forest; Huitz-Hok, the Lord of Hills and Valleys; Itzamna, the ruler of the sky; son of Hunab Kuh, the first god; Hun Ahau, god of the underworld; and Aychuykak, god of war. The hell of the people of Chichen Itza was Metnal — a cold, dank, gloomy place under the earth. The people of Chichen Itza also believed that demons and the spirits of the dead roamed the jungle at night.

Human sacrifice was a common part of their religion and took place often. The religious leaders of Chichen Itza used two forms of sacrifice and judgment. One was upon the altar of their temple; the other in their sacred well, which was a sheer walled volcanic crater filled with water. In the latter form, the victim was paraded through the city at night with drummers and trumpeters, and taken out by the east gate. The procession then followed one zig-zag trail up the side of the extinct volcano, and another into the mouth of the crater and down to a yawning hole. Just before dawn the priests began to chant to the accompaniment of flutes, drums and trumpets. And at dawn, the victim was cast into the hole and fell 70 feet into a pond at the bottom. If they survived the impact and could keep from drowning until noon that same day, they were found innocent and released. They were then given a place of high rank among the people and treated like a god. The spectators waited till noon came or the sacrifice drowned, brought food and drink and had a little fiesta to pass the time. For sacrifices upon the altar, people again played drums and trumpets, and they chanted. Victims were usually slaves or prisoners, although sometimes a citizen would offer one of their children to be used as a sacrifice. After being held in a wooden cage (if a prisoner) the victim was stretched out upon the altar on their back and held by four priests, one at each leg and arm. The high priest then killed the victim with a knife that had a blade made of obsidian. If a victim escaped before being sacrificed and was later found, they were still considered a chosen sacrifice and returned to the altar to fulfill their purpose.

Two other groups of people lived

on the island of Uxmal. One, a centrally located group of aboriginal cannibals, were there before the Mayans came. The other had a settlement on the north side of the island. They were the descendants of interracial marriages between the aborigines and some shipwrecked group. Both the Mayans and the aborigines considered them to be bad people, and there was no longer any interchange between them and the original aborigines. The aborigines and this interbred race were merely mentioned in *Tarzan and the Castaways*. They were never seen.

VALLEY OF DIAMONDS: *Tarzan and the Lion Man*. Out of a forest and across a river lay an open country with a barren cone-shaped volcanic hill. A mountain range ran to the northwest. At the base of the mountain range was the Omwamwi Falls that cascaded down a very tall and steep cliff. Over and beyond the cliff was the Valley of Diamonds and in it stood the English-speaking gorilla-populated city, London on the Thames of England. At the other end of the valley sat large piles of diamonds which gave the valley its name. The Valley of Diamonds could be reached by scaling the formidable cliff of the falls, or via the red granite column which was located directly west of a narrow canyon leading into the valley. The second way was the easier of the two, but even it had its problems. At one point, the trail through the canyon narrowed as the rock walls became closer and closer together. Then a short but precipitous wall had to be climbed by hand: the ascent was too steep for horses to make.

Inside the valley, the walled city of London on the Thames lay at the foot of the cliff it was partially

carved from, on the banks of a small river. The city wall was only about ten feet high but it had sharp stakes pointing down from the capstones to keep out intruders. The way into the city was lined with farms, fields and orchards where bamboo, celery, fruits, and berries were grown by the gorillas who labored in them with crude handmade tools. The buildings at the base of the valley were made of various materials. Some were circular and made of bamboo with thatched conical grass roofs. Others were rectangular and made out of sun-dried brick. Still others were made out of stone. Near the foot of the cliff stood a three-storied building with towers and ramparts in the medieval English style. Farther up the cliff, there was a larger but similarly constructed building.

The God and founder of London on the Thames based life in his city upon sixteenth century English society, monarchy, religion, customs, and characters — excepting the wearing of clothes. He taught the gorillas the English language, which they spoke in low gruff tones but with a marked English accent. These English gorilla citizens called the Omwamwi Falls the Victoria Falls, and the kings they always named after the kings of England. There was also a Privy Council, nobles, a cardinal, an archbishop, and priests who crossed themselves. Each gorilla considered himself an Englishman and bore an English name such as Cardinal Wolsey or the Duke of Buckingham. The king at the time of Tarzan was called Henry the Eighth and he was only permitted six wives whose names were the original names of the six wives of the original Henry the Eighth: *i.e.*, Anne Boleyn, Jane Seymour, Catherine of

Aragon (who was the reigning queen), and so on. The son of the king and queen was called the Prince of Wales. The wives of the king had different names before they married him, and these were changed when they became his wives. At the time of Tarzan King Henry the Eighth desired an additional wife and constantly argued with God about it.

The creature known as God was born a normal human in 1833 and graduated from Oxford in 1855. It was there that he first dreamed of and developed a way to prolong life based upon some of Charles Darwin's theories. He collaborated with Mendel for a while, but then went off on his own. God had discovered that he could prolong life by transplanting "deathless" human genes into the body cells of others. He had to work in secret, because in order to obtain the needed genetic material, he must lure young men into his laboratory and, after drugging them, extract it from them. He later began extracting deathless genes from the corpses and cadavers of deceased English royalty. He was caught, then persecuted and blackmailed which caused him to hate society. He fled to Africa and gorilla country. There he captured a number of gorillas and substituted their genetic material with that of humans which he had brought with him. At first there were no results, but after several generations he began to notice a change in the gorillas. They became more intelligent and human in their behavior, and they learned to speak. He trained them and built the city for them. Being an Englishman and for sentimental reasons, he called the city London and gave its inhabitants English names and taught them English customs.

By this time God was becoming old. Not wanting to die, he experimented and discovered that if he transplanted the body cells of young gorillas into himself, he could live forever. He also learned that to expedite the process he must eat the flesh and glands of the donor. The drawbacks of this longevity were that he took on a gorilla's physical characteristics, and he knew that he would eventually become a gorilla completely—at least physically. When Tarzan arrived God's transformation was well underway. He had the face of a man, but it was black like a gorilla's, and he had fangs. There were patches of black hair amidst patches of white all over his black-skinned body. His feet were those of a human, but his hands were wrinkled, with long curled claws. His eyes were sunken and looked very old. God's clothing consisted of a loincloth and an open shirt. He still enjoyed smoking cigarettes, however, and had a penchant for blonde women. After capturing Tarzan and Rhonda Terry, God hoped that he could regain his human characteristics by transplanting their cells into his body, and then eating them.

God lived in the larger castle above the king's castle. It was called the Golden Gates, or heaven. He taught the gorillas that their spirits would enter heaven after passing through the Golden Gates when they died, but only if they had believed in him and served him faithfully. The gorilla citizens were not allowed to question God, because he created them and they considered him omniscient. A few entered the Golden Gates before dying, though. Occasionally God sent for a young male or female, but they never returned. To reach God's castle, it was necessary to ascend the stone staircase known as the Holy Stairs, which rose from the lower castle of King Henry. There was also a secret stairway, known only to God, from his castle to the courtyard below.

The throne room of the king was large and had grass upon the floor. At one end was a large dais, but instead of a throne on it, there sat a thick tree trunk with leafless branches. There were no other items of furniture in the room. The chamber that housed the king's wives and their children was on the second floor and up a flight of stairs behind the throne room. It was large with grass covered floors. The king also had a secret passage that God did not know about. It led to a cave at the base of a cliff beyond the city wall.

Despite all their advancements, the gorillas were not entirely civilized. Besides not having any furniture or clothing (although God did), they still used their fangs and talons to fight with. However, they did possess a few weapons such as long shafted battle-axes, clubs and pikes. The only utensil they used for eating was a gourd for holding water. They had adapted a form of the Dum-Dum ceremony and they called it a dance. In it, they used actual drums (instead of an earthen mound), torches and a bonfire to light the scene, and they drank an alcoholic beverage.

As might be imagined, there were some throwbacks in the intelligent gorilla breeding process. Occasionally a more human looking hybrid gorilla would be born. Some even looked completely human, but had a totally wild gorilla mentality combined with the worst of human qualities. These misfits were all chased away or killed. They banded together, however, and created their own society in caves far away in the jungle of the valley. The members of this half-blooded society spoke the language of the Mangani.

The Valley of Diamonds presented several ironies. One was that Tarzan, a human Englishman who could speak the language of anthropoid apes, confronted anthropoid apes that could speak English. Another was that Tarzan, a man with a human mind who was raised by apes and learned their ways and language, confronted an apparent human with a gorilla's mind who was raised by civilized anthropoid apes.

VALLEY OF THE PALACE OF DIAMONDS: *Tarzan and the Golden Lion*. After ascending a narrow and rocky gorge leading up a mountainside behind Opar, a traveler could look down into a fertile basin in the heart of the mountain. Two or three miles distant, a sparkling building could be seen above the trees. This was the Palace of Diamonds, in the valley of the same name. Here dwelt the intelligent Bolgani who ruled over the less intelligent Gomangani who lived in fear and subserviency. Both these races spoke the language of the Mangani. The people of Opar feared to enter the Valley of the Palace of Diamonds because of the terrible monsters they believed inhabited it, and because all Oparians who had gone into the valley, had never come out. The narrow trail connecting Opar to the Valley of the Palace of Diamonds was occasionally used by the Oparians to capture the intelligent Bolgani and the lions that came out of the valley, to be used as sacrifices upon the altars of Opar. The Bolgani used the trail in turn to capture citizens of Opar for their purposes. There was only one other entrance into the valley: through a mining tunnel in its rear.

BOLGANI: The 1100 intelligent Bolgani who lived in the Valley of the Palace of Diamonds were larger than the average jungle gorilla and great ape outside, and were the Oparians' hereditary enemies. The Bolgani had human blood in them which made them more intelligent and cunning than normal apes or gorillas, and somewhat diabolical. They might have been a half-blooded mix of the people of Opar and the great apes they mated with. But instead of having more human form and features, as the priests of Opar did, they were anthropoid ape with human intellect. Through their intelligence, the Bolgani had enslaved and come to rule over a lesser form of themselves, the Gomangani, that dwelt in the valley with them. The Bolgani also walked erect like a man and never placed their knuckles upon the ground. They wore rich ornaments of gold and jewels, such as armlets, anklets, and a girdle of gold spangles imbedded with diamonds that reached to the ground in front and behind.

The city of the Bolgani was basically one extremely large building called the Palace of Diamonds. It consisted of various wings, apartments, towers, minarets, facades, and domes. The Palace of Diamonds appeared to be haphazardly put together, at different times and with various styles of architecture. Despite this incongruity it still maintained a unique and pleasing appearance. It sat upon an artificial rise with a broad staircase leading from the ground, and had many arcades and walkways surrounding it. The

main entrance was 30 feet wide and 15 feet high. Almost all the windows of the palace were barred. The most amazing aspect of this architecturally mad building of rendered, polished granite, was the fact that it was entirely encrusted with jewels and gold. One great tower in its northeast corner was entirely covered with ivy. It was called the Tower of Diamonds, because it was the repository of numberless bags of the mined precious stone. Another tower called the Tower of the Emperors housed the main throne room. The city was constantly under repair, and new towers and building additions were always under way. The granite blocks used for construction came from a quarry near the city.

The various interior floors of the towers were accessed by a vertical pole that passed through circular openings in the center of the floors and ceilings. The pole had horizontal pegs projecting from it, about a foot apart up its whole length, alternating from the left side to the right. Around the circular openings were three pillars to support the roof and ceilings. Each floor was circular, and at intervals along the curved walls were doors to the chambers. The interiors of all rooms were lit with tallow crescents. And they smelled strongly of incense. In fact, the smell permeated the air of the city. It was so strong within the buildings that it masked any other scents, and effectively rendered Tarzan's keen sense of smell useless. The Bolgani used woven cloth and animal skins for coverings and bedding. They also had furniture such as benches, tables, bedsteads, and chairs.

Encompassing the palace was a large granite wall that had a single immense gate in it, located on the east side of the building, which looked able to resist any attacking force. As a result of its stalwart appearance, sentries were never placed anywhere about the city — the Bolgani had no fear of attack. The gateway had posts on either side of it that were capped with large carved lions. The enclosing wall began about 50 feet from the jungle to prevent any overhanging of trees. Around the palace building, and just within the enclosure, grew trees, flowers, shrubbery and gardens where captive Gomangani of both sexes worked with several of the cruel Bolgani taskmasters overseeing them.

The Bolgani felt that they were the chosen race of their ruler, Numa, King of Beasts, Emperor of all Created Things, and that the simple Gomangani of the forest had been made to serve them and Numa. Consequently, the Bolgani treated the Gomangani like mindless unfeeling livestock. They performed all the construction and mining, under the supervision of the Bolgani. A few Gomangani acted as armed guards over the mass of their laboring fellows, but they were still under the command of the Bolgani. Behind the city were corrals for goats and chickens. There were also several hundred hanging beehive huts here — the Gomangani slaves that worked in the city lived in them. The Bolgani replenished or added to their supply of slaves by going to the Gomangani villages outside the city each month and collecting inhabitants. When approaching, the Bolgani gave voice to a hideous scream to alert the Gomangani that their village was about to be visited. Most of the Bolgani's advances and inventions were given to them

by an Englishman who they captured as a boy after he became lost and wandered into the valley. When the Bolgani realized his intelligence they gave him freedoms, but he was still an indentured servant. This Englishman helped them make and use tools and taught them craftsmanship, construction, farming and mining. No name was given him, but he had lived among the Bolgani for decades at the time of Tarzan and was then an old man.

In the throne room of the palace was a raised darkly polished wooden dais. Upon this, chained with four golden chains, was the large, but old, black maned lion known and worshipped as Numa, King of Beasts, Emperor of All Created Things. Stationed around him were four sturdy and rigid Gomangani. Behind Numa stood three thrones on which sat three gorgeously ornamented Bolgani. In front of and facing the dais, on either side of a central aisle, were rows of benches. The front two benches could seat 50 Bolgani. The windows of the chamber were long and reminiscent of a cathedral's. A ruling Bolgani used Numa, King of Beasts, Emperor of All Created Things, to pass judgments, claiming that the lion spoke to him. This of course was a strategy to allow the Bolgani to pass his own judgments. Often the judgment passed meant that the person being judged was to be eaten then and there by Numa.

When Numa, King of Beasts, Emperor of All Created Things, paraded through the city, two gorgeously ornamented Bolgani wearing headbands with white plumage, emerged and stood at either side of the main entrance portal. They cupped their hands to their mouths and gave a series of shrill sounds similar to a trumpet's. At this signal the Bolgani lined up on both sides of the walkway that led from the portal to a stairway, and all the Gomangani ceased work and lined up on either side of the stairway. This made a complete corridor of bodies from the entrance to the ground below the stairs. At this juncture more trumpet calls were heard from within the entrance, and presently four Bolgani came out abreast of each other carrying bludgeons held up right in front of them and wearing elaborate feather headdresses. They were followed by two more trumpeters. Then Numa, King of Beasts, Emperor of All Created Things, emerged held by the four Gomangani from the throne room by the four gold chains fastened to a diamond collar around his neck. Behind the lion 20 more Bolgani marching four abreast with spears came out. The Bolgani on either side of the walkway bowed low at the waist as their king passed between them. Once Numa reached the stairs with the slaves, the Gomangani prostrated themselves and placed their foreheads upon the ground. After Numa passed, the Bolgani and Gomangani went back to their interrupted duties. When Numa returned, the Gomangani and Bolgani resumed their positions along the stair and walkway, and paid their homage as before.

Southeast of the city, a trail wound through the precipitous cliffs of the bordering mountains, becoming narrower but less overgrown. Finally, it entered a narrow gorge devoid of underbrush. Here there was an open basin in the mountain where Gomangani brought sacks of dirt to other Gomangani to pan and sift for gold in a rivulet. Nearby was the granite quarry where the building blocks for the city were mined and cut. Deep in the richly gold-bearing quartz lay a large cache of diamonds. Even though they had more than they needed, the Bolgani continued mining for gold and diamonds, in the belief that the Atlantians who built ancient Opar would return and reward them for the precious metal and stones. Because of all the mining over the centuries, the mountains had become honeycombed with tunnels. As mentioned above, one tunnel extended through the mountain and offered the only other way in or out of the valley besides the trail from Opar. This open-ended shaft was used for ventilation purposes, and its entrance was constantly guarded by two Bolgani and 20 armed Gomangani. Their primary responsibility was to prevent the escape of slaves rather than to protect against invasion.

GOMANGANI: Dispersed in many small villages located in the forest surrounding the Palace of Diamonds were about 5000 Gomangani. Their villages consisted of a heavily stockaded compound with several beehive huts suspended above the ground by ropes tied to a branch of a tree. Each hut was seven feet wide and about six to seven feet high, and through an opening in the center of its floor, a rope hung down to the ground. The hut was entered by climbing this rope, and for privacy and protection, it could be readily drawn up. The hut also had small circular holes for windows about three feet from its bottom.

The Gomangani were tall and muscular, but had short disproportioned legs. They were entirely naked except for a few artificial spots of color put randomly about their body. They were also entirely hairless except for a patch of scraggly brown hair upon their heads. They had bestial faces with beetling brows and no forehead, the top of their heads running back almost flat to form a point behind. They had fangs and their jaw extended higher than their upper face. Even though they ate raw meat without utensils, the Gomangani did use short javelin-like spears and metal-bladed battle-axes as weapons.

Before Bolgani rule ever interfered with the Gomangani way of life, a Gomangani male arriving at maturity would leave his mother, make a hut of his own, and live out a solitary existence. The Bolgani changed this by teaching the Gomangani to stay together as a village of family units with a headman, and to use weapons. Even with this organization, the death toll was great among the Gomangani, because of various predators and the way their Bolgani masters treated them. The fact that the concept of community and family was still new to them played its part in keeping the population of the villages sparse. The males also did not seem to show affection or kindness to their mates and children; they simply used the females to propagate the race. This merely prevented the village from becoming extinct. Nonetheless, for some reason the Gomangani seldom ventured far from their settlements.

When a Bolgani came to a Gomangani village to fetch a monthly slave, he gave a few warning screams to alert the village. At this sound, the females and children hid themselves in the village in fear. Once the Bolgani reached the stockade, he was let in through a gate by several Go-

mangani warriors. He then demanded their women and children be brought before him. If they failed to appear, the Bolgani insisted that the male Gomangani force them out. This usually meant the hiders being dragged out by the hair. Besides being subject in this way, the Gomangani were also forced to hunt meat and gather fruits, nuts and other plant food for the Bolgani.

With such an existence, it is easy to see why Gomangani were a somber untalkative race. When excited, however, they would jump up and down and slap their sides with their arms. And despite living in fear of the Bolgani rulers and Numa, King of Beasts, Emperor of All Created Things, the Gomangani were very brave and powerful.

Because they lived in isolated ignorance, the Gomangani believed that there was nothing but fire outside their own valley basin, and none ever dared to go and see. They only knew that their Bolgani masters occasionally came back from the direction of Opar with a hairy white priest or a beautiful female priestess as captive. Where those people originated, they had no idea.

After uniting the Gomangani, Tarzan successfully led a revolt against the Bolgani that killed almost all but a hundred of them. He enlisted these survivors in his campaign to restore La to the throne of Opar. Thereafter, they were to remain as La's bodyguards. And the ruling of the Valley of the Palace of Diamonds and its Gomangani citizenry devolved upon the old Englishman.

VALLEY OF THE SEPULCHER: *Tarzan, Lord of the Jungle.* Near the southern border of Abyssinia, a thick forest teeming with life ended at the

Roy G. Krenkel illustration from *Tarzan and the Tarzan Twins* (© 1963 Edgar Rice Burroughs, Inc.).

base of a mountain range. Here, a small stream bubbled down out of the mouth of a canyon, and a well-worn trail ran alongside its waters. About three miles into the canyon, the path took a turn and led to a 60-foot-tall, white limestone cross with old English writing on it. It was so weathered and pockmarked with age that the writing was almost completely obliterated. The trail continued beyond the cross, where it narrowed with the canyon walls. At that point, the path passed between two boulders sitting very close together. As a person squeezed between the boulders, a black sentry would come out of hiding from behind, while another rushed in from the front, trapping him. This in itself was not unusual. But it was unusual that these black guards were adorned with medieval armor, clothing and accouterments, spoke in archaic English, and had names such as Peter Wiggs and Paul Bodkin.

These guards were from the city of Nimmr and were taking their turn in protecting and patrolling the southern entrance to the Valley of the Sepulcher. Their apparel consisted of extensively decorated leather jerkins with red crosses emblazoned upon their chests, close fitting lower garments, sandals cross-tied with doe-skin thongs to the knee, snug leopard skin bassinets that reached below the ears, a two-handed broadsword, and an elaborately tipped pike.

Further along the well-worn trail was the large mouth of a cavern that led into the valley. Its floor was well polished while its ceiling was dark from the torches that could be found just inside the entrance. The people of the Valley of the Sepulcher used flint and steel to light these torches

and any other fires. Inside, the floor sloped upward and the cavern became a tunnel. Several staircases continued to take the tunnel up to higher levels still. It ended at the brink of a sheer cliff overlooking a beautiful tree dotted valley. A hundred yards to the right along the cliff edge, the trail stopped abruptly. To the left rose a wall of masonry with two towers cut in it which flanked a tall gateway. The towers had long narrow embrasures in their walls, and the gate between them boasted a massive portcullis. Two more black guardsmen were on patrol there. Inside and to the left of the gate stood a guardhouse built into the side of the mountain. There was also a railing with horses tethered to it.

This was the Valley of the Sepulcher. It was a land seemingly transported from the middle ages, with people who had kept themselves cut off from the rest of the world and felt that the crusades were still going on. They had castles, wore armor and chain mail, fought with swords, daggers, pikes, lances, battle-axes and crossbows, and used long shields for protection. In the valley, though, the sword was used for cutting an opponent, not for thrusting or parrying as in fencing. The point of a sword was primarily used to finish off an adversary. Tournaments with jousts were held within the valley. There were kings and princes, queens and princesses, nobles, knights, and squires. The main part of the populace was Caucasians. There were also Negroes. Although they were of a lower class, they were not held as slaves or treated cruelly; indeed, they were almost equals. The slaves or serfs were the farmers. The freedmen were the craftsmen and artists. The men-at-arms herded cattle, and the knights defended the valley, competed in contests, and hunted.

Through the rugged northern mountains that bordered the valley, there was a little used trail entrance. This same mountain range provided the southern boundary of the Galla natives beyond. The Gallas feared the valley, because none who had entered it had ever returned. But they did have legends about the valley and its beautiful women and wealth. But the people of the Valley of the Sepulcher forbade entry anyway, because they believed that they were still surrounded by their enemies, Saracens — precisely their situation 735 years before when they first entered and settled the valley. So they thought that any stranger wanting to enter the valley could only be a Saracen or a spy.

The original founders of the valley left England under Richard the Lion Hearted's rule to fight in the crusades. After picking up several women in Cyprus, two of the ships that carried the knights to fight in the Holy Land were shipwrecked on the African coast while on their way to Jerusalem. The group from one ship was led by a knight named Bohun, and the group from the other by a knight named Gobred, the bastard son of Henry II. As they continued on foot towards Jerusalem, the two parties marched apart, and remained that way except when fighting an enemy. It was en route that they discovered the tunnel entrance to the Valley of the Sepulcher and beyond, the valley itself.

Bohun declared it to be the Valley of the Sepulcher and proclaimed the crusades over. In commemoration of this, he took the red cross that all crusaders wore upon the front of their tunics and placed it upon his back. His followers did the same and all were consequently dubbed Backers. Gobred on the other hand rejected Bohun's claim that they were in the real Valley of the Sepulcher, and he and his followers left their red crosses upon their fronts and became known as Fronters. Bohun then tried to leave the valley and head back to England. But Gobred blocked the tunnel entrance by force, preventing Bohun from leaving, because Gobred wanted all the shipwrecked crusaders to continue on to Jerusalem. Spitefully, Bohun fled across the valley toward the mountain range to the north and built a castle city there called the City of the Sepulcher to stop Gobred from pushing on to Jerusalem and the true valley of the sepulcher from that direction. (This northern range of mountains was rugged, but a rough, seldom used path led up through it from the valley.) Gobred also built a castle and city. He called his Nimmr, and it stood near the tunnel entrance. His followers protected and guarded the entrance, not only to keep out intruders, but to prevent Bohun from leaving the valley and returning to England. Bohun then proclaimed himself king, while Gobred proclaimed himself a prince under King Richard and through his descent from Henry II. These titles were later passed down from father to son. There were no nobles in the valley, since peerages could only be granted by the king of England. But there were knights, princes, and the pseudo-king, Bohun.

At the time of Tarzan the two cities were still at war with each other, with Bohun and his followers still desiring to return to England, and Gobred and his people wishing to continue on to Jerusalem. It had by then already been a standoff of 750 years or so. Within the valley were over 20 castles, each owned by a knight. These knights bore allegiance to either Nimmr and Prince Gobred, or to the City of the Sepulcher and King Bohun. Despite their constant warring, once each year a truce was declared for a week. During this time the two cities met for a grand tournament against each other where jousts and tilts were held. Fronters versus Backers. One year it was held in the plain before the city of Nimmr, and the next in front of the City of the Sepulcher.

The Great Tourney lasted three days, and usually only younger men participated in it. Since the people in the Valley of the Sepulcher were Christian, the Tourney started the first Sunday of Lent. As a rule and based upon tradition the knights of Nimmr and the knights of the Sepulcher did not dine together, and the visitors must remain camped a mile away from the Tourney grounds. The grand prize given to the winning city consisted of five maidens from the losing side. It was an honor for a maiden to be chosen, and many more volunteered than were needed. And in order that each city was best represented, only the most beautiful girls were selected. The losing city's maidens were put under the charge of Gobred or Bohun, taken back to the winning city, and never seen or heard from again. They were treated with respect, however, and given lawfully in marriage to a knight. By this method, new blood was always brought into the two societies.

The games began with a trumpet blast and both parties paraded to the Tourney grounds. The prince of Nimmr and the king of the Sepulcher rode alone and met in the center of the field. Here the visitor issued a rehearsed traditional challenge and the host accepted. Then the knights came out; they circled the grounds and viewed the five maidens brought from each city and the other lesser, yet valuable, prizes and awards. A point system was used and the city with the most points after the three days won. Contests were between individuals or groups of various sizes. Although it was commonplace for men to die in the Great Tourney, when an opponent was unhorsed he was considered defeated and the *coup de grâce* was never administered. To do so would have been a breach and an affront. The final event of the Tourney always pitted 100 mounted knights from each city against each other. For this event each one hundred warriors formed a line at their respective end of the field, and when a signal was sounded, the two groups charged at each other with lances. One hundred points were at stake in this final contest which could determine the outcome of the entire Tourney depending on how many points a side already had. During the fighting, broken lances could be replaced, but otherwise there were no rules to govern this mock battle.

Gambling was common at these events. Money, though, was almost unknown within the Valley of the Sepulcher, except for a few ancient coins that still existed from the time their ancestors first came there. They operated by barter, paying usually with services, produce or livestock. Jewels and precious metals were also often used in this barter system, because these normally rare items were mined in abundance by both cities from the mountains of their valley. To the people they were trinkets and decorations. Therefore, wealth per se was almost unknown. But influence, and the number of horses and servants a person had, gained advantage and favor. Of most value, however, was a person's honor, courage, talent, and virtue.

The valley also had a large population of leopards, so much so that one area was called the Wood of the Leopards.

NIMMR (FRONTERS): Down the road from the tunnel stood another barbican with guards, and beyond that rose the castle of Nimmr. A moat ran around the castle's outer wall. Between its water and the castle's outer wall was a poorly kept piece of land. A drawbridge across the moat led to a broad gateway with another portcullis. Inside the wall of the city were well-kept gardens. Practice jousts and other small contests were held weekly within the ballium. The ballium lay between the outer and inner walls of the castle, and entirely surrounded it. In Nimmr, the knights wore leopard skin bassinets.

A regular weekly jousting event was held with pomp and ceremony. The citizens turned out for it in their best clothes: women in bright dresses; men in colored apparel and polished armor. There were trumpeters and fanfare and banners and gay pennons. Before each contest, the combatants and their seconds rode to the prince's loge and saluted him by drawing their swords, raising them blade down, and kissing their hilts. The prince gave his address and the combatants returned to their respective sides. Mercy was almost unknown in these events, and it was customary to actually kill an opponent bested during the contest. A

portable grandstand for observers could be put in place for these events, and removed readily in case of a siege.

After the tournament a feast was held in the castle. The tables were arranged to form a T with the prince and his party at the top table. Because of the noise from the feasting hordes, it was necessary to shout to carry on a conversation with someone farther down the table. And if several people were shouting at once, the atmosphere became enormously loud and confusing. But if the prince began to talk, all lapsed into respectful silence. Toasts were made, lots of food was eaten, and there was much drinking.

CITY OF THE SEPULCHER (BACKERS): The people of the City of the Sepulcher considered their ruler, Bohun, to be a king. They were constantly at war with the city of Nimmr. Their bassinets were made of bullock hide to distinguish them from the leopard skin used by the knights of Nimmr. Although there were some small differences between their bucklers, and they wore and displayed different colors, the knights of the City of the Sepulcher were identically costumed and accoutered to the knights of Nimmr. Their castle city with its barbican was located near the seldom-used mountain trail in the north, which provided an alternative entry into the valley. Theirs was arranged similarly to the castle of Nimmr.

Waz-don: see **Pal-ul-don**

Waz-ho-don: see **Pal-ul-don**

Waziri: see **Natives**

XUJA: *Tarzan the Untamed.* Amid a desolate desert landscape cut by many gorges and littered with boulders, a canyon ran north and south, and upon its floor lay the skeleton of a large and ancient warrior. On his bones were a hammered brass helmet and a rusted breastplate of iron, and nearby rested a long straight sword and a harquebus. South, beyond the skeleton, the precipitous rock walls of the winding canyon widened then narrowed again, and the canyon sloped downward until, at a turn, a fertile valley came into view. This was the valley that contained the city of Xuja where Tarzan felt a sense of loneliness and danger. Vegetation covered the well-watered valley from end to end. At its southern extremity, a lofty mountain range rose, forming a natural border. The valley itself was about three or four miles from north to south, but longer east to west.

At the mouth of the canyon, a trail led down a cliff to the valley floor and to a forest of large trees where many and various birds of brilliant plumage screamed and called out among chattering monkeys. There were also a large number of snakes in the trees, and some crocodiles in the waterways. In addition, the forest was rich in fruits and nuts. All the fauna and flora here were similar to, yet slightly different from, those of the outer world. But despite all the abundance of the forest, there was hardly any game in the valley. The trail continued on to a stream which it followed in a southwesterly direction, then was joined by other trails. The tracks and scent of Numa, the lion, and Sheeta, the panther, were heavy upon the trail which, beyond the edge of the forest, ended at the walled city of Xuja.

Four hundred yards of open land lay between the edge of the forest and the wall of the city. This open land contained well-husbanded gardens arranged in neat symmetrical rows with irrigation canals among them. Through these canals, the original founders of Xuja, who had become lost and eventually settled in the valley, transported water from natural springs they had dug to irrigate their original trees which had proliferated to become the surrounding forest. At dusk these irrigation streams were closed with little gates by the workers in the gardens. Other gardeners brought in the freshly picked produce in large baskets that they bore upon their shoulders. They gained access to the city by beating on the wooden doors located in the arched gateway of the walls.

The city of Xuja had the shape of a long and narrow rectangle, yet the streets within the walls were winding. The outer wall stood about 30 feet high. It was plastered, painted cream, and broken by a few embrasures. Near an archway the wall was bare but for low shrubbery growing under it, but elsewhere it was vine covered. Throughout the great walled city there were towers, domes, and minarets. The largest central dome was gilded while the smaller ones around it were painted red, yellow, or blue. There was not much color or ornamentation to residences which were almost all two storied and flat roofed, with the upper floors being flush with the street. The ground floor was set back about ten feet, with pillars and columns supporting the floor above, which gave the whole street an arcade look on either side. The streets themselves were dirt, but the arcades under buildings, which effectively acted as sidewalks, were paved with well-worn, cut stones laid without mortar. The walls of a building were thick, and its openings small to help control the interior temperatures. The flat roof of each was accessible from within by climbing up a ladder through an aperture in the ceiling. Towards the middle of the city the buildings became larger, and there were shops with signs over their doors in a Greek-like written language. The city center had a large plaza and a placid lagoon. Here the buildings were the largest of all, and were ornamented with gold and painted many other colors. The street itself was one large paved mosaic of many patterns, colors, and designs. The dominant motif was that of the parrot, with those of lion and monkey being less prevalent.

At night the city streets and the interiors of buildings were lit by oil lamps. Inside homes, people used hangings instead of solid doors. Similar hangings decorated their walls. Wooden doors were used almost exclusively as exterior doors. Couches, chairs, tables, and benches made up their simple furniture. They used forks, spoons and knives to eat from bowls and plates.

The people of Xuja could best be described as rational maniacs. Each believed that he alone was sane and the others crazy. Their features and appearance suggested a stereotypical congenital insanity, yet their tone and demeanor seemed rational. And among them were skilled craftsmen and gardeners. Xujans were strongly built, and they had leathery skin that looked like yellow parchment, but they were not Asian. Their eyes were close set with small black irises that enhanced the whites of their eyes. The males' hair was black and typically cut about three to four inches long. It was stiff, stuck out of their heads at right angles, and grew low

down on the forehead giving them a brutish look. The males also had some scraggly hair on their chin and upper lip, but the rest of the face was smooth. Their upper lip was thin while, in contrasting, the lower was large and pendulous. Their canine teeth were longer than normal. Their noses were narrow. Xujans' arms were long, but not abnormally so, and their legs were short and straight. They wore snug nether garments or tights made from the hides of rodents, a woven loose sleeveless tunic that reached below the hips, and soft soled leather sandals that laced up to the knees. For weapons they carried a short heavy spear and a saber in a leather scabbard which they were very adept at using.

The females were shorter than the males and had longer hair which they held back from their faces with a piece of lace or fabric. The women went about topless and were even more plain than the men. They were also more violent and, consequently, did not live as long. They were usually kept in barred rooms. The women's single garment was made of a sheer gauzy material. It began below their bare breasts and wrapped around the body to the ankles. Bits of gold or other metal decorated the garment and their headdress. Otherwise they wore no other jewelry. The females' figure was more slender and symmetrical than the men's, especially in the arms, hands, and feet.

At any moment one of the usually depressed citizens of Xuja could become gripped by an uncontrollable berserk rage and attack anyone nearby including the children who played in the streets naked. When in such a rage, they hit, bit, and wrestled, while shrieking and screaming. On the other hand, Xujans were known to fall into a fit of mirthless maniacal laughter and dance about gibbering, or go running about naked while screaming. Some walked upon all fours; some jumped headforemost from rooftops. Since these attacks and antics were part of their daily lives, people indulging in them went practically unnoticed by the rest of the populace. Although there were citizens who actually did seem to be aware of their surroundings, most walked about oblivious to everything, wearing vacant stares. To compound the situation, many Xujans were epileptics.

Xuja had a king and queen, and they lived in a beautiful palace. The king could have many queens at the same time, but not all of them were necessarily human. While the kings, who came from a long line of lunatics, usually had short lives due to suicide and assassination, the queens continued on, being passed from king to king. The oldest queen at the time Tarzan arrived was a woman from the outside world who had been held captive in the palace for over 60 years. Her name was Xanila.

The palace was a very elaborately designed and decorated building. The parrot motif was used profusely there in all the hangings, mosaics, and carvings. The palace had many rooms and chambers and twisting hallways, and there were also secret passageways. One such went through a pool of water, beneath a wall, and into a canal that led out into the lagoon in the center of the city.

Other government officials, not of the royal blood, made up the ruling class. The guards and warriors amongst these nobles wore upon their tunics the emblem or symbol of the house they served. Princes wore a fillet of gold upon their head with a single parrot feather standing erectly in the front.

The people of Xuja took African natives as slaves when possible. Some of these were made eunuchs to guard the women's quarters in the palace. Outside Xanila's barred room a black eunuch stood constantly on guard. The rest of the palace was guarded by the king's warriors who wore yellow tunics with the emblem of a parrot on the back. They also patrolled the city. To call the king's guards and their lions, a bugle was used.

Xujans revered all birds, but mostly the parrot which was their god, and they even spoke the same language as the parrots that lived all about them. The parrot that the people of Xuja had actually made their god was supposed to have been over 300 years old. They kept it in the palace and worshipped him with disgusting religious practices. The Xujans also revered monkeys, and the myriad of them in the valley talked to the parrots. The parrots then flew to the city and told the people what the monkeys had said. When necessary, a bugle was used to call the parrots to the city's assistance. The people gave the parrots strategic instructions, and the birds heeded them. Usually, though, when the people walked through the forest they cast fearful glances at the parrots in the trees above them, and if a parrot swooped down at them, they would throw their arms over their face and fall flat on the ground. If anyone killed a parrot or monkey, the whole jungle cried out in protest and alarm. So to be safe, the people of Xuja did not eat any birds at all, and certainly not monkeys. Instead, they ate lions.

The eating lions were bred and raised by the Xujans just as cattle were in the beef-eating outside world. Lion was the only meat that they ate or craved, and they used it in all manner of palatable and well-prepared dishes. All herbivorous animals were raised for the lions to eat. Deer, boar, and antelope were chief among them, and they were all kept in corrals in the south part of the city. The Xujans used goats for milk.

There were, however, two types of lions in the valley of Xuja. One was a black-maned beast, larger than the normal lions outside the valley. These the Xujans were entirely unafraid of. They trained and domesticated them as men of the outer world did dogs. Once the lions were broken and obedient to their masters, they had free reign inside the city and walked about like familiar pets. They were also the lions the Xujans consumed. The other type of lion was black all over and larger than the domesticated variety. They were wild and ran loose in the valley, attacking the people and their trained lions. These ebony demons were not in the least afraid of humans, and struck fear in the hearts of both the Xujans and their trained lions. In fact, the citizens' fear of these lions was so great that they were loathe to go out of the city after dark. The trained lions of Xuja were actually half-breeds, born of the union of the valley's wild black lions and the normal beasts of the outer world.

When the trained Xujan lions hunted a man, they slowly gathered into a group near the victim and, where possible, circled him. The animals made no audible noise, but did not move by stealth either. Eventually their circle drew tighter until at a certain distance they decided to stop. They continued to watch their prey, and if he did not move they lay down facing him. This watching and waiting went on until one of the lions' human masters approached and gave them an order. Verbal commands were generally all that was necessary to control the cats, but occasionally they needed to be beaten with the haft of a heavy spear.

Zuli: see **Kaji and Zuli**

Cast of Characters

Abdul: A young male Arab aide and interpreter for Tarzan while the Apeman served as a special agent for the ministry of war in the desert of Algiers. Abdul was very faithful and fought alongside Tarzan in times of trouble. *The Return of Tarzan*

Abraham, the son of Abraham: The bearded, fanatic, epileptic Prophet of Paul, the son of Jehovah, and the leader of the South Midians. Abraham was jealous and suspicious of the parachuting Englishwoman, Barbara Collis, after the people supported her as a messenger from God. He attempted to have her killed as a sacrifice several times but failed. *Tarzan Triumphant*

Abu Néjm, Abdullah: An Arab who captured and sold Tarzan to Fritz Krause in revenge for the Jungle Lord putting a stop to Abdullah's raiding. Abdullah Abu Néjm knew of Tarzan's prowess and feared him. But when Tarzan was safely behind the bars of a cage, he spat upon him. When Tarzan finally escaped he put Abdullah into a cage. Then, when they were all marooned on the Mayan island of Uxmal, Abdullah

kept himself aloof from all the others. He was later shot and killed by Hans de Groote. *Tarzan and the Castaways*

Adendrohahkis: Thagosto (king) of the Minuni (Ant Men) city of Trohanadalmakus and father of Komodoflorensal who Tarzan rescued from a giant Alalus woman. Adendrohahkis was very fond of Tarzan and made him a prince in his city. *Tarzan and the Ant Men*

A'ht: see **Akut**

Aht, the son of Tha: The only brother of the cavewoman Nat-ul. Aht sided with Dag when the latter drew a line in the ground and vowed not to cross it until Nu, the son of Nu, was found. *The Eternal Savage (Lover)*

Ajax: see **Akut**

Akamen: A noble and cousin of Queen Atka in Ashair, the Forbidden City. Akamen was placed as the guard of Atan Thome and Lal Taask. At the request of Atan Thome, Akamen betrayed the queen and attempted to assassinate her with Lal Taask's assistance. The two would-be assassins were in turn betrayed to the queen by Atan Thome. Akamen

Virgil Finlay illustration for _Tarzan and the Castaways_ (© 1941 Edgar Rice Burroughs, Inc.).

was put into a cage in the temple throne room, and in an attempt to escape was killed by a _ptome_. _Tarzan and the Forbidden City_

Akut: A very large and strong Mangani possessed of above average intellect and curiosity. Akut became a great and devoted friend of Tarzan in _The Beasts of Tarzan_ after Tarzan bested him in battle with his infamous wrestler's full nelson. The Jungle Lord then lived with Akut and his tribe of Mangani on a jungle island off the coast of Africa until he could find a way off the island. Akut was instrumental in helping Tarzan find and rescue Jane and their supposed infant son, Jack. During this time they fought side by side and were great allies.

After Tarzan parted company with him Akut searched and waited ten years for the Ape-man to return. Because of this Akut was willingly,

and coincidentally, captured by Alexis Paulvitch who put him on display for profit in a traveling circus, and dubbed the great Mangani, Ajax. Akut was eventually seen in England and befriended by Tarzan's then teenage son, Jack. When Paulvitch attempted to murder the younger Greystoke for revenge on Tarzan, Akut, in Jack's defense, killed Paulvitch. Determined to return Akut to the jungle, Jack bought passage for both of them on a ship, and disguised Akut as his invalid grandmother, calling him Mrs. Billings, to fool the people on the boat. In a hotel in Africa, an attack by Akut foiled an attempted robbery by a wanted U.S. criminal named Condon and resulted in Condon's death. In fear of possible legal prosecution, Akut and Jack ran away into the jungle together to live in exile.

In the jungle Akut taught Jack the Mangani language and how to survive. Since Akut could not pronounce the name Jack, he chose the closest sounding word he could think of in the language of the Mangani. This was how Jack Clayton, the son of Tarzan, became Korak, the Killer. While spying on an Arab camp, Korak rescued a young abused girl named Meriem. Meriem called Akut by the easier name of A'ht and lived with the two jungle bachelors for some time. After several adventures Akut left Korak and Tarzan to become the king of, and live happily with, a new tribe of Mangani. *The Beasts of Tarzan* and *The Son of Tarzan*

Alam: The youngster who delivered food to Corrie van der Meer and Sing Tai when they were in a cave together hiding from the invading Japanese army in Sumatra, near the village of Tiang Umar. Alam was forced by the Japanese to divulge their hiding place. *Tarzan and the Foreign Legion*

Alextar: The brother of Nemone, the queen of Cathne, the City of Gold. In *Tarzan and the City of Gold* Alextar was the direct heir to the throne, but because of a conspiracy by M'duze and Tomos, he was kept locked up in the temple indefinitely. After Nemone killed M'duze and herself Alextar was released and given the throne. In *Tarzan the Magnificent* Alextar was found to be a cruel and weak king who was easily influenced by Tomos. Alextar, like his sister before him, became a little insane, and after killing Tomos turned his sword upon himself and committed suicide. *Tarzan and the City of Gold* and *Tarzan the Magnificent*

Ali: The fat sultan of the Galla Moslems who were the rivals of the lost

Portuguese city of Alemtejo. When Ali had Pelham Dutton, Sandra Pickerall, and the man who thought he was Tarzan as prisoners, he demanded a large ransom of 200 buffaloes from Alemtejo for Sandra alone. It was refused, so he claimed Sandra as his new wife. After an attack upon his village by the Tarzan-led Alemtejo, Ali was taken prisoner. *Tarzan and the Madman*

Ali-ben-Ahmed: The Arab sheik who respected Tarzan's bravery and almost let him go after capturing him for Nikolas Rokoff and Alexis Paulvitch. *The Return of Tarzan*

Althides: The strong underofficer of the guard in Cathne, the City of Gold, who escorted Tarzan to prison after the Ape-man was first captured. Tarzan showed Althides how to use a bow and arrow. *Tarzan and the City of Gold*

Amat: A cruel and conniving Sumatran who looked out for his own interests. Amat spied on Tarzan's camp and told the Japanese where it was. A cowardly liar Amat allowed some rogue Dutch guerrillas to abduct Corrie van der Meer. Amat was finally chased away by a murderous Tony Rosetti. *Tarzan and the Foreign Legion*

Ancient Mariner: The old sailor that Captain Billings angrily struck at after accidentally tripping over him upon the deck of the *Fuwalda*. After Black Michael defended the Ancient Mariner the captain attempted to shoot Michael, but his revolver was struck down by the nearby John Clayton. In repayment the Ancient Mariner forewarned the Claytons of an ensuing mutiny. *Tarzan of the Apes*

Andereya: The serving "boy" who was left to watch Kali Bwana when his master, Old Timer, went out hunting. When the Leopard Men came and attacked the camp Andereya was killed and Kali Bwana abducted. *Tarzan and the Leopard Men*

Anderssen, Sven: The Swedish cook on the ship *Kincaid* , on which Tarzan, Jane, and their infant son, Jack, were held captive on behalf of Nikolas Rokoff and Alexis Paulvitch. Sven carried a long greasy cooking knife in his apron, and was villainous and unintelligent looking with close set eyes and a large drooping mustache. His favorite saying was, "Ay tank it blow purty soon purty hard!" and he was proud of the fact that his last name was spelled with a double s. Despite his outward appearance, however, Sven had a heart of gold and was able to speak several languages, assisted Jane and the baby in escaping the *Kincaid*, and later gave his life for them while attempting to delay Rokoff and Paulvitch. Tarzan was with Sven for his last moments in this life and buried the chivalrous Swede in a shallow grave in the jungle. *The Beasts of Tarzan*

Andua: A Waziri warrior who was trained as a pilot and mechanic by Korak. *Tarzan and the Ant Men*

Annette: The pretty French maid to Princess Kitty Sborov on their ill-fated plane trip to Africa in search of a secret to longevity. The plane crash-landed, and when they were forced to go by foot through the jungle Annette and the American pilot, Neal Brown, fell in love. After Prince Alexis Sborov murdered his wife with a hatchet he made advances toward Annette. She was later lured off by one of the Kavuru and taken to their village. There she and Jane were saved by Tarzan, Brown, and Tibbs. Annette received an equal portion of the longevity pills

that were taken from the Kavuru. *Tarzan's Quest*

An-un: "Spear-eye," Pan-at-lee's father in the land of Pal-ul-don. *Tarzan the Terrible*

Aoponato: The number $800^3 + 19$ in the language of the Minuni, and the slave number assigned to Prince Komodoflorensal while he was a prisoner and slave in Veltopismakus. It was written in Minunian hieroglyphics. See illustration below. *Tarzan and the Ant Men*

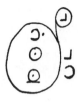

Aopontando: The Minuni word for the number $800^3 + 21$. This was Tarzan's assigned slave number after the Jungle Lord was captured by the warriors of the city Veltopismakus and shrunken to the Ant Men's size by the walmak Zoanthrohago. It was written in Minunian hieroglyphics. See illustration below. *Tarzan and the Ant Men*

Applosus, Appius: The faithful friend of Maximus Praeclarus who Appius replaced as captain of the Colosseum guards after Praeclarus was thrown in prison. Appius later informed Praeclarus that his fiancée, Dilecta, had been blackmailed into marrying the Caesar's son, Fastus. Praeclarus then informed Appius where his keys to the dungeon were located in his apartment. Appius went and retrieved them and set Praeclarus and Tarzan free. *Tarzan and the Lost Empire*

askari: Head bearers in a safari who were given guns to help defend, hunt, and enforce rules.

Asoka: The Lascar sailor on the *Saigon* who was assigned to routinely feed the captive and caged Tarzan along with the other prisoners. Tarzan attacked Asoka and took his keys to the cages, and after escaping put Asoka himself into a cage. *Tarzan and the Castaways*

Aswad, Ibn: The ivory and slave raiding Arab sheik who abducted Victoria Custer. *The Eternal Savage (Lover)*

Ateja: The beautiful Bedouin daughter of Sheik Ibn Jad who accompanied her father's raiding party in the search for the fabled lost city of Nimmr. Ateja was in love with a young Arab named Zeyd who was in her father's camp. Zeyd returned Ateja's love, but Fahd, who also desired Ateja, was jealous and framed Zeyd as an assassin. Upon hearing this Ateja forced Zeyd to flee the camp for his own protection. Later, Ateja met Tarzan and learned that Zeyd still lived. After her father's successful raid upon the Valley of the Sepulcher Tarzan dogged her father's footsteps and terrorized his safari. When everyone else abandoned him Ateja stood by her father's side and aided him. She was later happily reunited with Zeyd who was traveling with Tarzan's Waziri. *Tarzan, Lord of the Jungle*

Atewy: The shifty eyed Arab who was the right hand man to Sheik Ab el-Ghrennem. Able to speak broken English, Atewy associated with all the English speaking people in the motion picture safari who were on location in Africa and eavesdropped on them whenever possible. Atewy began to desire the stunt double, Rhonda Terry, and after she was abducted by the Arabs he began to plot against Ab el-Ghrennem to obtain her. Atewy was killed by English speaking gorillas during an ambush in the canyon that led to the Valley of Diamonds. *Tarzan and the Lion Man*

Atka: The cruel queen of Ashair, the Forbidden City, in the volcano valley of Tuen-Baka. Atka believed every stranger who came to the valley was attempting to steal the Father of Diamonds from her temple. She was, however, impressed with Tarzan and promised to free him if he swore loyalty to her. He would not, and after Tarzan led an attack against her with warriors from Thobos, a tribe of Mangani, and several of his friends from the outside world she was forced to surrender to him. *Tarzan and the Forbidden City*

Avan: Chief of the cliff dwelling people from the village of Clovi in Pellucidar. Avan was the father of Ovan who Tarzan saved from a *ryth,* and the husband of Maral who Avan had captured from Zoram. Avan allowed Tarzan to remain in peace until the village council decided what to do with him. *Tarzan at the Earth's Core*

Axuch: A white slave in the home of Dion Splendidus, and his daughter Dilecta, in the lost Roman city of Castra Sanguinarius. *Tarzan and the Lost Empire*

Baine, Jerrold: A crew member on the motion picture *Lion Man* which they were attempting to film on location in Africa. While traveling through a grass field in cannibal country Baine was killed in an ambush by the man-eating men. *Tarzan and the Lion Man*

Balando: Besides Muviro, Balando was the only Waziri who survived of the original ten who went searching for the Kavuru village. Balando helped Muviro salvage pistols from some dead pilots who had had the misfortune of landing near the Kavuru village. They used the guns against the Kavuru during an attack. *Tarzan's Quest*

Balza: "Golden girl," a blonde girl who was a half-blooded gorilla and human, created from the experimentation of the transformed man known as God, in the Valley of Diamonds. When she was born human in appearance and intellect she was cast out by her gorilla-looking parents, after living with them long enough to learn to speak the English language. Ostracized, she went to live with the other mutant outcasts and freaks in their jungle cliff dwellings. There Balza went about completely nude and learned to speak the language of the Mangani. She also learned to travel easily through the trees. When the movie stunt double, Rhonda Terry, was taken by Balza's mate, Malb'yat, the Golden Girl pursued them to reclaim her man, but was roped by Tarzan. The Jungle Lord then beat Malb'yat and rescued Rhonda. Because of this Balza felt she belonged to the Ape-man. Tarzan took both women back with him to the motion picture safari and explained to Balza that she was not his. Balza was accepted and clothed by the safari and in a surprise denouement, she became a big movie star in Hollywood. *Tarzan and the Lion Man*

Basuli: A Waziri chieftain who gave an answering lion roar to Tarzan at Opar. Basuli also led the Waziri against the Arabs of Achmet Zek. *Tarzan and the Jewels of Opar*

Batando: Chief of a Galla tribe of natives who welcomed back the returning Arab slave, Fejjuan. As agreed Batando gathered all the Gallas together to escort Sheik Ibn Jad's raiding party to the medieval Valley of the Sepulcher where he hoped the Arabs would all be killed. *Tarzan, Lord of the Jungle*

Batn, Abu: A somewhat cowardly sheik who distrusted whites even though he accompanied a group of communists into Africa to raid the treasure vaults of Opar. Abu Batn was insulted by the group's leader Peter Zveri and deserted the Russian after taking Zora Drinov and the exiled La of Opar to sell as slaves. Abu was killed by the American Wayne Colt while the Arab was attempting to rape Zora. *Tarzan the Invincible*

Baynes, Morison: A good-looking, healthy, and wealthy young English thrill seeker visiting the Greystoke estate. While there the Hon. Morison Baynes acted somewhat superior and pious. After seeing Meriem, Baynes was at first attracted to her, but was later turned off when he saw her talking to baboons. He still desired to marry Meriem, however, and told her that he loved her, but she did not return his love. Frustrated Baynes collaborated with Mr. Hanson (a.k.a. Sven Malbihn) to get Meriem from the Greystokes. Hanson tricked Baynes, though, and took Meriem for himself. Baynes followed the Swede and the two men exchanged shots. Baynes was wounded, but saved from death by Korak. Baynes was then caught by Arabs, but Korak again saved him. Baynes finally returned to the Arabs and was shot by them. *The Son of Tarzan*

Belthar: The royal pet lion and personal bodyguard of Queen Nemone in Cathne, the City of Gold. Belthar was a very large and ferocious lion that did not like Tarzan. Nemone entertained a personal belief that her life and Belthar's were somehow linked and that when one died the other would also. When Belthar was allowed to "hunt" Tarzan, the unarmed Jungle Lord was saved at the last instant by Jad-bal-ja, the Golden Lion. The two giant cats fought, and Jad-bal-ja won the battle and killed Belthar. When Nemone saw the dead Belthar she fulfilled her own belief by killing herself with a dagger on the spot. *Tarzan and the City of Gold*

ben Houdin, Achmet: An Arab criminal who was the ringleader of a raiding and killing group that was caught by Captain Armand Jacot of the French Foreign Legion. Achmet was promptly prosecuted and executed. His uncle, Sheik Amor ben Khatour, took revenge upon Jacot by kidnaping his daughter, Jeanne, who later became Korak's Meriem. *The Son of Tarzan*

ben Kadin, Ali: Sheik Amor ben Khatour's half brother (through a black slave mother) who had half of his face eaten away by disease. The repulsed Meriem was given to Ali ben Kadin by the sheik, and while he attempted to rape her in his tent, Korak entered and killed him with a knife. *The Son of Tarzan*

ben Khatour, Amor: An evil-eyed, older, and taller Arab known simply as the Sheik. Amor ben Khatour was the uncle of Achmet ben Houdin who was caught by Captain Armand Jacot of the French Foreign Legion, prosecuted as a criminal and executed, despite a bribe from Khatour. The Sheik then took vengeance

upon Jacot by kidnaping his seven-year-old daughter, Jeanne. Khatour changed Jeanne's name to Meriem and raised and abused her for several years while acting as her guardian. During a rescue attempt by Korak, Khatour was knocked out by the son of Tarzan. The Sheik did eventually get Meriem back and also succeeded in capturing Korak. But Tantor the elephant came to Korak's rescue and in the process trampled and killed the Sheik. *The Son of Tarzan*

Bertram: A knight of Nimmr in the lost medieval Valley of the Sepulcher. Sir Bertram was the friend of the American James Blake. Being a large man Bertram provided Tarzan with some of his clothing to wear when he escorted the Jungle Lord through the valley. *Tarzan, Lord of the Jungle*

Beyd, Mohammed: The Arab in charge of Achmet Zek's camp when Zek went to get the Oparian gold buried at the razed Greystoke estate. Later, when Albert Werper came back to camp with a tale of Zek being killed in battle, Beyd knew that Werper lied. Beyd also desired the captive Jane and wanted to kill Werper. When Beyd attempted to rape Jane in her tent Werper intervened and shot him with a pistol during their struggle. *Tarzan and the Jewels of Opar*

Billings: The captain of the small chimnied sailing vessel, *Fuwalda*, that was transporting Lord and Lady Greystoke to Africa, where they were going on military assignment. Captain Billings was a cruel bully, and after accidentally tripping over an old sailor called the Ancient Mariner, struck at him. Black Michael, a nearby sailor, defended the Ancient Mariner, but was shot at by the captain. Billings' revolver was struck

J. Allen St. John illustration from *Jungle Tales of Tarzan* (© 1919 Edgar Rice Burroughs, Inc.).

down by John Clayton, and thereafter he held a grudge against Clayton. The crew eventually mutinied, and Captain Billings received an axe to the head during the revolt. *Tarzan of the Apes*

Billings, Mrs.: see **Akut**

Billy: A small man with a distinguishing lump on his jaw who was the faithful and loyal askari to Jean and Eugene Hanson. He was also trusted by Tarzan. When the safari was ambushed by the warriors of Ur, Billy was left for dead along with Mr. Hanson. Both were later found by the cruel Wilson Jones and his even worse cohort, Cannon. The two bullies tortured both Eugene and Billy, but when the two unfortunates finally escaped Billy went into the jungle to hunt down Cannon. After lassoing and hanging the bully in the air, Billy slit his throat. *Tarzan: The Lost Adventure*

Black Michael: A bull necked bear of a sailor on the *Fuwalda* with large black mustaches. Michael defended an older sailor against the captain, and in the process was shot at by him. The revolver was struck down just in time by John Clayton, Lord Greystoke, and instead of being killed Michael was only wounded in the leg. Grateful to Clayton, Black Michael returned the favor during a mutiny he led by protecting the Claytons from the other sailors. He then humanely set them ashore on the west coast of Africa with supplies. Black Michael promised to inform the government of their whereabouts, but he was never heard of or seen again. *Tarzan of the Apes*

Blagh: A priest of Opar who was on traditional sentry duty when Esteban Miranda, a Spanish actor impersonating Tarzan, arrived with porters to steal gold from Opar's treasure vaults. Blagh believed Miranda was indeed the blasphemous Ape-man and informed Cadj, the rebellious high priest, of what he saw. *Tarzan and the Golden Lion*

Blake, James Hunter: A 25-year-old rich American whose favorite saying was, "I'll tell the whole world." Blake was on a photographic safari with Wilbur Stimbol, an older man on a hunting safari. Blake was kind to his porters, but Stimbol was not, and after several disagreements they decided to part ways. When Tarzan met Blake, the Jungle Lord was impressed by the young American and aided him. Blake later became separated from his safari and wandered into the hidden Valley of the Sepulcher. In this anachronism from the Middle Ages, where knights and castles still existed, he became Sir James, and quickly made both friends and enemies there. He fell in love with the beautiful princess Guinalda who was also attracted to him; after first spurning his love she later returned it.

When the Arab raiders of Sheik Ibn Jad arrived, they stole Guinalda and left Blake for dead. Tarzan entered the valley and saved Blake who rode out alone, of his own volition, in search of Guinalda. But Tarzan eventually saved Guinalda, in the outer jungle after she was abducted by a Mangani, and returned her to the valley. When Blake learned of this, he came home. It can be supposed that he married Guinalda, the woman he loved, and lived happily in the valley. *Tarzan, Lord of the Jungle*

Blk: One of the 20 priests who were cast out from Opar for supporting the traitorous high priest, Cadj. Blk found a location for the priests to live and build a new temple to the

Flaming God, and led them to it.
Tarzan and the Tarzan Twins

Bluber, Adolf: The short, overweight and bullnecked German who was one of the financial supporters, as well as the treasurer, of the expedition set up by Flora Hawkes to go in search of gold in the lost city of Opar. The red faced and thick accented Bluber was very concerned about how the expedition's finances were spent, and complained a lot about the money he wasted on his useless safari outfit. After many harrowing adventures, he was grateful to leave Africa with only his life. *Tarzan and the Golden Lion.*

Bobolo: A native chief who was also a member of the Secret Order of the Leopard Men. Bobolo was usually friendly to whites and would trade with them. But when the white woman, Kali Bwana, was captured by the Leopard Men, he wanted her. To fulfill this selfish desire he decided to help her and the white man, Old Timer, escape from the Leopard Temple. Bobolo recaptured Kali Bwana, however, and took her to the Betetes pygmy cannibal village for safekeeping. When Bobolo's wife, Ubooga, found out that he was a Leopard Man she blackmailed him. He was later arrested by soldiers for being a member of the order. *Tarzan and the Leopard Men*

Bodkin, Paul: A black sentry guarding the tunnel entrance to the medieval Valley of the Sepulcher, by the giant cross. He helped capture the lost American, James Hunter Blake, and escort him into the valley. Bodkin spoke the king's English and wore the garb of the Middle Ages. *Tarzan, Lord of the Jungle*

Bohun: The arrogant king of the Castle of the Sepulcher that guarded the canyon entrance at the north end of the hidden medieval Valley of the Sepulcher. King Bohun desired princess Guinalda of the rival city of Nimmr, and with several of his knights he boldly stole her after the Great Tourney between the two cities. *Tarzan, Lord of the Jungle*

Boleyn, Anne: One of the six English speaking gorilla wives of the gorilla king, Henry the Eighth, in the lost city of London on the Thames in the Valley of Diamonds. *Tarzan and the Lion Man*

1. Bolgani: The ruling class in the Valley of the Palace of Diamonds, which was located behind the valley of the Bolgani's hereditary enemies, the Oparians. These jewelry wearing apes, the Bolgani, walked upright and lived in a city. They dominated a lower order, the Gomangani, who they used as slaves and workers. The Bolgani's ruler was a lion they called Numa, King of Beasts, Emperor of all Created Things. See Valley of the Palace of Diamonds in Section Three. *Tarzan and the Golden Lion*

2. Bolgani: "Gorilla." Tarzan saved an unnamed gorilla from Histah, the snake. This same Bolgani returned the favor by protecting a helpless Tarzan from the knife of the murderous hunter Wilbur Stimbol. *Tarzan, Lord of the Jungle*

1. Bolton: The British lieutenant commander and skipper of the submarine *Union Jack* whose crew saved Tarzan and his "Foreign Legion" from being completely destroyed by the Japanese while in a boat on the ocean. Bolton was asked to perform the marriage ceremony for "Shrimp" Rosetti and Sarina, and for Jerry Lucas and Corrie van der Meer. *Tarzan and the Foreign Legion*

2. Bolton: The captain of the yacht *Naiad* when it was pirated and taken over by the motley crew of the mutinied *Saigon*. Bolton was later made the captain of the *Saigon* by Tarzan after the mutineers were overthrown with the Ape-man's assistance. *Tarzan and the Castaways*

Bolton-Chilton, Francis: The downed pilot who was made a porter and prisoner in the Ruturri Mountains by the Galla Moslems who were the rivals of the people of Alemtejo. Bolton-Chilton was later taken by the Alemtejos and made their slave. When Tarzan met him, during the period the Jungle Lord was pretending to be the true god of Alemtejo, he chose Bolton-Chilton to be his personal slave. Tarzan did this to gain information from the other man. He left Alemtejo with Tarzan, and during their time together it came out that Bolton-Chilton knew the true identity of the man who thought he was Tarzan. When they met up with Sandra Pickerall and the amnesiac, Colin T. Randolph, Jr., of West Virginia, the actual name of the man who thought he was Tarzan, Bolton-Chilton explained everything to them. It started when he had made a bet with Randolph that the West Virginian could not live alone in the jungle for a month like Tarzan. During the trip to carry out the requirements of the bet, Randolph and Bolton-Chilton had become separated after parachuting out of their defective plane, and the former had lost his memory. *Tarzan and the Madman*

Bourke, Billy: A friend of a Hollywood party crasher named Reece. While driving Bourke's car the two took Tarzan to a party where Bourke attempted to rape the hostess. Tarzan intervened and threw Bourke down the staircase. *Tarzan and the Lion Man*

Brown: The big game hunter staying at the Greystokes' while Barney and Victoria Custer were there. Brown seemed to have more woodcraft than Tarzan at the time, and believed that a dead zebra that they came across was killed by a man. Brown helped search for Victoria Custer after her disappearance. *The Eternal Savage (Lover)*

Brown, Horace: An American who invented an ignition disrupter which had military importance. Brown was murdered in a boarding house in London and his plans stolen, after his secretary, Mary Graham, told the wrong person about the invention. *Tarzan and the Jungle Murders* in *Tarzan and the Castaways*

Brown, Neal "Chi": The American pilot from Chicago who knew of the Kavuru longevity pills. Brown flew the plane that took Jane to Africa, along with Prince and Princess Sborov, who were searching for the pills; their English valet, Tibbs; and their French maid, Annette. During a storm he successfully crash-landed in some treetops. Because the Sborovs were selfish and condescending, Brown and the prince disliked each other. Brown was impressed with Jane's jungle knowledge and prowess, but he eventually fell in love with Annette. After Sborov murdered his sleeping wife with a hatchet and failed in his attempt to frame Brown for it, the prince tried to kill the pilot. Sborov failed at this too, and in fear ran off into the jungle where he was found by Tarzan. Sborov told the Jungle Lord that Brown had killed Jane (who in reality had been lured off into the jungle with Annette by the Kavuru). Tarzan ultimately learned the truth and befriended Brown, and together they searched for Jane and Annette.

At the Kavuru village, Brown piloted an abandoned plane that he and Tarzan crashed into the Kavuru's palace temple after they had safely parachuted out. They successfully raided the temple and saved the two women. Brown was given an equal portion of the longevity pills taken from the Kavuru. *Tarzan's Quest*

Brulor: An old priest who was the Father of Diamonds and the god in Ashair, the Forbidden City. Brulor was killed with a trident by the released prisoner, and former priest, Herkuf. *Tarzan and the Forbidden City*

Brynilda: The princess married to Prince Gobred, ruler of Nimmr, in the medieval Valley of the Sepulcher. Brynilda was the mother of Guinalda. *Tarzan, Lord of the Jungle*

Bubonovitch, Joe "Datbum": An educated and married staff sergeant from Brooklyn who was the assistant engineer and waist gunner aboard the B-24 bomber, the *Lovely Lady*. Bubonovitch and his good friend, Tony "Shrimp" Rosetti, were always teasing and insulting each other. After being shot down while flying with Tarzan over Japanese held Sumatra in the Dutch East Indies, Bubonovitch was caught by the Japanese. Just as they were about to behead him, he was saved by Corrie van der Meer and his captain, Jerry Lucas. *Tarzan and the Foreign Legion*

Buckingham, Duke of: An English speaking gorilla who was part of the council to King Henry the Eighth in the city of London on the Thames in the Valley of Diamonds. Buckingham was one of the gorillas that captured Rhonda Terry and gave her to the king. He later took Terry's look-alike, Naomi Madison, from some Arabs while they were attempting to enter the valley. Buckingham thought

Naomi was Rhonda and fled with her into the jungle so he could have her for himself. When Tarzan overtook them, the Jungle Lord slew Buckingham while Naomi watched. *Tarzan and the Lion Man*

Buira: The daughter of Muviro. After she was abducted by the Kavuru, Tarzan, Muviro and nine other Waziri went in search of her. Before she could be killed in the Kavuru temple, Tarzan and the American pilot, Neal Brown, saved her. *Tarzan's Quest*

Bukawai, the unclean: The repulsive, leprous, and reclusive witch doctor who lived in a cave near the village of Mbonga. Bukawai had two ill-tempered and hard to control hyenas that the natives thought were devils in the guise of pets. They said, therefore, that he entertained devils in his cave. Bukawai called Tarzan a devil-god. When the Jungle Lord abducted Tibo, a ten-year-old native boy, Momaya, Tibo's mother, sought out Bukawai for assistance. The unclean one agreed to help, and named his price. When Tibo was returned without the witch doctor's intervention, Bukawai still insisted on payment from Momaya. She refused and he kidnaped Tibo himself to force her to pay. He enclosed the boy in his cave, just out of reach of the hyenas. Tarzan rescued Tibo, and thus affronted Bukawai. Then, when Tarzan was knocked out in a storm, Bukawai came upon him and saw his chance to revenge himself on the young Jungle Lord. He tied him to a tree in his cave and loosed his hyenas on him. But Tarzan escaped and tied Bukawai to the tree. The hyenas ended up killing the witch doctor. *Jungle Tales of Tarzan*

Bukula: The enslaved porter of Arab sheik, Abu Batn. Bukula was later enlisted by Ibn Dammuk, the traitorous right hand man to Abu Batn, to help abduct La of Opar from the sheik. Bukula succeeded in luring La away from camp and into Dammuk's custody. *Tarzan the Invincible*

Bulabantu: The well-knit underchief to Mbonga, from the village of Mbonga. Tarzan thought Bulabantu a brave warrior because he courageously faced the glowing lion eyes that surrounded his campfire at night while his fellow warriors cowered in fear. When Bulabantu accidentally stumbled into the tribe of Kerchak, Tarzan did not want the Mangani to kill the native warrior, and when Bulabantu bravely faced the Mangani, Tarzan came and stood by his side. Taug joined the two, mainly to assist his friend Tarzan. Just when the apes were attacking, Tantor arrived and scared the Mangani away. *Jungle Tales of Tarzan*

Bulala: An ignorant west coast native who was a captive of the Bagalla cannibals along with the Tarzan Twins. Bulala was very generous and had a big heart, and despite his pigeon English he helped teach the Twins the native dialect of the Bagallas. He was the first chosen to be eaten by the cannibals and was taken away to a different hut. But the Twins helped Bulala escape. *Tarzan and the Tarzan Twins*

Bulland: A knight in the Castle of the Sepulcher in the lost medieval Valley of the Sepulcher. Sir Bulland was marshal of the guard of the castle during the Great Tourney. Complacent through years of peace, he carelessly left the portcullis open when Arab raiders entered the valley through the north pass and attacked. *Tarzan, Lord of the Jungle*

Bu-lot: "Moon-face." A Ho-don and the son of Mo-sar, chief of Tu-lur,

the Bright City. Bu-lot's great-great-grandfather was once king of Pal-ul-don and therefore Bu-lot had blood rights to the throne. Consequently, for political reasons, he was betrothed to O-lo-a, daughter of Ko-tan, king of the city of A-lur in the land of Pal-ul-don. At his "bachelor party" he got drunk and killed his future father-in-law with his knife. In the ensuing confusion he and his father went to the princess's quarters to kidnap O-lo-a and take her to their city. Pan-at-lee, a beautiful black Waz-don servant, defended O-lo-a. Before Bu-lot could kill Pan-at-lee Tarzan arrived and struck the Ho-don on the head from behind which killed him instantly. *Tarzan the Terrible*

bumude-mutomuro: "He-boy." The term, in the language of the Mangani, for the descriptive English name the young Tarzan chose for himself. *Jungle Tales of Tarzan*

Busuli: A native warrior of the Waziri tribe who Tarzan almost killed for his weapons. Instead, though, the Jungle Lord saved him from an attacking lion. Because of this Tarzan was accepted into the Waziri tribe. Busuli became a devoted friend and protector of Tarzan, even after the Ape-man became the chief of the Waziri. *The Return of Tarzan*

Butzow: A lieutenant, and friend of Barney and Victoria Custer and of Mr. William Curtis. Butzow accompanied Curtis to the Greystokes' African estate to visit the Custers who were already there. *The Eternal Savage (Lover)* and Barney Custer's own tale, *The Mad King*.

Buulaoo: The young son of Chief M'-ganwazam. He hated his mother, Tambudza, and after overhearing her offering aid to Tarzan, Buulaoo told his father. *The Beasts of Tarzan*

Bwana: Swahili for Lord.

Bwana, Kali: See **Kali Bwana**.

Cadj: The High Priest of Opar for most of La's reign. Cadj was upset that La loved Tarzan and not him, but due to political pressure he did eventually get La as his mate in *Tarzan and the Golden Lion*. In the same book when Cadj heard that the blasphemous and much hated Tarzan had entered Opar again the high priest set out with some of his warrior-priests to find and sacrifice the Jungle Lord. Although they saw the Spanish Tarzan impersonator, Esteban Miranda, they did actually find the real Tarzan lying unconscious after being drugged by Miranda's cohorts. Cadj immediately took it upon himself to blasphemously sacrifice Tarzan on the spot but La arrived to stop him. Tarzan was taken as a prisoner back to Opar where Cadj had been making plans with a traitorous priestess, Oah, to overthrow La and become king, making Oah the high priestess and his mate. Under the cover of darkness, La set Tarzan free and the two escaped together. Cadj then became the first king of Opar, and Oah his figurehead high priestess. After gathering a large army from the Valley of the Palace of Diamonds, Tarzan returned to Opar with La and overthrew Cadj. In the battle, however, Cadj captured the Ape-man and while attempting to sacrifice him again, the former high priest was attacked and killed by Jad-bal-ja, the Golden Lion. *Tarzan and the Jewels of Opar* and *Tarzan and the Golden Lion*

Caldwell, John: An alias Tarzan used on a boat from Algiers to London. *The Return of Tarzan*

Campbell, Joseph "Joe the Pooch": While in London, Campbell learned from Mary Graham, the talkative secretary of the inventor, Horace Brown, of an invention of military importance. After Brown was discovered dead and the plans missing Campbell met and collaborated with a Russian exile named Nikolai Zubanev to sell the plans to Italy. The plans were then taken from them by the British pilot Lt. Cecil Giles-Burton who flew them to Africa. The two pursued and shot down Giles-Burton's plane, but their own plane was shot down in the process. After wandering in the jungle separately, these two downed parties were taken in at different times by the Ramsgate safari. Campbell took on the alias of Smith and Zubanev the alias of Peterson. Smith/Campbell eventually killed Giles-Burton for the plans, and later killed his own cohort Peterson/Zubanev and tried to blame Tarzan for it. With the knowledge that the second finger was missing from Campbell's right hand, Tarzan was able to solve the murder mysteries, have Campbell arrested, and recover the plans. *Tarzan and the Jungle Murders* in *Tarzan and the Castaways*

Canler, Robert: The 40-year-old wealthy man who was in love with Jane before she went to Africa and met Tarzan. Canler loaned Jane's father, Professor Porter, $10,000 to finance his expedition to Africa. Jane mentioned him as *Mr.* Canler in a letter she wrote to her friend Hazel Strong while in Tarzan's cabin. Once Jane had been rescued and was back in America, Mr. Canler spoke often and insistently to Professor Porter about her marrying him. Since the professor could not repay the debt he owned Canler, he felt trapped and encouraged his daughter to marry Canler. Canler even went to

Wisconsin where Jane was living at her inherited farmhouse and there he got her to agree to marry him immediately. Even for her father's sake and with a minister present, she was still reluctant to marry Canler. Impatient, Canler grabbed Jane, and in her defense, Tarzan — who had traveled there for the ceremony — grabbed Canler and gave him a shaking that almost killed him. Through Tarzan's persuasion, Canler finally released Jane from her obligation. *Tarzan of the Apes*

Cannon: An overweight, sweaty white man without conscience or morals. Cannon was with Wilson Jones and Charles Talent when they came upon the Hanson safari, and on seeing Jean Hanson, he desired her. After a tornado, the cruel and ruthless Cannon found the decapitated head of one of his own men, and casually stole the gold teeth from its mouth. Cannon finally met his demise after being first hung and then having his throat slit by Hanson's askari, Billy. *Tarzan: The Lost Adventure*

Capell: The English colonel of the Second Rhodesians in British East Africa during World War I. Tarzan helped Colonel Capell's troops against the Germans. Later, Capell sent a plane out to search for Lt. Harold Percy Smith-Oldwick after he had made an emergency landing with his plane. By that time Smith-Oldwick had already joined with Tarzan and the German spy Bertha Kircher. When Smith-Oldwick's plane was discovered Capell, along with General Smuts, arranged for a rescue mission against the Xujan warriors who had the three cornered. Once they

had been rescued, Capell informed Tarzan that Bertha Kircher was not a German spy but an English one and that she had been a lifelong friend of his own family. He also told the Ape-man that she had promised to marry Smith-Oldwick. The final information Tarzan received from Colonel Capell came in the form of Hauptmann Fritz Schneider's diary. In it the Ape-man read that Jane was still alive. *Tarzan the Untamed*

Capietro, Dominic: A stocky, bearded, Italian communist who formed and led a slave raiding band of *shiftas*. Capietro captured a Russian named Leon Stabutch and befriended him. The two later captured Tarzan, but the Ape-man was rescued. When Capietro went on to capture the beautiful young Midian, Jezebel, he and Stabutch both desired her and played cards to determine who should possess her. Capietro won, but Stabutch fought him for her anyway and killed the Italian with a dagger. *Tarzan Triumphant*

Caraftap: A slave of Zoanthrohago in the same quarry as Tarzan and Komodoflorensal in the Minuni city of Veltopismakus. Caraftap wanted the beautiful female slave, Talaskar, to cook for him. But she refused, and voluntarily cooked for Tarzan and Komodoflorensal instead. This made Caraftap jealous, and after he was easily beaten by Tarzan in a fight, he became vengeful. When Tarzan and Komodoflorensal disguised themselves and escaped, Caraftap recognized them and reported their flight to the *vental*, Kalfastoban. While searching for the two escapees, Caraftap had his head twisted off by Tarzan. *Tarzan and the Ant Men*

Opposite: **Thomas Yeates illustration from *Tarzan: The Lost Adventure* (© 1995 Edgar Rice Burroughs, Inc.).**

Carb: A warrior with thin lips and unsympathetic eyes who was high in the council of the cave dwelling village of Clovi in Pellucidar. Carb was absent when Tarzan first arrived in the village with Ovan, the chief's son, who Tarzan had saved from a *ryth*. While away, Carb had captured the beautiful Jana, the Red Flower of Zoram, and was awarded her as his wife. After his return, Carb threatened Tarzan, and he wanted the villagers to kill him rather than accept him as a friend as they had done. But Tarzan escaped with Jana before any harm could befall either of them. *Tarzan at the Earth's Core*

Carl: The new servant of the Greystokes who kidnaped their infant son, Jack, for Nikolas Rokoff and Alexis Paulvitch in London. When Jack's heroic nurse jumped on the getaway car, Carl hit her in the face and knocked her loose. *The Beasts of Tarzan*

Catherine of Aragon: The first gorilla wife and, consequently, queen of the English speaking gorilla-king, Henry the Eighth of London on the Thames in the Valley of Diamonds. Even though Catherine disliked her husband, together they did have a son named the Prince of Wales. Catherine was jealous of the human female Rhonda Terry. *Tarzan and the Lion Man*

Cha, Itzl: A Mayan girl who was to be sacrificed in her city of Chichen Itza on the lost island of Uxmal. After Tarzan saved Itzl Cha from this religious death, he transported her back to his camp of castaways on an elephant's back. There she at first thought Tarzan and all his fellow castaways were gods. In the camp Itzl Cha was put under Patricia Leigh-Burden's care. The young Mayan maiden taught both Tarzan and Patricia the Mayan language while she learned how to speak English in return. Itzl Cha's association with Tarzan caused her to fall in love with the Jungle Lord, and when she saw that Patricia was in love with him also, Itzl Cha became jealous. This jealousy later caused her to run away from camp and return to Chichen Itza and warn the high priest that Tarzan was coming to rescue Patricia who had recently been taken prisoner. Tarzan was caught, and Itzl Cha was placed in a cage so she could still fulfill her duty as a human sacrifice. After Tarzan proved to the people that he was a god he ordered Itzl Cha released. *Tarzan and the Castaways*

Chan, Thak: A hunter on the lost Mayan island of Uxmal where Tarzan, two parties of castaways, and several non-native wild animals were marooned. While hunting one day Thak Chan was attacked by one of the lions let loose upon the island. But Tarzan saved him from this unfamiliar and savage creature. The Ape-man was also an unusual sight to the Mayan, and Thak Chan believed him to be Che, Lord Forest, one of the Mayan gods. Thak Chan believed that the orangutans that accompanied Tarzan — which he had never seen before either — were gods as well. So Thak Chan felt some importance when he escorted Tarzan to Chichen Itza, the main city upon the island. *Tarzan and the Castaways*

Chand: A Lascar sailor who collaborated with his shipmate, Jabu Singh, in a mutiny on the ill-fated *Saigon*. After their successful revolt was over, Tarzan led one of his own and put Chand into a cage along with the other mutineers. *Tarzan and the Castaways*

Charpentier: A lieutenant in the French Navy who rescued the marooned Porter party at Tarzan's cabin in Africa. Lt. Charpentier was the lifelong friend of Paul d'Arnot, and when d'Arnot was taken prisoner by the Mbonga cannibals Charpentier led the rescue party to their village. When d'Arnot could not be found, but bits of his clothes were, the tribe was almost completely massacred. *Tarzan of the Apes*

Chemungo: The son of Mpingu, chief of the Buiroo cannibals. In *Tarzan and the Forbidden City* Chemungo, along with three others, captured Helen Gregory while she wandered alone in the jungle after escaping Atan Thome. When they tried to kill and eat her in their village, Chemungo was hoisted overhead by Tarzan with a rope and held hostage until Helen was freed. As a result, he hoped someday to revenge himself upon Tarzan. And in *Tarzan and the Jungle Murders* his hope was realized. He came upon the oblivious Jungle Lord, cast a spear into his back, and took him captive to his village. *Tarzan and the Forbidden City* and *Tarzan and the Jungle Murders* in *Tarzan and the Castaways*

Chon: An old bearded man who cursed a lot. Although deposed, he was considered to be the true god in the lost volcano crater land of Tuen-Baka which contained Ashair, the Forbidden City, and its rival city, Thobos. Chon and a following of his priests lived in a cave near Ashair, biding their time until he could return as the true god. Chon captured Helen Gregory under the surface of lake Horus where she was waiting for Tarzan and Paul d'Arnot. Magra and Mr. Gregory, Helen's father, were also caught. In order for Chon to determine whether they spoke the truth about their purpose in Tuen-Baka, he wanted to read the entrails of Mr. Gregory. Chon was reinstated as the true god after Queen Atka was overthrown by Tarzan and the Thobotian navy. *Tarzan and the Forbidden City*

Chuldrup: A Lascar sailor who hated whites and was knocked down by a temperamental Wilhelm Schmidt upon the ill-fated *Saigon*. After the *Saigon* was shipwrecked upon the lost Mayan island, Uxmal, and the passengers, prisoners, and crew divided into two camps. Chuldrup was sent to spy on Tarzan's. While on his way through the jungle to the others' camp, Chuldrup was killed by a tiger that had been released by Tarzan from the *Saigon*. *Tarzan and the Castaways*

Chulk: A young and strong Mangani bull that possessed greater intelligence than most. He dressed as an Arab at Tarzan's bidding to help them better infiltrate Achmet Zek's camp. But when Chulk heard the Arab guns, he fled in fear. Later, when he came across a sleeping Mugambi, he stealthily took back Tarzan's pouch of jewels from him. Chulk then rescued Tarzan from Belgian soldiers, and after being shot by them, he still managed to carry Albert Werper away before dying. Once Chulk died, Werper took the pouch of jewels from him. *Tarzan and the Jewels of Opar*

Clayton, Alice: Tarzan's beautiful biological mother whose maiden name was Rutherford, and who was also called Lady Alice and Lady Greystoke. While pregnant Alice and her husband, John Clayton, Lord Greystoke, were stranded in the jungle on the west coast of Africa by the mutinous sailors of the *Fuwalda*. When John was attacked by a large great ape, Alice managed to shoot and kill the creature with a rifle as it charged her husband. The night her son was born she suffered a breakdown. This, coupled with the trauma of childbirth and their life in a savage jungle, caused the beautiful young mother to become delusional. A year after the birth of their son John, who became Tarzan, Lady Alice passed away in her sleep. Her husband was killed that same day in the cabin next to her body. The remains of both were later buried beside their jungle home by the Porter family and, ironically, the Claytons' nephew, William Cecil Clayton. *Tarzan of the Apes*

Clayton, Jack: see **Korak**

Clayton, Jack (Jackie), Jr.: Korak's first son and the grandson of Tarzan. *Tarzan and the Ant Men*

Clayton, Jane: see **Porter, Jane**

1. Clayton, John: The given name of Lord Greystoke, Tarzan's handsome biological father, as well as Tarzan's. The senior Clayton was appointed to investigate the unfair treatment of native recruits in a British colony on the west coast of Africa. His wife of three months, the former Alice Rutherford, was determined to go with him even though she was pregnant. On the way, the crew of their vessel, the *Fuwalda*, mutinied. Because Clayton had saved the life of one of them, they let him and his young wife live, but set them ashore with supplies at the edge of the jungle on the west coast. There Clayton built a cabin and provided for the couple. All during this time he dedicatedly kept a diary. Due to the stresses of childbirth and their life in the jungle, Lady Alice died in her sleep a year after the birth of their son. While mourning her loss, the distracted John Clayton was killed

by Kerchak, the king of the Mangani, who had entered the cabin for just that purpose. *Tarzan of the Apes*

2. Clayton, John: The given name of Tarzan, as it was his biological father's. See Tarzan and Section One.

Clayton, William Cecil: The eldest son of the younger brother of John Clayton (Tarzan's father). This made William the first cousin of Tarzan. Because he was in love with Jane Porter and wanted to marry her, William was with Jane, her father, and their entourage when they were first marooned near Tarzan's cabin. In *The Return of Tarzan* he found the discarded note Paul d'Arnot had written to Tarzan that proved the Ape-man was the rightful heir to the Greystoke estate. William selfishly kept it to himself.

He and Jane eventually became engaged, and on a cruise together they met up with, and were befriended by, Nikolas Rokoff who was using the alias M. Thuran. When the yacht was shipwrecked, they floated helplessly in lifeboats, suffering starvation and thirst to the point of death, until they were miraculously washed ashore on the African coast near Tarzan's cabin. There they lived in a tree house that Thuran and Clayton built. In this primitive existence Jane finally was honest with herself and Clayton. She broke off their engagement after admitting her love for Tarzan, even though she believed the Ape-man dead.

After Jane was kidnaped by the 50 frightful priests of Opar, Clayton contracted a fever and was cruelly abandoned by M. Thuran. A few days later the still living Tarzan, and the recently rescued Jane, returned to witness William Cecil Clayton's last moments in mortality. Before his final breath was taken, however, in an act of deathbed repentance, he gave Jane the note from d'Arnot that proved Tarzan's birthright. William Cecil Clayton's remains were buried next to those of his aunt and uncle (Tarzan's parents) near their cabin in Africa. At Tarzan's request, William was given a military gun salute at his graveside by a rescue party of soldiers. *Tarzan of the Apes* and *The Return of Tarzan*

Coh Xiu, Cit: The king of Chichen Itza upon the lost Mayan island, Uxmal. Cit Coh Xiu desired the marooned Patricia Leigh-Burden when she was captured by his warriors and brought to the city. *Tarzan and the Castaways*

Collis, Lady Barbara: A beautiful woman with a great smile, and the daughter of the Earl of Whitney. While flying her plane over the Ghenzi Mountains in Africa, Barbara ran out of fuel with no suitable place to land. So she parachuted out and landed in the lost and isolated land of Midian. With such an entrance, the fanatic Christian Midianites thought that she was a messenger from god and treated her as such at first. While there Barbara learned the Midianite language from the ostracized golden haired girl named Jezebel. In return she taught Jezebel to speak English. The Midianite prophet, Abraham, the son of Abraham, was suspicious as well as jealous of Barbara and wanted her done away with even after she "miraculously" saved a drowned sacrificial victim. As part of Abraham's ploy he had Barbara thrown into the Lake Chinnereth and left for dead, but she escaped. She was then to be crucified and burned at the stake, but was rescued from this by the lost and wandering American, Lafayette Smith. Together they escaped but were captured by the North Midians who Tarzan rescued them from. Smith and Barbara fell in love. *Tarzan Triumphant*

Colt, Wayne: The leftist American who became a part of Peter Zveri's communist treasure raiding expedition to Opar. Colt joined in time to rescue the beautiful Zora Drinov from the burly East Indian, Raghunath Jafar. When the expedition made its way into Opar, Colt was captured by the Oparians, but was secretly released by the priestess, Nao, who became infatuated with him because of his good looks. Colt then wandered lost in the jungle until he came upon a fleeing Zora who was being pursued by Sheik Abu Batn. Colt slew the Bedouin with a knife that Nao had given him and stayed with Zora in the jungle. He then became separated from her, but met La of Opar who was with Jad-bal-ja, the Golden Lion. In the end it was revealed that he was not a communist but a special agent in the employ of the United States government. He then professed his love for Zora Drinov which she returned. *Tarzan the Invincible*

Condon: The wanted U.S. criminal who attempted to rob young Jack Clayton and Akut (the Mangani disguised as Jack's invalid grandmother, Mrs. Billings) when they landed in Africa. At night Condon entered the apartment of Jack and Akut and was attacked and killed by the great Mangani. After the two fled, Condon's body was discovered by the hotel's proprietor, Herr Skopf. The criminal's death and the disappearance of Jack and his invalid grandmother remained a mystery at the hotel. *The Son of Tarzan*

Constantine: The father at the French mission that was the first civilized place the young Tarzan came to after he and Paul d'Arnot first left the jungle on foot. Father Constantine welcomed them, and they stayed there a week. He also provided Tarzan with clothes to replace his loincloth. *Tarzan of the Apes*

Cranmer: An English speaking gorilla in the city of London on the Thames in the Valley of Diamonds. Cranmer was one of the gorillas who captured the American stunt double actress, Rhonda Terry, and brought her to the king. He was also a confidant to the half-man, half-gorilla they considered to be God. *Tarzan and the Lion Man*

Crouch: The doctor on the yacht *Naiad*, owned by the Leigh family, when it was pirated by the mutinying crew of the *Saigon*. *Tarzan and the Castaways*

Crump, Tom: The older notorious ivory poacher who had been previously run out of the country by Tarzan. Crump shot at Tarzan, wounding him in the head and knocking him out. He took Sandra Pickerall back to Pelham Dutton who was searching for her, but later plotted with Dutton's guide, Bill Gantry, to take Sandra and earn a greater reward for themselves. Along the way Crump was captured and enslaved by the people of Alemtejo. Together with his cohort, Ivan Minsky, they escaped during a raid and came upon the gold mine of the Galla Moslems. Their greed caused them to take more gold than they could easily carry. Paranoid that someone (including themselves) would try to take their gold, they traveled without taking time to find food and water. Eventually Crump went crazy from hunger, fatigue, and paranoia and dashed out Minsky's brains with a gold nugget. Crump died soon

thereafter of thirst and hunger. *Tarzan and the Madman*

Curtis, William: A friend of Barney and Victoria Custer's who visited them at the Greystokes' African estate. William came close to being the dream man that Victoria had recurring visions of. Although he at first never spoke to her of his love, William finally proposed. Before she could respond in the affirmative, though, an earthquake struck and she fainted.

During her unconsciousness, Victoria had another vision of her dream man. When she awoke she went looking for him, and was captured by Arabs. Later, when something, or someone, was suspected of killing and eating the Greystoke livestock, Curtis fired a shot in the direction of a movement in the night and ended up hitting Nu, the son of Nu, from the Niocene — the man of Victoria's dreams. The Greystokes nursed Nu back to health and tried to learn from him the possible whereabouts of Victoria. Curtis did not like or trust Nu, and felt the troglodyte was responsible for Victoria's disappearance. When they all went searching for her, Nu found her first and saved her. When Curtis saw them together he became jealous and attempted to shoot at Nu, but Terkoz, the Greystoke wolfhound, attacked and killed Curtis.

This series of events turned out to be part of a dream or alternate reality of Victoria's that played itself out during the time she was unconscious from the earthquake. When she really awoke, it was only a few minutes after Curtis' original proposal and he was still alive. But after that "dream," Victoria did not feel that she could ever marry Curtis. *The Eternal Savage (Lover)* and the non–Tarzan adventure *The Mad King*

Custer, Barney: A man from Beatrice, Nebraska. He and his sister, Victoria, visited the Greystokes in Africa to hunt and to help Barney try to forget about something in his life. Barney was the only one who was understanding about Victoria's recurring visions of a dream man or caveman lover, and her fear of earthquakes. When the caveman Nu, the son of Nu, arrived after an earthquake and was taken in by the Greystokes, Barney realized that this troglodyte might actually be the man of his sister's dreams. Consequently, he befriended Nu and helped him learn to speak English. When it was discovered that Victoria had been taken by Arabs, Barney went with the others to search for her. (To learn more of Barney Custer and what he is trying to forget at the Greystokes' read *The Mad King*.) *The Eternal Savage (Lover)*

Custer, Victoria: A woman from Beatrice, Nebraska. She was beautiful, hearty and usually calm. She was also a great shot with a rifle, and considered very brave except when it concerned mice and earthquakes. Victoria often had bouts of a lost and longing feeling that occurred after an earthquake or after seeing evidence of one. She would then have romantic dreams of a caveman. This was one reason why she had not yet married, even though there were many eager and eligible men around. While Victoria and her brother, Barney, were visiting the Greystokes in Africa, she was contemplating marriage to William Curtis who was the closest living thing to the dream man of her recurring visions. After he proposed to her, an earthquake struck and she fainted.

Upon awakening, she was inspired to go alone to a cave. There she found, lying unconscious, Nu, the son of Nu, of the Niocene, the caveman of her dreams. While succoring him near the cave, she was captured by Arabs. Nu was later found by the Greystokes and with their help recovered completely. Together, they then searched for Victoria. Nu found her first and saved her. When Curtis saw them together, he became jealous and attempted to take a shot at the troglodyte. But Terkoz, the Greystokes' wolfhound, attacked and killed Curtis before he could fire. Victoria then went away with Nu and somehow, through another earthquake, became the cavewoman Nat-ul, the daughter of Tha. But this was Victoria in an alternative reality, in which she was in love with Nu during the Niocene period of Earth's history.

In the midst of her adventures as Nat-ul in this past or other life, another earthquake struck and brought her back to the present where, in reality, only minutes had gone by. Victoria then went directly to a cave that had been uncovered by the earthquake and found the remains of a giant caveman with his broken spear and a saber-toothed tiger skull. As a result of her dreamlike experiences, she was also unable to accept Curtis' marriage proposal. See **Nat-ul**. *The Eternal Savage (Lover)* and the non–Tarzan adventure *The Mad King*.

Dag: A warrior friend of Nu, the son of Nu, of the Niocene. During the tribe's trek for a better place to live, Dag drew a line on the ground and said he would not go past it until Nu, the son of Nu was found. They all agreed and went back to look for Nu who was searching for Nat-ul.

Once he had Nat-ul, Dag protected her from Zor, the large lion. *The Eternal Savage (Lover)*

da Gama, Cristoforo (Chris): The fat king of the lost city of Alemtejo who desired their captive goddess, Sandra Pickerall, for himself. Da Gama hated and was jealous of his high priest, Pedro Ruiz, who also desired Sandra. With the assistance of Tarzan, da Gama was dethroned by Osorio da Serra, a favorite of the people. Da Gama ended up fleeing the city with Ruiz. *Tarzan and the Madman*

Daimon: The name of a demon that Tarzan pretended to be while searching around Athne, the City of Ivory. *Tarzan the Magnificent*

Dak-lot: "Fat-face." The Ho-don sentry who led Tarzan to King Kotan of A-lur in Pal-ul-don while the Jungle Lord was pretending to be Dor-ul-Otho, the son of god. *Tarzan the Terrible*

Dalfastmalo: The breeder of *diadets* (royal antelopes) in the Minuni city Veltopismakus. Dalfastmalo made a wager with Zoanthrohago about the duration of Tarzan's shrunken state. *Tarzan and the Ant Men*

Dammuk, Ibn: A son of a sheik, and of the same tribe as Abu Batn who Dammuk worked for as a right hand man. Together they served the communists, led by Peter Zveri, who raided Opar for treasure. When La, high priestess of Opar, wandered into their camp, Dammuk desired her. He abducted her and took her away from the camp. While he attempted to rape her in the jungle, La killed Dammuk with his own dagger. *Tarzan the Invincible*

Dareyem: An Arab tribesman who was faithful to Ibn Dammuk. Dareyem assisted in the abduction of La of Opar. *Tarzan the Invincible*

d'Arnot, Paul: A wealthy French navy lieutenant who was part of the group that pursued the mutineers of the *Arrow* and found the stranded Porter party at Tarzan's cabin. While searching for Jane, and possibly Tarzan, Lt. d'Arnot was ambushed and taken prisoner by the cannibals of the Mbonga village. In the village he was tied to a stake and almost killed. But Tarzan rescued him right before the death stroke was administered in the ceremonial Mbonga dancing rite. While convalescing in the jungle in Tarzan's care, d'Arnot mistakenly taught Tarzan to speak his native French, even though the Jungle Lord wrote notes to him in English. Realizing his mistake, d'Arnot taught Tarzan to speak English as well. During this time the Porter party left, along with the rest of d'Arnot's crew because they thought he was dead.

Once d'Arnot was fully recovered, he and Tarzan trekked out of the jungle and into civilization. On the way, the Frenchman became curious about Tarzan's origin and existence, and read the diary of John Clayton, Lord Greystoke, which Tarzan had with him. Once in Europe, d'Arnot proved Tarzan was the son of Lord Greystoke by comparing the adult Tarzan's fingerprints with those of an infant's found in the senior Clayton's diary. After Tarzan renounced his birthright, d'Arnot helped support him financially in Europe and assisted him in obtaining his first job, as an agent for the minister of war. During their time together, d'Arnot, who was considered one of the best swordsmen in Europe, taught the Lord of the Jungle how to fence.

In *Tarzan and the Forbidden City* d'Arnot fell in love with the beautiful Helen Gregory. He went with her

J. Allen St. John illustration from the *Tarzan and the Jewels of the Opar* newspaper serialization (© 1918 Edgar Rice Burroughs, Inc.).

safari, led by Tarzan, into the jungle to search for her lost brother, Brian, who happened to look like Tarzan. Helen at first denied his love, but later returned it. *Tarzan of the Apes, The Return of Tarzan, The Beasts of Tarzan,* and *Tarzan and the Forbidden City.*

Darus: An older and faithful high priest to La in the lost City of Opar. Darus was the feeder of the captured lions used in Opar, and was enlisted by the usurped and recently escaped La to aid her in reclaiming her throne. *Tarzan the Invincible*

da Serra, Osorio: The popular noble and the captain-general of the warriors in the lost Portuguese city of Alemtejo who desired the throne. When Tarzan saved da Serra from an enraged water buffalo, he befriended the Ape-man. Seizing the opportunity at hand, the crafty noble then enlisted Tarzan in overthrowing the ruling king and high priest. As part of the plan da Serra had Tarzan pretend to be the true god of Alemtejo. After the ensuing revolt the people made Osorio da Serra their king. *Tarzan and the Madman*

Davis, Bill: The staff sergeant from Waco, Texas, aboard the B-24 bomber, the *Lovely Lady,* over Japanese held Sumatra in the Dutch East Indies. After their plane was shot down by the Japanese, Bill was made a prisoner of war and was to be executed on the day of his twenty-fifth birthday. But Tarzan saved him and his comrade, Carter Douglas, by rescuing them from their prison. *Tarzan and the Foreign Legion*

de Coude, Olga: Of Russian birth and the sister of Nikolas Rokoff. Olga became a countess through marriage to the much older Count Raoul de Coude. Not only was she a lovely young brunette she also pos-

sessed a disarming sweet smile. She met Tarzan on an ocean liner and admired his youth, good looks and bravery. After Tarzan saved her husband from a blackmail attempt at the hands of Nikolas Rokoff and Alexis Paulvitch, the Jungle Lord also saved her from a similar fate, and possibly worse as well.

A friendship developed and in Paris Tarzan became a regular visitor to the de Coude home. Through this familiarity, Rokoff attempted to revenge himself on Tarzan and Olga by having her husband catch them alone together in a compromising situation. Rokoff's plan worked better than expected, because even though Olga and Tarzan realized what was going on, they gave into their passion for each other and really were caught in each other's arms by the count. Even though the virtue of the countess was still intact, to protect the honor of all involved a duel with pistols was arranged between Tarzan and Count de Coude. In a display of self-sacrifice and contrition, Tarzan willingly lost the duel but, miraculously, not his life. This gallant act gained him the undying respect and admiration of the count and countess. *The Return of Tarzan*

de Coude, Raoul: The French Count who married Nikolas Rokoff's sister, Olga, even though she was many years younger than him. Count de Coude was a high official in the French ministry of war, and was purported to be the best swordsman in France and the best shot in Paris. Tarzan saved him and his wife from blackmail by Rokoff and his cohort, Alexis Paulvitch, on an ocean liner, and because of this Tarzan became a frequent and welcomed visitor to the de Coude home in Paris.

The Count's wife, Olga, became

enamored with Tarzan because of his looks, youth and bravery. Capitalizing upon this, her brother and Paulvitch concocted a vengeful scheme wherein she and Tarzan were caught in each other's willing arms by her husband. The count immediately attacked Tarzan, but the Ape-man almost killed him. Even though the countess's virtue was intact, the count challenged Tarzan to a duel with pistols on the field of honor. Knowing that he had tarnished the de Coude family name, and in atonement, Tarzan allowed himself to be shot without returning fire. Miraculously, he lived and his attempted self-sacrifice only raised him further in the eyes of the count and countess. Tarzan became one of their most respected and admired friends, and the count gave him his first job, as an agent for the minister of war. *The Return of Tarzan*

de Groote, Hans: The good-looking Dutch first mate on the ship *Saigon* that transported a caged Tarzan for exhibition in a wild animal show. De Groote wanted Tarzan to be treated humanely while in his cage, but after a mutiny he himself was put in a cage, together with Fritz Krause, the man who purchased Tarzan for exhibition. Hans also began liking the French girl, Janette Laon, and told her so. She liked him back.

After Tarzan took over the vessel, they were all shipwrecked on an island and separated into two camps. De Groote and Janette were in Tarzan's camp. But she was abducted and taken to the other camp. Hans went after her, and shot and killed Abdullah Abu Néjm, the Arab who had originally captured Tarzan and sold him.

De Groote was the first to realize that Tarzan was Lord Greystoke and informed the others. He also hinted that a marriage between him and Janette could be immediately performed by the captain of the yacht that ultimately rescued them. *Tarzan and the Castaways*

de Lettenhove: A leader of the good Dutch guerrillas under Captain van Prins in Japanese held Sumatra in the Dutch East Indies. When Tarzan walked freely into their camp, de Lettenhove was at first suspicious of his identity and story. But his fears were later allayed. *Tarzan and the Foreign Legion*

Dick: The Tarzan Twin who had black hair and was nicknamed Tarzan-go by his classmates. His American mother had married an Englishman who was a cousin of Tarzan's. She then moved to England with her husband, and there gave birth to Dick. That same day her identical twin sister had given birth in America to a boy she named Doc. Because of their same birthdays and the fact that they looked alike through their twin mothers, the boys were also called the Tarzan Twins by their classmates. Attempting to live up to the name of Tarzan, Dick and Doc became very athletic, and agile tree climbers.

At the age of 14 Dick and Doc were both invited to visit Tarzan on his African estate for a few months. During the train ride in Africa the train was derailed and the curious boys wandered off into the jungle where they quickly became lost. After being captured by cannibals they escaped with the help of some other captives. In the jungle Dick was attacked by a lion but luckily it impaled itself upon his spear and died. Tarzan soon found them and took them back to his estate.

While waiting for their luggage

Dick and Doc wore a loincloth and headband, and carried a spear, bow and arrows, and a knife. They were later separated from Tarzan while out exploring and ran into 20 rogue priests of Opar. The priests had with them a captive 12-year-old girl named Gretchen who they were forcing to be their new high priestess. Dick and Doc rescued Gretchen, but the Oparian priests recaptured her along with Dick, while Doc managed to remain free. Then, at one point, Gretchen was forced to sacrifice Dick upon an improvised altar, but Jad-bal-ja, the Golden Lion, saved him. *Tarzan and the Tarzan Twins*

Dilecta: The beautiful daughter of senator Dion Splendidus, whose family was the second most powerful in the lost Roman city of Castra Sanguinarius. Although desired by the crafty Fastus, Dilecta was engaged to the honorable patrician officer, Maximus Praeclarus, who aided Tarzan in escaping and gave him refuge. Tarzan protected Dilecta from the advances of Fastus, and after Praeclarus and Tarzan were betrayed and imprisoned, Dilecta was blackmailed into marrying Fastus. As a reward, though, her family and Praeclarus and his family were to be protected. During the marriage ceremony but before the vows could be exchanged, Tarzan and Praeclarus, along with other escaped prisoners, stormed the throne room and saved Dilecta. *Tarzan and the Lost Empire*

Din, Xatl: A noble on the lost Mayan island of Uxmal who saw Tarzan and his marooned party of castaways when they were trying to find refuge on the island. When Thak Chan, the hunter, befriended Tarzan and brought him to the city, Xatl Din admitted him and acted as his escort. *Tarzan and the Castaways*

Doc: The Tarzan Twin who had blond hair and was nicknamed Tarzan-tar by his classmates. The twin sister of Doc's American mother had married an Englishman, who was a cousin of Tarzan's. She had moved to England and gave birth to Dick. On the very same day, Doc was born in America. Because of their common birthday and the fact that they looked alike through their twin mothers, the boys were also called the Tarzan Twins by their classmates. Attempting to live up to the name of Tarzan, Doc and Dick became extremely athletic, and agile tree climbers.

At the age of 14 they were invited to visit Tarzan on his African estate for a few months. During the trip through Africa, their train was derailed and the curious boys wandered off into the jungle where they quickly became lost. After being captured by cannibals, Doc showed the natives some sleight-of-hand magic tricks and was considered a witch doctor with stronger medicine than Intamo, the village witch doctor. Because of this, the twins were feared and, as prisoners, given certain freedoms within the village until the day they were to be eaten. With the help of some other captives and a native youth the boys escaped into the jungle after the jealous Intamo attempted to kill Doc. Tarzan soon found them and took them back to his estate.

There, while waiting for their luggage, Doc and Dick wore a loincloth and headband, and carried a spear, bow and arrows, and a knife. They were later separated from Tarzan while out exploring and ran into 20 rogue priests of Opar. The priests had with them a captive 12-year-old girl name Gretchen who they were forcing to be their new high priestess. Dick and Doc rescued Gretchen, but the Oparian priests recaptured her along with Dick. Doc followed the party and began killing the priests one by one, shooting them from the trees with his arrows. Nevertheless, Jad-bal-ja and Tarzan arrived and saved Gretchen and the twins. Besides Tarzan and his family, Doc was the only other person Jad-bal-ja showed affection to, which he did by rubbing his head against the youth. *Tarzan and the Tarzan Twins*

Dogman: One of the Arabs under Sheik Abu Batn involved with the communist, Peter Zveri, and his treasure raid on Opar. After La, the high priestess to the Flaming God of Opar, entered the Arabs' camp, a group of them including Dogman, approached her. When the unfortunate Dogman reached out and, in unwitting sacrilege, laid a hand on her, La instantly stabbed and killed him with her knife. *Tarzan the Invincible*

Dongo: The headman of Dominic Capietro's scouting party of black *shiftas* who captured the Russian Leon Stabutch. *Tarzan Triumphant*

Dooth: The elder priest of Opar who counseled Cadj, the traitorous high priest, not to slay Tarzan in *Tarzan and the Golden Lion*. In *Tarzan the Invincible*, Dooth conspired with Oah—a traitorous priestess whom he desired and made love to—to usurp High Priestess, La of Opar. After successfully taking over Opar, Dooth ruled the lost city with a tyrant hand. When the Oparians saw La returning with Tarzan, they killed Dooth and reinstated La. *Tarzan and the Golden Lion* and *Tarzan the Invincible*

Dorf: A former officer in the imperial

Air Force who became a mate on the dirigible O-220 that took Tarzan and Jason Gridley into Pellucidar to rescue David Innes. *Tarzan at the Earth's Core*

Doria: The daughter of Thudos and one of the most beautiful women in Cathne, the City of Gold. Because of her beauty Doria was kept hidden by her family from Queen Nemone who was jealous of all women who could be considered prettier than herself. If Nemone found her out Doria would be killed or disfigured. Doria loved Gemnon, and he and Tarzan visited her at home. But when a spying Erot saw her, he hurried and told Nemone. Doria was subsequently imprisoned and sentenced to be sacrificed in the active volcano, Xarator. While in her prison cell, Erot attempted to rape her, but Tarzan arrived and killed him. The Jungle Lord then hid Doria in the hut of the slave Niaka, the brother of Hafim who Tarzan had saved. *Tarzan and the City of Gold*

Dorsky, Michael: A communist Russian in Peter Zveri's treasure raid on Opar. Dorsky was left to kill Tarzan as he lay a bound captive in their camp. In the ensuing struggle, the Ape-man bit Dorsky on the wrist and knocked him down before Tantor arrived and killed the Russian and rescued Tarzan. *Tarzan the Invincible*

Dor-ul-Otho: "Son of god" in the language of Pal-ul-don. Tarzan successfully pretended to be Dor-ul-Otho, the son of Jad-ben-Otho, the tailless god of the Pal-ul-donians, to gain entrance into the city of A-lur while searching for Jane in the land of Pal-ul-don. *Tarzan the Terrible*

Douglas, Carter: A 20-year-old staff sergeant from Van Nuys, California, who was aboard the B-24 bomber the *Lovely Lady* when it was shot down in Japanese held Sumatra in the Dutch East Indies. Carter was taken prisoner by the Japanese and about to be executed when Tarzan saved him and his comrade, Bill Davis. *Tarzan and the Foreign Legion*

Drinov, Zora: The beautiful wavy-haired Russian atheist who was part of the expedition of communists that wanted to cause world turmoil after gaining fantastic riches by looting the treasure vaults of Opar. Even though Zora was loyal to the group's leader, Peter Zveri, she began liking the American communist, Wayne Colt. When the exiled High Priestess, La of Opar, was taken into their camp, she and Zora become friends. Zora taught La to speak English. She eventually killed Zveri and announced she hated him because he had murdered her family. She then denounced communism and revealed her love for Wayne Colt, who in turn disclosed that he was not a communist but a special agent for the U.S. government. *Tarzan the Invincible*

Dufranne: The captain of the French naval cruiser that rescued the Porter party from the jungle at Tarzan's cabin. *Tarzan of the Apes*

Dutton, Pelham: An American who led a safari in search of his love, Sandra Pickerall, who was supposed to have been abducted by Tarzan. After being separated from his safari, Dutton was attacked by a lion and saved by Tarzan. Together with some Mangani, they searched for Sandra and for the man impersonating Tarzan who was the one who had really kidnaped Sandra. Dutton deserted Tarzan and was captured by cannibals. Tarzan again saved him. Together once more, they reached the lost mountain city of Alemtejo where Dutton was captured by Alemtejo's enemies, the Galla Moslems, and made a slave. In their stronghold, he was imprisoned with the Tarzan impostor, and the two planned an escape. During their breakout, Dutton was attacked and killed by the Mangani friends of the man impersonating Tarzan. His corpse was then eaten by a lion. *Tarzan and the Madman*

Dyaus: The name for the elephant god of Athne, the City of Ivory. The Athneans used an actual living elephant to represent Dyaus. *Tarzan and the City of Gold* and *Tarzan the Magnificent*

Ebopa: A large praying mantis that bore the names the Stick That Walks and the Undying God of Ur. The people of Ur worshiped this terrible insect, and kept it trapped in caves and caverns under their city until they allowed it to come to the surface to fight and kill in their arena. When fighting Ebopa used typical praying mantis moves that the warriors of Ur mimicked when they fought hand to hand.

When Hunt and Jad-bal-ja became trapped in the caves where Ebopa lived, the Stick that Walks pursued them. Eventually they found their way to the opening of an arena sewer and pushed their way out, as Jad-bal-ja tried to fight back the holy mantis. Once loose in the arena, Ebopa confronted and fought Tarzan. After the Jungle Lord mortally wounded the Undying God of Ur, Ebopa attempted to escape, and in the process ran amok sending the citizens scrambling in a panic. During the chaos oil lamps and torches were knocked over which set the city on fire. The flaming remains of Ur finally collapsed into its underground caverns and passages which Tarzan had followed Ebopa into. In a sealed-off tunnel, Ebopa died next to one of its hatching eggs, while the Jungle Lord watched. Tarzan then realized why Ebopa had been considered undying: he saw that the Stick That Walks was both male and female, and able to impregnate itself to create more mantises to take its place. He also speculated that the large insect was probably from Pellucidar, from whence it had walked to the surface via one of the many tunnels under the Earth's crust. *Tarzan: The Lost Adventure*

Edward: The young squire for the American, James Hunter Blake, when he fought in the Great Tourney in the lost medieval Valley of the Sepulcher. *Tarzan, Lord of the Jungle*

Eight Hundred Cubed Plus Nineteen: See **Aoponato**

Eight Hundred Cubed Plus Twenty-one: See **Aopontando**

el adrea: "The Lord with the large head." The Arabic name for the black-maned desert lion. El adrea lived primarily in the mountains, but would descend to the desert valleys and steal livestock from the nomadic Arab tribes. The Arabs feared el adrea, and anyone who could kill him was highly respected.

el-Aziz, Abd: The leader of the party of Arab raiders from the group of Sheik Ibn Jad that went farther into the lost medieval Valley of the Sepulcher looking for treasure and women. Abd el-Aziz and his followers were defeated by the knights of Nimmr. *Tarzan, Lord of the Jungle*

el-fil: The Arabic name for elephant.

el-Ghrennem, Ab: The sheik of the Arabs that accompanied the *Lion Man* movie crew on location in Africa. Ab el-Ghrennem and his fol-

lowers believed that the prop treasure map of stunt double Rhonda Terry was real. To get hold of it, they kidnaped Rhonda and the leading lady, Naomi Madison, because they could not tell the two apart. The map turned out to be authentic, and when Ab el-Ghrennem and his Arab followers entered the canyon that led to the treasure city, they were attacked and killed by the intelligent English speaking gorillas that dwelled there. *Tarzan and the Lion Man*

Elija, the son of Noah: The leader of the fanatical Christian North Midian village. Elija was short, stocky, blue eyed, wore a single goat skin garment and carried a club. After capturing Lafayette Smith, Lady Barbara Collis, and the South Midian golden haired girl named Jezebel, Elija was curious about Smith's pistol. In explaining how it worked, Smith lied and had the son of Noah put the barrel to his eye and pull the trigger. He killed himself. *Tarzan Triumphant*

Elkomoelhago: The lazy, self gratifying tyrannical Thagosto (king) of the Minuni city of Veltopismakus. King Elkomoelhago believed he was a walmak and claimed to have been instrumental in developing the shrinking machine that he hoped would actually increase his height and that of his people, from their standard 18 inches. The king spent time and tax dollars on superficial pomp and circumstance, such as beautifying the city and having exact military precision in parades, but failed to prepare the city and people for more practical things like war. His daughter was the beautiful Janzara. *Tarzan and the Ant Men*

Erot: A common warrior in Cathne, the City of Gold, until Queen Nemone took a liking to him and made him a noble and her favorite. When Tarzan came and the queen took a liking to him, Erot became jealous of the Ape-man and plotted with Tomos and M'duze to kill him. Their first try failed and Erot was banished. In an attempt to get back in good graces with the queen, Erot spied on Tarzan and his friend Gemnon. He found out about Doria, a pretty girl Gemnon loved and who he was hiding from the vain and jealous Nemone. Erot reported this to the queen, and after Doria was imprisoned and sentenced to be sacrificed in the volcano, Xarator, he tried to rape her. Tarzan arrived and killed Erot and put his body in the sacrificial leather bag meant for Doria. Even after Erot's body was discovered in the bag, it was still thrown into the active crater. *Tarzan and the City of Gold*

Eshbaal: A goat herding member of the fanatical Christian North Midian village of Elija, the son of Noah. Eshbaal was short, stocky, blue eyed, wore a single goat skin garment, and carried a club. He saw the escaping Lafayette Smith, Barbara Collis, and Jezebel fleeing from the land of the South Midians, and informed his people. After capturing the trio, Eshbaal desired Jezebel for himself. *Tarzan Triumphant*

Esmeralda: The heavy-set black maid who worked for the Porter family when they first entered Tarzan's world. Esmeralda's most used saying when terrified was, "O Gaberelle!" Afterwards she would usually swoon. She remained as the Greystokes' maid in England and for a while at their African estate. Esmeralda positively identified the infant Jack after he was returned in *The Beasts of Tarzan*. *Tarzan of the Apes, The Return of Tarzan, The Beasts of Tarzan, The*

Son of Tarzan, and *The Eternal Savage (Lover).*

Es-sat: "Rough-skin." The wicked ruler of the cliff dwelling Waz-don from the village of Kor-ul-ja in the land of Pal-ul-don. Es-sat desired Pan-at-lee, a beautiful female from the tribe, to be his mate. When Pan-at-lee's true love, Om-at, was away Es-sat snuck into her apartment and made advances toward her while she was changing clothes. She fended him off, and by using her gold breastplates knocked him out with a blow to the head. Om-at returned with Tarzan, and after finding Es-sat regaining consciousness in Pan-at-lee's apartment, the two Waz-don fought each other in what they called a *gund-bar*, or chief-battle, which determined who would be the next chief. This sort of battle could only be waged with nature's weapons, but when Om-at began to win, Es-sat cheated by using a knife in his tail. Despite this Om-at prevailed, and after killing Es-sat, he became the new *gund* or chief of Kor-ul-ja. *Tarzan the Terrible*

Eyad: A sinister eyed Arab with a fat lower lip in Sheik Ab el-Ghrennem's group that escorted a movie company shooting on location in Africa. When the Arabs kidnaped the movie's star, Naomi Madison, and her lookalike stunt double, Rhonda Terry, Eyad did not care for them, and voiced this to a fellow Arab named Atwey. When his band went off and were killed by the English speaking Gorillas of the Valley of Diamonds, Eyad escaped death by having been assigned to stay behind to watch the horses. He then wandered around until he was discovered by Bill West and Thomas Orman who were out searching for the missing women. *Tarzan and the Lion Man*

Fahd: A French speaking Arab from the tribe of el-Harb who worked with Sheik Ibn Jad on a search for the fabled treasure filled city of Nimmr. Fahd desired Ibn Jad's daughter and set up Zeyd, the man she loved, as an attempted murderer. He later collaborated with Wilbur Stimbol to steal the Nimmrian princess, Guinalda. Fahd was eventually killed by Zeyd with a khusa knife. *Tarzan, Lord of the Jungle*

Fastus: The rat faced son of Caesar Sublatus in the lost Roman city of Castra Sanguinarius. Fastus desired the beautiful Dilecta even though she loved and was engaged to Maximus Praeclarus. Despite this Fastus made physical advances toward her, and when Tarzan discovered this, he saved her. This angered Fastus, and when Praeclarus aided the Ape-man, Fastus sought to betray them both by having them imprisoned to fight in the gladiator games. He then blackmailed Dilecta into marrying him in return for the protection of her family and Praeclarus's. His plan almost succeeded, but before the end of the wedding ceremony, Tarzan and Praeclarus, along with other prisoners of the games, escaped and stormed the throne room. Fastus was killed by natives during the ensuing battle. *Tarzan and the Lost Empire*

Favonia: The beautiful daughter of the scholarly Septimus Favonius in the lost Roman city of Castra Mare who was desired by the evil Fulvus Fupus. Favonia met the lost archeologist from the outer world, Erich von Harben, when he was a guest of her father and her cousin Mallius Lepus. Favonia fell in love with Erich and he with her, and the two ended up marrying and living together in the outer world. *Tarzan*

and the Lost Empire and mentioned in *Tarzan at the Earth's Core*

Favonius, Septimus: The eccentric scholar, uncle of Mallius Lepus, and the father of the beautiful Favonia. Septimus loved to entertain guests and threw a party to present the outsider, Erich von Harben, to his friends. *Tarzan and the Lost Empire*

Fejjuan: A Galla slave of the Arab sheik, Ibn Jad of the Beny Salem fendy el-Guad, who was stolen when he was a boy from his native tribe. Fejjuan was well trusted and liked by the Arabs, but he longed to go back to his people. Finally, his dreams came true when he was permitted to return to his tribe by his Arab masters, to enlist their aid in locating the fabled lost city of Nimmr. Fejjuan agreed to do this for the Arabs, but on condition that they release all the Galla slaves they held, which they did. Upon entering his native village, it was revealed that his original tribal name was Ulala. It was Fejjuan who found the lost American Wilbur Stimbol. *Tarzan, Lord of the Jungle*

Feng, Wong: A Chinese shopkeeper in Loango and a healer who used only natural methods. Wong Feng assisted Atan Thome and Lal Taask in kidnaping Helen Gregory. *Tarzan and the Forbidden City*

Fernando: One of the Mangani tribe of Ho-den who were known as the servants of God in the lost land of Alemtejo. They traveled with and aided the man who thought he was Tarzan. Fernando assisted Sandra Pickerall in scaling the steep cliff entrance to Alemtejo. On the way he lost his hold and fell to his death, and became food for the lions that prowled as guards below. *Tarzan and the Madman*

Festivitas: The mother of Maximus

Praeclarus in the lost Roman city of Castra Sanguinarius. While his family gave Tarzan refuge in their house she taught the Jungle Lord how to speak Latin. *Tarzan and the Lost Empire*

Firg: A priest and the Keeper of the Keys to the dungeons and prison cells of Opar. Firg was killed in his sleep by Nao, a young priestess, who was attempting to take the keys from him to set free the American, Wayne Colt. *Tarzan the Invincible*

Flaubert: See **Monsieur Flaubert**

Fodil: An Arab faithful to Ibn Dammuk who assisted in the abduction of High Priestess La of Opar. *Tarzan the Invincible*

Frecoult, M. Jules: see **Albert Werper**

Fupus, Fulvus: A short, dark, greasy looking man in love with Favonia in the lost Roman city of Castra Mare. Fulvus was jealous of Erich von Harben (from the outside world), because he and Favonia liked each other. Fulvus wormed his way into favor with the Caesar, Validus Augustus, who ultimately announced Fulvus as the heir to his throne, even though the people disliked him. Fulvus Fupus then had von Harben imprisoned. After Augustus was killed by von Harben's porter, Gabula, Fupus laid claim to the throne of Castra Mare. When the true heir to the throne, Cassius Hasta, arrived with Tarzan and troops, Fulvus went into hiding. *Tarzan and the Lost Empire*

Gabula: A member of the native Batoro tribe in the Urambi country. Gabula was the personal body servant of Erich von Harben when he was searching for the Lost Tribe of the Wiramwazi Mountains. Afraid, he and the rest of the porters deserted von Harben. But guilt-ridden, Gabula overcame his fears and

returned to accompany von Harben into the valley of the Lost Empire. Imprisoned in the empire, Gabula escaped and, during the great games, snuck into the loge of Caesar Validus Augustus, Emperor of the East, and killed him with a dagger. Gabula was rescued by Tarzan along with von Harben. *Tarzan and the Lost Empire*

Galla Galla: The old, fat, bleary-eyed chief of the Bagalla cannibals who captured the Tarzan Twins to hold them until they were fat enough to eat. After seeing Doc's magic tricks Chief Galla Galla was afraid of the youth and felt Doc had strong medicine. *Tarzan and the Tarzan Twins*

Gantry, Bill: The hunter and guide for Pelham Dutton when he was searching for Sandra Pickerall. Gantry and Tom Crump plotted to take Sandra for themselves to get a greater reward. He eventually left Crump and their other cohort, Ivan Minsky, and it is assumed that he was eaten by cannibals. *Tarzan and the Madman*

Gault, Gerald: The guide for Mr. Romanoff's hunting safari when they merged with the Ramsgate photographic safari. Gault was rude to Lt. Cecil Giles-Burton when they came across him lost and emaciated in the jungle. He was also cruel to the porters in the safari. When he knocked one down, Giles-Burton interfered and knocked Gault down. *Tarzan and the Jungle Murders* in *Tarzan and the Castaways*

Ga-un: A Mangani from the tribe of Ungo. In *Tarzan and the Forbidden City* Ga-un entered the forbidden volcano land of Tuen-Baka at Tarzan's behest. But once there he seized the Tarmangani-she, Helen Gregory, from the priests of Chon, the true god, and dragged her away by the ankle. Fearing punishment from Tarzan for abducting her, Ga-un attempted to kill Helen, but the brave girl escaped by jumping from a cliff into the lake Horus. *Tarzan and the Forbidden City* and *Tarzan and the Madman*

Gayat or **Ga-yat**: A Mangani bull from the tribe of Toyat. He was of an easygoing disposition and was an ally of Tarzan because the Jungle Lord saved him from Numa when Gayat was but a *balu* or baby. In *Tarzan and the Lost Empire*, it is revealed that Gayat was captured, along with other members of his tribe, to be used as part of the gladiator games in the Colosseum of the lost Roman city of Castra Sanguinarius. When the Mangani were sent out to attack Tarzan during the games, he recognized them and renewed his friendship with them. Tarzan then used them to help start a revolt, and they all escaped the Colosseum. In *Tarzan the Invincible* Gayat was one of the few who was not afraid to be around Jad-bal-ja, the Golden Lion. Then in *Tarzan and the Leopard Men*, it is revealed that Gayat and Zutho left Toyat's tribe to form their own. Ga-yat also went to find a human to untie the wire bonds that secured Tarzan's wrists. *Tarzan, Lord of the Jungle; Tarzan and the Lost Empire; Tarzan the Invincible* and *Tarzan and the Leopard Men*

Gazan: "Red skin." The reddish haired *balu* or baby of Tarzan's childhood Mangani playmates, Taug and Teeka, from the tribe of Kerchak. Tarzan was very interested in Gazan and often played with the little *balu* once Teeka trusted and allowed him to. The Lord of the Jungle saved Gazan from Sheeta, the panther, and Histah, the snake.

When Toog, a rogue bull from another tribe, attempted to steal Teeka for himself, he shook Gazan loose from a tree and the *balu* fell. He was knocked out and left lifeless. *Jungle Tales of Tarzan*

1. Geeka: The name of Meriem's ugly doll. It had an ivory head, a body of rat skin, stick arms and legs, and wore a grass skirt. Meriem loved the doll nonetheless, and named it after the native boy who had made it and given it to her. It was her only confidant during the period she was an abused prisoner in the Arab village of Sheik Amor ben Khatour. *The Son of Tarzan*

2. Geeka: The native boy who made an ugly ivory headed doll which he gave to Meriem. She named it after him. *The Son of Tarzan*

Gefasto: A *zertol* (prince or noble) of King Elkomoelhago's in the Minuni city of Veltopismakus. Gefasto was a fearless military genius and was the Chief of Warriors for the city. *Tarzan and the Ant Men*

Gemba: The Negro slave messenger of Doria, the beautiful daughter of Thudos, in Cathne, the City of Gold, in *Tarzan and the City of Gold*. In *Tarzan the Magnificent* Gemba was captured in a raid and taken to Athne. In the Athnean dungeon he met and remembered Tarzan who was also a prisoner. Gemba escaped and returned to Cathne where he told them of Tarzan's plight. A rescue party was immediately sent. *Tarzan and the City of Gold* and *Tarzan the Magnificent*

Gemnon: A young and intelligent noble by birth who took a liking to Tarzan when the Ape-man was a prisoner in Cathne, the City of Gold, in *Tarzan and the City of Gold*. After Tarzan won a fight in a tournament, he became Gemnon's charge and responsibility. The two grew to be friends and even roommates in Gemnon's quarters. In *Tarzan the Magnificent* Gemnon secretly gave Tarzan a dagger while the Apeman was a prisoner under the new king, Alextar. *Tarzan and the City of Gold* and *Tarzan the Magnificent*

Gerard: The captain who became a friend of Tarzan's while with Lt. Gernois in a company of *spahis* stationed in Algiers. *The Return of Tarzan*

Gernois: A taciturn traitor and a lieutenant in the French military, commanding the *spahis* stationed in Sidi Aissa, Algeria. He had vital stolen information for the government, and Tarzan was sent to keep an eye on him as part of his first assignment for the ministry of war. Gernois was later blackmailed by Nikolas Rokoff and Alexis Paulvitch into helping them murder Tarzan. But the Jungle Lord foiled their plans. When Gernois saw Tarzan alive, he took his own life, after giving the stolen information to Rokoff and Paulvitch. *The Return of Tarzan*

Gerooma: A sentry in the lost city of Ur who loved to play games of chance. Gerooma was shot in the mouth by one of Tarzan's arrows and then had his throat slit by the Jungle Lord. *Tarzan: The Lost Adventure*

Giles-Burton, Cecil: A British lieutenant in the Royal Air Force who stole the plans for an invention of military significance from Joseph "Joe the Pooch" Campbell and Nikolai Zubanev. Giles-Burton then flew alone to be with his father in Bengasi. On the way he was shot down by the machine gun of a pursuing plane carrying Campbell and Zubanev. But he managed to shoot and kill their pilot with his revolver,

forcing them down, too. Giles-Burton parachuted out and wandered lost in the jungle where he became emaciated. But he still retained the plans. Tarzan found his plane, and while investigating the crash, labeled Lt. Cecil Giles-Burton, Pilot Number Two. Giles-Burton eventually stumbled upon the Ramsgate safari and was taken in. But right away he got into three separate fights with Sergei Godensky, Duncan Trent, and Gerald Gault. By winning each encounter, he made enemies of them all. He then began to like Lady Barbara Ramsgate, whom he knew previously, and she him. Before anything further could develop between them, Giles-Burton was killed for the plans, stabbed one night in his tent by Joseph Campbell who was in the safari under an alias. *Tarzan and the Jungle Murders* in *Tarzan and the Castaways*

Giles-Burton, Gerald: A British colonel stationed in Bengasi and a friend of Tarzan's. Colonel Giles-Burton was the father of the murdered Lt. Cecil Giles-Burton of the Ramsgate safari. Tarzan informed the senior colonel of his son's death and received his aid in returning to the safari and seeking out the murderer. *Tarzan and the Jungle Murders* in *Tarzan and the Castaways*

Gluf: A member of the lowland tribe of Pheli in Pellucidar. He went with his chief, Skruk, and a few others to steal a wife from Zoram. On the way they found and pursued Jana, the Red Flower of Zoram, and almost had her captured when the lost American, Jason Gridley, came to her rescue. When Gluf attacked the American, Jason shot the primitive dead with a pistol. *Tarzan at the Earth's Core*

Gobred: The prince and ruler of the

castle of Nimmr in the lost medieval Valley of the Sepulcher. He liked the American, James Hunter Blake. While Gobred's daughter, the lovely princess Guinalda, fell in love with Blake. *Tarzan, Lord of the Jungle*

Gobu: "Black-he." A Mangani killed by the Tarzan impersonator, Esteban Miranda. *Tarzan and the Golden Lion.*

Go-bu-balu: see **Tibo**

1. God: The title and position given to the half-man, half-gorilla ruler and "creator" of the English speaking gorillas in the lost city of London on the Thames in the Valley of Diamonds. Once a normal human being, he studied and experimented at a young age with evolution and genetics and learned how to transfer cells and genetic material from human to human. Fleeing persecution for his work and looking for seclusion to continue his experimenting, he went to gorilla country in Africa and began to transfer human cells into gorillas. After several generations the gorillas became more intelligent and human in nature, but not in form, and learned to speak. God then educated them and formed a society that he patterned after England's, using the names of English people and places. Beginning to grow old, and wanting to ward off death, God injected gorilla cells into himself. This caused him to live indefinitely, but he took on many of the physical characteristics of the gorilla while remaining human intellectually. With the capture of Rhonda Terry and Tarzan, God decided to take some of their cells in an attempt to regain his human form. And to expedite the procedure, he planned on eating some of the organs of his two human victims. But Tarzan and Rhonda escaped. *Tarzan and the Lion Man*

2. God: The name of the man who thought he was Tarzan of the Apes, given to him by King Cristoforo da Gama and his high priest, Pedro Ruiz, in the lost city of Alemtejo. The man called God had lost all memory of any former life except the idea that he was Tarzan. But he went around the jungle doing very un–Tarzan-like things, thereby ruining the real Jungle Lord's reputation. Because of this Tarzan sought to take his life. God also had a group of Mangani called the Servants of God as companions who he could communicate with.

One of the things he did was capture Sandra Pickerall and take her to Alemtejo to be his mate and their goddess. After truly falling in love with Sandra, he felt bad and sorry for capturing her, and decided that they should flee the city together. While escaping they were both captured by Galla Moslems and made their slaves. But God and Sandra got away and both expressed their love for each other. When the real Tarzan came upon them, he ended up liking this false Tarzan and did not kill him.

Accompanying Tarzan then was Francis Bolton-Chilton. He had been a friend of the man who thought he was Tarzan, before God got amnesia. Bolton-Chilton told Tarzan and Sandra that the man known as God was actually Colin T. Randolph, Jr., of West Virginia who had been obsessed with the Tarzan mythos in his former life, and had trained and studied to be like the Jungle Lord. He had made a bet with Francis Bolton-Chilton that he could live alone like Tarzan for a month in the African jungle.

Bolton-Chilton took him up on the bet and together they flew to Africa so they could let Randolph off in the jungle. Over the Ruturri Mountains, the plane developed problems and they both had to parachute out. Bolton-Chilton landed safely and was captured by some Galla warriors, but Randolph was knocked unconscious on landing in the lost Portuguese city of Alemtejo. The primitive people took his parachuting descent as divine and proclaimed him God. When he regained consciousness Randolph had lost all memory except for the notion that he was the real Tarzan of the Apes. After the party found the downed plane, Randolph regained his memory and flew them all out of the country. *Tarzan and the Madman*

Godensky, Sergei: A Russian professional photographer in the Ramsgate safari when it joined with the safari of the Russian expatriate, Mr. Romanoff. The two Russians immediately disliked each other. Then when Godensky made unwelcome advances toward Violet, Lady Barbara Ramsgate's maid, Lt. Cecil Giles-Burton intervened and knocked Godensky down. The Russian was furious and drew his knife on Giles-Burton, but Lady Barbara came upon them and stopped the fight. *Tarzan and the Jungle Murders* in *Tarzan and the Castaways*

Gofoloso: A *zertol* (prince or noble) and the chief of chiefs for King Elkomoelhago in the Minuni city of Veltopismakus. *Tarzan and the Ant Men*

Go-lat: "Black-nose." An older king of a tribe of Mangani that Tarzan wished to gain peaceful acceptance into. At first Go-lat attacked the Ape-man, but Tarzan forced the old king to say "kagoda" by tossing him

to the ground several times. After this, Tarzan was accepted into the tribe. *Tarzan the Untamed*

Golato: The hulking native headman in Kali Bwana's safari. Golato attacked Kali in her tent and during their struggle she shot him in the arm. Consequently, he and all the other members of the safari deserted Kali, leaving her alone in the jungle. *Tarzan and the Leopard Men*

Goldeen, Ben: The production manager for the movie company Prominent Pictures when they were casting for a Tarzan film. Goldeen dismissed John Clayton (Tarzan) as the wrong type to play the role of Tarzan in the movie, but hired him as a hunter. On the set, the Ape-man killed a lion attacking Cyril Wayne (the actor playing Tarzan). Goldeen was so upset that he fired Clayton (Tarzan) because, as he bitterly complained, the lion would cost him $10,000 to replace. *Tarzan and the Lion Man*

Golden Lion: see **Jad-bal-ja**

Goloba: The headman of Leon Stabutch's safari who deserted because of an attack by a rogue band of *shiftas* led by Dominic Capietro. *Tarzan Triumphant*

Go-lot: "Black-face." A young and insubordinate bull Mangani in the tribe of Zu-yad. When the she–Tarmangani, Jean Hanson, and her father, Eugene, were discovered by the tribe, Go-lot desired her for a slave. So he abducted her, after knocking her father down. Go-lot then fought and killed Zu-yad for possession of Jean. When Tarzan arrived, he killed Go-lot by disemboweling him. *Tarzan: The Lost Adventure*

1. Gomangani: "Black great ape." See the Ape Language in Section Two above.

2. Gomangani: A lower order in the

Valley of the Palace of Diamonds. The Gomangani lived in subservience to the more intelligent Bolgani behind the lost city of Opar. The Gomangani were tall and well muscled with long arms and short legs. Their bullet heads had almost no forehead, and receded back to a point. Their homes were beehive huts hung from ropes in a tree. They lived in terror of the Bolgani, distrusted everyone, and did not laugh or seem very happy. Their weapons consisted of javelins and axe-like devices. When Tarzan arrived, he was able to rally them to overthrow the Bolgani. For more information see Valley of the Palace of Diamonds in Section Three. *Tarzan and the Golden Lion*

Gonfal: The great mind-controlling diamond of the Kaji. The Gonfal was used tyrannically by Mafka, the Kaji magician–witch doctor, to control anyone within the range of its power including the Kaji warrior women and their male slaves. The only person besides Mafka's twin brother who was able to control the diamond and not be affected by it was Tarzan. After Tarzan took it from Mafka, Spike and Troll unknowingly stole its artificial duplicate from him to use to their advantage. Tarzan planned on giving the real one to Stanley Wood and his wife, Gonfala, to sell in civilization. See **The Great Emerald of the Zuli**. *Tarzan the Magnificent*

Gonfala: The beautiful daughter of the lost Mountfords who was raised to be queen and goddess of the Kaji warrior women from the moment she was born. Gonfala was believed to be the personification of the mind-controlling diamond, the Gonfal, which Mafka, the magician–witch doctor, used to control the Kaji people, including Gonfala. This mind control by Mafka gave Gonfala a seeming Jekyll and Hyde-like personality.

Gonfala fell in love with the prisoner, Stanley Wood, whom she helped escape the land of the Kaji. After Tarzan aided her and the other prisoners in their flight, Gonfala ran away because she felt Wood did not like her. Tarzan brought the two back together. But when they were on their way to Railhead, Gonfala was captured by Spike and Troll who wanted to make her their queen. After the three wandered around lost they entered the land of Athne, the City of Ivory, and were made prisoners. There the king, Phoros, desired her. Then, willingly, Gonfala was married to Stanley Wood by a priest in Athne by order of Menofra, the jealous wife of Phoros, in the hope that her unfaithful husband would not try to seduce the newlywed. But Phoros did try, nonetheless, and Gonfala ended up killing him with a dagger. *Tarzan the Magnificent*

Goob: One of the mountain Tongani (baboons) enlisted by Korak to attack the Kovudoo cannibal village of Gomangani and rescue Meriem. *The Son of Tarzan*

Go-yad: "Black-ear." A big bull Mangani of the tribe of Toyat who was in the tribe of Kerchak when Tarzan first took over as its king. When Guinalda, the Tarmangani princess from the Valley of the Sepulcher, was abandoned in front of Go-yad and Toyat by the frightened Tarmangani, Fahd and Wilbur Stimbol, Go-yad was ready to kill her. Toyat stopped him, however, then abducted Guinalda for himself. Go-yad at first challenged Toyat, then chased after him.

Go-yad was later captured, along

with other members of the tribe, for the gladiator games in the Colosseum of the lost Roman city of Castra Sanguinarius. When they were sent out to attack Tarzan during the games, he recognized the Mangani and renewed his friendship with them. The Jungle Lord then used them to form a revolt, and they all escaped the Colosseum. *Tarzan, Lord of the Jungle* and *Tarzan and the Lost Empire*

Gozan: "Black skin." A bull Mangani in the tribe of Kerchak. He was on sentry duty when the brave Gomangani, Bulabantu of the tribe of Mbongo, entered the Kerchak feeding grounds. Gozan alerted the rest of the tribe by calling, "Kreegah." When Tarzan spoke in an effort to save the Gomangani, Gozan protested and tried to demean Tarzan by telling the rest of the tribe that he had once seen the Ape-man dancing alone in the moonlight with Sheeta, the panther. Gozan then called Tarzan a Gomangani with his skin off. *Jungle Tales of Tarzan*

Graham, Mary: The homely, yet talkative, secretary for the inventor Horace Brown. Mary unintentionally divulged the inventor's plans for an invention of military importance to Joseph "Joe the Pooch" Campbell at a party. *Tarzan and the Jungle Murders* in *Tarzan and the Castaways*

Great Emerald of the Zuli: see **The Great Emerald of the Zuli**

Gregory: Mr. Gregory formed a safari along with his daughter, Helen, to search for his missing son, Brian, who was supposed to be a prisoner in Ashair, the Forbidden City. Gregory enlisted Paul d'Arnot who in turn enlisted Tarzan to lead and guide their safari. Once they reached the crater valley of the Forbidden City, Mr. Gregory was put into a prison in Ashair's rival city, Thobos, and left there while Tarzan and the French pilot, Lavac, went to Ashair itself. Mr. Gregory was eventually released by Thetan, the nephew of the king of Thobos, who was indebted to Tarzan for saving his life. Mr. Gregory then went to Ashair with his fellow prisoner, Magra. *Tarzan and the Forbidden City*

Gregory, Brian: The missing brother of Helen Gregory who looked very much like Tarzan. Brian's father organized a safari led by Tarzan to find his son, if he still lived. Brian was alive, but he had been imprisoned in the temple of Ashair, the Forbidden City, for attempting to steal the Father of Diamonds. When they rescued him, Brian was pessimistic, bearded, and extremely emaciated. He was reunited with his sister and father. *Tarzan and the Forbidden City*

Gregory, Helen: A beautiful, very vivacious, 19-year-old blonde. She and her father asked Paul d'Arnot to assist them in forming a safari to search for her lost brother, Brian. D'Arnot readily fell in love with Helen. She at first denied his love, but later accepted and returned it. Along the way Helen was abducted and rescued several times by various people, and was eventually taken a prisoner to the Forbidden City and made a handmaid to their god, Brulor, and forced to marry the priest, Zytheb. After the ceremony, she killed Zytheb with a vase and took his dagger and keys. With these she released all the prisoners including Paul d'Arnot and her emaciated brother, Brian. After a few more abductions, she was safely reunited with everyone. *Tarzan and the Forbidden City*

Gridley, Jason: From Tarzana, California, the inventor of the Gridley Wave which enabled him to make radio contact with the prehistoric land of Pellucidar at the center of our Earth, as well as the planet Mars (Barsoom). After hearing a message of distress from the Earth's core, Jason enlisted Tarzan's aid to take a rescue mission into the inner world in a specially built and equipped dirigible, the O-220, through a polar opening he theorized existed. Their objective was to rescue David Innes, the first Emperor of Pellucidar. During the expedition, Tarzan was in charge and Jason his lieutenant. In Pellucidar Jason went searching for a missing Tarzan in a plane that they had brought with them. The plane was attacked and wrecked in the air by a *thipdar* (pteranodon), but Jason parachuted to safety. On the ground, he saved the cavegirl Jana, the Red Flower of Zoram, from some prehistoric men. The two fell in love, but Jana feigned a lack of interest and ran away. After several adventures with pirate-like Korsars and snake men called Horibs, Jason was reunited with Tarzan and Jana. Even after David Innes was rescued, Jason remained in Pellucidar to continue searching for one of his original crew members, Von Horst, who had become lost. At this juncture, Jana finally announced her love for Jason and stayed with him. The book *Back to the Stone Age* (original title: *Seven Worlds to Conquer*) in the Pellucidar series, details Von Horst's further adventures and reveals that Jason did actually leave in the O-220 without the lost crew member, but only after receiving a promise from David Innes to search for him. *Tarzan at the Earth's Core*

Gromvitch: A small wiry white man who was left in charge of the bearers

of Wilson Jones' safari. Gromvitch was later swept up and decapitated in a tornado. His head ended up stuck in a tree where his gold teeth were taken out by Cannon, one of his merciless former comrades. *Tarzan: The Lost Adventure*

Gron: The pretty, but tragically jealous wife of Tur, of the Boat Builders, in the Niocene period of Earth's history. When Tur captured and brought the beautiful Nat-ul to the village as a second wife, Gron was extremely jealous. Nu, the son of Nu, came to rescue Nat-ul but was captured in the attempt and made a prisoner. Gron attacked him, and for this Tur beat her. In revenge she killed their infant son and helped Nu escape. Gron then began to fall in love with Nu, and in hopes of winning his affection she decided to accompany him to the island where Tur had taken Nat-ul. When Nu refused her love, Gron first killed Tur with her knife, then took her own by jumping from a cliff. *The Eternal Savage (Lover)*

Grotius: The second in command of Hooft's band of bad guerrillas in Japanese held Sumatra in the Dutch East Indies. *Tarzan and the Foreign Legion*

gryf: An evolved carnivorous Triceratops-like dinosaur in the land of Pal-ul-don. For more information, see *gryf* in the Language of Pal-ul-don in Section Two and Pal-ul-don in Section Three. *Tarzan the Terrible*

Guinalda: A princess of Nimmr, the daughter of Prince Gobred, in the lost medieval Valley of the Sepulcher. She fell in love with the lost American, James Hunter Blake, after he was brought into her society. She was then abducted by King Bohun of the rival City of the Sepulcher at the end of the Great Tourney. Blake gave pursuit and recaptured her. But then the two were set upon by Arab raiders who left Blake to die after taking Guinalda with them out of the lost valley.

Guinalda was subsequently abducted and taken into the jungle by the greedy Arab, Fahd, and the American, Wilbur Stimbol. There they stumbled upon a few of the Mangani of the tribe of Toyat. Terrified, the two men fled leaving Guinalda at the mercy of the apes. Toyat immediately desired Guinalda and took her for himself. Then Jad-bal-ja, the Golden Lion, arrived and scared Toyat away. After Tarzan joined them, he carried her back to the Valley of the Sepulcher. When Blake, who had survived and gone in search of Guinalda, heard from Tarzan that she was alive and had been returned to the Valley of the Sepulcher, he returned there to live with her. *Tarzan, Lord of the Jungle*

Gulm: The self-elected leader of 20 priests who were cast out from Opar because they supported the traitorous former high priest, Cadj. After they captured Dick, one of the Tarzan Twins, Gulm took an arrow in the leg from Doc, the second twin. Then, after failing to force Kla, (a.k.a. Gretchen von Harben), the new La, to sacrifice Dick upon an improvised altar, Gulm decided to sacrilegiously offer the sacrifice himself, but was killed in the attempt by Jad-bal-ja. *Tarzan and the Tarzan Twins*

Gunto: A Mangani who bit his wife, Tana, in *Tarzan of the Apes* because he thought that she was lazy. As a result of this Tana ran to Tarzan, the new king of the tribe of Kerchak, for help. He counseled both of them. In *Jungle Tales of Tarzan*, when Tarzan

brought the native boy Tibo to the tribe as his own, Gunto wanted to kill the youth. Later, when Tarzan stole the corpse of Mamka from Numa, the lion, Gunto caught the young Jungle Lord as he leapt into the trees, and helped him reach safety. Gunto was the sentry who discovered the lion Tarzan was disguised as entering the tribe's territory. He was finally killed by Taug for wanting to murder Tarzan. *Tarzan of the Apes* and *Jungle Tales of Tarzan*

Gupingu: The witch doctor of the Bukena who lived near the Kavuru village. When the Bukena captured Tarzan, who they thought was a Kavuru, Gupingu was afraid to kill him for fear of future punishment from the Kavuru. So he secretly set Tarzan free on the promise that the Ape-man would not steal any more of their girls. Shortly thereafter, Naika, the daughter of Gupingu, was taken by the Kavuru. This infuriated him because he thought he had been betrayed by Tarzan who he still believed to be a Kavuru. After this the Waziri arrived looking for Tarzan and Gupingu made a potion that drugged them. *Tarzan's Quest*

Gust: A Swede who masterminded the mutiny of the *Crowie* and then thought to become the leader of the group of mutineers. When Gust saw his men coming to kill him on Jungle Island, he ran away. He observed his former shipmates abduct Jane and the Mosula woman, and informed Tarzan and Mugambi. Gust then traveled safely back to Europe with Tarzan. *The Beasts of Tarzan*

Guy: A knight from the Castle of the Sepulcher in the medieval lost Valley of the Sepulcher. Sir Guy fought the American, James Hunter Blake,

J. Allen St. John illustration from *Jungle Tales of Tarzan* (© 1919 Edgar Rice Burroughs, Inc.).

in the Great Tourney, but was stabbed in the throat and lost. Instead of finishing him off, or leaving him lying on the ground, Blake administered to Sir Guy's wounds and saved him. Returning the favor, Sir Guy, along with Sir Willard, who Blake had also defeated and aided, secretly freed the American from the dungeon of King Bohun. *Tarzan, Lord of the Jungle*

Hafim: A large Galla native slave in Cathne, the City of Gold. Because he could not be easily handled and disciplined by his masters, Hafim was to be disposed of by being used as the quarry in a Grand Hunt with lions. Tarzan overtook him before the lions could, and carried him out of the forest hunting grounds. Hafim asked Tarzan to tell his brother, Niaka, the headman of the slaves in the Cathne quarry, that he had escaped. This Tarzan did. *Tarzan and the City of Gold*

Hajellan: An Arab sentry who left his post at the tent of Zora Drinov and La, the high priestess of Opar, as part of Ibn Dammuk's plan to abduct La. Hajellan was later killed by Jad-bal-ja. *Tarzan the Invincible*

Hanson, Mr.: see **Sven Malbihn**

Hanson, Eugene: An older, but still husky and strong, former football player and amateur boxer with a Ph.D. from Texas University. He was on a photographic safari with his daughter, Jean, looking for the Mangani. After his safari was taken from him by Wilson Jones and his thugs, Tarzan took it back from Wilson and returned it to Hanson. When Hanson and Jean were found by a tribe of Mangani, she was taken by a young bull named Go-lot, after Hanson had punched the Mangani and in turn been knocked down by him. Later, during a native ambush,

Hanson was knifed and left for dead. When he was found alive by the cruel Wilson and his even worse cohort, Cannon, they tortured him and he lost a finger. After Hanson escaped with his trusted askari, Billy, they took Wilson with them as their prisoner. Hanson and Wilson ultimately fought it out in a boxing match, and the former knocked the latter out. *Tarzan: The Lost Adventure*

Hanson, Jean: Lean, blonde and beautiful, and the stubborn, take-charge daughter of Eugene Hanson. Father and daughter were on a photographic safari together in Africa searching for the Mangani when a tribe of them came upon the two. Go-lot, a bull, abducted Jean after knocking her father down, and then had to fight and kill the king, Zu-yad, who also desired her. Tarzan tracked them, killed Go-lot, and saved Jean. She was later captured by warriors from Ur and taken to their lost city and cast into a dungeon. Jeda, one of Jean's large female guards, liked to played cruel tricks on her, and when the two women were paired to fight each other in the arena games, Jean killed her overconfident opponent by putting a knife in her eye. Jean later escaped Ur with Tarzan's help. *Tarzan: The Lost Adventure*

Hasta, Cassius: The nephew of the tyrannical Caesar, Vladius Augustus, of the lost Roman city of Castra Mare. Hasta was hereditarily in line to the throne, and was well liked by all the people of the city except his uncle. Consequently, the jealous Caesar always sent Hasta on missions to remove him from the city. On one such mission Hasta was captured and thrown into prison by the people of Castra Sanguinarius and placed in the same cell with Tarzan. After both survived the great games of that city, they caused a revolt and overthrew the Caesar. With a strong army behind them they marched upon Castra Mare to make Cassius Hasta the ruler of both cities. The people there willingly surrendered because of their love of Cassius. *Tarzan and the Lost Empire*

Hawkes, Flora: A young and beautiful former maid in the Greystokes' London townhouse and in their African bungalow. After leaving their employ, Flora decided to organize an expedition to Africa to obtain gold from the lost city of Opar that she had heard so much about while working for Tarzan and Jane. To accomplish this, she found four men to help financially support her, and a Tarzan look-alike named Esteban Miranda. Along the way Miranda fell in love with Flora.

Their treasure hunt safari went well, and Miranda played his part very convincingly, but rumors of it started to filter back to the Greystoke bungalow and the true Tarzan. After he discovered Flora's camp near the walls of Opar he boldly entered it alone. Flora recognized him and hid. She then had him drugged and left behind. Once the gold was taken from Opar, Miranda stole it back from the safari and hid it for Flora and himself. While Miranda was away, Flora and her other four cohorts were betrayed by their askari and porters, and after fleeing into the jungle they came upon Jane and some Waziri searching for Tarzan. Jane took them in and protected them. But Miranda entered their camp, plucked Flora out of their midst, and set up camp with her by a river. When the exhausted Flora did not return Miranda's love, he

abandoned her. Tarzan discovered her alone and learned where Miranda had gone. After pursuing him, he believed the impersonator drowned. To repay all the wrong she had done them, Flora pledged to work in the Greystokes' home once more.

In *Tarzan and the Ant Men*, Flora was still employed with the Greystokes in Africa when the still living Miranda again tried to impersonate Tarzan to Jane. Flora recognized him and revealed that he was not the Lord of the Jungle. *Tarzan and the Golden Lion* and *Tarzan and the Ant Men*

Henry the Eighth: The king of the English speaking gorillas in the city London on the Thames in the Valley of Diamonds. He and the rest of the intelligent gorillas were created by a half-man, half-gorilla being known only as God. King Henry was jealous of God and always wanted to become god himself, but was too fearful at first. When Rhonda Terry was captured by his sentries Henry the Eighth desired her to be his seventh wife, even though he was only allowed six by God. In revolt King Henry took Rhonda and attempted to force her to be his wife. During the ensuing mayhem he fled the city with her and was pursued by Tarzan. To further his escape he discarded Rhonda, but was attacked and killed by a lion. *Tarzan and the Lion Man*

Herat: The large and cruel looking king of Thobos, the rival city of Ashair, the Forbidden City, in the lost volcano land of Tuen-Baka. Herat was the uncle of Thetan and married to the jealous Mentheb. Herat made prisoners of Tarzan and the other members of the Gregory safari, despite Thetan's recommendation to the contrary, and would only release them if three conditions were met. Herat took a liking to Magra from the Gregory group and made advances toward her until Mentheb found out. *Tarzan and the Forbidden City*

Herkuf: A priest to the god Brulor, the Father of Diamonds, in Ashair, the Forbidden City. Before that he was a priest to Chon, the True God and Father of Diamonds. After offending Brulor, Herkuf was made a prisoner in the temple room, but was released from his cage, along with the captives of the Gregory safari, by Helen Gregory. Herkuf joined their group and showed them how to escape the temple through a secret exit. In revenge, he killed Brulor with a trident. While walking along the lake bottom with Tarzan, Herkuf found a chest in a sunken galley. It contained the actual over-sized diamond that was the genuine Father of Diamonds. Herkuf then assisted in getting the king of Thobos's aid in attacking Ashair and saving Tarzan and his party. *Tarzan and the Forbidden City*

Hines: Once an officer in the Imperial Air Force, Lieutenant Hines became the navigator on the dirigible O-220 that carried Tarzan and Jason Gridley to Pellucidar in search of David Innes. *Tarzan at the Earth's Core*

Hiram: see **Old Timer**

Hirfa: The wife of Sheik Ibn Jad and mother of the beautiful Ateja. *Tarzan, Lord of the Jungle*

Hoesin: The chief of the Sumatra mountain kampong where the fleeing van der Meer family sought rest and guides. After only giving them guides, Hoesin sent them away and betrayed them to the Japanese. *Tarzan and the Foreign Legion*

Hooft: The leader of the bad Dutch guerrillas in Japanese held Sumatra. The wiley Hooft got Amat, a native Sumatran, to trick Corrie van der Meer so he could collect the reward for her offered by the Japanese. His plan succeeded and he captured Corrie, but she later escaped. *Tarzan and the Foreign Legion*

Howard: An English speaking gorilla noble loyal to King Henry the Eighth in the lost city of London on the Thames in the Valley of Diamonds. *Tarzan and the Lion Man*

Hud: A young warrior in the Niocene cave tribe of Nu who desired Nat-ul and abducted her for himself. Nat-ul, however, was in love with Nu, the son of Nu, and mortally wounded Hud with a stone knife while escaping from him. Still alive, Hud was found by Nu and lived long enough to tell his rival what had happened. *The Eternal Savage (Lover)*

Hugo: The Dutch guerrilla killed by Tarzan while on sentry duty in a tree near Hooft's camp. *Tarzan and the Foreign Legion*

Hunt: A blond white man who was in love with Jean Hanson and supposed to meet up with her safari in the jungle. But Hunt and his friend, Elbert Small, became lost, and their safari was found by the cruel Wilson Jones and his even worse cohort, Cannon, and taken over by them. Hunt and Small escaped by running into the jungle where Hunt met Tarzan and traveled with him. He talked entirely too much for the Ape-man, though, and Tarzan left him in a cave with Nkima and Jad-bal-ja to watch over him while he searched for Hunt's friends. Hunt did not trust Jad-bal-ja and attempted to follow Tarzan through the trees. But he failed miserably and returned to the cave. While exploring it, he fell into a pit with interconnecting tunnels, oil lamp gutters, and ancient writings. Jad-bal-ja followed him in, and when they heard something following them, they ran. What was stalking them was the giant praying mantis, Ebopa, the Stick That Walks, the Undying God of Ur. It chased them up a sewer tunnel that led to the arena where Tarzan was then fighting. Hunt escaped through Tarzan's intervention and gained Jean Hanson's affection. *Tarzan: The Lost Adventure*

Hyark: A large warrior of the low born Eythra class of people in Athne, the City of Ivory, who proclaimed that he could kill Tarzan in the arena. When Tarzan countered and declared that he could kill both Hyark and a lion at the same time, the Athnean showed his cowardice and unsuccessfully tried to get out of the event. In the inevitable arena battle, Tarzan shoved Hyark toward the lion. Hyark ran from it and the beast gave chase and killed him. *Tarzan the Magnificent*

Ibeto: The husband of Momaya and the father of ten-year-old Tibo, the native boy who was abducted by the maternally yearning Tarzan, from the village of Mbonga. *Jungle Tales of Tarzan*

Id-an: "Silver-spear." A Waz-don from the cliff village of Kor-ul-ja in the land of Pal-ul-don, and one of Pan-at-lee's two brothers. *Tarzan the Terrible*

Imba: The name of Kali Bwana's "boy," or native cooking servant. Imba was a sullen middle aged man who eventually deserted her. *Tarzan and the Leopard Men*

Imigeg: The old and forgetful high priest in the Secret Order of the Leopard Men. The crafty Imigeg used ventriloquism to make a chained leopard ostensibly speak as their god. *Tarzan and the Leopard Men*

Innes, David: With the scientist Abner Perry, David Innes discovered the lost and primeval land of Pellucidar, located at our Earth's core, by riding down in a drilling machine called an iron mole. There Innes married Dian, the Beautiful, and became the first Emperor of Pellucidar. His imprisonment and captivity by the pirate Korsars caused Jason Gridley to get Tarzan to assist in outfitting and to accompany a rescue expedition into the savage land. Their mission was successful and David Innes was freed. (More can be learned about the adventures of David Innes and Abner Perry and their discovery of Pellucidar, by reading Burroughs' Pellucidar series starting with *At the Earth's Core*.) *Tarzan at the Earth's Core*

In-sad: "Dark-forest." The Waz-don warrior from the cliff village of Kor-ul-ja in the land of Pal-ul-don who accompanied Tarzan, Ta-den, Om-at, and O-dan in search of Pan-at-lee. *Tarzan the Terrible*

Intamo: The crafty old witch doctor who wielded more power than the chief in the cannibal village of Bagalla when the Tarzan Twins were brought in as captives. When Doc performed a magic trick that the natives felt was more potent than anything Intamo could do, the witch doctor became jealous and plotted against the Twins. After attempting to poison the boys Intamo went to their hut to finish them off, but was killed in the attempt by the pygmy Ukundo. *Tarzan and the Tarzan Twins*

In-tan: "Dark-warrior." The unfortunate Waz-don who was left to guard Tarzan in the village of Kor-ul-lul after the Ape-man was knocked unconscious during a fight against them. When he secretly regained consciousness and broke his bonds, In-tan came over to inspect him. Tarzan attacked him and during the battle the Ape-man cut off In-tan's tail at the base. After killing him, the Jungle Lord also cut the Waz-don's head off and took it with him to spook the rest of the village. *Tarzan the Terrible*

Isaza: The Waziri serving "boy" and cook of Lord Passmore (Tarzan). *Tarzan Triumphant*

Iskandar: A Sumatran leader of ten who captured Corrie van der Meer for the reward that had been offered by the Japanese. Corrie escaped and Iskandar killed the sentry on duty who let her slip past. When he and his men approached Tarzan's "foreign legion," the Ape-man shot Iskandar in the leg with an arrow as a warning. A brief skirmish ensued which the "foreign legion" won. They then let Iskandar go on his way with his dead and dying. *Tarzan and the Foreign Legion*

Ivitch, Paul: A communist Russian in Peter Zveri's Opar raiding safari. Ivitch mistook Tarzan, who was wearing a leopard skin G-string, for a real leopard in a tree. He shot at the Jungle Lord, grazing his head and knocking him unconscious. Tarzan recovered and, after all was said and done, commanded that natives escort Ivitch and others of his group through the jungle to the nearest railroad. *Tarzan the Invincible*

Ja: A *mezop* from Anoroc in Pellucidar. Ja commanded the viking-like armada that was sent to Korsar to rescue his good friend, David Innes, First Emperor of Pellucidar. On the way they came across Tarzan and company also heading to Korsar. They joined forces and successfully rescued Innes. (More can be learned about Ja by reading the Pellucidar series by Burroughs, starting with *At the Earth's Core*.) *Tarzan at the Earth's Core*

Jacot, Armand: The Prince de Cadrenet and father of Meriem (Jeanne), Korak's wife. While a captain in the French Foreign Legion he was nicknamed "the Hawk" because of his keen eyesight. Jacot offered a reward for his daughter and made an intensive search for her after she was kidnaped by the Arab sheik, Amor ben Khatour, in revenge for Jacot's execution of his nephew, Achmet ben Houdin. Jacot was ultimately promoted to the rank of general and became a respected friend of Tarzan's. *The Son of Tarzan*

Jacot, Jeanne: see **Meriem**

Jad, Ibn: The sheik of the Beny Salem fendy el-Guad who led his *menzil* of Arabs to the fabled lost treasure city of Nimmr in the Valley of the Sepulcher. After looting one of the medieval castles, Ibn Jad made his escape. Tarzan caught up with the Arabs and began shooting them one by one from the trees with arrows until they returned the treasure. Despite the fact that they thought Tarzan a *jinn*, or evil spirit, Ibn Jad's terrified men and Galla slaves marched on until, finally, they all refused to carry the treasure any further. Ibn Jad then carried it himself, with his beautiful daughter, Ateja, remaining by his side to help him. They were finally corralled by Tarzan's Waziri. Ibn Jad was turned over to the Galla natives and, presumably, sold into slavery. *Tarzan, Lord of the Jungle*

Jad-bal-ja: "The-golden-lion" in the language of Pal-ul-don. Jad-bal-ja had an unusual golden hue to him when he was found as a cub by

Roy G. Krenkel illustration from *Tarzan and the Tarzan Twins* (© 1963 Edgar Rice Burroughs, Inc.).

Tarzan, and having just returned from Pal-ul-don, the Lord of the Jungle named him in the language of that land. Jad-bal-ja grew to be an irregularly large and strong black-maned forest lion, and was trained and raised by Tarzan. Because of the fear the natives at the Greystoke estate held for Jad-bal-ja, he was usually caged at night; otherwise he was left free to roam the jungle at will. Jad-bal-ja showed his affection for a person by rubbing his head against his body, but he only did this with Tarzan and his family, and with Doc, one of the Tarzan Twins. The Golden Lion often followed and searched for Tarzan and saved the Ape-man's life several times. During these he would also aid other friends of Tarzan such as La, the High Priestess of Opar, and Nkima. In some lion worshiping societies, Jad-bal-ja took the place of their lion gods. In *Tarzan and the Lion Man*, the Golden Lion found a mate. *Tarzan and the Golden Lion, Tarzan, Lord of the Jungle, Tarzan the Invincible, Tarzan and the City of Gold, Tarzan and the Lion Man, Tarzan and the Tarzan Twins,* and *Tarzan: The Lost Adventure*

Jad-ben-Otho: "The great God" of the Waz-don and Ho-don in Pal-ul-don. Tarzan pretended to be Dor-ul-Otho, the Son of God, to gain entrance to A-lur, the capital city of the Ho-don. The half-crazy Lt. Erich Obergatz later used the same concept when he pretended to be the tailless Jad-ben-Otho, by going totally naked except for flowers in his hair. *Tarzan the Terrible*

Jad-guru-don: "The terrible man" in the language of Pal-ul-don. The Waz-don in the city of Kor-ul-ja called Tarzan this after he cut off the tail of one of their warriors in a fight.

Once they learned his name, they called him Tarzan-jad-guru or Tarzan-the-terrible. *Tarzan the Terrible*

Ja-don: "Lion-man." The mighty Ho-don chief of Ja-lur, the Lion City, and the father of Ta-den, Tarzan's friend. Ja-don defied Ko-tan, the king of A-lur, and Lu-don his high priest. When the Jungle Lord pretended to be Dor-ul-Otho, the Son of God, Ja-don took a liking to him. The chief of Ja-lur also gave assistance to a captive Jane. He then led his warriors in a revolt against the city of A-lur after Ko-tan was assassinated by Bu-lot. Once the fighting was over, Ja-don was made king of the Ho-don. Ja-don made a pact with Om-at, the *gund* (chief) of some Waz-don, to work out peace between the two habitually warring peoples. *Tarzan the Terrible*

Jafar, Raghunath: A burly East Indian Hindu who was part of the Opar treasure seeking safari under the Russian communists, Peter Zveri and Zora Drinov. Jafar desired Zora and attempted to rape her, but was stopped by the American, Wayne Colt. When he attempted to kill Colt, Tarzan ended the Hindu's life with an arrow. After Jafar was buried, Tarzan dug up his body and threw it into the camp from a tree to spook the Zveri-Drinov party. *Tarzan the Invincible*

Jana, the Red Flower of Zoram: The sister of Thoar from the city of Zoram in the Mountains of the Thipdars in Pellucidar. Jana was considered the most beautiful of the beautiful women of Zoram, and was pursued by the men of Pheli because of her loveliness. She was saved by the lost American, Jason Gridley. They fell in love, but she did not at first verbalize it, and after Gridley affronted her, she deserted him. Jana was then captured by the men of Clovi and met Tarzan who also became their prisoner. With the assistance of a friendly youth, Tarzan and Jana escaped and traveled together until they were captured by the snake-like Horibs. The Lord of the Jungle easily escaped the Horibs and after finding his Waziri nearby quickly returned and rescued Jana from them as well. During the rescue they were reunited with Jason who was also a captive of the Horibs. Jana finally announced her love for Jason after he decided to remain in Pellucidar to search for a missing member of his expedition. *Tarzan at the Earth's Core*

Jane: see **Porter, Jane**

Janzara: The beautiful, but spoiled, gray-eyed, brunette daughter of King Elkomoelhago of Veltopismakus in the land of the Minuni. In an attempt to elicit a response from Tarzan, Janzara stabbed him in the arm. The beautiful princess ended up desiring the Jungle Lord, but when he did not return her love she opened a trapdoor in her chambers and he fell through it into a wildcat pit. Soon after during a physical battle between Janzara and the slave woman, Talaskar, both women rolled through the same trapdoor. Already a prisoner in the cat pit was Zoanthrohago who loved Janzara. After escaping the pit, she discovered how wrong she had been about Tarzan and his friends. She helped everyone get away to the rival city of Trohanadalmakus, after they promised not to enslave her and Zoanthrohago who, she finally realized, she loved too. *Tarzan and the Ant Men*

Jar-don: "Stranger," the Pal-ul-donian name given to Korak by the Waz-don *gund* (chief), Om-at, after

the son of Tarzan entered the land of Pal-ul-don in search of his father. *Tarzan the Terrible*

Jean C. Tarzan: Tarzan's French name given him by Paul d'Arnot. The initial was for Clayton. *The Return of Tarzan*

Jeda: The large female guard from the lost city of Ur who captured Jean Hanson and played cruel tricks on her. She incurred Hanson's hatred. When the two faced each other in the arena, the overconfident Jeda at first easily handled her opponent, but then Jean managed to kill the Urian by stabbing her in the eye with a knife. *Tarzan: The Lost Adventure*

Jenssen, Carl: A large, yellow bearded Swede who searched for Jeanne Jacot (Meriem) for the reward offered by her father. Unable to find her Jenssen became an ivory raider with Sven Malbihn, and while trading with some Arabs he saw the missing Meriem among them. Later, when Jenssen saw her as a prisoner of the Kovudoo cannibals, he bought her from them. He did not want Meriem harmed and had to protect her from Malbihn. While attempting to save her from being raped by his partner, Jenssen was shot by Malbihn with a pistol and killed. *The Son of Tarzan*

Jerome, Jerry: see **Kid**

Jerome, Jessie: see **Kali Bwana**

Jervis: The English foreman who consorted with Mr. Hanson (a.k.a. Sven Malbihn) at the Greystoke estate in *The Son of Tarzan*. Jervis was put in charge of rebuilding the Greystoke estate and bungalow after their destruction by the Germans. *The Son of Tarzan* and *Tarzan the Terrible*

Jezebel: A golden-haired, gray-eyed girl from the lost epileptic land of Midian. She was not epileptic like the others of her village, and this combined with her beauty made her an outcast. Her smile and laughter were also considered sinful. Jezebel was the first to approach the parachuting English lady, Barbara Collis, and used the ploy of Barbara being a messenger from God to her own advantage. She taught Barbara the language of Midian and learned English in return. The golden haired girl ended up falling in love with the American gangster, Danny "Gunner" Patrick, and he with her. Outside her valley, Jezebel was captured by *shiftas,* and then taken from them by the Russian Leon Stabutch. After Tarzan saved her, she and "Gunner" planned to live happily ever after in America. *Tarzan Triumphant*

Jobab: An apostle in the epileptic fanatic Christian land of Midian. Jobab encouraged the people to crucify both the beautiful golden haired Jezebel and the English woman Barbara Collis after claiming to have talked with Jehovah during a seizure. When the lost American geologist, Lafayette Smith, tried to rescue the girls, he shot at Jobab with his pistol and missed. Because of this Jobab thought he was protected by divine intervention. But a moment later he was shot and killed with the same pistol by Barbara Collis, who had a better aim. *Tarzan Triumphant*

1. Joe: The scenarist on a jungle picture being shot on location in Africa. *Tarzan and the Lion Man*

2. Joe: The name of the host of a party that Tarzan unwittingly crashed while out riding with two young men who were looking for a good time in Hollywood. *Tarzan and the Lion Man*

Jones: A sailor on the *Kincaid* who was

nicer than the rest. *The Beasts of Tarzan*

Jones, Robert (Bob): A Negro from Alabama who became the cook on the dirigible O-220 that Tarzan and Jason Gridley flew in on a rescue mission into Pellucidar. Jones was superstitious and took along his lucky rabbit's foot. He was also confused by the eternal noonday sun of Pellucidar and always wrote "noon" in his journal at the beginning of each entry. *Tarzan at the Earth's Core*

Jones, Wilson: A tall black man who, even though he was a former boxer, was easily and quickly rendered *hors de combat* by Tarzan after the Lord of the Jungle came upon him and his cohorts. Because of this humiliating defeat, Wilson was anxious for a one-on-one rematch with Tarzan. His gang took over Eugene Hanson's safari, but Wilson did not want to kill Hanson and left him in the jungle. They went on to take over Hunt and Small's safari after that. Then Wilson ran into Tarzan again. He shot the Ape-man, tied him to a tree with leather straps, and left him to die. Later, Wilson and a cohort found Hanson again with his askari, and they held the two men captive and tortured them. But they escaped and, ironically, captured their former captor, Wilson. Under their guard, he was escorted to the lost city of Ur. On the way there, Wilson angered Hanson so much that the latter released him to fight with him hand to hand, and knocked him out. *Tarzan: The Lost Adventure*

Kabariga: The chief of the Bangalo natives who came to Tarzan seeking aid in ridding their country of a raiding band of Abyssinian *shiftas* led by a white man. *Tarzan Triumphant*

Kahiya: The acting headman for Peter

Zveri's communist treasure seeking safari to Opar when the usual headman, Kitembo, was gone. *Tarzan the Invincible*

Kala: The young yet large and intelligent foster Mangani mother of Tarzan. After the tragic loss of her newborn, Kala felt a maternal sympathy and longing for the crying infant, John Clayton, Jr. (Tarzan), after her tribe of apes broke into his father's cabin and killed the elder Clayton. Kala took the infant, called him Tarzan, and raised, nursed, and protected the young human as her own. After she was killed by the poison tipped arrow of Kulonga, a black native warrior from the tribe of Mbonga, Tarzan killed the native in revenge. Tarzan considered Kala his only true mother and the only creature that imparted love to him in the jungle. *Tarzan of the Apes* and *Jungle Tales of Tarzan*.

Kalfastoban: The loud mouthed braggart *vental* (leader of ten men) in charge of Zoanthrohago's slave quarry that Tarzan was placed in after the Ape-man was shrunk to the size of the Minuni. When Kalfastoban saw the beautiful female slave, Talaskar, he purchased her for himself. While Komodoflorensal and Tarzan were attempting to rescue Talaskar, Komodoflorensal killed Kalfastoban in a sword fight. *Tarzan and the Ant Men*

Kali Bwana: "Hard Lord," the Swahili title for the platinum blonde, blue-gray eyed American woman, Jessie Jerome. The name was given to her by her native safari when she was searching for her older brother, Jerry Jerome. After she shot her headman in the arm for making unwelcome advances toward her, the safari deserted her. She then met up with an American named Old Timer and be-

came his friend. After the Leopard Men captured Kali Bwana, they attempted to make her their high priestess. Old Timer helped her escape, but she was soon taken captive to a cannibal pygmy village where she was almost eaten. Old Timer again helped her escape. Afterwards he announced his love for her, but she was offended. And then the Mangani abducted him. When he got free and was reunited with Kali Bwana, she realized she loved him and told him so. The couple then met up with Old Timer's original male companion, Kid, who turned out to be Kali's missing brother, Jerry Jerome. *Tarzan and the Leopard Men*

Kam, Lum: A faithful Chinese servant to the van der Meer family in Japanese held Sumatra. When the van der Meer family fled from the Japanese, Lum Kam carried the exhausted Elsje van der Meer. Lum Kam and Hendrik van der Meer were eventually killed by bayonet wielding Japanese soldiers. *Tarzan and the Foreign Legion*

Kama: A female Mangani in the tribe of Kerchak. *Jungle Tales of Tarzan*

Kamak, Abdul: A young and handsome, though sinister looking, Arab new to Sheik Amor ben Khatour's group. Abdul Kamak desired Meriem after she was returned to the sheik's *douar* as a mature young woman. He told her of his love, but she could not and did not return it. Regardless he was determined to have her. When Amor ben Khatour overheard Abdul tell Meriem that he hated him, the sheik confronted him. This resulted in Abdul hitting the sheik hard enough to knock him down. He then fled the camp after taking with him a photo of Meriem as a young girl. Abdul immediately went and informed Meriem's father, Capt. Armand Jacot, about his daughter's captivity. *The Son of Tarzan*

Kamudi: The native "boy" of Stanley Wood who helped make bows and arrows after they escaped from the Kaji. *Tarzan the Magnificent*

Kandos: The right-hand man and cohort of Phoros, the dictator of Athne, the City of Ivory. *Tarzan the Magnificent*

Kaneko, Kenzo: The second lieutenant in the Japanese camp where Tarzan was taken as a prisoner in Sumatra. When Kenzo Kaneko questioned Tarzan and received no answers, the Japanese decided to torture him by dragging him behind a horse. Before the torture could commence, though, Kaneko was shot by Tarzan's rescuing "foreign legion." *Tarzan and the Foreign Legion.*

Kapopa: The witch doctor in Chief Bobolo's village who took the American white woman, Kali Bwana, to a tribe of cannibal pygmies as the prisoner of Bobolo. *Tarzan and the Leopard Men*

Karnath: The king of the tribe of Kerchak when Tarzan returned to them after his first adventures in civilization. To help Karnath remember who he was so that he could be accepted into the tribe again, Tarzan reminded him of how they used to throw sticks at Numa. Karnath remembered and allowed Tarzan to re-enter the tribe. *The Return of Tarzan*

Kavandavanda: The king, witch doctor, high priest of priests, and god of the Kavuru. He was described as an extremely good looking, young, blond haired man. In reality he was possibly hundreds of years old, because Kavandavanda had invented longevity elixir pills that, if taken every month, gave eternal life and beauty. When he first met Jane, Kavandavanda thought he loved her. He offered her his same eternal youth and beauty if she would be his mate and high priestess, even though he had taken a vow of celibacy. She refused. When the temple was attacked by Tarzan and others, Kavandavanda attempted to kill Jane with a dagger, but was shot and killed by Tarzan instead. *Tarzan's Quest*

Kaviri: The chief of a tribe of natives along the Ugambi River. After being poorly treated by Nikolas Rokoff, Kaviri attacked Tarzan and his beasts in their canoes. The Ape-man choked Kaviri until he was unconscious. When he came to, Tarzan made the chief assign some warriors to paddle his canoes. *The Beasts of Tarzan*

Kavuru: White warriors with the secret of eternal youth and longevity. See Kavuru in Section Three. *Tarzan's Quest.*

Keewazi: The Waziri warrior in charge of feeding Jad-bal-ja and cleaning his cage while Tarzan was gone searching for Esteban Miranda. When Jad-bal-ja escaped during one of the feedings to go after Tarzan, Keewazi felt he deserved punishment for allowing it to happen. When they returned together, he was much relieved. *Tarzan and the Golden Lion*

Kerchak: The seven foot tall king of the tribe of Mangani that adopted Tarzan. Originally, during a berserk rage, Kerchak chased the Mangani female Kala and caused her newborn to fall to its death. Soon thereafter he killed Tarzan's biological father, John Clayton, Lord Greystoke, when the Lord of the Jungle was a year old. He would have killed the infant Tarzan then, too, had not

Kala rescued the babe to raise as her own. Kerchak hated Tarzan, and in another fit of berserk rage, challenged him. The Lord of the Jungle duly killed the Mangani king. *Tarzan of the Apes* and *Jungle Tales of Tarzan*

Keta: A little monkey Tarzan made friends with in Japanese held Sumatra. It reminded Tarzan of Nkima, and like Nkima, Keta traveled with the Ape-man. The only member of Tarzan's "foreign legion" that Keta accepted was Tony "Shrimp" Rosetti, and when Tarzan was captured by the Japanese, the monkey alerted the group through Rosetti. With Tarzan, Keta survived a boat attack and subsequent submarine rescue. *Tarzan and the Foreign Legion*

Khamis: The witch doctor in the cannibal village of Chief Obebe upon the banks of the Ugogo River. When the Tarzan impersonator, Esteban Miranda, was abducted to his village, Khamis told the villagers that their prisoner was the river devil, not Tarzan. Chief Obebe disagreed and said that he was indeed Tarzan, not the river devil. To prove who was right, they chained Miranda in a hut. If he escaped, they said, he was the river devil. if he died a natural death, he was Tarzan, their hated enemy.

In *Tarzan and the Ant Men* Uhha, Khamis' young daughter, spoke to Miranda. He scared her into helping him escape, then forced her to go with him. While searching for his daughter, Khamis stumbled upon the real Tarzan lying unconscious and took him prisoner. Back in the village, Khamis and Obebe decided to torture Tarzan until he revealed Uhha's whereabouts. The Lord of the Jungle broke his bonds, and after seizing Khamis and chasing Obebe

away, he threw the witch doctor through the roof of the hut that Obebe had run into. Obebe, thinking the falling body was Tarzan attacking, blindly stabbed the body until the witch doctor was dead. *Tarzan and the Golden Lion* and *Tarzan and the Ant Men*

Kid: An American about 22 years old who was poaching ivory in Africa. His accomplice was another American who, although not much older, was named Old Timer. The pair had not had much luck and decided to separate to cover more territory. After a while, Old Timer became missing. The Kid went searching for him and ended up at the village of Chief Bobolo. Bobolo was not too friendly and desired to kill Kid. Fortunately, a young native girl who liked the young American warned him of the chief's intentions. Kid also learned that there was a white woman involved in Old Timer's disappearance. When all were reunited, it was revealed that the white woman was Kid's sister, Jessie Jerome, and that Old Timer and she were in love. It was also revealed that Kid's real name was Jerry Jerome. *Tarzan and the Leopard Men*

King: The large original leader of the mutinying crew of the *Arrow* which put Jane Porter's party on shore at Tarzan's cabin. King was shot in the back at the cabin by the cowardly Snipes. *Tarzan of the Apes*

Kip, Lum: A Chinese sailor and cook on the ill-fated *Saigon*. He spoke the Lascar language, and when he overheard his Lascar shipmates discussing a mutiny, the faithful Lum Kip told the first mate about it. The mutineers were successful nevertheless, and when they found out that the Chinaman had informed on them, they strung him up by his thumbs and lashed him. After the *Saigon* was shipwrecked on the lost island of Uxmal, Lum Kip was made the cook for the people in Tarzan's camp. *Tarzan and the Castaways*

Kircher, Fräulein Bertha: A beautiful young woman who Tarzan hated because he believed her to be a German spy after a German regiment destroyed his estate and apparently killed Jane. Tarzan discovered that Kircher carried his mother's locket which he had given to Jane in token of his affection, and which had been missing from what was supposedly her charred body at their burned and pillaged bungalow. Kircher used the locket as identification to get behind German lines. When Tarzan caught up with her, he took the locket from her. He spared her life, however, because he could not bring himself to kill a woman, even though she was a hated German.

Tarzan and Kircher's paths crossed several more times. He spared and saved her life again, but berated himself for showing this weakness. But the Fräulein returned the favor by saving and aiding the Jungle Lord a few times. She also showed great courage and resourcefulness under extreme conditions. Consequently, he could not help but admire her, and even started to like her despite his earlier prejudice. At the same time she could not help but fall for the heroic Lord of the Jungle. She was deeply saddened and hurt, however, by Tarzan's prejudicial hatred of Germans, including her. In spite of his anti–German feeling, at one point he did hold hands with Kircher to comfort her.

Their adventures together included lion and ape attacks, capture by cannibals and other natives, and captivity and separation in the lost maniac city of Xuja. While in Xuja, Kircher was dressed and prepared by an old English woman to become another queen to the king of the city. On her way to the king's chambers, she was kidnaped by the prince and taken away. But Tarzan saved her again.

During this time they also met and helped a stranded pilot named Harold Percy Smith-Oldwick who, himself, could not help but fall in love with Bertha. Smith-Oldwick went so far as to voice his feelings to her. She at first rejected him, because of her love and admiration for Tarzan. But in the end she promised to marry the lost pilot. After she and Smith-Oldwick safely departed, Tarzan learned the truth about Fräulein Kircher — that she was, in fact, the Honorable Patricia Canby, one of the most valuable members of the British intelligence service attached to the forces in East Africa. *Tarzan the Untamed*

Kitembo: The chief of the Basembos and headman to Peter Zveri's safari. Kitembo hated whites, but wanted to become the King of Kenya through Zveri's influence, while Zveri only wanted to use Kitembo as a puppet chief over the natives. When Kitembo attempted to take Zora Drinov from Zveri, Tarzan shot an arrow through the chief's chest. *Tarzan the Invincible*

Kla: An Oparian contraction that means "New La." See **Gretchen von Harben**

Komodoflorensal: Purported to be the greatest swordsman in all the land of Minuni. He was the son of Adendrohahkis, the king of Trohanadalmakus, and thus the zertolosto or prince royal. Komodoflorensal was the first Minunian that

Tarzan ever saw. This occurred when the Jungle Lord rescued him from the grasp of an Alalus woman. After welcoming the giant Ape-man into his city, the grateful prince helped teach him the language of the Minuni.

Komodoflorensal and Tarzan were both captured and taken prisoner in a battle between Trohanadalmakus and their rival city, Veltopismakus. And, because he would not reveal who he was to the enemy, Komodoflorensal was assigned and called by a slave number, Aoponato, which translated represents $800^3 + 19$. The beautiful female slave, Talaskar, volunteered to cook for both Komodoflorensal and Tarzan. During that time she fell in love with Komodoflorensal and he with her. Together with Tarzan, the couple escaped from Veltopismakus. Komodoflorensal and Tarzan later found out that she was a princess, the daughter of a captured queen. *Tarzan and the Ant Men*

Korak: The Mangani name given to Tarzan's first son, Jack, by the great ape Akut. It literally meant "the killer," and was the word most similar to "Jack" that Akut could pronounce. Korak (Jack) was the first and only known son of Tarzan and Jane. He first appeared in the non–Tarzan book *The Eternal Savage (Lover)*. In the Tarzan series itself, his first appearance was in the third book, *The Beasts of Tarzan*, where he was kidnaped as an infant by Nikolas Rokoff and Alexis Paulvitch. Living in civilization, his mother tried to keep him from any knowledge of his father's wild upbringing and any repetition of it. But Jack's destiny was to become a lord of the jungle himself, as revealed in *The Son of Tarzan*.

In this book, a young Jack ran away with Akut, an old Mangani friend of Tarzan, to escape possible criminal prosecution as well as to help return the ape to the jungles of Africa. The pair ended up living in the jungle together for several years, where Jack learned to speak the language of the Mangani and became in all respects the equal of his father in jungle craft and animal lore, as well as in physical and mental prowess. The similarities between father and son also included a strong friendship with Tantor, the elephant, and in Korak being considered a demon by the natives of the jungle. The main difference between the two was that Korak gave merely a silent victory cry.

Korak also met, rescued, and married a captive Arab girl named Meriem. In reality, and unbeknownst to Korak, she was a lost French princess, the daughter of General Armand Jacot, Prince de Cadrenet.

When Jane was taken by the Germans in *Tarzan the Untamed*, it was learned that Korak participated in the war at the Arginine Front. In *Tarzan the Terrible*, Korak left the army and began searching for Tarzan who, in turn, was searching for Jane. Korak's search led him into the land of Pal-ul-don with his Enfield rifle and some ammunition. On entering Pal-ul-don, he was befriended by the hairy black Waz-don, Om-at, and given the name Jar-don which meant "stranger." With the aid of the Waz-don, Korak arrived in time to save Tarzan from being sacrificed alive at the hands of Erich Obergatz and Lu-don, the high priest of A-lur. He killed both men with his rifle. The sound and results of the rifle were taken for miraculous powers of God, and Korak became known as the Messenger of Death and the Messenger of the Great God.

Through his military training Korak learned to fly planes, and taught his father, Tarzan, this skill at the beginning of *Tarzan and the Ant Men*. In the same book, it is revealed that Korak and Meriem had given birth to a son named Jack "Jackie" Jr. *The Beasts of Tarzan, The Son of Tarzan, Tarzan the Terrible, Tarzan and the Golden Lion, Tarzan and the Ant Men*, and *The Eternal Savage (Lover)*

Ko-tan: The father of the beautiful O-lo-a and king of the Ho-don city A-lur, the City of Light, in the land of Pal-ul-don. Ko-tan held Jane captive in his city and desired her to be his queen, but High Priest Lu-don, also desired her. When Tarzan arrived to find out if Jane were in the city, he pretended to be Dor-ul-Otho, the son of their great god, Jad-ben-Otho. Ko-tan believed he was Dor-ul-Otho and did him honor. But before he could rescue Jane, Tarzan was exposed by Lu-don and an anxious Ko-tan began making wedding preparations for Jane and himself. At a bachelor party of sorts for Bu-lot, who was betrothed to O-lo-a, the future son-in-law of the king got drunk, and in a moment of uncontrolled anger threw a knife at Ko-tan and killed him. *Tarzan the Terrible*

Kovudoo: The brave middle-aged chief of a tribe of cannibals that the young Korak at first attempted to befriend. After being attacked by them, the son of Tarzan repeatedly raided and terrorized the tribe. When the natives had had enough of this, they hunted Korak down, hit him with their spears, and stole

Meriem from him. Kovudoo then planned to sell Meriem to the Sheik, but was informed by two lying Swedes that the Sheik was dead. So Kovudoo sold Meriem to the Swedes. Having enlisted several Tongani (baboons) as troops, Korak returned to the cannibals' village looking for Meriem and razed the place to the ground. The remainder of the tribe of Kovudoo relocated out of the country. *The Son of Tarzan*

Kraski, Carl: A young, good looking Russian with wavy brown hair who was one of four men who supported and accompanied Flora Hawkes on a treasure stealing safari to the lost city of Opar. Kraski had feelings for Flora. After surviving several harrowing experiences, and barely escaping with their lives, the members of the safari became separated from Flora. Tarzan found them and led them to some natives who he wanted to escort the outsiders to the coast. On the way to the natives' village, Kraski saw a pouch of jewels that Tarzan had taken from the Valley of the Palace of Diamonds, and while the Ape-man slept the Russian took the pouch and headed into the jungle alone. There, he eventually stumbled upon Flora and the jealous Tarzan impersonator, Esteban Miranda, she had hired. Miranda immediately killed Kraski with a spear and took the pouch. *Tarzan and the Golden Lion*

Krause, Fritz: The man who purchased a caged Tarzan from Abdullah Abu Néjm to put the Ape-man on display as a wild man in a traveling animal show. After Tarzan escaped he put Krause in a cage, and when they were all shipwrecked, Krause was placed in a separate camp from Tarzan and the rest of the

Ape-man's chosen companions. While Tarzan was away, Krause went back to the Jungle Lord's camp and forcefully abducted Janette Laon. When Tarzan returned he killed Krause with an arrow. *Tarzan and the Castaways*

Krause, Kitty: see **Kitty Sborov**

Kraut: A large red faced German general. Tarzan knocked a burning oil lamp onto him when, seeking vengeance, the Ape-man unceremoniously snatched Major Schneider from a military headquarters in German East Africa. *Tarzan the Untamed*

Kulonga: The son of Chief Mbonga from the cannibal village of Mbonga who killed Kala, Tarzan's ape foster mother. Prince Kulonga was also noteworthy because he was the first human being the Lord of the Jungle ever saw (and almost ate). After Kulonga killed Kala, Tarzan stalked him and observed him with curiosity. Before the native prince could get away, the vengeful Ape-man hung him by a grass rope and stabbed him through the heart. Tarzan then took Kulonga's bow and arrows and some of his clothing. *Tarzan of the Apes*

Kurvandi: The nearly seven foot tall black king of Ur who was born somewhat insane due to inbreeding. Because of this mental imbalance Kurvandi was cruel, merciless and bathed in human blood. As king he had two jet-black lions as guardian pets, and would take many women to wife if the mood struck him. While in his arena box he was killed by Jad-bal-ja after the Golden Lion came up from a sewer opening on the back of Ebopa, the large praying mantis god of Ur. For more information see Ur in Section Three. *Tarzan: The Lost Adventure*

Kwamudi: The headman of the porters for the *Lion Man* motion picture safari in Africa. After several attacks by the cannibal Bansutos, Kwamudi deserted the safari with his fellows. He was later caught by the cannibals and placed in a hut with the actor and Tarzan look-alike, Stanley Obroski. Kwamudi acted as interpreter for Obroski, but was eventually tortured and eaten by the Bansutos. *Tarzan and the Lion Man*

Kyomya: The 19-year-old slave boy assigned to the new captive goddess, Sandra Pickerall, in the lost Portuguese city of Alemtejo. Believing Sandra to be a real goddess, Kyomya was faithful to her even when the high priest, Pedro Ruiz, attempted to force himself upon her. While defending his goddess from Ruiz, Kyomya was killed by the high priest with a dagger. *Tarzan and the Madman*

La: The High Priestess of the Flaming God in the lost city of Opar, last bastion of Atlantis. La was a beautiful Caucasian woman with gray eyes who wore little clothing. What she did wear was gold and jewel encrusted. La spoke the language of the Mangani as well as her ancient Atlantian, although the latter mainly for religious ceremonies. She made her first appearance in *The Return of Tarzan* where she almost succeeded in sacrificing the Lord of the Jungle upon the altar of the Flaming God (the sun). Tarzan escaped, and La developed a great and undying love and desire for him. In *Tarzan and the Jewels of Opar*, she offered him his freedom if he would return her love. He would not, but she released him anyway. Her priests called her a traitor and tried to usurp her.

In *Tarzan and the Golden Lion*, Tarzan was again captured by the priests of Opar and La was forced to decide between his death and losing the throne and her life. She decided to escape with Tarzan by leading him out of Opar and into the Valley of the Palace of Diamonds. While there, Tarzan told some Gomangani that La was his mate, to keep them from harming her. Later in the valley, he overthrew the intelligent ruling Bolgani, and enlisted their surviving members to go with him to Opar to return La to the throne. This they succeeded in doing and La became the ruler over all who lived in Opar.

In *Tarzan the Invincible*, La was usurped again and went with Tarzan out of Opar, into his world. There she became the captive of Arab slave traders, made friends with the communist, Zora Drinov, learned to speak English, and developed a crush on the American, Wayne Colt. She was even befriended and aided by Jad-bal-ja, the Golden Lion. But finally, with the aid of Tarzan, La was restored again to the throne of the Flaming God. For more information see Opar in Section Three. *The Return of Tarzan, Tarzan and the Jewels of Opar, Tarzan and the Golden Lion*, and *Tarzan the Invincible*.

Lady: The name given to Jane by the Waziri. See **Jane Porter**

Lady Barbara: see **Barbara Collis** or **Barbara Ramsgate**

Lady Greystoke: see **Jane Porter** and **Alice Clayton**

Lajo: A respected Korsar pirate in Pellucidar who was among the party that captured Jason Gridley and Thoar. Lajo was somewhat kinder and more sympathetic than the other

Korsars and cut the two men's bonds. After they were all rescued from the Horibs and taken aboard the O-220 dirigible, Lajo was selected to be the parachuting messenger to the Cid in the city of Korsar, and pushed out of the ship. *Tarzan at the Earth's Core*

Lamech: The first of the fanatic epileptic Christian South Midians shot with a pistol by the American geologist, Lafayette Smith, while the latter attempted to save Barbara Collis and Jezebel from a burning crucifixion. *Tarzan Triumphant*

Lana: The sister of Thoar and Jana, The Red Flower of Zoram. Lana was from the city of Zoram located in the Mountain of the Thipdars in Pellucidar. She was abducted by a male member of a rival tribe to be his wife. *Tarzan at the Earth's Core*

Lang, Freeman: A radio reporter in Hollywood. *Tarzan and the Lion Man*

Laon, Janette: A very pretty brunette French woman who had a questionable past, and may have been a prostitute. Janette wanted the caged Tarzan treated decently aboard the ship *Saigon* and cut Tarzan's bonds herself. She was later put into the cage with him by the mutinous Wilhelm Schmidt as a punishment, but Tarzan did not harm her and they made friends. Janette shot the Lascar sailor, Jabu Singh, after he shot Tarzan from behind. During this time she began liking the first mate, Hans de Groote, and he her. Upon the Mayan island of Uxmal, Janette was abducted by members of the camp of mutinous sailors, but rescued by Tarzan. De Groote and she were

Opposite: **J. Allen St. John illustration from the *Tarzan and the Jewels of Opar* newspaper serialization (© 1918 Edgar Rice Burroughs, Inc.).**

later married by the captain of the pirated yacht *Naiad*. *Tarzan and the Castaways*

Lara: A native Sumatran in a village where Corrie van der Meer stayed with Tarzan and his men. When the two-faced Amat betrayed Corrie and had her captured by the bad Dutch guerrillas. Lara revealed the truth about Amat and his lies. *Tarzan and the Foreign Legion*

Larsen: The captain of the ill-fated ship *Saigon* who stayed in his cabin with a fever most of the cruise. Captain Larsen did not care for Fritz Krause. *Tarzan and the Castaways*

Lavac, Jacques: The French lieutenant and seaplane pilot who flew the Gregory safari and Tarzan into the interior. When the plane ran out of gas, Lavac successfully landed it on a lake. He began to like Helen Gregory, and was jealous of Paul d'Arnot and made disparaging remarks about him to Helen. He finally voiced his love for her, but she rejected him. When Helen and d'Arnot became a couple, Lavac attempted to kill the other Frenchman. After being put in prison in Thobos, Lavac went with Tarzan to Ashair, the Forbidden City to try and help the Ape-man get the Father of Diamonds. In trying to make amends to d'Arnot for his earlier selfishness and evil, Lavac saved him from a giant attacking seahorse, but was killed in the process. *Tarzan and the Forbidden City*

Leigh, Penelope: The overweight and captious aunt of Patricia Leigh-Burden. Penelope was on the yacht pirated by the *Saigon*, which had a caged Tarzan aboard it. She believed the Jungle Lord to be a cannibal and complained about his lack of attire. After her niece developed a romantic liking for Tarzan, she disap-

proved of the relationship until informed that he was an English Lord. *Tarzan and the Castaways*

Leigh, William Cecil Hugh Percival: An older retired mustached colonel and the uncle of Patricia Leigh-Burden. His yacht, the *Naiad*, was pirated by the *Saigon* which had a caged Tarzan aboard it. After the *Saigon* foundered and its mutinous crew were subdued and put in a different camp, Colonel Leigh was placed in charge of Tarzan's camp by the Ape-man. Leigh believed in the Jungle Lord even though his complaining wife, Penelope, did not trust him. *Tarzan and the Castaways*

Leigh-Burden, Patricia: A physically fit young woman from the *Naiad*, the yacht that was pirated by the *Saigon* on which Tarzan was being held in a cage. Patricia started liking Tarzan more than she should and he downplayed it. After they were shipwrecked, Tarzan rescued the young Mayan maiden, Itzl Cha, and brought her back to camp. He asked Patricia to watch over her, and she did. She taught the girl English and picked up a good knowledge of the Mayan tongue in return. When Tarzan left to go searching in the jungle Patricia stubbornly followed him and was promptly taken captive by Mayan warriors. She tried to fool the king and priest of the Mayan city into thinking that she was a goddess and Tarzan's mate. After Tarzan rescued her, Patricia voiced her love for him, not knowing that he was already married. When she was informed of this fact, it did not change her feelings for the Jungle Lord at all. *Tarzan and the Castaways*

Leo: The lion used in a Prominent Pictures production of a Tarzan film. For the movie John Clayton (Tarzan) was cast as the white hunter and not as himself. During production, Leo became nervous and tried to attack the actor hired to portray Tarzan, and the real Tarzan (Clayton) intervened and killed the beast. The production manager fired Clayton on the spot because, he bitterly complained, to replace the lion would cost him $10,000. *Tarzan and the Lion Man*

Lepus, Mallius: The centurion in charge of Porta Decumana of the lost Roman city of Castra Mare. He was the nephew of the old scholar Septimus Favonius and cousin of the beautiful Favonia. Lepus took a liking to Erich von Harben of the outer world and introduced him to Favonius. *Tarzan and the Lost Empire*

1. Lion-man: see **Ja-don**

2. Lion Man: The name Zora Drinov gave Tarzan after spending some time with him in the jungle. *Tarzan the Invincible*

3. Lion Man: The name of the lead Tarzan-like character in the motion picture of the same name being shot on location in Africa. The actor cast for the part, Stanley Obroski, happened to look identical to Tarzan. After Stanley died Tarzan took his place in the movie without any of the cast or crew knowing. *Tarzan and the Lion Man*

Lobongo: The chief of the Tumbai village of Utenga natives and father of Orando. *Tarzan and the Leopard Men*

Lord: An English captive of the Zuli warrior women who led the hunting party that captured Tarzan. Woora, the magician witch doctor of the Zuli, thought Lord was a fool and put him in the same cell as Tarzan. After Tarzan helped Lord escape, the Ape-man was immediately retaken by Woora. But Lord killed the old magician and freed Tarzan. Then, however, because of his greed for the Great Emerald of the Zuli, the Englishman betrayed the Lord of the Jungle and took the precious stone from him while he slept. Lord was subsequently captured by the Kaji and beheaded by Mafka, the identical twin of Woora. *Tarzan the Magnificent*

Lord Greystoke: see **John Clayton**

Lorro: One of the Amazon-like warrior women from the village of Zuli. *Tarzan the Magnificent*

Lucas, Jerry: A 23-year-old captain from Oklahoma City and pilot of the ill-fated B-24 bomber, the *Lovely Lady*, that Tarzan was on, and which was shot down over Japanese held Sumatra. Jerry was the first member of his party to realize that Colonel Clayton was actually Tarzan of the Apes. Despite being a self-proclaimed woman hater (because of a girl who left him for another man) Jerry still fell in love with Corrie van der Meer, and became jealous of Corrie and Tak van der Boss. During an ambush Jerry was shot and developed a fever from his wounds. After escaping he and Corrie were married aboard the submarine that rescued them from the ocean. *Tarzan and the Foreign Legion*

Lu-don: "Fierce-man." The high priest of the Ho-don in the Temple of the Gryf in A-lur, the City of Light, in Pal-ul-don. Lu-don wanted to get ride of the king and rule all the Ho-don himself. He also desired Jane who was a prisoner there, but because King Ko-tan also desired her, Lu-don held back. When Tarzan arrived claiming to be Dor-ul-Otho the suspicious Lu-don did not believe that he was the Son of God. He exposed Tarzan as an impostor and had him imprisoned. After Ko-tan was assassinated Lu-don made his play for the throne by having

Mo-sar be his puppet king. Tarzan escaped and helped lead the revolution against Lu-don. When the almost completely insane Eric Obergatz showed up proclaiming to be The Great God, Jad-ben-Otho, Lu-don realized the political advantage of having "God" on his side. So he acknowledged Obergatz as Jad-ben-Otho, knowing full well that the German was also an impostor. After Tarzan was again captured, Lu-don and Obergatz attempted to sacrifice him, but Korak showed up and killed both men with his Enfield rifle. *Tarzan the Terrible*

Lukedi: A youth from the native Bagego tribe in the Wiramwazi Mountains near the west end of the canyon containing the Lost Empire. He served food to Tarzan after the Apeman was captured by his tribe. Both Lukedi and Tarzan were subsequently taken prisoner by the Romans of Castra Sanguinarius. *Tarzan and the Lost Empire*

Lulimi: see **Sobito**

Lupingu: A native from Kibbu village. Lupingu was the rival of Nyamwegi for the same girl, until Nyamwegi was killed by the Leopard Men. Being a turncoat, Lupingu consorted with Sobito, the recently defamed witch doctor of the nearby village of Tumbai, to discourage their fellow natives from attacking the Leopard Men. They did not succeed. So in an effort to curry favor, Lupingu informed the Leopard Men of the avenging army of his own people approaching them. When Tarzan observed him telling this secret to the Leopard Men, he exposed Lupingu to the villagers. In punishment, Tarzan bound Lupingu, slit his throat, and threw him into the Leopard Men's village as a warning. *Tarzan and the Leopard Men*

Lu-tan: The husband of Tha and the mother of Nat-ul and Aht (Nat-ul's only brother) in the Niocene period of Earth's history. *The Eternal Savage (Lover)*

Luvini: A large native who took the crooked Owaza's place as headman of the treasure hunting expedition fronted by Flora Hawkes. Under Luvini the safari joined some Arab ivory and slave raiders in order to steal their booty, so that their disastrous trip to Africa would not be a total loss. But Luvini wanted it all for himself and decided that his men would kill not only the Arabs but the white members of the expedition too, except Flora Hawkes who he lusted after and desired. But Flora and her cohorts escaped into the jungle and stumbled into Jane, Lady Greystoke's safari of Waziri. While the Waziri were defending against Luvini's pursuing natives, Luvini himself snuck around behind and abducted Jane, not Flora.

With Jane held captive in a hut, Luvini entered to rape her. But, having loosened her bonds, she attacked him and killed him with his own knife. She then escaped from the village by climbing the palisade. The Waziri soon arrived and attempted to rescue her by burning the village and flushing everyone out. Not seeing Jane amid the panicked masses, they went into the smoldering village to look for her. They discovered the hut where she had been held, saw Luvini's corpse burnt beyond recognition with some of Jane's clothes nearby, and believed the body to be hers. They took the charred body away and buried it. *Tarzan and the Golden Lion*

Mabunu: A toothless, filthy, old Negro hag who scolded and abused Meriem while she was in the custody of the

Arab sheik, Amor ben Khatour. *The Son of Tarzan*

Madison, Naomi: The blonde leading lady in a Tarzan-like jungle motion picture to be shot on location in Africa. "The Madison," as she was called, was proud and selfish and not considered a very good actress by all but herself. She was prone to faint in dangerous situations. Naomi pretended to like the film's director, Thomas Orman, but really liked the leading man, Stanley Obroski, a Tarzan look-alike. She and Rhonda Terry, her almost identical stunt double, were eventually abducted by the group of Arabs who were escorting the company in Africa. The two women escaped, but they became separated during a lion attack and Naomi was retaken by the Arabs. She was then captured by the English speaking gorilla, Buckingham, who wanted her for himself. Tarzan saved her, though, and returned her to Orman. All the hardships that the Madison went through finally began to humble the movie star, but in a twist ending, she married a prince named Mudini. *Tarzan and the Lion Man*

Mafka: The great mind-controlling Columbian witch doctor–magician of the Kaji warrior women. Mafka's identical twin brother, Woora, ruled the rival Zuli warrior women. Mafka used the Gonfal diamond to control his people and bend them to his will. He also raised up Gonfala as a queen, but controlled her too. He was unable to mentally control Tarzan, though, and the Ape-man had Mafka bound and gagged and turned over to the people the old magician had so tyrannically ruled. They summarily killed him. *Tarzan the Magnificent*

Magra: The tall, svelte and beautiful brunette consort of Atan Thome. Magra mistook Tarzan for the missing Brian Gregory, who she thought she loved, then helped kidnap the Jungle Lord for Atan Thome. When Thome attempted to shoot Tarzan who he also thought was Brian, Magra knocked the weapon up causing Thome to miss. Even though Tarzan repeatedly denied that he was Brian Gregory, Magra did not believe him until he saved her from a lion. She then fell in love with him for who he really was, and Tarzan had to gently rebuke her for her love. After betraying Atan Thome, she willingly aided and accompanied Tarzan and the Gregory safari. While searching for and traveling in the land of Ashair, the Forbidden City, Magra was desired and abducted on several occasions, but escaped or was rescued each time. *Tarzan and the Forbidden City*

Makahago: The Chief of Buildings and a zertol (prince or noble) of King Elkomoelhago in the Minuni (Ant Men) city of Veltopismakus. Makahago was not very knowledgeable in his assignment. *Tarzan and the Ant Men*

Malbihn, Sven: A bearded Swede who searched for the kidnaped Jeanne Jacot (Meriem) for the reward offered by her father, and always carried a faded newspaper clipping with Meriem's picture on it. After becoming an ivory raider, he and his partner in crime, Carl Jenssen, first saw Meriem in an Arab camp. Later, when she was discovered in a cannibal village, the two Swedes lied to the chief and bought her for themselves. Malbihn desired Meriem, and after tricking Jenssen into leaving their camp, he attempted to rape her. She fought him off until the suspicious Jenssen returned and discovered them. Malbihn then killed his partner with a pistol. Tarzan arrived shortly thereafter and gave Malbihn a good shaking, and when the Jungle Lord saw Meriem he took her away.

Malbihn then shaved his beard and took on the name of Mr. Hanson to fool Meriem and Tarzan when he approached them at the Greystoke estate. The disguise worked and Malbihn collaborated with the Hon. Morison Baynes, who was in love with Meriem, to steal the young girl away from Tarzan and Jane. This they succeeded in doing, and after the Swede treacherously took Meriem from Baynes, he again attempted to rape her. This time Meriem knocked him out and escaped. Malbihn was later gored, trampled, and tossed by Tantor, the elephant, when the pachyderm saved Korak from an Arab camp. *The Son of Tarzan*

Malb'yat: "Yellow head." A blond haired man born with a human body and the mind of a gorilla. Malb'yat was created through the experimentation of the half-man, half-gorilla, God, in the Valley of Diamonds. Malb'yat became an outcast because he was born human in form and gorilla in mind instead of the other way around like the rest of his family. He went to live with the other mutant outcasts and freaks in cliff dwellings in the jungle where he became their king. Malb'yat spoke the Mangani language and traveled easily through the trees and behaved like a gorilla. Balza was his mate, and when Tarzan bested Malb'yat and took Rhonda Terry from him, Balza accompanied and aided the Ape-man. *Tarzan and the Lion Man*

Mal-gash: "Yellow-fang." The king of the Mangani of Ho-den, who were also known as the Servants of God to the man who thought he was Tarzan and to the people of Alemtejo. In order to communicate with them, the Alemtejos taught the apes some of their own language. *Tarzan and the Madman*

Malud: An arrogant knight in the lost medieval Valley of the Sepulcher. Sir Malud courted Princess Guinalda and was affronted by the American James Hunter Blake after Blake was accepted in the valley as a friend. To save face Malud challenged Blake to a duel. The American surprised all not only by beating Sir Malud but by succoring the wounded knight instead of killing him. *Tarzan, Lord of the Jungle*

Maluma: The white servant girl and hairdresser of Nemone, the queen of Cathne, the City of Gold. Whenever Maluma overheard Nemone talking about Tarzan, she would pass any vital information to Phobeg who would relay it to the Jungle Lord. *Tarzan and the City of Gold*

Mamka: An unfortunate female Mangani from the tribe of Kerchak that was killed by Numa, the lion. Tarzan decided that Numa must not be allowed to feel that he could kill Mangani with impunity so, with the help of other Mangani, he tormented the lion and daringly took Mamka's body away from him. *Jungle Tales of Tarzan*

Mangani: The great manlike anthropoid apes of the Tarzan adventures. For further information see Mangani in Section Three.

Manu: "Monkey" in the language of the great apes. The Manu spoke the language of the Mangani and often provided the Jungle Lord with information although it was usually gossip. Nkima was one of Tarzan's closest friends and monkey associates, but there were others. His first

Thomas Yeates illustration from *Tarzan: The Lost Adventure* (© 1995 Edgar Rice Burroughs, Inc.).

known monkey friend was a Manu without a name in *Jungle Tales of Tarzan*. This little primate saved Tarzan on one memorable occasion. Overcoming its fear of the larger Mangani of the tribe of Kerchak, the Manu pulled away the lion skin which disguised an unconscious Tarzan before the apes accidentally killed him, thinking he was an actual lion. And there was another Manu named Keta in the jungles of Sumatra in *Tarzan and the Foreign Legion*.

Maral: The wife of Avan, chief of the cave dwelling people of Clovi in Pellucidar. She was the mother of Ovan, who Tarzan saved from a *ryth*. Maral was originally from Zoram (which was known for its beautiful women), but was abducted by Avan to be his wife. She was kind to the captive Jana, the Red Flower of Zoram, and to Tarzan. *Tarzan at the Earth's Core*

Marcus, Gordon Z.: An older actor who played the part of the father of Naomi Madison's character in the *Lion Man* motion picture shot on location in Africa. *Tarzan and the Lion Man*

Marks, Joey: The boxing manager of the world champion "One Punch" Mullargan. Mullargan made Marks go with him on an African big game hunting trip. He had hay fever during it and sneezed all the time. After Marks lost the management of the arrogant champ, he and Mullargan got themselves and Tarzan captured by cannibals. With the Ape-man's aid, they escaped and Marks, impressed by the Jungle Lord, offered him an opportunity to be the next world champion. *Tarzan and the Champion* in *Tarzan and the Castaways*

Martha: A girl in the land of Midian who asked several questions. *Tarzan Triumphant*

Matsuo, Tokujo: The captain of the invading Japanese army in the Dutch East Indies who pursued the van der Meer family as they fled into the interior. After capturing Corrie van der Meer, Matsuo desired her. *Tarzan and the Foreign Legion*

Maya: A blonde girl Tarzan danced with at a Hollywood party that he crashed with some young acquaintances of his. Maya introduced Tarzan to some moviemakers. She also knew Rhonda Terry. *Tarzan and the Lion Man*

Mbeeda: The traitorous headman of Sheik Amor ben Khatour. Mbeeda was bribed by Carl Jensson and Sven Malbihn to steal Meriem from the Sheik. After leaving to get her, though, he was returned dead on a stretcher as a warning to the two Swedes. *The Son of Tarzan*

Mbonga: The chief of a cannibal tribe

that moved into Tarzan's jungle. Mbonga's son, Kulonga, killed Kala, Tarzan's ape foster mother, and was the very first human Tarzan had seen. As a result of the killing, the tribe of Mbonga became Tarzan's favorite people to terrorize and play tricks on.

As a young man seeking answers about God, Tarzan entered the village of Mbonga and confronted the village witch doctor, Rabba Kega. When Rabba Kega turned and fled, Tarzan pursued him and was almost killed by the spear-wielding chief himself, Mbonga. The Ape-man in turn almost killed Mbonga, but had pity on the old man and let him live. Later, the tribe of Mbonga captured Paul d'Arnot and began torturing him at the stake, but Tarzan rescued the Frenchman before they could kill and eat him. Not knowing that d'Arnot and Tarzan were alive and gone from the village d'Arnot's fellow troops entered in search of the two. When only bits of d'Arnot's clothing could be found, they believed their comrade had already been killed and eaten. So they massacred the whole village. *Tarzan of the Apes* and *Jungle Tales of Tarzan*

Mbuli: The headman of Atan Thome's safari who informed Thome that Tarzan sometimes gave the victory cry of the bull ape. *Tarzan and the Forbidden City*

M'duze: A gnarled old Negress who was the real power behind the throne of Nemone, the queen of Cathne, the City of Gold. Through blackmail M'duze was able to manipulate the beautiful queen who, it was rumored, might actually be M'duze's daughter. M'duze became concerned about Tarzan's increasing influence with Nemone and feared that the Ape-man would give the queen the

courage to get rid of her, so she constantly interrupted the two when they were left alone. M'duze then plotted with Tomos, the captain of the guard, and Erot, the one time favorite of the queen, to kill Tarzan. Their plots failed, but in a fit of rage, Nemone killed M'duze with a dagger. *Tarzan and the City of Gold*

Medek: A fat black eunuch slave in the temple of Kavandavanda in the village of the Kavuru. Medek, with an unclean sound, called the guardian leopards into the garden of the temple to feed or to attack anyone trying to escape. The large eunuch was posted as the sentry outside Jane and Annette's door, and Ogdli killed him when he came to help the two women escape. *Tarzan's Quest*

Melrose: The tail-gunner of the B-24 bomber, *Lovely Lady*. He was killed while the pilot, Captain Jerry Lucas, was speaking to him when the plane came under attack. In the delirium of his later fever, Jerry spoke to the dead Melrose. *Tarzan and the Foreign Legion*

Melton: A guide for the world heavyweight boxing champion "One Punch" Mullargan and his manager, Joey Marks, when they were hunting big game in Africa. He did not care for Mullargan or Marks. When Tarzan approached him, Melton did not recognize the Jungle Lord and attempted to draw his pistol on him. But the Ape-man grabbed his gun hand and gave him a good shaking. Melton then became cooperative. *Tarzan and the Champion* in *Tarzan and the Castaways*

Mem-sahib: A native term, similar to Bwana, for female leaders and masters. The Waziri used it in reference to Jane.

Menofra: A prostitute, considered masculine and not very pretty, but who became the wife of Phoros, the usurping dictator of Athne, the City of Ivory. When Phoros got drunk, he attacked and wounded Menofra because he feared her jealousy of the beautiful warrior woman, Gonfala. To try and stop her unfaithful husband from making advances toward Gonfala, she ordered a priest to marry Gonfala to Stanley Wood in the hopes that Phoros would not violate their marriage vows. Menofra was killed during a battle with Cathne, the City of Gold. *Tarzan the Magnificent*

Mentheb: The wise, but jealous, wife of King Herat in Thobos, the rival city of Ashair, the Forbidden City, and the aunt of Thetan. Queen Mentheb took a liking to Tarzan and his physical prowess, and after falling into an arena where he was battling two lions, she was saved by the Jungle Lord. *Tarzan and the Forbidden City*

Meredonleni: A sentry in the lost city of Ur who was shot in the chest by Tarzan's arrow. *Tarzan: The Lost Adventure*

Meriem: Korak's black-haired and black-eyed beautiful French wife whose real name was Jeanne Jacot. As a seven year old, she was kidnaped by the Arab sheik Amor ben Khatour in revenge against her father, Capt. Armand Jacot, Prince de Cadrenet, of the French Foreign Legion for having prosecuted and executed the Sheik's nephew, Achmet ben Houdin. Capt. Jacot posted a reward for his daughter's return.

Sheik Khatour changed her name to Meriem and abusively raised her for several years. Through time Meriem almost completely forgot her past and her native French language as she lived with the Arabs and learned their tongue. Her only

friend and confidant during this period was her ugly ivory headed doll named Geeka, which was also the name of the native boy who gave it to her. When Korak discovered Meriem and rescued her from the abusive Sheik, the two lived in the jungle for several years along with Akut, the great ape. Meriem learned the language of the Mangani from them, how to live in the jungle and travel through the trees. During this time she loved Korak as a brother.

After Tarzan rescued her from some Swedish hunters who sought the reward for her, he took Meriem to his bungalow and placed her under the loving care of Jane who, unbeknownst to Meriem, was Korak's mother. At this time she was 16 years old. She called Tarzan "Bwana" after hearing the Waziri use that term, and called Jane "My Dear," because she had heard Tarzan refer to his wife by that endearment. Jane educated Meriem by teaching her English and French. The latter learned quickly because it was her forgotten native tongue. When a young Englishman, Morison Baynes, visited the Greystokes he fell in love with Meriem and courted her. She considered the marriage, only because she was starting to forget about Korak. But then she was kidnaped again by one of the Swedes in cahoots with Baynes. Although she soon escaped, she was taken again by Sheik Khatour. This time she was saved from the dreadful Arab by Korak and Tantor.

Meriem finally realized that she was in love with Korak and they were married. She was then reunited with her father at the Greystokes' in England. Meriem and Korak had at least one child named Jack "Jackie"

Jr. *The Son of Tarzan* and *Tarzan and the Ant Men*

Mesnek: The female slave to Queen Mentheb in Thobos. *Tarzan and the Forbidden City*

Messenger of Death: One of the Pal-ul-donian names given to Korak, the Killer, by Ta-den, the Ho-don. With his Enfield rifle, the son of Tarzan killed High Priest Lu-don, the German Erich Obergatz, Chief Mo-sar, and the priest, Pan-sat. He slaughtered them all in the altar room of the Temple of the Gryf in the city of A-lur before they could offer Tarzan as a sacrifice. *Tarzan the Terrible*

Messenger of the Great God: One of the Pal-ul-donian names given to Korak, the Killer, by Ta-den, the Ho-don. With his Enfield rifle, the son of Tarzan killed High Priest Lu-don, the German Erich Obergatz, Chief Mo-sar, and the priest, Pan-sat, in the altar room of the Temple of the Gryf in the city of A-lur before they could offer Tarzan as a sacrifice. *Tarzan the Terrible*

Metak: The powerful son of Herog XVI, king of the maniac city Xuja. At the sight of the beautiful and bare-breasted Bertha Kircher, Metak went into a lustful frenzy and after picking her up bodily he fled with her through the palace. When Tarzan arrived he attacked Metak and a tremendous battle ensued. The great strength of the Ape-man finally won out and he pitched Metak out of a window and into a lion pit. *Tarzan the Untamed*

Metellus, Caecilius: One of the nobles and a centurion in the lost Roman city of Castra Mare. Metellus was the best friend of the heir to the throne, Cassius Hasta. The jealous and conniving Fulvus Fupus revealed his suspicions about Erich von Harben being a spy to Metellus in the baths, to try to spread propaganda against the visitor. Caecilius Metellus was later captured by warriors of the rival city Castra Sanguinarius and imprisoned with Tarzan and several others in the dungeons to await the great games. After surviving the games Metellus accompanied the triumphant Tarzan and the new and true Caesar, Cassius Hasta, back to Castra Mare. *Tarzan and the Lost Empire*

M'ganwazam: The chief of the cannibal village of Waganwazam. M'-ganwazam betrayed both Jane and Tarzan at separate times in their respective escapes from, and search for, Nikolas Rokoff. *The Beasts of Tarzan*

Mgungu, Gato: The older, fat chief of the Secret Order of the Leopard Men who used a regular looking village as a front for the organization. Before becoming the chief of the Leopard Men, Gato Mgungu had been the chief of a regular village. When Utenga villagers, accompanied by Tarzan, attacked Gato Mgungu and the Leopard Men in force, their village was razed and burned to the ground. *Tarzan and the Leopard Men*

Michel: The serving boy and personal body servant to the American James Hunter Blake after Blake was accepted as a friend in the Valley of the Sepulcher. *Tarzan, Lord of the Jungle*

Miltoon: The unfortunate little crooked legged servant of King Kurvandi in the lost city of Ur. Miltoon mentioned that Tarzan was very strong. But in an insane test to determine if Miltoon was lying about Tarzan's strength, the jealous king had his old servant stand with fruit on the top of his head so that he could shoot an arrow at it. Miltoon took the arrow in the eye and died. *Tarzan: The Lost Adventure*

Minsky, Ivan: A Russian cohort of the ivory poacher Tom Crump who he plotted with to abduct Sandra Pickerall for a reward. As time went by Minsky began hating and resenting Crump. After their porters deserted them, the two surrendered to the Alemtejos and were made their slave prisoners. During a raid they escaped and discovered the Galla Moslem gold mine. In greed they took more than they could easily carry, and after suffering much fatigue and hunger, Crump went crazy and dashed Minsky's brains out with a gold nugget. *Tarzan and the Madman*

Miranda, Esteban: A very well-built Spanish actor who stood six foot three inches tall and looked remarkably like Tarzan. In *Tarzan and the Golden Lion* Esteban was recruited to impersonate Tarzan by Flora Hawkes, to help her and some henchmen steal gold from the lost city of Opar. Along the way Esteban fell in love with Flora and became jealous of their male companions.

In Africa, Esteban plunged into his role. All who encountered him—humans and animals alike—believed him to be the real Tarzan, although they were surprised by his unusual cruelty. Esteban even fooled the Waziri and Jane, and he started to believe that he really was the Jungle Lord. But after several adventures Jad-bal-ja, the Golden Lion, and the real Tarzan met up and finally hunted Esteban down. He ran and they believed he drowned in a river, but he did not. He was captured by the Obebe tribe of cannibals, chained, and held captive.

At the beginning of *Tarzan and*

the Ant Men it was revealed that Esteban was held a captive of the Obebe for a year. During that time the resourceful Spaniard learned the Obebe language and used the superstitious fears of the natives to his advantage by convincing Uhha, the young daughter of the witch doctor, to release him, give him weapons and show him the way out of the village. He also knavishly took her hostage. After wandering around in the jungle for a while, Uhha knocked Esteban out while he slept, and escaped. He awakened with amnesia and was mentally unstable. In this condition he was found by a Waziri warrior who mistook him for Tarzan. He was taken to the Greystoke bungalow and all there believed him to be Tarzan, too, including Jane. They sent for a surgeon who performed an operation which cured Esteban of his amnesia and mental derangement. But, the crafty Spaniard decided to continue to fool everyone that he was the Lord of the Jungle. A reformed Flora Hawkes, however, was again working for the Greystokes and revealed the truth about Esteban. *Tarzan and the Golden Lion* and *Tarzan and the Ant Men*

Mirando: The unfortunate warrior from the tribe of Mbonga who ran unexpectedly into Tarzan in the jungle near the village. In surprise Mirando ran screaming back home, attracting the attention of the other villagers. In the meantime, Tarzan did not have time to completely escape. Coming into the village itself, he threw his noose around Mirando and hoisted the warrior into the air, frightening the onlookers. From high in a village tree Tarzan killed Mirando and then hurled his body at the startled villagers. *Tarzan of the Apes*

Molak: The Mangani king of the tribe of Akut who Tarzan killed shortly after the Jungle Lord was marooned on Jungle Island. *The Beasts of Tarzan*

Momaya: The mother of Tibo and wife of Ibeto. Momaya distrusted her witch doctors and felt Tarzan's power was greater. But when Tibo was taken by Tarzan, Momaya steeled herself and sought out the reclusive leper witch doctor Bukawai. On the way she found Tibo on her own, but Bukawai took credit for it and demanded payment. Momaya refused to pay and Bukawai kidnaped Tibo himself. *Jungle Tales of Tarzan*

Momulla: A Maori sailor aboard the *Crowie* who helped lead a mutiny. After abducting Jane and the Mosula woman from Tarzan on Jungle Island, Momulla was forced to work the ship when the Ape-man took over. *The Beasts of Tarzan*

Monsieur Flaubert: Count Raoul de Coude's second in his pistol duel with Tarzan. *The Return of Tarzan*

Monsieur Thuran: see **Rokoff, Nikolas**

Montmorency, Richard: A knight and the Keeper of the Gate the day James Hunter Blake was escorted under guard into the medieval Valley of the Sepulcher. Once Blake was accepted as an ally, Sir Richard helped train him in the customs and ways of war of his lost civilization. *Tarzan, Lord of the Jungle*

Moore, Harold: The studious young tutor of Jack Clayton (Korak) who retired after being attacked and tied up by Jack who desired to see the circus. *The Son of Tarzan*

Mori, Antonio (Tony): A not very well educated communist Filipino who wanted independence for the Philippines and joined Peter Zveri's communist fund-raising expedition to Opar. Mori eventually became disillusioned with the whole communist ideal and disavowed it. Because of this he received protection from Tarzan while being guided out of the Jungle. *Tarzan the Invincible*

Morley: A knight in the Castle of the Sepulcher under King Bohun's rule in the lost medieval Valley of the Sepulcher. Sir Morley was on guard with Sir Bulland at the portcullis near the pass out of the north end of the valley when the Arab raiders of Sheik Ibn Jad attacked. *Tarzan, Lord of the Jungle*

Mo-sar: "Short-nose." A Ho-don chief from Tu-lur, the Bright City. His great-grandfather was the king of Pal-ul-don and therefore he had a real claim to the throne of A-lur, the City of Light, the Pal-ul-don's capital. For political reasons Ko-tan, king of A-lur, allowed Mo-sar's son, Bu-lot, to be betrothed to his daughter, O-lo-a. After Bu-lot killed Ko-tan in a drunken rage, he and his father, Mo-sar, rushed to the royal chambers to abduct O-lo-a. When they arrived there, Mo-sar took one look at the prisoner, Jane Clayton (who was being held in the chambers), and abducted her for his wife.

Knowing that Mo-sar was the next in line to be king, Lu-don, the high priest of A-lur who wanted to be the absolute political and religious power in all Pal-ul-don, decided to set Mo-sar up as a puppet king under him. When Tarzan was captured and put on the altar to be sacrificed, Korak arrived with his Enfield rifle and shot and killed Lu-don and Mo-sar before they could slay the Jungle Lord. *Tarzan the Terrible*

Mosula Woman: After running away from an undesirable marriage in her village, the Mosula Woman found shelter in the bottom of a canoe along the Ugambi River. She was taken in by Mugambi and the beasts of Tarzan who were traveling by canoe to the *Kincaid*. She was then abducted along with Jane by the mutineers of the *Crowie*. After being rescued, the Mosula Woman decided to remain with the Waziri and be Mugambi's wife. *The Beasts of Tarzan*

Motlog: Originally from the Arab tribe of el-Harb Motlog rode with Sheik Ibn Jad on the search for the fabled treasure-filled city of Nimmr. *Tarzan, Lord of the Jungle*

Mountford, Lady: Killed by the Kaji warrior women because she gave birth to a daughter — Gonfala — and not a son. *Tarzan the Magnificent*

Mountford, Lord: Presumed lost in Africa for 20 years with his wife. Trying to escape the Kaji country, he was discovered by Stanley Wood, Robert van Eyk, Troll, and Spike. Before he died, Lord Mountford warned them of the danger there. *Tarzan the Magnificent*

Mourak, Abdul: The large commander of some Abyssinian soldiers in the jungle searching for Achmet Zek. Mourak captured Albert Werper, but decided to let him go if the Oparian gold that Werper said was buried at the razed Greystoke estate was actually there. They met up with Zek and his Arabs, also looking for the gold, and a battle ensued that resulted in almost all of Mourak's men being killed. Mourak later found and captured a lost and wandering Jane Clayton. While camping, he and the remainder of his men were attacked by hungry lions, but Tarzan saved Jane and carried her off. *Tarzan and the Jewels of Opar*

1. Mpingu: A Bagego slave in the household of Dion Splendidus in the lost Roman city of Castra Sanguinarius. Mpingu interpreted for the hiding Tarzan until the Jungle Lord learned the Latin language fluently. The suspicious Romans took Mpingu and tortured him until he revealed where Tarzan was hiding. *Tarzan and the Lost Empire.*

2. Mpingu: The chief of the Buiroos cannibal tribe and father of Chemungo. When Mpingu's vengeful son brought a wounded Tarzan to his village, Mpingu let the Ape-man live to see if any evil would come of it. While captive, Tarzan swayed and chanted, then called Tantor to his rescue. *Tarzan and the Forbidden City* and *Tarzan and Jungle Murders* in *Tarzan and the Castaways*

Mpugu: The native chief of a village friendly to whites where Tarzan left his feverish look-alike, Stanley Obroski. Obroski died of the fever while in the chief's keeping. *Tarzan and the Lion Man*

Mr. Hanson: see **Sven Malbihn**

Mrs. Billings: see **Akut**

Muda, Taku: The chief of a Sumatra kampong that gave asylum to the fleeing van der Meers. When the Japanese arrived and discovered that they had given assistance to the Dutch family, the village was burned. *Tarzan and the Foreign Legion*

Mugambi: A huge, intelligent chief of the Wagambi of Ugambi who Tarzan waylaid and made assist him and his "beasts" in *The Beasts of Tarzan*. After some time, these beasts of Tarzan began following and obeying Mugambi. The chief of the Wagambi became a devoted friend of the Ape-man, joined the Waziri, and took a Mosula woman to wife. Well-built and valiant, Mugambi fought side by side with Tarzan on several occasions and defended both him

and Jane. In *The Jewels of Opar* Mugambi searched for Jane and stole Tarzan's pouch of jewels from Albert Werper. They were later stolen from Mugambi by Chulk, the Mangani. *The Beasts of Tarzan* and *Tarzan and the Jewels of Opar*

Mukarram, Abdul: The young right-hand man of Sheik Ibn Aswad. After Aswad's group abducted Victoria Custer, Abdul desired her and became obsessed with her. At first he tried to make friends with her, eventually professing his love for her. But Victoria refused him. So after killing her guard, he abducted her for himself, and while traveling through the jungle, attempted to rape her. She was saved by Nu, the son of Nu, of the Niocene, who killed Abdul by biting through his jugular. *The Eternal Savage (Lover)*

Mullargan, "One Punch": The arrogant, dirty-fighting, heavyweight boxing champion of the world. After winning the title, he fulfilled a long-time dream by going to Africa to do some big game hunting. There he bullied and hit the native porters working in his safari. He also used the same unfair style in his hunting, slaughtering herds of animals with a machine gun. After tracking Mullargan and his manager, Joey Marks, Tarzan fought One Punch one on one. The Ape-man got the better of the world champion, but before he could finish the fight , they were attacked and captured by the Babangos cannibal tribe. Mullargan was impressed with Tarzan's strength, and apologized for killing the animals. They helped each other escape, but were discovered leaving. After a great defensive struggle,

Mullargan was retaken. One Punch made another attempt at escape, but it too failed. When a lion entered the village and scared the natives away, it went for Mullargan, but Tarzan saved him. The Jungle Lord then ordered the champ and his party to leave Africa. *Tarzan and the Champion* in *Tarzan and the Castaways*

Mulungu: The native name for God, used by many tribes including the Waziri.

1. Mumga: An old toothless female Mangani in the tribe of Kerchak. *Jungle Tales of Tarzan*

2. Mumga: The old toothless priestess in the temple of the Leopard Men who helped prepare Kali Bwana to be the high priestess of the Leopard God. *Tarzan and the Leopard Men*

Munan-go-Keewati (or Munango-Keewati): The name given to Tarzan by the cannibal tribe of Mbonga. It meant forest god, devil god, white devil god, or demon.

Mungo: A bull Mangani who stole one of the wives of Thaka in the tribe of Tarzan (Kerchak). *Tarzan of the Apes*

Mutimbwa: Chief of the cannibal Waruturi tribe. Mutimbwa's tribe captured God, the man who thought he was Tarzan, and Sandra Pickerall. *Tarzan and the Madman*

Muviri: A Waziri warrior who was with Tarzan when he first found Meriem and saved her from rape in the camp of Sven Malbihn. *The Son of Tarzan*

Muviro: A member of the Waziri tribe and a faithful friend of Tarzan. Muviro was the hereditary chief of the Waziri and the subchief to Tarzan, their war chief. He and the Waziri

Opposite: **J. Allen St. John illustration from *The Beasts of Tarzan* (© 1916 Edgar Rice Burroughs, Inc.).**

often came to Tarzan's rescue and accompanied him on many adventures. His son, Wasimbu, became Jane's personal bodyguard and servant. Muviro went in search of the Kavuru, who he believed had abducted his daughter, Buira. *Tarzan and the Lost Empire, Tarzan at the Earth's Core, Tarzan the Invincible, Tarzan Triumphant, Tarzan's Quest, Tarzan and the Champion* in *Tarzan and the Castaways,* and *Tarzan and the Tarzan Twins*

muzimo: A native term for the protecting spirit of an ancestor. A *muzimo* often took the form of animals such as birds and monkeys, and natives prayed and made offerings to these spirits for protection. In *Tarzan and the Leopard Men* the Apeman was thought to be the *muzimo* of the native youth Orando. The monkey Nkima was also thought to be a *muzimo* in the same book, and in *Tarzan and the Lost Empire.*

M'walot: An old Mangani friend of Tarzan from the tribe of Toyat. M'walot remembered the Ape-man as an ally and freed him from the bonds that Arabs had put on him after the Jungle Lord had been rescued by Tantor, the elephant, and taken into the jungle. *Tarzan, Lord of the Jungle*

M'wa-lot: The leader of the tribe of club-wielding Sagoths in the land of Pellucidar that caught Tarzan in one of their snares. *Tarzan at the Earth's Core*

Mweeza: A native from the village of Mbonga who, after Tarzan impersonated a lion, was attacked by a real lion inside the village and taken into the jungle to be eaten. Because of his impersonation, the villagers thought Tarzan was a shape-changer. *Jungle Tales of Tarzan*

My Dear: The name given to Jane by

Meriem after she heard Tarzan refer to his wife by this term of endearment. *The Son of Tarzan*

Naika: The daughter of Gupingu, the witch doctor of the Bukena village, near the Kavuru country. Naika was taken by the Kavuru warrior, Ydeni, but Tarzan came and took her from him and returned the girl to her village. When she learned that her village had captured some Waziri friends of Tarzan, she tried to persuade her people not to kill them. *Tarzan's Quest*

Naliny: A Galla native who was the father of Tabo and Ulala (Fejjuan). *Tarzan, Lord of the Jungle*

Nao: A young priestess of Opar who experienced love at first sight with the captured American, Wayne Colt. Nao served Colt his food. In order to free him she killed Frig, the keymaster of Opar, took his keys and released Colt. Before the American left, they kissed, and Nao gave him her dagger. *Tarzan the Invincible*

Naratu: The large jealous wife of the runaway native sergeant, Usanga, who feared Naratu's wrath. *Tarzan the Untamed*

Natando: One of the native scouts searching with Dr. Karl von Harben for the his daughter, Gretchen. *Tarzan and the Tarzan Twins*

Nat-ul: The daughter of Tha, and the sister of Aht (her only brother). Nat-ul was a beautiful cavewoman from the Niocene. She looked like, and was some how linked with, the modern day woman Victoria Custer. In some way, they were one and the same. In the Niocene Nat-ul loved Nu, and he went off to prove his worthiness by slaying Oo, the saber-toothed tiger. When, through the effects of an earthquake, Victoria of the present became Nat-ul in the Niocene, she was waiting for Nu to return with the head of Oo. At that point, Nat-ul was abducted by a rival to Nu named Hud. She killed Hud and ended up being pursued by Tur of the boat building people. Nu gave chase and he and Nat-ul finally got back together after several adventures. Despite all this Nu stubbornly went out again to hunt for the head of Oo to prove his love for Nat-ul. While he was gone another earthquake struck and Nat-ul became Victoria Custer in the present time. See also **Victoria Custer**. *The Eternal Savage (Lover)*

Neeta: A young Mangani from the tribe of Kerchak who drowned. *Tarzan of the Apes*

Nemone: The beautiful, but jealous, temperamental queen of Cathne, the City of Gold. She became queen at the age of 12 and was manipulated and blackmailed by an old black woman named M'duze who, it was speculated, was Nemone's mother. The queen was also considered a bit unstable mentally. She was jealous of her beauty and had all good-looking women either mutilated or killed.

Queen Nemone always had a rather large and ferocious lion by her side named Belthar who she felt linked to in life. Belthar did not particularly like Tarzan, but Nemone desired the Jungle Lord and offered him nobility in her kingdom if he would be her mate. Tarzan had a difficult time resisting Nemone's allure and beauty, but any liaison was always interrupted by M'duze. Nemone finally became fed up with M'duze's control and killed her in a fit of rage. Tarzan then pushed her too far and she imprisoned him. Afterwards she had Belthar attack the Lord of the Jungle in an arranged hunt. But Jad-bal-ja, the Golden Lion, arrived just in time and killed

Belthar. When Nemone saw her lion dead, she killed herself with a dagger to fulfill her own belief of their lives being inextricably linked. Tarzan buried Nemone and Belthar next to each other. *Tarzan and the City of Gold*

Niaka: A Galla slave and the brother of Hifam, an unruly slave, in Cathne, the City of Gold. Niaka was made the headman of the slaves in the quarry of Cathne and lived alone with his wife in his own hut. When Tarzan informed him that he had helped Hifam escape, Niaka was grateful and returned the favor to Tarzan by hiding Doria, the beautiful daughter of Thudos, from Queen Nemone in his hut. *Tarzan and the City of Gold*

Nkima: The name of a small monkey that accompanied Tarzan on several adventures and often assisted him. Nkima believed that all creatures were out to eat him and, alone, he was usually miserable and afraid. But in the security of Tarzan's arms or safely on his shoulder, Nkima became boastful, scolding, and rather bloodthirsty. He screamed for the Jungle Lord to kill everything, and boldly threatened anyone and anything. Nkima helped Tarzan on several occasions by biting through his bonds or scampering off to find and bring Muviro and the Waziri to his assistance whether at the Jungle Lord's behest or not.

Nkima was mistaken a few times for the spirit of various dead relatives of different natives and, more specifically, the spirit of Nyamwegi, a native killed by the Leopard Men, in *Tarzan and the Leopard Men*. He was also known and trusted enough by Jad-bal-ja to be allowed to ride on the Golden Lion's back. In *Tarzan's Quest* Nkima finally found a mate, but he later abandoned her to save himself from being attacked by the rest of her tribe. In the same book, Nkima, for his part in the adventure, received an equal portion of the life-prolonging elixir pills that Tarzan and four others got. In *Tarzan and the Foreign Legion* it was confirmed that he had received the pills and that they had worked. *Tarzan and the Lost Empire, Tarzan the Invincible, Tarzan and the Leopard Men, Tarzan's Quest,* and *Tarzan: The Lost Adventure*

Noice, Clarence: The sound director for the *Lion Man*, a motion picture he and his fellow crew members were trying to shoot on location in Africa. Noice was killed in an ambush in a grass field by the heart-eating cannibals, the Bansutos. *Tarzan and the Lion Man*

Nsenene: A happy and good natured native girl from the village of Bobolo. Nsenene was secretly in love with the white trader, Kid, and when Nsenene learned that Chief Bobolo was intent on killing Kid, she went out and warned him. She also informed him of the capture of a white woman named Kali Bwana. When Nsenene learned that Kid was interested in this woman the young native girl became a little jealous. Kid sensing her hurt and jealousy lied and told Nsenene that Kali was his sister, which, as it turned out, she really was. *Tarzan and the Leopard Men*

Ntale: The self-appointed chief of the previously leaderless slave raiding band of *shiftas* after their Italian leader, Dominic Capietro, was murdered by Leon Stabutch, and their original headman was killed by Tarzan. Ntale decided to kill the Chicago gangster Danny "Gunner" Patrick, who was his prisoner, but

Gunner shot and killed him instead. *Tarzan Triumphant*

Nu: The father of Nu. The senior Nu was the chief of chiefs, or king, of their cave village in the Niocene period of Earth's history. He went to look for his son after the village began moving to a new location. *The Eternal Savage (Lover)*

Nu, the son of Nu: A large man from the Niocene period of Earth's history. Nu's father was the chief of chiefs of his tribe. Nu spoke the Mangani language as well as his own tribal tongue.

Nu, the son of Nu, was in love with the cavewoman, Nat-ul. With his only weapons being a stone-tipped spear, an axe and a knife, he found and slew Oo, the saber-toothed tiger, to prove his love to her. During this hunt Nu was knocked out and trapped in a cave by an earthquake where he remained hermetically sealed for 100,000 years. He was reawakened by another earthquake in the present not knowing that any time had elapsed.

Victoria Custer, a young girl who looked just like Nat-ul and was visiting the Greystokes' African estate, was led to Nu in the cave and cared for him. She was then abducted by Arabs, and Nu was found by a search party and taken in by the Greystokes who believed the troglodyte knew where Victoria was. Barney, Victoria's brother, taught Nu English so that they could obtain information from him about Victoria's disappearance. Once they learned that Nu knew nothing, the caveman escaped from the Greystoke bungalow to track Victoria because he believed that she was his Nat-ul.

When the two met, Victoria "became" Nat-ul and they were back in the Niocene period of Earth's existence. There Nu and Nat-ul were still in love and the troglodyte was still going off to hunt for the head of Oo. After another caveman carried Nat-ul off, Nu pursued them. Several adventures later, Nat-ul and Nu were finally reunited but Nu stubbornly went off yet again for the head of Oo. Another earthquake struck and Nat-ul woke up as Victoria Custer at the Greystokes'. She went directly to a nearby cave that had been unearthed by the earthquake and found the skeleton of a large caveman with the skull of a saber-toothed tiger nearby. *The Eternal Savage (Lover)*

Numa, King of Beasts, Emperor of All Created Things: The name of the lion installed as the ruler of the Bolgani in the Valley of the Palace of Diamonds which was located behind Opar. The Bolgani would offer human sacrifices to Numa, and when they attempted to offer High Priestess La of Opar, Tarzan entered the room and with his spear killed the King of Beasts, Emperor of All Created Things. When Jad-bal-ja arrived Tarzan proclaimed the Golden Lion the new ruler of the Bolgani. *Tarzan and the Golden Lion*

Numa of the Gulch: While wreaking his vengeance on the German army Tarzan discovered a small cave that led into a gulch with steep cliff-like sides. The only way in and out of the gulch was through the cave, although someone with the climbing ability and strength of Tarzan could gain access to it by scaling its steep sides. Tarzan discovered, the hard way, that the cave and gulch were the lair of Numa, the lion. After escaping this black-maned demon by climbing the sheer walls of the gulch, Tarzan went around to the cave entrance and blocked it with rocks and boulders and trapped Numa inside. After capturing Major Schneider, who he thought was the leader of the regiment that killed Jane, the Jungle Lord put the German officer in the gulch for the famished Numa to eat. Later Tarzan subdued Numa and led him on a leash into a German machine gun trench to attack the enemy. The lion fed well and escaped from Tarzan.

Later, Numa attacked and killed the horse ridden by Bertha Kircher, the German spy, and she became trapped under the dead horse's body. Tarzan arrived on the scene and saved Kircher by momentarily driving the familiar lion away without a battle. After Kircher knocked Tarzan unconscious and left him lying on the jungle path, Sheeta, the leopard, took a hungry interest in the prostrate and defenseless Ape-man. As it was about to dine on him, Numa of the gulch appeared and killed the leopard, because the great cat had gained respect for this human king of beasts. *Tarzan the Untamed*

Numa of the pit: Tarzan fed and then rescued a young but impressively large and completely black lion that was trapped in a pit. Later, after the plane they were flying in was forced to land in a desert gorge, Bertha Kircher and Lt. Harold Percy Smith-Oldwick were approached by Numa of the pit. After they succeeded in eluding the carnivore, Tarzan, who had tracked their plane, arrived. The great black Numa remembered the Ape-man's kindnesses to him and was submissive to the Jungle Lord. Numa of the pit helped Tarzan escape the maniac citizens of the lost city of Xuja, but later wandered away from the Jungle Lord, Kircher, and Smith-Oldwick before their final standoff with the lions and people of Xuja. *Tarzan the Untamed*

Numabo: The chief of the cannibal Wamabos who aided and befriended Usanga and his soldiers. Numabo and his warriors captured the downed English pilot Lt. Harold Percy Smith-Oldwick and were preparing to eat him when Tarzan literally fell into their hands from a broken branch. Numabo decided to make it a two-course banquet and added the Lord of the Jungle to the menu. Tarzan and Smith-Oldwick escaped with the aid of the German spy, Bertha Kircher, and several bulls from the Mangani tribe of Go-lat. *Tarzan the Untamed*

Numgo: An old bull Mangani from the tribe of Kerchak who told Tarzan that he, Numgo, was God when Tarzan questioned the great ape about deity. *Jungle Tales of Tarzan*

Nyalwa: The new chief of the Betetes cannibal pygmy tribe after their old chief, Rebega, was killed by Tarzan's arrow when they attempted to kill and eat the white woman, Kali Bwana. Nyalwa was considered brave, but when Tarzan, who later became a prisoner in the village, called the Mangani tribe of Zutho to his aid, the new chief showed his fear. *Tarzan and the Leopard Men*

Nyama: A beautiful, English speaking native girl who was a prisoner in the dungeons of the lost city of Ur with Jean Hanson. Nyama had been made the wife of Kurvandi, the king of Ur, but because she did not want to be his wife she made him miserable. She helped Tarzan and Jean escape Ur. *Tarzan: The Lost Adventure*

Nyamwegi: A native from Tumbai village who was killed by the Leopard Men while traveling back to his home after courting a girl from Kibbu village. Orando, the son of the chief of the Kibbu, thought that Nkima was the new physical manifestation of the spirit of Nyamwegi, or his *muzimo*. *Tarzan and the Leopard Men*

Nyuto: The chief of the native Bagego tribe of the Buliso clan at the west end of the valley of the Lost Empire in the Wiramwazi Mountains. *Tarzan and the Lost Empire*

Oah: A traitorous priestess of Opar who collaborated with Cadj to overthrow La. After La fled with Tarzan, Cadj proclaimed himself king of Opar and made Oah his new figurehead high priestess. When Tarzan and La returned with an army of the intelligent Bolgani and simpleminded Gomangani from the Valley of the Palace of Diamonds, Cadj was killed by Jad-bal-ja and Oah was forgiven by La. In *Tarzan the Invincible* Oah proclaimed herself High Priestess of the Flaming God and made Dooth her high priest after imprisoning La. Because they reigned with a tyrant hand they were both subsequently killed by the Oparians when La was seen returning with Tarzan. *Tarzan and the Golden Lion* and *Tarzan the Invincible*

Obambi: The serving "boy" and cook of the American geologist Lafayette Smith. Lafayette ordered Obambi to leave him while he studied the rock formations of the Ghenzi Mountains. When Smith did not reappear, Obambi went with the American gangster Danny "Gunner" Patrick to look for him. *Tarzan Triumphant*

Obebe: The old chief of a cannibal tribe on the Ugogo River. In *Tarzan and the Golden Lion* Obebe captured the actor and Tarzan impersonator, Esteban Miranda, and wanted to kill and eat him because he believed him to be the real Tarzan. The witch doctor, Khamis, however, believed that Miranda was the river devil in the form of Tarzan. Until it could be decided which he was, they chained Miranda in a hut. In *Tarzan and the Ant Men* he escaped the Obebe, and the real Tarzan was captured and brought back to the village to be tortured. But the Ape-man broke his bonds and chased Obebe into a hut. Then Tarzan threw Khamis through the roof of the same hut. Obebe, thinking it was Tarzan breaking in, repeatedly stabbed the body and killed the witch doctor. *Tarzan and the Golden Lion* and *Tarzan and the Ant Men*

Obergatz, Erich: The lieutenant in the German army, and second in command to Hauptmann Fritz Schneider in the company that raided and pillaged the Greystoke estate while Tarzan was away. After the Germans took Jane alive in the attack, Obergatz was put in charge of transporting her as they went deep into the interior. There they stumbled into the land of Pal-ul-don during the dry season and were attacked by a band of Ho-don warriors. They captured Jane but Obergatz got away. While searching through the valley for a way out Obergatz stumbled onto the cross-bred tribe of Waz-ho-don. He learned their language and beliefs and pretended to be a deity. They treated him well, until a woman attempted to stab him as proof that he was mortal. Obergatz fled in fear.

After being alone for a while his mental stability began to falter. In this condition, he stumbled onto Jane, who had escaped and was living primitively on her own. She warned him off, but when the lustful Obergatz attempted to invade her tree house she stabbed him with her spear. The German, wounded

and now almost completely insane, wandered to the city of A-lur and pretended to be their god, Jad-ben-Otho. In his unstable condition, he started to believe that he really was "The Great God," and when Tarzan was captured he attempted to sacrifice the Ape-man upon an altar. Before the sacrifice could take place, though, Korak arrived and shot and killed Obergatz with his Enfield rifle. *Tarzan the Terrible*

Obroski, Stanley: A muscular world champion marathoner who was a Tarzan look-alike. Obroski was cast to play the role of the Lion Man in a Tarzan-like Hollywood motion picture of the same name to be shot on location in Africa. During the production he became romantically interested in his leading lady, Naomi Madison. On the trek to the location Obroski slept a lot. When they were ambushed in a grass field by Bansuto cannibals, he ran blindly in fear.

Obroski was captured by the Bansutos and was about to be tortured and eaten when he finally started to fight back. Tarzan, watching from a tree, admired the man's courage and was surprised by his likeness to himself. He rescued Obroski and the two men traveled together. Obroski contracted a fever, so Tarzan took him to a native village to be taken care of. But the former marathoner eventually died. All of the cast and crew mistook Tarzan for Obroski. Not wanting to reveal his true identity and shame Obroski's name, the Jungle Lord finished shooting the picture in the place of his erstwhile companion. *Tarzan and the Lion Man*

O-dan: "Like a rock." A Waz-don warrior of the village of Kor-ul-ja in the land of Pal-ul-don who accompanied Tarzan, Ta-den, Om-at, and

In-sad in search of Pan-at-lee. *Tarzan the Terrible*

Ogabi: A native friendly to Tarzan who became an askari in the safari searching for Brian Gregory. He was sent to find Tarzan to gain his assistance in their search. During a plane flight over Africa Ogabi got flying sickness. In a fight on the waters by Ashair, the Forbidden City, he was lost overboard. *Tarzan and the Forbidden City*

Ogdli: The Kavuru warrior priest who captured Jane, and after becoming infatuated with her decided to help her. After killing the sentry in front of Jane's room Ogdli took both her and Annette (who was with Jane) to a secret tunnel leading out of the temple. There they were set upon by warriors of Kavandavanda. Jane and Annette were recaptured, but Ogdli escaped. In the Jungle outside the Kavuru village Ogdli was seized by Tarzan and questioned. The Kavuru was then left in Muviro's custody, and presumably released upon the successful return of Tarzan with Jane. *Tarzan's Quest*

1. Ogonyo: The native sentry outside the hut in which Tarzan was imprisoned in the village of the Bagegos at the west end of the valley of the Lost Empire. Ogonyo believed that Tarzan was a demon, and when he saw Nkima leave Tarzan's hut the superstitious native thought that the monkey was the ghost of his dead grandfather. Ogonyo was also imprisoned with Tarzan in the lost Roman city of Castra Sanguinarius and escaped with the Jungle Lord. *Tarzan and the Lost Empire*

2. Ogonyo: The headman of the safari for Lafayette Smith and Danny "Gunner" Patrick. After being captured by a slave raiding band of *shiftas*, Ogonyo aided "Gunner" when

they made their escape. *Tarzan Triumphant*

O'Grady, Pat: The jolly assistant director on the Tarzanesque *Lion Man* picture being shot on location in Africa. When the savage and naked Balza was brought to camp by Tarzan, O'Grady became very interested in her romantically. *Tarzan and the Lion Man*

Oju: A large young orangutan in Uglo's tribe in Sumatra who did not trust Tarzan and got into a fight with him. The Jungle Lord made him say "kagoda," or "I surrender." But when Oju abducted Corrie van der Meer, Tarzan killed the orangutan. *Tarzan and the Foreign Legion*

Old Man from the Valley of the Palace of Diamonds: As a boy, the old man became separated from his camp, got lost, and was captured by unfriendly natives. He managed to escape, though, and after wandering in the jungle for months, he stumbled into the Valley of the Palace of Diamonds. There he was captured by the intelligent ruling caste, the Bolgani. They realized the value of the knowledge he possessed, and let him live as one of them and taught him the language of the great apes. When Tarzan met him in the top of the ivy tower of the Palace of Diamonds, he was an old man. Despite his affiliation with the Bolgani, the Old Man gave the Jungle Lord information to help him rescue La, because he wanted to escape with him, if escape were possible, and go back to the civilized world of man. After Tarzan overthrew the Bolgani, he talked the Old Man into staying and being the new king of the valley. The outside world had changed so much, the Ape-man knew, and he felt that the Old Man would never adjust to it nor find happiness there. *Tarzan and the Golden Lion*

Old Raffles: The name given to a huge old wild lion that was killing the Greystoke livestock. *The Eternal Savage (Lover)*

Old Timer: A 30-year-old American who was ivory poaching in Africa with a younger man named Kid. They had both sworn off women. After separating to cover more ground for poaching, Old Timer came upon Kali Bwana who had been deserted by her entire safari. Against his first instincts, he decided to accompany and assist her. But having gone a long time without female companionship, he began to desire her. They were both captured by the Leopard Men, and at one point Old Timer was going to be sacrificed to the Leopard God. After Tarzan rescued him, Old Timer went to a cannibal pygmy village to rescue Kali Bwana who he had earlier helped escape from the Leopard Men. He was successful, and the two wandered in the jungle together. In their conversation, it was revealed that his real name was Hiram, or Hi for short. After a while, Old Timer was unable to resist his natural urges and made a pass at Kali Bwana. But she was offended by it, and that made him ashamed.

In the meantime Tarzan had been captured by the pygmies, but had escaped with the aid of the Mangani. The great apes, however, were unable to unlock the secret of the copper wire Tarzan was bound with, so Tarzan sent one of them, Ga-yat, to find a human to assist him. When Ga-yat came upon Old Timer and Kali Bwana, he abducted Old Timer and knocked Kali down. Old Timer untied Tarzan and together they went back for Kali. When Kid, Old Timer and Kali were all together again, it was revealed that Kali and

Kid were brother and sister. Kali also finally returned Old Timer's affection. *Tarzan and the Leopard Men*

O-lo-a: "Like-star-light." A Ho-don princess, the daughter of King Ko-tan of A-lur, the City of Light, in the land of Pal-ul-don. O-lo-a was very beautiful and in love with the self-imposed exile, Ta-den, who had been befriended by Tarzan. She was, however, betrothed to Bu-lot, son of Mo-sar, for her father's own political reasons. During a bachelor party of sorts, Bu-lot got drunk and threw his knife at her father, Ko-tan, and killed him. Bu-lot then went to O-lo-a's quarters and attempted to abduct her, but Pan-at-lee, O-lo-a's Waz-don slave, tried to protect her. Luckily, Tarzan burst in and saved them both. Because of the assassination of her father a revolution began, and Ta-den returned to aid his own father and Tarzan. Ta-den and O-lo-a were married along with Om-at and Pan-at-lee in the throne room of A-lur. *Tarzan the Terrible*

Om-at: "Long-tail." A Waz-don and the second Pal-ul-donian who Tarzan met. In their first encounter, Om-at ambushed the Ho-don, Ta-den, who was with Tarzan. The two fought until a *jato* (saber-toothed tiger) attacked them. After Om-at helped Tarzan kill the *jato*, the Ape-man had all three of them make a pact to help each other and be friends. Om-at then took them to his village, Kor-ul-ja. Before they arrived, however, Om-at's love, Pan-at-lee, had fled in fear of Es-sat, the wicked chief of the village, who desired her. When Om-at found this out, he killed Es-sat in a *gund-bar* (chief-battle) and became the new chief of the village. He led an attack upon A-lur as part of the revolution started by Tarzan. There he and

Pan-at-lee were reunited and married. Om-at also befriended Korak after he entered the land of Pal-ul-don searching for Tarzan. *Tarzan the Terrible*

Orando: The son of Lobongo, the chief of the Tumbai native tribe. Orando discovered Tarzan after the Jungle Lord was knocked unconscious and pinned down by a felled tree during a storm. Instead of killing him, he helped him to get out from under the tree. Tarzan awoke with amnesia and was unable to remember his name. After hunting a while with him, Orando decided that the Lord of the Jungle was his *muzimo* (the protecting spirit of a deceased ancestor). With this powerful *muzimo*'s assistance, he gathered an army of natives and attacked the stronghold of the hated Leopard Men, eventually winning the battle. *Tarzan and the Leopard Men*

Oratharc: The loyal slave of the princess Janzara in the Minuni (Ant Men) city of Veltopismakus. To escape the city, Oratharc obtained *di-adet* mounts for himself, Janzara, Tarzan, Komodoflorensal, Zoan-throhago, and Talaskar. *Tarzan and the Ant Men*

Orman, Thomas: A stocky tanned film director who drank too much. Because of his drinking and the harsh conditions of location shooting in Africa, Orman was cruel to the native porters. After a few people were killed, though, he sobered up and quit drinking. When the film's leading lady, Naomi Madison — who Orman thought he was in love with — and her stunt double, Rhonda Terry, were taken by Arabs, the director and his chief cameraman Bill West, went after them. In a surprise twist, Orman ended up marrying Rhonda Terry and making

pictures in Samoa. *Tarzan and the Lion Man*

Otobu: The captured giant Wamabos slave in the lost maniac city of Xuja. Tarzan enlisted him in his service by whispering to him through a tapestry when Otobu was serving food to Vesa, the mayor of Xuja. While trying to escape, Otobu was knocked unconscious and believed dead. But when he came to he went with Tarzan, Bertha Kircher, and Smith-Oldwick as they fled the city and valley of Xuja. Tarzan accompanied Otobu back to the Wamabos country. *Tarzan the Untamed*

Oubanovitch: The communist Russian engineer who spread propaganda while collaborating in a mutiny with the psychopathic second mate, Wilhelm Schmidt, on the ill-fated ship *Saigon*. When the vessel was shipwrecked, the survivors separated themselves into two camps. At one point, several from Oubanovitch's camp went back to Tarzan's and stole provisions and weapons, and abducted the French girl, Janette Laon. When her companions discovered this, they went to Oubanovitch's camp to rescue her. During the ensuing fight, Oubanovitch was shot and killed by Tibbet, the second mate of a yacht which the *Saigon* had pirated. *Tarzan and the Castaways*

Ouled-Nail: The term used for girls who had been kidnaped and sold as slaves to dance for money. One in particular befriended Tarzan because of his kindness to her and helped him escape a mob attack in a cafe in Sidi Aissa, Algeria. After their escape Tarzan returned her to her father, Kadour-ben-Saden, who was an Arab sheik. When the Ape-man was captured by another sheik for Nikolas Rokoff, the *Ouled-Nail* again risked her own life for him. Although her real name was never revealed, she had feelings for Tarzan, and he considered her a fit and wonderful companion. Tarzan was very tempted to stay and live with her people indefinitely. *The Return of Tarzan*

Ovan: A youth from the cave dwelling city of Clovi in Pellucidar where his father was the chief. Ovan was almost killed by a giant prehistoric bear called a *ryth*, but Tarzan saved him from it. They became friends and Ovan cleaned Tarzan's *thipdar* talon wounds. Together they went to Clovi where they both hoped Tarzan would be received as a friend. The Ape-man was at first accepted, but later imprisoned. In gratitude for saving his life, Ovan showed Tarzan and the female prisoner, Jana, a secret back exit to the cave where they were being held captive. *Tarzan at the Earth's Core*

Owaza: The crooked headman of the askari that accompanied Flora Hawkes and Esteban Miranda, a Spanish actor impersonating Tarzan, and their four male cohorts on their trip to steal gold from the treasure vaults of Opar. When Miranda took the gold from the rest of his party, he enlisted the crafty old Owaza to aid him. Owaza agreed, but later stole the gold from Miranda and hired some natives to help him take it to the coast. On the way, he and his bearers stopped at a village to rest. The village chief was an ally of Tarzan's and turned the group over to the Ape-man. Owaza was given some compensation and sent on his way with an admonition never to return to Tarzan's country. *Tarzan and the Golden Lion*

Paabu: The Bagalla cannibal youth who tried to hit Doc while the Tarzan Twin was being escorted into the village. Doc reacted by giving Paabu a bloody nose. Doc later performed a magic trick by which he made a pocketknife apparently disappear into Paabu's ear. After this the natives avoided Paabu, because they believed the white witch doctor boy had put big medicine in him. Chief Galla Galla wanted to prove that Paabu did not have the pocketknife in his ear by knocking the youth's head in and having a look inside. Doc stopped this from happening by causing the knife to reappear. In gratitude Paabu warned the Twins of the witch doctor's revenge, and aided them in their escape by supplying them with weapons. *Tarzan and the Tarzan Twins*

Pagth: A king of Tarzan's old Mangani tribe of Kerchak who believed the actor and Tarzan impersonator, Esteban Miranda, was the Ape-man when the Spaniard killed a member of the tribe. When the real Tarzan arrived searching for Miranda, Pagth drove him away. *Tarzan and the Golden Lion*

Pan-at-lee: "Soft-tailed-doe." The beautiful black and hairy female Waz-don who was in love with Om-at. While Om-at was away, Es-set, the village chief, made advances toward Pan-at-lee, but she knocked him out with her gold breastplates and ran away. She ended up hiding in some old abandoned caves where Tarzan trailed her, arriving in time to save her from a Tor-o-don. After Tarzan and Pan-at-lee went hunting together, the two became treed by a *gryf*. They escaped, but she was immediately captured by a Ho-don slave raiding party and taken to A-lur. There she became the personal body servant of Princess O-lo-a. A revolution began with Tarzan's assistance, and when it was over, Pan-at-lee was freed. She ended up

marrying Om-at in a double ceremony along with O-lo-a and Ta-
den. *Tarzan the Terrible*

Pan-sat: "Soft-skin." A Ho-don priest
under the evil High Priest Lu-don
in the Temple of the Gryf in A-lur,
the City of Light, in the land of Pal-
ul-don. Pan-sat appeared to be Lu-
don's favorite cohort and consultant,
and he had grand visions for himself
once Lu-don became ultimate ruler
of Pal-ul-don. Lu-don disguised
Pan-sat as a warrior and sent him to
Ja-lur, the Lion City, to kidnap Jane
Clayton and return her to him. This
Pan-sat succeeded in doing. Then
Korak killed Lu-don with his Enfield rifle. Pan-sat, seeing his dreams
of power and wealth crumble before
him, attempted to complete their
sacrifice by killing Tarzan with the
sacrificial knife. But Korak shot him
dead, too. *Tarzan the Terrible*

Parr, Catherine: An English speaking
gorilla and the youngest and most
recent wife of the gorilla king,
Henry the Eighth. Catherine was the
friendliest queen to the American,
Rhonda Terry. When the other
wives would have attacked Rhonda,
Catherine Parr protected her and
was kind to her. *Tarzan and the Lion
Man*

Passmore, Lord: An alias used by Tarzan when he and his Waziri, pretending to be a hunting safari, were
investigating rumors about a cruel
band of *shiftas* led by a white man.
Tarzan Triumphant

Patrick, Danny "Gunner": A good-
looking blue-eyed gangster from
Chicago who was the right-hand
man to a "Big Shot." Danny loved to
use a Thompson submachine gun,
which was how he earned his nickname, "Gunner." After getting caught
trying to double-cross his boss,
Danny decided to leave America.
While on a boat to England he met
and became acquainted with the
young geologist, Lafayette Smith,
who was on his way to Africa, and
decided to go along with him for
fun. In Africa Danny met and was
impressed with Tarzan. They saved
each other on different occasions,
and when Danny and Tarzan entered
the lost land of Midian looking for
Smith, the Chicagoan met the lovely
young golden haired Jezebel. They
fell in love with each other and, after
getting out of Africa, they planned
to run a filling station in America
and live happily ever after. *Tarzan
Triumphant*

Paulvitch, Alexis (Alexander): A
Russian who became one of Tarzan's
most tenacious antagonists along
with his cohort Nikolas Rokoff.
After serving as Rokoff's valet, Paulvitch became Rokoff's lieutenant
and co-conspirator. When the pair
first met Tarzan in *The Return of
Tarzan* the Ape-man foiled several
attempts by them to blackmail the
Count and Countess de Coude. Because of his interference, the two
sought vengeance. They undertook
many attempts to hurt him, and the
majority failed. The most successful
involved the kidnaping of Tarzan
and Jane's first child, Jack (Korak),
to lure Tarzan to them, in *The Beasts
of Tarzan*. They ended up capturing
not only Tarzan but Jane as well. In
the ensuing situations and adventures, Tarzan did not die, and Paulvitch and Rokoff failed to get the
great ransom and rewards they
wanted for Jane and Jack. It was, in
fact, Rokoff who died, at the fangs
and claws of Sheeta the Terrible.
Paulvitch was stranded in the jungles
of Africa as a captive of a tribe of
cannibals who tortured and abused
him for ten years. After that decade,

the much leaner, older, and somewhat disfigured Russian was rescued by a passing ship in *The Son of Tarzan*.

At this juncture Paulvitch took on the alias of Michael Sabrov. During a stop on the way back to civilization he was discovered and confronted by a curious and somewhat docile great ape. Coincidentally, it was Akut, the Mangani friend of Tarzan from *The Beasts of Tarzan*. Naming the great ape Ajax, the entrepreneurial Paulvitch became Akut's owner and trainer, and put the animal in a traveling circus. While at a stop in London, Tarzan's then teenage son, Jack, met and befriended the great ape. Realizing that he was once more in Tarzan's sphere, Paulvitch again sought to revenge himself and Rokoff upon the Ape-man, by attempting to murder the younger Greystoke. Akut, defending Jack, finally put an end to the life of Alexis Paulvitch. See also **Nikolas Rokoff**. *The Return of Tarzan, The Beasts of Tarzan,* and *The Son of Tarzan*

Peebles, John: A big and meaty ex-prizefighter who, along with three others, was enlisted by Flora Hawkes to help form a treasure hunting expedition to the lost city of Opar. Peebles survived the ordeal and gratefully returned to Europe with nothing except his life. His favorite saying was, "'ere we are 'nd that's that." *Tarzan and the Golden Lion*

Perry, Abner: The scientist who invented the giant drilling machine or iron mole that he and David Innes used, and accidentally discovered the savage and primeval land of Pellucidar at our Earth's core. When the pirate Korsars imprisoned Innes in Pellucidar, Perry contacted the American, Jason Gridley, through the Gridley Wave radio and asked for assistance. (More can be learned about Abner Perry and David Innes' discovery of Pellucidar and their adventures there, by reading the Pellucidar series by Burroughs beginning with *At the Earth's Core*.) *Tarzan at the Earth's Core*

Philander, Samuel T. "Skinny": The secretary and assistant to Professor Archimedes Q. Porter who was Philander's childhood friend. Over time he became more of a caretaker than an aide to the ailing and aging professor. Philander accompanied the Porters to Africa and could verify, with Professor Porter, that the tiny skeleton found and buried with the remains of Lord and Lady Greystoke was that of an infant primate and not a human. *Tarzan of the Apes* and *The Return of Tarzan*.

Phobeg: A not so intelligent braggart who was very large and muscular and purported to be the strongest man in Cathne, the City of Gold. Phobeg was stockier but a few inches shorter than Tarzan, and had beady eyes, a low forehead, and a prominent jawbone. In *Tarzan and the City of Gold*, Phobeg desecrated the temple, while serving there as a guard, by stepping on the tail of Thoos, the lion god of Cathne, and was imprisoned with Tarzan. Phobeg bragged that he could easily kill Tarzan in the arena battle that was to take place between them to amuse Queen Nemone. When they finally fought, Tarzan handily beat Phobeg. Instead of killing him, which was the custom and what the crowd wanted, the Jungle Lord spared the stocky temple guard and won his undying friendship, respect and loyalty. In gratitude Phobeg gave Tarzan information about the temple and the queen. In *Tarzan the Magnificent* his loyalty continued even under the cruel leadership of the new king, Alextar, and he incited the populace to riot and revolt against the king and his followers. *Tarzan and the City of Gold* and *Tarzan the Magnificent*

Phordos: The father of Tarzan's friend, Gemnon, in Cathne, the City of Gold. Phordos was the hereditary captain of the hunt for the rulers of Cathne, and let Tarzan stay at his home for a while. *Tarzan and the City of Gold*

Phoros: A large bestial man who usurped the throne of Athne, the City of Ivory, and became a dictatorial ruler. When the beautiful Gonfala was taken prisoner Phoros desired her, but he feared the jealousy of his homely wife, Menofra. After a bout of heavy drinking he attacked and wounded his wife, and thought her dead. When he then attempted to rape Gonfala she killed him with a dagger. *Tarzan the Magnificent*

Pickerall, Sandra: She was of Scottish descent. Sandra believed that the man who thought he was Tarzan and who had abducted her was actually the real Jungle Lord. She then learned that he was the god of the lost city Alemtejo, and that he had captured her to be their goddess and his mate. On the way to Alemtejo she was seized by the Waruturi cannibals but saved by the real Tarzan. After a few rescues, escapes, and recaptures she ended up again with the man who thought he was Tarzan, in Alemtejo. There she played her role as the new goddess, and won the affection of the man who thought he was Tarzan. Later, in atonement for capturing her, he decided that they should flee the city together. After a few more adventures, abductions, and escapes, she realized that she loved the man who thought he was

Tarzan. She declared her love and he returned it. It was then revealed that he was the American, Colin T. Randolph, Jr., and that he had suffered a head injury that caused him to forget his past. *Tarzan and the Madman*

Pierce: The valet for the Russian expatriate, Mr. Romanoff, who was on safari in Africa. Theirs joined the Ramsgate photographic safari and Pierce fell in love with Lady Barbara Ramsgate's maid, Violet. *Tarzan and the Jungle Murders* in *Tarzan and the Castaways*

Pilot Number One: see **Torlini**

Pilot Number Two: see **Cecil Giles-Burton**

Pindes: A one time palace guard in Cathne, the City of Gold. Pindes was considered good looking, but was weak and easily influenced. Even though he disliked Erot, Pindes collaborated with him and Xerstle to try and kill Tarzan on a hunt with lions. Tarzan figured it out and foiled their plans. *Tarzan and the City of Gold*

Pithecanthropus: The evolutionary term given to the Waz-don of Pal-ul-don because of their close resemblance to this stage of man's human evolution, in *Tarzan the Terrible*. It was also used to describe the Sagoths in *Tarzan at the Earth's Core*.

Porter, Archimedes "Ark" Q.: The bespectacled, aging, intellectual professor of science from Baltimore, Maryland, who was the father of Jane. Professor Porter was occasionally given to delusions, hallucinations and talking to himself. He borrowed money to form an expedition to seek treasure in Africa. The treasure hunt was successful, but knowledge of the money caused the crew of their ship to mutiny and put the Porter party ashore in the jungle near Tarzan's cabin. There Porter and his assistant, Samuel T. Philander, examined the skeletons of Lord and Lady Greystoke as well as that of Kala's ape baby. Both of these educated men saw that the infant was not human, but they held their tongue. When the bones were buried near the cabin Professor Porter, who had been ordained as a minister earlier in his life, performed the funeral ceremony. He later had to do the same for William Cecil Clayton, the nephew of the Greystokes and Tarzan's cousin, as his emaciated remains were buried next to those of his aunt and uncle, in *The Return of Tarzan*. The professor also performed the wedding ceremonies for Tarzan and Jane, and Lord Tennington and Hazel Strong. In *Tarzan and the Golden Lion* Jane heard that her father was very sick and she left for Nairobi to fly back to him. He recovered. *Tarzan of the Apes* and *The Return of Tarzan*

Porter, Jane: The first white woman Tarzan ever saw and who eventually became his wife. Jane was an American from Baltimore, Maryland, and the daughter of Professor Archimedes Q. Porter. She was named after her mother, and was described as a blonde woman of surpassing beauty. Jane liked and was courted by Tarzan's cousin, William Cecil Clayton. When Tarzan first saw Jane she and several others, including William, had just been marooned by mutinous sailors on the very shore by his parents' cabin. The Jungle Lord became instantly enamored of Jane and spied on her. After she was abducted by his rogue Mangani foster brother, Terkoz, and carried into the jungle, the Ape-man pursued them. He fought and killed Terkoz in a terrific battle that won Jane's gratitude and love, even though this was the first time she had seen him.

Jane and her marooned party were eventually rescued and taken back to America before an absent Tarzan could be told. Jane made her companions wait as long as they could for her forest man to return. She would not believe, as they did, that he was a savage cannibal. After she left, Tarzan learned English and French, then followed her to America. When he found her she had already promised herself to Robert Canler for her father's sake. But, in defense of Jane, Tarzan almost killed Canler at the wedding and broke up the ceremony. Tarzan also knew that his cousin, William Cecil Clayton, was in love with Jane, and decided to walk away.

But Jane really loved Tarzan. Even though she went forward with plans for marrying William, she never gave up on the Lord of the Jungle. And after ending up back in Africa, she finally broke off her engagement to William because she could not deny her love for Tarzan any more, although, at the time, she thought him dead. Jane was then captured by the priests of Opar and almost offered as a sacrifice to the Flaming God by La before Tarzan saved her.

After William died of hunger and thirst, Jane and Tarzan were married by her father at Tarzan's cabin. Together they had a boy they named Jack who Jane tried to shield from any knowledge of his father's past primitive life and upbringing. But she failed — Jack became Korak, the Killer. He married Meriem and gave Tarzan and Jane a grandson they named Jackie.

Throughout the series Jane was captured or thought dead several times, most notably in *Tarzan the Untamed* and its sequel *Tarzan the*

Terrible. Being a beautiful woman she was desired by many men, but she always remained true to Tarzan. Her woodcraft, hunting and tree climbing skills improved greatly in her life with Tarzan. And in both *Tarzan the Terrible* and *Tarzan's Quest* these proved to be invaluable assets that helped her survive adventures she had in the jungle while assisting others. Also, in *Tarzan's Quest* she obtained for herself an equal portion of the immortality elixir pills from the Kavuru.

"My Dear" was a term of endearment Tarzan used for Jane. Her daughter-in-law, Meriem, began calling her it as well. The Waziri usually called her Lady. *Tarzan of the Apes, The Return of Tarzan, The Beasts of Tarzan, The Son of Tarzan, Tarzan and the Jewels of Opar, Tarzan the Untamed, Tarzan the Terrible, Tarzan and the Golden Lion, Tarzan and the Ant Men, Tarzan's Quest,* and *The Eternal Savage (Lover)*

Potkin, Abe: A moviemaker in Hollywood who, along with another movie man, Dan Puant, did not think John Clayton (Tarzan) to be the right type for their Tarzan picture. *Tarzan and the Lion Man*

Praeclarus, Maximus: After Tarzan was captured in the Lost Empire he was presented to Caesar Sublatus Imperator, Emperor of the West in the city of Castra Sanguinarius, by Praeclarus who liked and admired the Ape-man. Tarzan protected Maximus Praeclarus' fiancée, Dilecta, from the treacherous Fastus. In return Praeclarus aided Tarzan in his escape, and allowed him to hide in his home. Praeclarus and Tarzan were then betrayed by Fastus and imprisoned together for the gladiator games. They survived the games

and led a revolt against the throne. *Tarzan and the Lost Empire*

Preswick: An English major and friend of Tarzan's. He served under Colonel Capell in the Second Rhodesians in British East Africa. Major Preswick recognized Tarzan when he, literally, dropped into their headquarters. He then presented Tarzan to Colonel Capell. *Tarzan the Untamed*

Prince of Wales: The gorilla son of the intelligent English speaking gorilla, King Henry the Eighth, and his gorilla wife, Queen Catherine of Aragon. *Tarzan and the Lion Man*

Puant, Dan: A famous movie scenarist and screenwriter in Hollywood. Puant and another movie man, Abe Potkin, did not think John Clayton (Tarzan) to be suitable to play the role of the Jungle Lord in their Tarzan picture. *Tarzan and the Lion Man*

Quesada: A priest in the lost Portuguese city of Alemtejo. He was made high priest by Captain-General Osorio da Serra after da Serra overthrew the king and former high priest and was given the throne by the voice of the people. *Tarzan and the Madman*

Rabba Kega: The original witch doctor for the tribe of Mbonga. When a young Tarzan entered the village in search of God, Rabba Kega tried to use voodoo magic on him. When it did not work, he ran from the Lord of the Jungle. When Tarzan caught him the frightened witch doctor swooned. Later, when the tribe had made a lion trap, Tarzan, as a cruel joke, caught Rabba Kega and replaced him as the bait in it. A lion duly came and killed the witch doctor. *Jungle Tales of Tarzan*

Ra-el: The daughter of Kor whose family made the finest spear tips and best balanced spears in the Niocene cave tribe of Nu. Ra-el desired Nu, the son of Nu. She lied when she said that Nat-ul, the woman Nu loved, had gone willingly with Hud, when really she had been forcibly abducted by him. *The Eternal Savage (Lover)*

Ramsgate, Barbara: While with her brother's photographic safari, the young and beautiful Lady Barbara found their old acquaintance, Lt. Cecil Giles-Burton, wandering alone in the jungle. Because of his emaciated state she at first did not recognize him. After a while Lady Barbara began to like Burton and he her. But he was murdered before the relationship could go anywhere. *Tarzan and the Jungle Murders* in *Tarzan and the Castaways*

Ramsgate, John: The leader of a photographic safari with his sister, Lady Barbara, that combined with the Romanoff hunting safari. When they stumbled upon an old acquaintance, Lt. Cecil Giles-Burton, wandering in the jungle Ramsgate at first did not recognize him because of the his emaciated state. *Tarzan and the Jungle Murders* in *Tarzan and the Castaways*

Randolph, Colin T., Jr. (Rand): The man who thought he was Tarzan and who was known as God by the people of Alemtejo. See **2. God**. *Tarzan and the Madman*

Rateng: The Galla warrior from Sultan Ali's village who helped capture Sandra Pickerall and the man who thought he was Tarzan. When the village was attacked by the Alemtejos, Rateng was out hunting. On his way back to the village he stumbled upon the escaped Sandra and took her as his captive, and desired her for himself. As they traveled Rateng's surveillance of Sandra became

lax, and she was able to take an arrow from his quiver and kill him with it. *Tarzan and the Madman*

Rebega: The older chief of the cannibal pygmies known as the Betetes. Rebega agreed to watch and protect the white woman, Kali Bwana, for Chief Bobolo, but when Bobolo did not return as he promised Rebega decided the village would eat her. In attempting to kill Kali Bwana, Rebega was shot dead by an arrow from Tarzan. *Tarzan and the Leopard Men*

Red Flower of Zoram: see **Jana**

Reece: The name of a young man who pretended to know John Clayton (Tarzan) from London and volunteered to show him around Hollywood. The Jungle Lord accepted, and together they went to a movie premiere. Later they joined up with a buddy of Reece's, Billy Bourke, and all three crashed a Hollywood party. *Tarzan and the Lion Man*

Rela: The sister of Ovan and daughter of Avan, the chief of the cliff dwelling village of Clovi, in Pellucidar. Rela's mother was Maral, who was captured from Zoram. Rela accepted Tarzan into the tribe without suspicion. *Tarzan at the Earth's Core*

Reyd: The doctor aligned with the friendly Dutch guerrillas in Japanese held Sumatra. The only medical tool Dr. Reyd had was an oral thermometer that he kept in a metal case. *Tarzan and the Foreign Legion*

Rokoff, Nikolas: A vile Russian who caused Tarzan no end of trouble and became the Jungle Lord's arch nemesis. His partner in crime was the equally obnoxious Alexis Paulvitch. Rokoff was the brother of Countess Olga de Coude. After being cashiered from the Russian army, he used his father to get back into government service, this time as a secret agent. When Tarzan foiled several attempts by Rokoff and Paulvitch to blackmail Count Raoul de Coude on an ocean liner, Rokoff developed a deep-seated hatred of the Ape-man and swore to take vengeance on him. The two Russians followed and stalked Tarzan from Paris to the desert of Algiers and finally onto the ship back to London. On board, Rokoff shaved his beard off and assumed the alias of Monsieur Thuran to conceal his identity. He and Paulvitch ultimately succeeded in pitching Tarzan overboard.

After switching ships without his partner, Rokoff began courting Hazel Strong for her money. He then met up with Jane Porter and William Cecil Clayton who he became shipwrecked with on the African coast. After Jane was kidnaped by 50 frightful priests of Opar, Clayton contracted a fever. Rokoff cruelly abandoned the helpless man and set off on his own. He was then surprised by Tarzan, who was still alive, and imprisoned.

After escaping, Rokoff collaborated with Alexis Paulvitch again to take vengeance on Tarzan. Rokoff's main plan involved kidnaping Jack Clayton, the infant son of Tarzan and Jane, in order to lure the Ape-man into their trap and seize him. It worked, but in the process they accidentally acquired Jane as well. After marooning Tarzan on a jungle island and several other adventures, Rokoff finally met a grisly end at the claws and fangs of Tarzan's panther friend, Sheeta the Terrible. See also **Alexis Paulvitch**. *The Return of Tarzan* and *The Beasts of Tarzan*.

Romanoff: A Russian expatriate who merged his hunting safari with the Ramsgate photographic safari. Romanoff had a valet with him while on safari. He disliked the professional photographer, Sergei Godensky, in the Ramsgate safari who also happened to be Russian. *Tarzan and the Jungle Murders* in *Tarzan and the Castaways*

Romero, Miguel: A brave Mexican communist who accompanied Peter Zveri and other communists to Opar to loot the lost city's treasure vaults to fund their cause. Once at Opar, Romero went the farthest into the lost city and was still able to escape when attacked by the Oparians. Romero and his friend, Antonio Mori, became disillusioned with communism and were protected by Tarzan after they disavowed it. *Tarzan the Invincible*

Rosetti, Tony "Shrimp": The short staff sergeant and ball turret gunner aboard the B-24 bomber, the *Lovely Lady*, who hailed from Chicago and prayed a lot to Mary. Rosetti and Joe "Datbum" Bubonovitch were always teasing and poking fun at each other. Rosetti at first disliked Colonel Clayton (Tarzan) because he was British. After he heard that Clayton was Tarzan, he thought that it meant the Ape-man was Johnny Weismuller, the actor. He ended up liking Tarzan. Even though he was a self-proclaimed woman-hater Rosetti fell in love with the half–Dutch, half–Sumatran guerrilla, Sarina.

The Chicagoan was a brave man, and at one point distracted a rhinoceros to save the rest of the group. When Tarzan made friends with a new monkey, Keta, Shrimp was the only other human it liked. He and Sarina were married by the captain of the rescuing British submarine. *Tarzan and the Foreign Legion*

Rufinus: The underofficer at the gateway into the eastern Roman city of Castra Mare in *Tarzan and the Lost Empire*.

Ruiz, Pedro: The high priest of the lost Portuguese city of Alemtejo who did not care for the king, Cristoforo da Gamma. Ruiz had hawk-like features and a dark visage. As part of the religion in Alemtejo, he offered human sacrifice and used black magic. Ruiz desired the new found captive goddess, Sandra Pickerall, and at one point entered her chambers and attempted to seduce her. Ruiz was eventually forced out of his position during a revolt by Tarzan and Osorio da Serra, a crowd favorite. *Tarzan and the Madman*

Rungula: The chief of the heart-eating cannibal tribe of Bansutos. Rungala and his warriors repeatedly ambushed and harassed the crew of the movie, *Lion Man*, who, while on location, were attempting to pass through their country. When the Bansutos captured the leading man, Stanley Obroski, Rungula took the white man's clothes for himself. Just before they were to kill Obroski, Tarzan lassoed Rungula and hoisted him into a tree. There the Jungle Lord made the terrified chief promise never to harm white men again. *Tarzan and the Lion Man*

Rutherford, Alice: See **Alice Clayton**

Sabrov, Michael: see **Alexis Paulvitch**

Sancho: One of the Mangani known as the Servants of God who spoke both the ape language and a language taught to his tribe by the people of the lost city of Alemtejo. When the Tarmangani known as God attacked the Servants of God, Sancho took the she–Tarmangani, Sandra Pickerall, from him and carried her off. Sancho then stumbled upon the Mangani tribe of Ungo, who were allies of the real Tarzan, and had to battle them for possession of Sandra. *Tarzan and the Madman*

Sarus: A servant or guard in the house of Dion Splendidus in the lost Roman city of Castra Sanguinarius. *Tarzan and the Lost Empire*

Sarina: A 35-year-old Eurasian of Sumatran and Dutch heritage who was a member of Hooft's rebel guerrillas in the jungles of Sumatra. She became disgruntled with Hooft and his band of thieves, and when they captured Corrie van der Meer, Sarina helped her escape, because she used to work for the van der Meers when she was younger and liked them. She then led Hooft's group purposely down the wrong trail. Sarina later joined Corrie and Tarzan's group in their escape from Sumatra. The healthy and pretty Eurasian later fell in love with the American, Sergeant "Shrimp" Rosetti, and they were married by the captain of a rescuing British submarine. *Tarzan and the Foreign Legion*

Sborov, Alexis: A Russian prince who married Kitty Krause, a widowed friend of Jane's who had inherited millions. Sborov, Kitty, Jane and a few others took a plane to Africa to search for a secret to longevity. After it crashed-landed and they were forced to trek through the jungle, Sborov's cowardliness showed through. He later killed his wife with a hatchet while she slept and attempted to frame the pilot, Neal Brown, who Sborov disliked. Immediately after this, the prince made advances toward Jane, and also tried to sow discord in the company. Sborov finally attempted to kill Brown, but failed and was scared away. When Tarzan found him alone, the Russian lied to the Jungle Lord about his circumstances to protect himself. When Tarzan tried to reunite him with Brown, Sborov ran away in terror. Once more wandering alone in the jungle, he finally snapped and went mad. He was captured and taken to the village of the Kavuru. There he leapt out of a second-story window of the temple and was eaten by the leopards kept in the garden below. *Tarzan's Quest*

Sborov, Kitty: An old friend of Jane's, a social climber who was widowed and inherited millions of dollars. As Kitty Krause, she married the Russian prince, Alexis Sborov. On hearing that a secret to longevity was to be found in Africa, the vain Kitty decided to go searching for it. On the way, the plane carrying her and her party made a crash-landing in a storm, ending up lodged in a tree. Overweight and used to being waited on, the stranded Princess Sborov was not physically or emotionally able to endure the inconveniences of jungle travel. So she and her husband complained a lot and slowed the rest of the party down. Soon after this her selfish and greedy husband killed her with a hatchet during the night. *Tarzan's Quest*

Schmidt: A sailor aboard the *Kincaid* who plotted with Schneider to abduct Jane and abandon Tarzan on Jungle Island. The two then joined the mutineers on the Crowie. After their plan succeeded, Tarzan made it back to the ship, took it over, and forced Schmidt to work as a hand on their voyage back to Europe. *The Beasts of Tarzan*

Schmidt, Wilhelm: The second mate on the *Saigon* who spat upon Tarzan while the Ape-man was held captive in a cage. The psychopathic Schmidt hated the first mate, Hans de Groote. Eventually, he mutinied and took over the ship. After Tarzan escaped the cage, he put Schmidt in it. When the ship was wrecked and the

people marooned on an island, Tarzan separated them all into two camps. He assigned Schmidt to one, and himself and de Groote to the other. When Tarzan was away Schmidt led a group to the Apeman's camp and took weapons, provisions and the French girl, Janette Laon. While rescuing Janette, Tarzan shot and killed Schmidt with an arrow. *Tarzan and the Castaways*

1. Schneider: The mate of the *Kincaid* who plotted with Schmidt to abduct Jane and abandon Tarzan on Jungle Island. They later joined the mutineers on the *Crowie*. After successfully executing their plan, Schneider attacked Jane in the *Crowie's* cabin. At this point, Tarzan arrived and wrung Schneider's neck despite Jane's objection. *The Beasts of Tarzan*

2. Schneider: The unfortunate brother of Hauptmann Fritz Schneider. A major in the German Army stationed in Africa, Major Schneider was described as being of medium build and having upstanding mustaches. He was mistaken for his brother by a vengeance seeking Apeman and became the first to be thrown into the small enclosed gulch where Tarzan had trapped a hungry Numa, the lion. *Tarzan the Untamed.*

Schneider, Fritz: The huge, bull-necked Hauptmann (captain) of the German army company sent to Tarzan's estate in British East Africa. While Tarzan was away, Schneider and his company—which included the two lieutenants, Obergatz and von Goss—brutally attacked and razed the Greystoke estate, killing most of the Waziri guards and people living there. The Germans kidnaped Jane and faked her death to fool Tarzan. The Lord of the Jungle was enraged, then became obsessed with hunting down and killing Schneider and his regiment in revenge for what they had done. After mistakenly killing Schneider's brother, Tarzan finally found the Hauptmann and killed him with his knife in a hand-to-hand struggle. *Tarzan the Untamed*

Scrab: The chief of the boat building tribe that Tur belonged to. When Gron, Tur's mate, attacked the prisoner Nu, the son of Nu, Scrab told Tur to beat her and take a new mate. *The Eternal Savage (Lover)*

Servants of God: The Mangani tribe trained by the people of Alemtejo and taught their language. They followed and obeyed the man who thought he was Tarzan who was also the god of the people of Alemtejo. *Tarzan and the Madman*

Shah, Alauddin: The chief of Moeke-moeko in Sumatra who helped get a boat and provisions for Tarzan and his Foreign Legion. Alauddin did this because of Sarina, who was part of Tarzan's group, and in memory of her father, Big Jon. *Tarzan and the Foreign Legion*

Shang, Kai: A Chinaman from Fachan. Kai Shang, along with Momulla the Maori and Gust the Swede, led a mutiny aboard the *Cowrie*. After successfully kidnaping Jane, Kai Shang was killed by Sheeta the Terrible. *The Beasts of Tarzan*

Sheeta the Terrible: Sheeta means leopard or panther in the language of the Mangani. In *The Beasts of Tarzan* the Lord of the Jungle saved a sheeta from a felled tree. It became a faithful friend to him, and followed and assisted him in his search for Jane, their son Jack, Nikolas Rokoff and Alexis Paulvitch. Sheeta the Terrible, as the cat became known, stayed with Tarzan even when its hereditary enemy, the Man-

gani, went with them, and when they had to travel in canoes. Sheeta even went along with the Mangani when Tarzan was not there and followed Mugambi's lead. When the Jungle Lord called them, Sheeta and the Mangani came to him. It was Sheeta the Terrible that killed Nikolas Rokoff. *The Beasts of Tarzan*

shiftas: White-robed black men on horseback who banded together as robbers and raiders after being cast out from their own tribes and countries.

Shorty: A member of the crew on location in Africa shooting a Tarzan-esque jungle picture. After the native porters and servants deserted his safari, Shorty was assigned to assist in cooking because he used to run a hot dog stand on Ventura Boulevard in California. *Tarzan and the Lion Man*

Simba: A native term for lion.

Simpson: A sailor on the ship *Marjorie W.* that found Alexis Paulvitch on the beach and later Akut, the Mangani. When Simpson saw how docile Akut seemed, he decided to play a joke upon the great ape and stuck him with a pin. Akut bit him on the shoulder in retaliation. *The Son of Tarzan*

Singh, Jabu: A Lascar sailor on the *Saigon* who collaborated with the psychopathic second mate, Wilhelm Schmidt, in a mutiny. When the caged Tarzan was facing the other way, Jabu Singh shot him in the back. In return the Lascar was shot in the right arm by the French girl, Janette Laon. *Tarzan and the Castaways*

Sir Galahad: The name of the obedient horse the American, James Hunter Blake, used in the lost medieval Valley of the Sepulcher. *Tarzan, Lord of the Jungle*

Skopf: The German proprietor of the

Thomas Yeates illustration from *Tarzan: The Lost Adventure* **(© 1995 Edgar Rice Burroughs, Inc.).**

African hotel where Jack Clayton stayed with his invalid grandmother, Mrs. Billings (who was really Akut the Mangani in disguise). Herr Skopf was the one who discovered the body of Condon, a wanted U.S. criminal, in Jack's room after Jack and Akut disappeared. Both the disappearance and the body baffled Herr Skopf. *The Son of Tarzan*

Skruk: The bullet-headed chief of the lowland village of Pheli. Along with a few other males of his tribe, he was pursuing the beautiful Jana, the Red Flower of Zoram, so he could make her his wife. Then the lost American, Jason Gridley, arrived and helped protect Jana, not only from Skruk and his companions, but from some *hyaenodons* as well. Gridley's intervention frightened Skruk away. *Tarzan at the Earth's Core*

Small, Elbert: A small Negro who became lost with Hunt in a safari in Africa while searching for the Hanson safari. After their safari was taken over by Wilson Jones and his cohort, Cannon, Small and Hunt escaped by running blindly into the jungle. Small was later found by Tarzan in a tree, almost completely naked. The Jungle Lord placed him back in the tree for his own protection. Then Wilson and Cannon came along, and Small successfully attacked them by swinging down on a vine. But Cannon escaped and ended up slitting Small's throat. *Tarzan: The Lost Adventure*

Smith: see **Joseph "Joe the Pooch" Campbell**

Smith, Lafayette (Lafe) A.M., Ph.D., Sc. D.: A professor of geology at the Phil Sheridan Military Academy who looked very young and wore glasses. Smith decided to go to Africa to study the great rift valleys of the Dark Continent, and on his

way there he met the gangster Danny "Gunner" Patrick. On a whim they decide to travel together. Once in Africa Smith got himself trapped in a fissure by a lion, and while retreating found a secret way into the valley of Midian. There he saved Barbara Collis and the Midianite Jezebel from crucifixion despite his poor marksmanship. All of them were then caught by the North Midians and were saved by Tarzan. Smith fell in love with Collis and she with him. *Tarzan Triumphant*

Smith, Milton: The Executive Vice President in Charge of Production for the B.O. Studio that decided to send a movie crew to Africa to make a jungle picture. *Tarzan and the Lion Man*

Smith-Oldwick, Harold Percy: The boyish faced lieutenant who was a pilot with the English forces in East Africa. He was fair haired, blue eyed and slender. Smith-Oldwick's airplane stalled while on a mission over the jungle and he was forced to land. While attempting to fix it, he was captured by the Wamabos tribe of cannibals. When the duty bound Tarzan attempted to rescue him, he was captured as well. They were both rescued by the charging, spear-wielding German spy, Bertha Kircher, along with several Mangani bulls from the tribe of Go-lat. Lt. Smith-Oldwick fell in love with Fräulein Kircher and expressed his feelings to her. She rejected them at first, because she had feelings for Tarzan. Despite this, the brave young officer valiantly helped and defended Bertha and Tarzan through many adventures. Once they were rescued and safe, his affections were finally returned by Fräulein Kircher and she promised to marry him. *Tarzan the Untamed*

Smuts: The general commanding Colonel Capell of the Second Rhodesians in British East Africa. General Smuts launched a rescue mission for the lost pilot, Lt. Harold Percy Smith-Oldwick. *Tarzan the Untamed*

Snipes: The cowardly sailor with a face that reminded Tarzan of Pamba, the rat. He led the mutineers of the *Arrow* who put the Porter party ashore at Tarzan's cabin. Snipes killed King, the original leader of the mutiny, by shooting him in the back. When Snipes had a disagreement with William Cecil Clayton, the rat faced sailor attempted to shoot him in the back, too. Snipes was stopped by Tarzan who, from the cover of the jungle, threw a spear through the man's shoulder. While burying the Porter treasure chest further down the shore from the cabin, Snipes was killed by a shipmate wielding a pickax. *Tarzan of the Apes*

Sobito: A witch doctor in the Utenga village of Tumbai who was part of the Secret Order of the Leopard Men in which group he was a high priest with the name of Lulimi. When an amnesiac Tarzan was brought into Tumbai village by the chief's son, Orando, who claimed that the Ape-man was his own *muzimo,* the old witch doctor was skeptical and challenged Tarzan. In the process Sobito was humiliated and almost killed by the Ape-man in front of the villagers. Because of this Sobito became very angry and sought to take vengeance on Tarzan. Later, Tarzan abducted Sobito from the Leopard Men's temple. He turned him over to the Utengas and revealed his dual identity. The wiley witch doctor escaped, however, and went to the village of Bobolo for asylum. Tarzan

recaptured him and took him back to Tumbai village where the vengeful villagers killed him. *Tarzan and the Leopard Men*

Sokabe, Hideo: The lieutenant in the Japanese invading army that pursued the van der Meer family into the interior of the Dutch East Indies. He was a subordinate of Captain Tokujo Matsuo. When Sokabe found Corrie van der Meer, he desired her. *Tarzan and the Foreign Legion*

Son of Tabernarius: One of the escaped prisoners from the Colosseum in the lost Roman city of Castra Mare. With eight to ten other escapees, the son of Tabernarius kidnaped the beautiful Favonia for ransom. When he was betrayed by his cohorts, he told the new Caesar, Fulvus Fupus, who was in love with Favonia, where she could be found. *Tarzan and the Lost Empire*

Son of Tarzan: see **Korak**

Son of The First Woman: A 16-year-old docile and effeminate Alali male who was imprisoned, along with his siblings, in the stone-walled corral nursery of his large barbaric mother, The First Woman. The son of The First Woman stood up for Tarzan when the Ape-man was put into the corral, but the youngster was chased away by his more numerous and savage sisters. After the death of The First Woman, The Third Woman came to check the corral and on seeing Tarzan she desired him for a mate. But Tarzan escaped and took the son of The First Woman with him.

In the jungle, the son of The First Woman wanted to learn to use and make the unfamiliar weapons of the Ape-man which included a knife, a bow and arrows, and a spear. After mastering their usage the youth gained much greater confidence and courage. With these new weapons he killed game and defended himself against the Alalus women. When he became separated from Tarzan he met other subordinate males and taught them to make the same weapons. The son of The First Woman banded the males together, and for the first time captured their much larger female counterparts to be their mates and cooks. With his new tribe of male dominated Alali the son of The First Woman ambushed a party of Minuni who were being pursued by other Minuni. To his surprise he discovered that one of the 18-inch-tall Ant Men was his long lost friend and mentor, Tarzan of the Apes, who had been shrunken to the Ant Men's size. The son of The First Woman aided Tarzan and his Minuni friends and escorted the Jungle Lord to the edge of the Great Thorn Forest surrounding the land. *Tarzan and the Ant Men*

Spider: One of the crew on Lord Tennington's yacht, the *Lady Alice*. On a lifeboat, Spider was the loser in the Nikolas Rokoff–rigged lottery of death between himself, William Cecil Clayton, and M. Thuran (Rokoff). He was to be eaten by the other two starving men. The full realization of his grisly loss caused the emaciated Spider to throw himself overboard and drown rather than be eaten. *The Return of Tarzan*

Spike: The white hunter with the Wood and van Eyk safari when they were captured by the Kaji warrior women. Spike accompanied Tarzan in an escape from the Kaji, and desired to possess the mind-controlling Gonfal diamond and the Great Emerald of the Zuli which the Ape-man had in his possession. While Tarzan slept Spike and his cohort, Troll, took both jewels from the

Ape-man and fled. On the way they stumbled across the beautiful Kaji goddess, Gonfala, and abducted her to make her their queen as they ruled with the Gonfal. Spike ended up fighting with Troll about Gonfala and the Gonfal. They were then made prisoners in Athne, the City of Ivory. After Tarzan helped them escape they were escorted out of Africa after promising never to return. *Tarzan the Magnificent.*

Splendidus, Dion: A senator and head of the second most powerful family in the lost Roman city of Castra Sanguinarius. His daughter was the beautiful Dilecta and his slave was the Bagego native Mpingu who interpreted for Tarzan. After Tarzan was betrayed and thrown in prison Dion Splendidus was also imprisoned. Tarzan escaped and saved the senator. Once Caesar Sublatus was usurped and killed Tarzan suggested Dion Splendidus become the new Caesar. This he did. *Tarzan and the Lost Empire*

Stabutch, Leon: A Russian who was sent to Africa to avenge Peter Zveri's death by hunting down and killing Tarzan. Stabutch was deserted by his safari and captured by *shiftas,* but was befriended by their white leader, Dominic Capietro. When the beautiful golden haired Midianite, Jezebel, was captured by them, they both desired her and played cards to see who would get her. Stabutch lost but killed Capietro and left the camp with Jezebel. When Tarzan arrived Stabutch shot at the Ape-man but missed. He fled in fear, but was pursued by Tarzan who shot him with arrows until he was dead. *Tarzan Triumphant*

Stalin, Joseph: The communist dictator of Russia who gave the order for Leon Stabutch to avenge Peter

Zveri's death by killing Tarzan. *Tarzan Triumphant*

Stanlee: see **Stanley Wood**

Stimbol, Wilbur: A scion of Stimbol & Co. of New York, the 50 year old was on a hunting safari with James Hunter Blake, a man 25 years his junior. During the safari Stimbol was abusive and arrogant to his porters, and because of this he and Blake parted ways. After Tarzan humiliated him, Stimbol attempted to kill the Ape-man. Finally his porters deserted him and left him alone. He found his way to the Arab raiding camp of Sheik Ibn Jad and struck up an alliance with him. When Tarzan came to the Arab camp, Stimbol was talked into killing him. The terrified Stimbol attempted to do as he was bid, but instead of the Jungle Lord, Stimbol killed an Arab by mistake. Later, Stimbol and another Arab, Fahd, abducted princess Guinalda and fled into the jungle. After losing Guinalda to some Mangani , he became separated from the Arab. Blake discovered Stimbol lost, sick and helpless and took him to a native village from which he was escorted from Africa by the Waziri. *Tarzan, Lord of the Jungle*

Stone, Jimmy (or Jimmie): An ex-marine who knew how to cook. After the desertion of their native porters and cooks he was assigned to help Rhonda Terry cook for the cast and crew of the *Lion Man* motion picture being shot in Africa. Stone later became the second assistant production manager for the B.O. Studio in Hollywood. *Tarzan and the Lion Man*

Strong, Hazel: An American and the best friend of Jane Porter. Jane wrote Hazel faithfully even while marooned in Tarzan's cabin in the African jungle. Tarzan met up with Hazel on a ship from Algiers to London while he was under the pseudonym of John Caldwell, London, and she admired him greatly. When Nikolas Rokoff and Alexis Paulvitch pitched him overboard, she mistook his body falling past her porthole for refuse. Nonetheless, she was the only one who saw anything amiss in his disappearance from the ship. Using the pseudonym of M. Thuran a shaven Rokoff fell in love with and courted Hazel in the hope that he might obtain her wealth, but she was only interested in him as a friend. She did fall in love with Tennington, an English Lord, who was captaining his own yacht. Hazel and Tennington were married in a double ceremony along with Tarzan and Jane that was performed next to Tarzan's cabin by Jane's father. *The Return of Tarzan* and *Tarzan's Quest*.

Sublatus: The cruel and tyrannical Imperial Caesar and Emperor of the West in the city of Castra Sanguinarius who was disliked by most of his citizens. Sublatus was affronted and humiliated by Tarzan several times and wanted revenge. Once Tarzan was imprisoned Sublatus sentenced him to the great games in the hope that he would be killed. After Tarzan won every battle and was, according to the rules, supposed to be given his freedom, Sublatus denied it because of his hatred. The crowd was displeased by this decision and began shouting for the death of Sublatus. Tarzan then formed a revolt and laid siege to the palace. In the ensuing battle, Sublatus was slain by natives. *Tarzan and the Lost Empire*

Suffolk: An English speaking gorilla and part of the Privy Council to King Henry the Eighth in the city of London on the Thames in the Valley of Diamonds. Suffolk followed Buckingham (another gorilla) when the latter ran off with the American actress Naomi Madison. *Tarzan and the Lion Man*

Sullivan: One of the nicer members of the crew of the *Kincaid*. *The Beasts of Tarzan*

Taask, Lal: The tall, thin East Indian who was the right-hand man to Atan Thome, and who mistook Tarzan for the missing Brian Gregory. When Tarzan refused to cooperate with Thome, who also believed him to be Brian, Taask attempted to stab him from behind, but the Ape-man lifted the Indian and threw him. Taask then kidnaped Helen Gregory, Brian's sister, for ransom. On safari with Thome, Taask began to dislike his master and did not want to go any further with him. When they were both captured and taken into Ashair, Thome betrayed the Indian by persuading him to attempt to assassinate the queen after forewarning her of his coming. Despite this betrayal, Thome and Taask escaped together from Ashair. When Taask attempted to kill Thome, the latter killed him instead. *Tarzan and the Forbidden City*

Tabo: A Galla native and the brother of the Arab slave, Fejjuan (Ulala). *Tarzan, Lord of the Jungle*

Tada, Kumajiro: A Japanese lieutenant who spoke English which he had learned while working in Oregon. In Japanese held Sumatra, Lt. Tada was informed by Amat about Tarzan's stranded group. The Japanese captured Rosetti and Bubonovitch, and while attempting to behead them, was shot dead by Jerry Lucas. *Tarzan and the Foreign Legion*

Ta-den: "Tall tree." A Ho-don and the first Pal-ul-donian that Tarzan met when he entered their land in search of Jane. Ta-den was in self-imposed exile from A-lur because of his forbidden love for the princess O-lo-a. His father was Ja-don, chief of Ja-lur, the lion city. Tarzan and Ta-den became friends after the Ape-man saved him from a lion in their first encounter. The Ho-don helped teach Tarzan the language of Pal-ul-don, and its customs. Tarzan also befriended Om-at, a Waz-don (the furry black variety of the Ho-don), and had all three of them make a pact of peace and loyalty to each other. Ta-den stayed with Om-at's people until needed in the revolution started by Tarzan in A-lur. Ta-den and O-lo-a finally got together and were married in a double ceremony with Om-at and Pan-at-lee in the throne room of A-lur. *Tarzan the Terrible*

Taglat: "Neck-nose." A sullen, cruel and crafty older Mangani bull who accompanied Tarzan even though he hated him. When Taglat saw the Tarmangani-she, Jane, he desired her. A little later, Tarzan dressed him in Arab clothes and sent him into Achmet Zek's village to save Jane who was a prisoner there. But the Mangani stole her for himself, and while attempting to untie her bonds, he was attacked and killed by Numa. *Tarzan and the Jewels of Opar*

Tai, Sing: The loyal Chinese servant of the van der Meers in Japanese held Sumatra. Sing Tai fled with Corrie van der Meer and protected her for two years. When the Japanese finally discovered them, they bayoneted Sing Tai, but did not mortally wound him. Tarzan found the injured man and helped him get to the village of Tiang Umar where he left him to recover from his wounds. During a later ocean escape, the faithful Sing Tai was blown in half by a Japanese ship's guns, but his companions were ultimately rescued. *Tarzan and the Foreign Legion*

Tajiri, Kanji: The Japanese colonel of the main body of soldiers in Japanese held Sumatra in the Dutch East Indies. When the two-faced native Sumatran, Amat, told Tajiri the name of the village where Tarzan and his "Foreign Legion" were camped, he personally led two companies to attack it. After Tarzan's band ambushed the Japanese, Tajiri chased Amat with a sword, but was shot by Rosetti. *Tarzan and the Foreign Legion*

Talaskar: The beautiful second generation Mandalamakus slave girl in the Minuni (Ant Men) city of Veltopismakus. Talaskar remained unmolested by the rulers and freemen of the city by contorting her features at will to make herself appear ugly and old. She was imprisoned in the same quarry that Tarzan and Komodoflorensal were sent to, and she volunteered to cook for both of them, and eventually fell in love with Komodoflorensal. Her beauty was finally discovered, however, by the *vental*, Kalfastoban, who purchased her to be his mate, but she was rescued by the escaping Tarzan and Komodoflorensal. After deciding to become Komodoflorensal's wife it was revealed that she was a princess through her mother. *Tarzan and the Ant Men*

Talent, Charles: A tall black man who, in his youth, had killed his abusive father. But Talent loved killing, and never looked a person in the eye unless he was about to take his life. Tarzan killed Talent by using a series of quick moves that created a shock overload to his system. *Tarzan: The Lost Adventure*

Tambudza: The old first wife of M'ganwazam in the cannibal village of Waganwazam. Tarzan declined to take the old woman's hut for the night (which was proffered him by her husband), because it would have left her out in the cold. In return for this kindness Tambudza assisted Tarzan by warning him of her husband's sinister intentions toward him. *The Beasts of Tarzan*

Tana: The lazy wife of the Mangani, Gunto, in the tribe of Kerchak. She ran to Tarzan, the new king of the tribe, because her husband bit her for her neglect. Tarzan counseled them both. *Tarzan of the Apes*

Tanar: The son of Ghak, the Hairy One, King of Sari in Pellucidar. Tanar was captain of one of the ships that discovered Tarzan, Jason Gridley, and their company in a long boat on their way to rescue David Innes from the Korsars. (More can be learned about Tanar's personal story by reading *Tanar of Pellucidar* in the Pellucidar series.) *Tarzan at the Earth's Core*

Tantor: "Elephant" (whether African or Indian) in the language of the Mangani. Tantor was one of Tarzan's (and later Korak's) truest and most faithful friends. It showed Tarzan the greatest amount of love, outside of Kala. The Jungle Lord wiled away many hours on Tantor's back, scratching its thick hide and talking soothingly to the great pachyderm in the language of the Mangani, which it seemed to understand. This friendship was proven on many occasions when the Jungle Lord had to call upon Tantor to rescue him from life threatening situations. Tarzan even saved Tantor from an elephant pit once. To Tarzan, Tantor had no rival in the jungle (except perhaps man) and every creature made way for the great monarch of the forest as he passed by.

Tar-gash: "White-fang." The leader of the party of Sagoths (club-wielding and tree-swinging Neanderthal manlike apes who spoke the Mangani language) that caught Tarzan in a snare in Pellucidar. Tar-gash stood up for Tarzan, and the Jungle Lord returned the favor by standing by Tar-gash's side against the Sagoth's own tribe. Throwing their lots together the two escaped the rest of the Sagoths and traveled together. Tar-gash then tried to help Tarzan find his way back to the O-220 dirigible. During this time they hunted together and were impressed with each other, and Tarzan taught Tar-gash how to make and use the bow and arrow and the spear. When they came upon the *gilak* (human), Thoar, Tarzan made friends with him also and kept the peace between him and Tar-gash, two habitual enemies. The three traveled together amicably, but when Tarzan was taken away by a *thipdar* (pteranodon) the two Pellucidarians parted ways. *Tarzan at the Earth's Core*

Tarrant: One of the crew of the *Arrow* that mutinied and put the Porter party on shore at Tarzan's cabin. When they were burying the Porters' treasure chest further up the coast, Tarrant killed the leader of their party, the cowardly Snipes, with a pickax. *Tarzan of the Apes*

Tarzan: "White skin" in the language of the Mangani. Kala, a bereaved female great ape who had lost her own infant, rescued the one-year-old son of the deceased Lord and Lady Greystoke from certain death at the hands of Kerchak, the king of her tribe. She then took the human babe to her bosom as her own. Little John Clayton, renamed Tarzan, was raised by Kala and the tribe of Kerchak, never knowing of his real parentage or ever seeing another human being until his mid-teens. During that time, Tarzan did not know that such a thing as man existed or that he was anything other than a great ape himself. The youngster grew slowly, but wonderfully, and because he possessed human intellect, curiosity and ingenuity, and with the almost superhuman strength he had developed, Tarzan soon became the king of the apes.

As a youth, he eventually discovered his human father's cabin, although he did not know it was such. From it he obtained his actual sire's hunting knife and personal diary, and his mother's jeweled locket; and he taught himself to read and write the English language from the many children's primers that were there. He also learned that he was more than a pale skinned Mangani — he was a "M-A-N."

Then, as a teenager, other men finally entered Tarzan's world: first in the form of African natives and later in the form of an American female from Baltimore named Jane Porter. After many adventures, Tarzan accepted his birthright and inheritance. He and Jane married and had a son named Jack who later earned the Mangani name Korak, the Killer. See **Jane Porter, Paul d'Arnot**, and **Korak**. In addition, see Section One and Mangani in Section Three.

Tarzan-jad-guru: "Tarzan the terrible" in the language of Pal-ul-don. This was the name given to Tarzan after he cut off the tail of one of the attacking Waz-don warriors of Korul-ja. The name stuck after the people saw what a fierce fighter he was. *Tarzan the Terrible*

Tarzan, Jean C.: Tarzan's French name given him by Paul d'Arnot.

J. Allen St. John illustration for *Tarzan and the Golden Lion* (© 1923 Edgar Rice Burroughs, Inc.).

The initial is for Clayton. *The Return of Tarzan*

Taug: A large Mangani from the Jungle Lord's youth who was the only bull of the tribe of Kerchak who had any affection for the Tarmangani, Tarzan. Taug was the third member of a love triangle along with Tarzan and Teeka, the she-ape. At first, Teeka chose the Ape-man over Taug, but the Mangani eventually won over the Tarmangani. Taug and Teeka had a *balu* (baby) they named Gazan because of its reddish coloring. When Sheeta, the panther, attempted to capture Gazan, Tarzan attacked it and Taug joined in the fight. When Tarzan wore the skin and head of Numa to surprise the tribe of Kerchak, Taug attacked what he thought was the lion, hit him with a rock, and knocked the young prankster out. When they discovered that it was Tarzan in disguise, many of the tribe wanted to kill him, but Taug protected the young man. Taug also went with Tarzan to recapture Teeka from a bull Mangani of another tribe. *Jungle Tales of Tarzan.*

Taurus, Claudius: For five years running he was the champion professional gladiator, and crowd favorite, in the lost Roman city of Castra Mare. *Tarzan and the Lost Empire*

Teeka: A female Mangani in the tribe of Kerchak. Teeka was one of the young Tarzan's playmates. Later she became his first love as he matured physically and hormonally, and began to find her beautiful looking. He had a rival in Taug, another onetime playfellow, but when Tarzan saved Teeka from Sheeta, the panther, she chose him over Taug as a mate. Nonetheless, the fickle Teeka ultimately decided on Taug as her mate, rather than the Tarmangani, Tarzan. Taug and Teeka had a *balu* (baby) they named Gazan because of his reddish coloring. At first Teeka was protective of Gazan and bristled even when Tarzan approached him. But after Tarzan, with Taug's assistance, saved Gazan from Sheeta, Teeka allowed the Tarmangani to come near the infant. After Tarzan captured a young Gomangani named Tibo to raise as his own, Teeka was the only one of the tribe of Kerchak who accepted the frightened native youth. When Teeka was taken as a mate by Toog, a Mangani from another tribe, Tarzan and Taug pursued them. When they were set upon by several of the Mangani from Toog's tribe, Teeka found some rifle cartridges that Tarzan had taken from his father's cabin, and threw them. Some hit a boulder and discharged, scaring the enemy Mangani away and saving Tarzan and Taug's lives. *Jungle Tales of Tarzan*

Tennington: A very positive and optimistic English Lord and friend of William Cecil Clayton and Jane Porter. Lord Tennington loved to sail his yacht, the *Lady Alice*, and took Jane Porter, William Cecil Clayton, Hazel Strong, M. Thuran (a.k.a. Nikolas Rokoff) and several others on a cruise down the African coast. After the yacht was wrecked and they had to abandon ship, the various members of the party became separated in the ocean. Tennington and Hazel's lifeboat eventually made shore not far from Tarzan's cabin. Tennington and Hazel fell in love and were married by Jane's father next to Tarzan's cabin in a double wedding ceremony with Tarzan and Jane. *The Return of Tarzan*

Tennington, Hazel: see **Hazel Strong**

1. Terkoz: Tarzan's Mangani foster brother, the son of Tublat and Kala in the tribe of Kerchak. Terkoz was a large and truculent Mangani who hated Tarzan greatly. He questioned the Jungle Lord's kingship and was insubordinate to him. During the first fight between them, the Ape-man stumbled on the wrestling holds, the half nelson and the full nelson (which served him in later battles). Instead of killing Terkoz, he applied the full nelson to his spine and allowed the Mangani to surrender by saying "ka-goda." But before that point, Terkoz gave Tarzan the forehead wound that became the identifying telltale scar which turned crimson when the Ape-man was angry. Later, when Terkoz abducted Jane Porter, Tarzan and the great Mangani had a rematch. This time Tarzan killed him. The second battle between them was also noteworthy for being the first time Jane actually set eyes on Tarzan. *Tarzan of the Apes*

2. Terkoz: The name of one of Tarzan's great wolfhounds at his African estate. Terkoz liked Victoria Custer and accompanied her in a search for her dream man, Nu, the son of Nu, of the Niocene. The great wolf-hound did not like Mr. William Curtis, who was in love with Victoria. But when Nu was found, Terkoz immediately took to the Troglodyte. When Victoria was abducted by Arabs Terkoz attempted to defend her, but was knocked out by an Arab rifle. After Curtis found Nu and Victoria together, he attempted to shoot at Nu, but Terkoz attacked and killed the jealous man. *The Eternal Savage (Lover)*

Terry, Rhonda: The blonde stunt double of Naomi Madison, the star of a Tarzanesque motion picture a studio was attempting to shoot on location in Africa. Rhonda was a better actress than Madison, more athletic and of a much tougher constitution. During the shooting Rhonda developed a liking for the chief cameraman, Bill West, and he did for her. For a prop in the movie, Rhonda used a treasure map she had found in a book. She did not consider the map to be genuine, but it turned out to be. And the Arabs who accompanied the movie expedition certainly believed it was. Consequently, Rhonda and Madison were both abducted by the Arabs because they wanted the map and could not tell the two women apart.

After Terry instigated their escape the two women became separated. Rhonda was captured by English speaking gorillas and taken to their gorilla king, Henry the Eighth. King Henry desired Rhonda, but so did the half-man, half-gorilla god of these educated apes. Tarzan arrived and after helping Rhonda escape he returned her to the movie crew. In a surprise denouement, it was revealed

that Rhonda had ended up marrying the film's movie director, Thomas Orman, and was making pictures in Samoa as his leading lady. *Tarzan and the Lion Man*

1. Tha: The disgruntled priest in the lost city of Opar who was rebuked by La before she attempted to sacrifice Tarzan. This censure caused Tha to go into a berserk rage and attack the other priests, the votaries and the priestesses. The disturbance allowed Tarzan to break his bonds without being seen. Tha then lustfully abducted La, but Tarzan pursued and rescued her, killing Tha in hand-to-hand combat. *The Return of Tarzan*

2. Tha: The husband of Lu-tan and the father of Nat-ul and her only brother, Aht. Tha was second only to Nu, the chief, in their cave village of the Niocene, and was the one that wanted the tribe to move out of the earthquake prone locale they were in. Tha liked Nu, the son of Nu, and thought he would be the ideal mate for Nat-ul, and accompanied the senior Nu in the search for the chief's son. *The Eternal Savage (Lover)*

1. Thaka: A male Mangani in the former tribe of Kerchak who complained to their new king, Tarzan, that Mungo, another Mangani, had stolen one of his wives. *Tarzan of the Apes*

2. Thaka: A female Mangani in the tribe of Kerchak. *Jungle Tales of Tarzan*

The First Woman: The name applied to the bulky and barbaric Alalus woman (or *Zertalacolol* in the language of the Minuni) who found Tarzan unconscious after the small plane he was piloting crashed beyond the Great Thorn Forest which encompassed the land of the Minuni. The large and hairy The First

Woman carried the inert Tarzan to her village to keep as a seasonal mate. When other females of the tribe saw her with him, they challenged her and tried to take Tarzan from her forcibly. The First Woman prevailed and after stripping the still unconscious Ape-man, she deposited him in her stone-walled corral where she had her children living in confinement. Later, when The Third Woman came back to the village with her own mate and bringing an antelope for food, The First Woman challenged the larger female and was killed in the ensuing struggle. *Tarzan and the Ant Men*

The Giant: *Zuanthrol* in the Minuni language. It was the name given to Tarzan by the warriors of Veltopismakus after he fought against them in battle on the side of the Trohanadalmakus warriors. Tarzan was known by this name even after he was shrunk to the size of the Minuni by Zoanthrohago, the *walmak*, he never told them what he was really called. He was able to withhold this information by feigning a complete lack of knowledge of their language. *Tarzan and the Ant Men*

The Great Emerald of the Zuli: The large mind-controlling stone used tyrannically by Woora, the magician–witch doctor of the Zuli, to subjugate anyone in the range of its power, including the warrior women of his village and their male slaves. The only person — other than Woora and his jealous twin brother, Mafka — who was able to control the gem and not be affected by it was Tarzan. When Tarzan defeated Woora he took the emerald with him. It was then taken from him by Lord who lost it to Mafka, the ruler of the Kaji. After the Ape-man retrieved it, the stone was taken from him again,

by the escaped prisoners Spike and Troll. The two thieves were then attacked by the Bantango cannibals. Although they escaped, they were forced to leave the emerald with the natives. Tarzan later entered their village and took the stone from the chief, and buried it. He then promised to give it to Gonfala and Stanley Wood to sell in civilization. See Gonfal. *Tarzan the Magnificent*

The Man: A certain lion named Numa used this term to distinguish Tarzan of the Apes from other humans. *Tarzan and the Tarzan Twins*

The Man Who Thought He Was Tarzan: See **2. God**

The Second Woman: The second Alalus woman (or *Zertalacolol* in the language of the Minuni) spoken of in *Tarzan and the Ant Men*. The Second Woman challenged The First Woman who had brought an unconscious Tarzan back to the village as her mate. During the ensuing fight, The First Woman knocked The Second Woman unconscious with her club. Later when she and The First Woman challenged The Third Woman, they were both killed by The Third Woman. *Tarzan and the Ant Men*

The Sheik: see **Amor ben Khatour**

The Spirit of Nyamwegi: Nyamwegi was a native from Tumbai village who was killed by the Leopard Men. When Orando, the son of the village chief, discovered that Nyamwegi was dead, he thought that the monkey, Nkima, was the *muzimo*, or new physical manifestation of Nyamwegi's spirit. *Tarzan and the Leopard Men*

The Third Woman: One of the largest and broadest barbaric Alalus women (or *Zertalacolol* in the language of the Minuni). When The Third Woman came back to her village with one of the effeminate and docile males and an antelope for food, she was challenged by The First Woman and the Second Woman. She killed both challengers. *Tarzan and the Ant Men*

Thetan: The nephew of King Herat of the lost city of Thobos in the volcano crater land of Tuen-Baka. Because Tarzan saved Thetan from a miniature Tyrannosaurus Rex, the Thobotian was impressed with the Ape-man and befriended him and his followers. Thetan helped lead an attack against a fleet from the rival city of Ashair, in a bid to rescue Helen Gregory. He then took Tarzan and the rest to Thobos and vouched for them with the king. Despite his advocacy, everyone was imprisoned, and Tarzan had to perform various feats to regain their freedom. Thetan helped Mr. Gregory and Magra escape. He then led an army against Ashair, the Forbidden City, to help Tarzan. *Tarzan and the Forbidden City*

Thoar: A Pellucidarian from the city of Zoram in the Mountains of the Thipdars and the brother of Jana, the Red Flower of Zoram. After Tarzan and the *sagoth*, Tar-gash, helped save Thoar (a *gilak*) from a *Dyal* (a Phororhacos of the Niocene) the Ape-man made peace between the two habitual enemies. The three traveled together until the Jungle Lord was carried off by a *thipdar* (pteranodon), whereupon Thoar and Tar-gash parted company. During their time together Thoar taught Tarzan the language of Pellucidar. When the lost American, Jason Gridley, stumbled upon Thoar being attacked by a *dyro-dor* (stegosaurus) he helped him defeat it with his pistols. While searching for Jana together they were both captured by the Ko-

rsar pirates and then the snakelike Horibs. With the unintended assistance of Tarzan, Thoar and Jason escaped the underwater caves of the Horibs and were reunited with the Ape-man, Jana, and the lost Waziri. They then traveled by boat and were found by the fleet out to rescue David Innes, then by the dirigible O-220. *Tarzan at the Earth's Core*

Thome, Atan: A suave-looking, thin-lipped Eurasian who desired the Father of Diamonds from Ashair. The plump, greasy Thome attempted to beat the Tarzan-led Gregory safari to the Forbidden City to obtain the jewel. After capturing Helen Gregory, Thome desired her, but Helen escaped. Thome's porters deserted him in fear, and the only one who remained was Lal Taask, his always faithful right-hand man. Thome's avarice for the Father of Diamonds drove him on until they were captured by the Ashairians. After Thome betrayed Taask, both were placed in cages in the throne room of the temple where the Father of Diamonds was kept in a casket. When they made their escape Thome took the casket and Taask attempted to kill him. By this time Thome was completely mad from greed and killed Taask with a rock. When the casket was opened Thome saw that it only contained a lump of coal. He immediately suffered a heart attack and died. *Tarzan and the Forbidden City*

Thompkins: One of the crew on Lord Tennington's yacht, the *Lady Alice*. While adrift on a lifeboat with Jane Porter, William Cecil Clayton, and M. Thuran (Nikolas Rokoff), and two other crewmen, Thompkins was the first to die of thirst and starvation. *The Return of Tarzan*

Thompson: The pilot of the search

plane that sighted Lt. Harold Percy Smith-Oldwick's plane downed in the desert gorge that led to Xuja, the maniac city. After his return to base, Lt. Thompson, Colonel Capell and General Smuts planned and executed a rescue mission. *Tarzan the Untamed*

Thoos: The name of the lion god of the people of Cathne, the City of Gold. Thoos was manifested in the form of an old mangy lion. *Tarzan and the City of Gold* and *Tarzan the Magnificent*

Throck, Dick: A big, meaty ex-prizefighter who, along with three others, was enlisted by Flora Hawkes to form a treasure hunting expedition to the lost city of Opar. After numerous ordeals, Throck survived and gratefully left Africa with nothing but his life. *Tarzan and the Golden Lion*

Throk: A sentry guarding the prisoners in the village of the Lake Dwellers when Nu, the son of Nu, searched it for Nat-ul. Nu talked to Throk in his dark hut just before he went on duty, and, after fooling him that he was also of the village, Nu told Throk that he would take the shift for him. At first, Throk was glad to get out of sentry duty, but then he became suspicious and aroused the village. When he attacked Nu, Throk got a stone axe in the face. *The Eternal Savage (Lover)*

Throwaldo: A zertol (prince or noble) and the unknowledgeable Chief of Agriculture in the Minuni city of Veltopismakus under King Elkomoelhago. *Tarzan and the Ant Men*

Thudos: A handsome middle-aged noble in Cathne, the City of Gold who was the father of the beautiful Doria. As a youth Thudos beheaded the king of their rival city, Athne, and had it prominently displayed on his door archway. In *Tarzan and the City of Gold* Thudos hid Doria from the jealous and vain Queen Nemone. For this he was imprisoned as a traitor along with Gemnon, Doria's suitor. In *Tarzan the Magnificent* Thudos was made king of Cathne by Tarzan after Nemone's brother, Alextar, killed himself as Nemone had done before him. *Tarzan and the City of Gold* and *Tarzan the Magnificent*

Thuran: See **Rokoff, Nikolas**

Tib, Tippoo: An old member of a tribe whose witch doctor gave Tarzan an immortality treatment as payment for saving his life. Tippoo Tib was used by the youthful looking witch doctor in an effort to prove to the Jungle Lord both the efficacy of the treatment and his own advanced age. With corroborating testimony from the chief, the witch doctor tried to establish that he was older than Tippoo Tib because he had been a contemporary of Tippoo Tib's grandfather and that Tippoo Tib himself had been born as early as the 1830s. Tippoo Tib was not a defined character in any of the Tarzan novels, and was only mentioned by the Jungle Lord. *Tarzan and the Foreign Legion.*

Tibbet: The second mate of the yacht *Naiad* that was pirated by the *Saigon*. After the *Saigon* was taken over by Tarzan, the Jungle Lord made Tibbet the second mate. Then the ill-fated *Saigon* was shipwrecked upon an island and the parties separated themselves into two camps. During an attempt to save the beautiful French girl, Janette Laon, from the men of the other camp, Tibbet shot and killed the Russian, Oubanovitch. *Tarzan and the Castaways*

Tibbs: The English valet of the Russian prince, Alexis Sborov. Tibbs accompanied Sborov when the prince and his wife took a party to Africa, where the couple hoped to find the secret of longevity. However, the plane carrying the group crash-landed in the jungle. Afterward, while the survivors were wandering around lost, Sborov tried to make Tibbs do all the work for him until the valet finally had enough and announced his resignation. Tibbs and the American pilot, Neal Brown, ended up the only ones left of the original party after Princess Sborov was killed by her husband, Jane and Annette were taken by the Kavuru, and Prince Sborov himself ran off into the jungle in fear. Ultimately, when everyone had escaped the Kavuru, Tibbs reluctantly accepted an equal portion of the longevity pills. *Tarzan's Quest*

Tibo: The ten-year-old son of Momaya and Ibeto of the village of Mbonga. Under the influence of an overpowering parental feeling, Tarzan took Tibo to raise as his own child. He named him Go-bu-balu, which meant Black-he-baby in the language of the Mangani. Tibo was terrified living among the Mangani, would not eat properly and consequently became thin and sickly. After learning some of the ape language, he asked to go back to his mother, and Tarzan finally complied. The village of Mbonga promised to make a tribute to Tarzan for returning the boy. Tibo was later taken by the leprous, hermit witch doctor, Bukawai, to force his mother to pay up for services which had not actually been rendered. Tarzan subsequently rescued Tibo from Bukawai. *Jungle Tales of Tarzan*

Timothy: One of the old bearded leaders in the epileptic and fanatic land of Midian. *Tarzan Triumphant*

Tobin: An older English speaking gorilla who was the high priest in the lost city London on the Thames in the Valley of Diamonds. Father Tobin was faithful to the half-man, half-gorilla ruler named God. *Tarzan and the Lion Man*

Tollog: The pockmarked, shifty-eyed brother of Sheik Ibn Jad. Tollog accompanied his brother's group on a treasure hunting quest to the fabled lost city of Nimmr. When Tarzan was captured by them Tollog crept into the Ape-man's tent and attempted to kill him. The Jungle Lord escaped by calling Tantor, the elephant. After the great pachyderm burst into the compound and tore the tent away, he hurtled Tollog onto another tent, but the lucky Arab landed virtually unharmed. Later, when Tarzan was again in their camp, he took Tollog, bound and gagged him, and left him in his tent. The older American, Wilbur Stimbol, crept into the tent to slay the Jungle Lord, but in the darkness, he killed Tollog by mistake. *Tarzan, Lord of the Jungle*

Tomar: A youth in the cave dwelling village of Clovi in Pellucidar. Tomar was the messenger who announced the return of Carb. *Tarzan at the Earth's Core*

Tomlin: The valet of John Ramsgate while the Ramsgates were on a photographic safari. Tomlin was in love with Violet, Lady Barbara Ramsgate's maid. *Tarzan and the Jungle Murders* in *Tarzan and the Castaways*

Tomos: An older, cruel and ruthless captain of the guard who was one of Queen Nemone's councilors in Cathne in *Tarzan and the City of Gold*. Tomos wanted to marry the queen and collaborated with old M'duze to control the city. It was rumored that he was the sire of Erot, a handsome commoner who was made a noble by the queen. Tomos did not like Tarzan. In *Tarzan the Magnificent* Tomos was made Prime Minister of the City of Gold through his manipulative influence in the life and dealings of Alextar, the new king of Cathne after Queen Nemone committed suicide. In a fit of vengeance and madness Alextar cleft Tomos' skull. *Tarzan and the City of Gold* and *Tarzan the Magnificent*

Toog: A rogue bull Mangani who had been beaten when he challenged the king of his original tribe for the kingship. After wandering into the territory of the tribe of Kerchak, Toog saw the lovely Teeka and abducted her for himself. In the process he shook Teeka's child, Gazan, loose from a tree and the *balu* was left lying lifeless. Teeka did not go willingly and Toog had to beat her into submission. Tarzan and Taug, Teeka's mate, pursued Toog and overtook him near his old stomping grounds. A battle ensued and many of Toog's original tribe came to help him. Tarzan and Taug would have been killed had not Teeka thrown some of Tarzan's rifle cartridges at a boulder, accidentally discharging them. The noise scared Toog and his tribe away. *Jungle Tales of Tarzan*

Torlini: A lieutenant, and pilot for Joseph "Joe the Pooch" Campbell and Nikolai Zubanev when they were pursuing Lt. Cecil Giles-Burton who had some stolen invention plans. Lt. Torlini was shot in the air by Giles-Burton's revolver, but managed to land the plane before dying. His body and plane were discovered by Tarzan who dubbed Torlini Pilot Number One. *Tarzan and the Jungle Murders* in *Tarzan and the Castaways*

Torndali: A *zertol* (prince or noble) in the Minuni city of Veltopismakus under King Elkomoelhago. Torndali was made Chief of Quarries even though he knew little about his assignment. *Tarzan and the Ant Men*

Tor-o-don: "Beast-like-man." A lower form of evolving man, living in Pal-ul-don. They were similar to the "Java man" and more like the *Pithecanthropi* than were the Ho-don or Waz-don. The Tor-o-don were slow moving, hairy creatures with tails. For more information see Pal-ul-don in Section Three. *Tarzan the Terrible*

To-yad: Of the Sagoth tribe of M'walot in Pellucidar. To-yad was a member of the group that found Tarzan trapped in their snare and about to be eaten by a saber-toothed tiger. A fellow Sagoth, Tar-gash, led this small party and decided to treat Tarzan humanely. To-yad questioned the authority of Tar-gash in relation to the Ape-man, and was summarily beaten by Tar-gash for doing so. At the first opportunity To-yad brought the matter up with M'walot the king of the tribe. *Tarzan at the Earth's Core*

Toyat (To-yat): The king of a Mangani tribe. Toyat hated and feared Tarzan because the Jungle Lord had kept him from becoming king at an earlier juncture. In *Tarzan, Lord of the Jungle* Toyat saw the Arab, Fahd, and the American, Wilbur Stimbol, with their prisoner, Princess Guinalda from the Valley of the Sepulcher, fleeing into the jungle. After scaring off the Tarmangani males Toyat took the she–Tarmangani, Guinalda, for himself. In *Tarzan the Invincible* Toyat stumbled upon another she–Tarmangani, Zora Drinov, alone in the jungle and seized her for himself, but Tarzan's Tantor, the elephant, scared the king Mangani away. *Tarzan, Lord of the Jungle,* and *Tarzan the Invincible*

J. Allen St. John illustration for *The Son of Tarzan* **(© 1915 Edgar Rice Burroughs, Inc.).**

Trent, Duncan: A member of the Ramsgate safari who liked Lady Barbara Ramsgate and was a bit jealous of the attentions given to her by Lt. Cecil Giles-Burton. When Trent approached Giles-Burton and told him to keep away from Barbara, a fight ensued in which Trent was knocked down. When Tarzan came to the safari he was accused of murder. Trent drew his pistol on the Jungle Lord, but he did it too slowly. Tarzan caught the man up and dragged him as a shield into the jungle. He later released him unharmed. *Tarzan and the Jungle Murders* in *Tarzan and the Castaways*

Troll: A white hunter with the Wood and van Eyk safari who looked like a gorilla and was captured by the Kaji warrior women. Troll had six wives among the Kaji. But he escaped from the tribe anyway, along with Tarzan, who he disliked. Troll and his cohort, Spike, took what they thought was the real mind-controlling Gonfal diamond and the Great Emerald of the Zuli from a sleeping Tarzan, and fled. In the jungle they were attacked by the Bantangos cannibals. Although they escaped, they left the Great Emerald of the Zuli with the natives. Troll and Spike then stumbled upon Gonfala and captured her with the intention of making her a queen and allowing her to rule with the Gonfal. The two men ended up fighting about the Gonfal and Gonfala. Spike knocked Troll silly, and thereafter Troll thought that Gonfala was his sister. All three were made prisoners in Athne, the City of Ivory, and after being rescued, the two men were escorted out of Africa after promising never to return. They were also given the artificial duplicate Gonfal diamond that they still believed was real. *Tarzan the Magnificent.*

Tublat: "Broken nose." The husband of Kala, Tarzan's ape mother. Tublat hated his Tarmangani foster son, and became Tarzan's childhood enemy. The young Ape-man added to this enmity by often making Tublat the victim of his pranks. Tarzan eventually killed Tublat after the latter attacked Kala in a berserk fit of jealous rage during a dum-dum ceremony. *Tarzan of the Apes* and *Jungle Tales of Tarzan*

Tubuto: An apprentice to the witch doctor, Rabba Kega, in the village of Mbonga who wanted to succeed his master. After Rabba Kega was found killed by a lion in a trap, Tubuto correctly suspected Tarzan, the white devil-god, of being behind it. In *Tarzan and the Jewels of Opar*, the Jungle Lord almost saved an itinerant witch doctor from an attack by Numa, the lion, but the man was mortally wounded. Before he died, though, he told Tarzan that he remembered him from the time he was practicing as the witch doctor in the village of Mbonga. And he prophesied some future doom as a gift to Tarzan for trying to save his life. Then he died. Although the name of this witch doctor was not given, by deductive reasoning, he could have been Tubuto. He was to be Rabba Kega's successor. And not long after Rabba Kega's death, the entire tribe was scattered by the French Navy searching for Paul d'Arnot, which left no village of Mbonga for another witch doctor to belong to. *Jungle Tales of Tarzan* and possibly *Tarzan and the Jewels of Opar*

Tur, of the Boat Builders: Tur came upon Nat-ul watching his tribe and desired her, even though he already had a wife named Gron and a son by her. Tur tried to capture Nat-ul and while he was pursuing her she was abducted by a pterodactyl and taken to an island. He took a canoe to the island in the hope of finding her still alive. He finally captured her and brought her back to his village; Gron became extremely jealous. Nat-ul escaped, while Nu, the son of Nu, was captured attempting to rescue her. Gron attacked Nu, and Tur beat her for it. In jealous revenge Gron killed their infant son and set Nu free. Tur found Nat-ul again and after tricking her he took her to another island. Together Nu and Gron went in pursuit of Tur and Nat-ul. Once they were all together, the heartbroken Gron killed Tur, then took her own life. *The Eternal Savage (Lover)*

Ubooga: The toothless old wife of Chief Bobolo. When Ubooga found out her husband's dual identity as a Leopard Man she held his secret over his head to get what she wanted. *Tarzan and the Leopard Men*

Udalo: The chief of the Bukena whose young women were constantly hunted by the Kavuru because of the close proximity of the two tribes. The Bukena hated the Kavuru, and when Tarzan came into their village they thought he was one and captured him. He escaped, though. When the Waziri came looking for him, Udalo had them all drugged and imprisoned. Tarzan returned and helped the Waziri escape. He then made Udalo promise not to harm any strangers, including himself and the Waziri, ever again. *Tarzan's Quest*

Uglo: The king of his tribe as well as the oldest and largest orangutan in it. After he saw Tarzan kill Histah, the snake, in order to rescue an orangutan balu, Uglo made friends with the Ape-man. *Tarzan and the Foreign Legion*

Uhha: The young daughter of Khamis, the witch doctor, in the cannibal village of Obebe on the banks of the Ugogo River. Uhha's village had imprisoned the Spanish actor and Tarzan impersonator, Esteban Miranda, until they could prove whether he was the river devil or the Jungle Lord. Esteban succeeded in convincing Uhha that he was the river devil and had her release him and give him weapons. The fearful Spaniard then forced her to go with him into the jungle where

they wandered for some time. After witnessing Miranda's cowardly ways and lack of woodcraft, Uhha realized that this person was neither the river devil nor the legendary Tarzan. So she knocked Miranda over the head while he slept, and after taking the pouch of jewels he had on him (which happened to belong to the real Tarzan), she left him lying unconscious. But alone in the jungle, Uhha was killed and eaten by a lion. *Tarzan and the Golden Lion*

Ukundo: A pygmy who was a captive along with the Tarzan Twins in the Bagalla cannibal village. After being the Twins' interpreter, Ukundo helped teach them to speak the Bagalla dialect. Even though he knew the jungle well and had great woodcraft knowledge, he was afraid of the jungle at night because of his superstitious belief in demons. Ukundo defended Doc by killing the jealous witch doctor, Intamo. He then accompanied and assisted the Twins in their escape from the Bagalla. *Tarzan and the Tarzan Twins*

Ulala: see **Fejjuan**

Ulan: A youthful friend of Ovan in the cave dwelling village of Clovi in Pellucidar. Ulan was a thinker and seemed more intelligent than others of his tribe. He was also a storyteller and an artist who made cave wall paintings. Ulan defended Tarzan as Ovan's friend and rescuer and accepted the Ape-man into the village. *Tarzan at the Earth's Core*

Ulp: One of the 20 priests who had been cast out from Opar for supporting the traitorous high priest, Cadj. Ulp came into disfavor with the group's leader, Gulm, who was advocating sacrificing Ulp to the Flaming God. While on sentry duty Ulp decided to let the group's captive high priestess, Kla (Gretchen von Harben), loose in the jungle so she would be eaten by a lion, and therefore not available to sacrifice him on Gulm's order. To explain what had happened, Ulp told Gulm that the Flaming God had come down and taken Kla away. But Gulm was suspicious. He had Ulp walk at the end of the line as they marched through the jungle so he might be killed by the arrows of Doc, which he was. *Tarzan and the Tarzan Twins*

Umar, Tiang: The chief of the Sumatran village where Sing Tai and Corrie van der Meer sought asylum and hid for two years from the Japanese army. Tiang Umar was tortured by the Japanese to tell them where the two refugees were, but he did not break. *Tarzan and the Foreign Legion*

Una: The sister of Nu, the son of Nu, of the Niocene. *The Eternal Savage (Lover)*

Ungo: The king of the tribe of Mangani in *Tarzan and the Forbidden City* that attacked the Gregory safari and carried off the Tarmangani-she, Magra. During the dum-dum ceremony in which they were to kill Magra, Tarzan arrived and saved her after fighting Ungo. He made the king surrender by putting him in a wrestler's full nelson. After the defeat Tarzan became king of the tribe and had the Mangani follow him and the safari to the volcano valley of Tuen-Baka. There Ungo saw Atan Thome running with the casket that the Tarmangani thought contained the Father of Diamonds. Ungo, thinking it a game, took the casket from Thome, but later dropped it. He then went into a cave and attacked the priests of Chon.

In *Tarzan and the Madman*, after Ungo found Tarzan unconscious from a bullet wound to the head, he carried the Ape-man away to safety. *Tarzan and the Forbidden City* and *Tarzan and the Madman*

Usanga: The burly, black sergeant in charge of a group of native soldiers who ran away from their German leaders. Usanga had kidnaped Fräulein Bertha Kircher and, at various times, had attempted to seduce her, rape her, and make her his wife. He had failed in all his attempts due to the intervention of his jealous wife, Naratu, or the sheer fear of her. After the Wamabos tribe he was staying with captured the stranded English pilot Lt. Harold Percy Smith-Oldwick, Usanga forced the flier to teach him how to fly his airplane. Once he learned the basics Usanga took off with Fräulein Kircher to start a new life with her: he left Naratu and Smith-Oldwick behind. His plan failed, however, because Tarzan lassoed the flying plane and climbed in, then killed Usanga by tossing him out. *Tarzan the Untamed*

Usula: A Waziri warrior who spoke broken English which he had picked up in Europe while there with Tarzan. Usula believed that the Spanish actor and Tarzan impersonator, Esteban Miranda, was indeed Tarzan and spoke to him in English. In *Tarzan and the Ant Men* Usula came upon a mentally unstable Esteban Miranda eating an old dead buffalo carcass, and mistaking him for the real Tarzan again, took him back to the Greystoke estate. *Tarzan and the Golden Lion* and *Tarzan and the Ant Men*

Valthor: A noble and an elephant man of the house of Xanthus in Athne, the city of Ivory. Valthor was about six feet tall, well-built, brown eyed, and had handsomely rugged strong features. He wore many ornaments and armor made of ivory. In *Tarzan and the City of Gold* Tarzan rescued Valthor from a band of *shiftas*. The two became friends and admired and respected each other. On the way to his country Valthor taught the Ape-man his language and in exchange Tarzan taught the Athnean how to make and use the bow and arrow. After both were taken captive in Cathne, the City of Gold, the Ape-man saved Valthor from a lion in a pit and won the Athnean's freedom from Cathne.

In *Tarzan the Magnificent* Valthor was made a prisoner after a successful usurpation of the Athnean throne. In the dungeon he befriended Stanley Wood, a prisoner from the outside world who was also a friend of Tarzan's. In captivity Valthor helped train Wood in the use of elephants. When the Ape-man was captured, the three friends were reunited. Tarzan then helped start a revolution and returned the throne to the king. *Tarzan and the City of Gold* and *Tarzan the Magnificent*

van der Bos, Tak: The reserve officer with a bad bunch of Dutch guerrillas in Japanese held Sumatra. Van der Bos led the guerrillas to believe that he was an ally, but he was not. After Tarzan fell from a tree near their camp and was knocked unconscious and taken prisoner, van der Bos confided his true allegiance to the Ape-man and together they escaped. Van der Bos knew Corrie van der Meer from childhood and was her good friend. Jerry Lucas was jealous of the relationship between the two until he found out that van der Bos was married. During an ocean escape attempt, the Dutchman's leg was blown off, and he later died aboard the rescuing submarine. *Tarzan and the Foreign Legion*

van der Meer, Corrie: A pretty 16-year-old blonde Dutch girl who, with her family, fled the invading Japanese in Sumatra. Slender and healthy, Corrie eventually became the only remaining member of her family, and for two years she and the van der Meers' faithful Chinese servant, Sing Tai, successfully hid in a native village. When they were finally discovered by the Japanese Corrie cut her hair short and dyed it black to look like a native boy. Despite her disguise she was identified and taken captive by the Japanese who she had developed a deep-seated hatred for and prejudice against.

After Tarzan, under the name of Clayton, saved her from the Japanese she joined his band of downed American forces. There she met the pilot, Jerry Lucas, and they fell in love. By this time Corrie was in great physical condition and demanded to be treated like the men. After several adventures, abductions and rescues, they all finally escaped, and Corrie and Lucas were to be married by the captain of the British submarine that took the party to safety. *Tarzan and the Foreign Legion*

van der Meer, Elsje (maiden name Verschoor): The Dutch wife of Hendrik van der Meer who was a rubber planter in Japanese held Sumatra in the Dutch East Indies. Together they had a daughter named Corrie. While fleeing the invading Japanese, Elsje became weak and contracted a fever from the exposure and the constant running. She was then carried by their faithful Chinese servant, Lum Kam, but eventually died nonetheless. *Tarzan and the Foreign Legion*

van der Meer, Hendrik: A stubborn Dutchman who planted rubber in

Japanese held Sumatra in the Dutch East Indies. He and his family had to flee their home when the Japanese invaded the island. During their flight his wife, Elsje, died from exposure and fever. Later, in the village where he sought refuge, Hendrik was bayoneted to death by the pursuing Japanese. His daughter, Corrie, and a faithful family servant, ultimately survived the Japanese occupation. *Tarzan and the Foreign Legion*

van Eyk, Robert (Bob): Stanley Wood's faithful friend and companion who was captured along with him by the Kaji warrior women. Van Eyk and Tarzan helped all of their party escape, and after staying at the Greystokes', he left for Railhead alone after Gonfala disappeared. *Tarzan the Magnificent*

van Prins, Kervyn: The captain and commanding officer of the friendly Dutch guerrillas in Japanese held Sumatra in the Dutch East Indies who helped Tarzan and his group. *Tarzan and the Foreign Legion*

Vanda: The orangutan mother of the balu Tarzan saved from Hista, the snake, in Sumatra. *Tarzan and the Foreign Legion*

Vesa: The mayor of Xuja, the city of maniacs. When Vesa caught his wife making advances toward the English pilot, Lt. Harold Percy Smith-Oldwick, he attacked them, but Smith-Oldwick killed him with his pistol. With Smith-Oldwick's help, Vesa's wife hid her husband's body behind some furniture in an alcove of her apartment. *Tarzan the Untamed*

Vestako: The manipulative and oily major-domo of King Elkomoelhago in the Minuni city of Veltopismakus. Vestako's official title was Chief of the Royal Dome. *Tarzan and the Ant Men*

Victor: A Filipino cabin boy aboard the dirigible O-220 that went into Pellucidar in search of David Innes. *Tarzan at the Earth's Core*

Violet: The maid of Lady Barbara Ramsgate. On a photographic safari in Africa, Lord Ramsgate's valet, Tomlin, and Mr. Romanoff's valet, Pierce, both fell in love with Violet. While the Russian professional photographer, Sergei Godensky, made unwanted advances toward her. *Tarzan and the Jungle Murders* in *Tarzan and the Castaways*

von Goss: An underlieutenant in the German company commanded by Hauptmann Fritz Schneider and Lt. Erich Obergatz which razed the Greystoke estate. When Tarzan finally caught up with von Goss in a machine gun trench in a war zone, the Ape-man snapped the German's vertebrae. *Tarzan the Untamed*

von Harben, Erich: The son of the medical missionary, Dr. Karl von Harben, and the sister of Gretchen. Erich was an archeologist who studied dead languages as well as the native Bantu dialects, and was an accomplished mountain climber. After hearing about the legend of the Lost Tribe of the Wiramwazi Mountains from the natives at his father's mission, Erich became very curious about the tribe and set out on an expedition to find them. After all but one of his safari deserted him he stumbled upon the Lost Empire in a large mountain canyon. In this throwback to Roman civilization, Erich made some quick friends high in the hierarchy, as well as a few enemies. He also fell in love with the beautiful Favonia, daughter of the old scholar Septimus. Tarzan eventually found him after several adventures and returned him to his father.

In *Tarzan at the Earth's Core*, it was revealed that Erich did marry Favonia and made several trips into the Wiramwazi Mountains to visit and explore her country there. On one such trip he discovered canoes made of a light, but strong metal. Tarzan suggested the use of this metal, dubbed *Harbenite*, in the construction of the dirigible that took the Jungle Lord and a crew into the Earth's core. *Tarzan and the Lost Empire* and mentioned in *Tarzan at the Earth's Core*

von Harben, Gretchen: The daughter of Dr. Karl von Harben and the sister of Erich. At 12 years old the pretty Gretchen wandered away from her father's mission and was captured by 20 outcast priests of Opar. These priests decided to make Gretchen their new high priestess and gave her the name of Kla, which is a contraction of "the New La." While traveling to the chosen site of their new temple they taught Gretchen their language and the duties she was to perform. They also began treating her with the respect due her new sacred role. Gretchen was rescued from the priests by the Tarzan Twins, Dick and Doc, but was later recaptured along with Dick. At the new temple site Gretchen was forced to sacrifice Dick, but swooned before completing the ritual. Tarzan and Jad-bal-ja arrived and saved them from the priests and returned Gretchen to her worried father. *Tarzan and the Tarzan Twins*

von Harben, Karl: A medical missionary running a mission in the Urambi country of Africa. After his 12-year-old daughter, Gretchen, was captured by outcast priests of Opar to be their new high priestess, Dr. von Harben relentlessly searched the jungle for her for weeks. There he met Tarzan looking for the Tarzan Twins, Dick and Doc. The Apeman found and rescued the Twins and Gretchen, and reunited the girl with her father. Dr. von Harben later sought Tarzan's help in locating his missing son, Erich. *Tarzan and the Tarzan Twins* and *Tarzan and the Lost Empire*

von Horst, Frederich Wilhelm Eric von Mendeldorf und: Of German heritage and once an officer in the German Imperial Air Force, von Horst became a lieutenant on the dirigible O-220 that flew into the land of Pellucidar to rescue David Innes. During a search for a missing Tarzan in Pellucidar, von Horst went hunting a boar and got separated from the ten Waziri who were with him. (To learn what happened to Von Horst, see *Back to the Stone Age* [original title: *Seven Worlds to Conquer*] in the Pellucidar series.) *Tarzan at the Earth's Core*

Walumbe: Native dialect for "God of death."

Wamala: The "boy," or personal servant, of the communist Zora Drinov. Wamala was faithful to Zora, but was forced away from her by the traitorous headman Kahiya. *Tarzan the Invincible*

Waranji: A Waziri warrior. *Tarzan the Magnificent*

Wasimbu: The giant Waziri, son of Tarzan's faithful friend Muviro. Wasimbu had been Jane's personal bodyguard for over a year when a German military company, led by Hauptmann Fritz Schneider, attacked and razed the Greystoke estate. The Germans crucified Wasimbu on the living room wall of the Greystoke home. *Tarzan the Untamed*

Wayne, Cyril: The actor cast by

Prominent Pictures to play Tarzan in preference to Tarzan himself (John Clayton). During a scene with a real lion, the animal attacked Cecil, but Tarzan intervened and killed it. *Tarzan and the Lion Man*

1. **Waziri**: A physically and intellectually superior tribe of brave and fearsome African natives. For more information see Natives in Section Three.

2. **Waziri**: The name of the chief of the Waziri when Tarzan entered their tribe. Chief Waziri was the last member of the tribe who had seen the lost city of Opar when they initially discovered it back in his youth. He described to Tarzan how to get there. Chief Waziri was killed during an attack by his tribe upon some ivory and slave raiding Arabs. *The Return of Tarzan*

3. **Waziri**: The name Tarzan took for himself as the newly elected chief of the Waziri after Chief Waziri's death. *The Return of Tarzan*

Werper, Albert: A tall lieutenant in the Belgian army who was assigned to duty in the Congo instead of being court-martialled. In a fit of jungle madness Werper shot his captain in cold blood, then fled his military compound and joined a group of Arabs led by Achmet Zek. Werper became one of Zek's trusted lieutenants and the two conspired against the Greystokes. Taking on the alias of M. Jules Frecoult, Werper pretended to be a lost hunter and was taken in by Tarzan and Jane. He then followed Tarzan to Opar and ended up stealing a pouch of jewels from him that the Ape-man had retrieved from the fabled city. After Werper had a falling out with Achmet Zek, he tried to take Jane (whom he desired) with him out of Africa by lying to her. He killed Zek

but lost the jewels. After a few captures and escapes, though, he regained the pouch of gems from the body of Chulk, the Mangani. Werper then fled alone into the jungle. His skeleton was found by Tarzan, the pouch of jewels still with it. *Tarzan and the Jewels of Opar*

West, Bill: The chief cameraman in the production crew attempting to shoot the motion picture, *Lion Man*, on location in Africa. Bill liked the stunt woman, Rhonda Terry, and she liked him, but he became jealous of the Tarzan look-alike, Stanley Obroski. When Rhonda and the actor Naomi Madison were kidnaped by Arabs, Bill went with the film's director, Thomas Orman, to try to find them. *Tarzan and the Lion Man*

"Whale": The nickname given to the five foot six inch Japanese officer in charge of the unit which captured Tarzan in Sumatra. Whale had been a truck gardener in Culver City and spoke English. *Tarzan and the Foreign Legion*

White: An English big game hunter employed as a technical advisor on the motion picture, *Lion Man*, which a studio was attempting to shoot on location in Africa. Major White was also cast to play the white hunter in the picture. In an ambush by the savage Bansuto cannibals, White was killed by a native arrow. *Tarzan and the Lion Man*

Wiggs, Peter: A black sentry at the cross near the tunnel entrance to the medieval Valley of the Sepulcher. Wiggs spoke old English and was dressed as a knight when he captured the lost American, James Hunter Blake. *Tarzan, Lord of the Jungle*

Willard: A knight from the Castle of the Sepulcher in the lost medieval Valley of the Sepulcher. Sir Willard went against the American, James Hunter Blake, in a joust in the Great Tourney. Blake won, but instead of finishing Sir Willard off, the American tended to his wounds. Returning the favor, Sir Willard and Sir Guy, who Blake also defeated and aided, secretly freed Blake from the dungeon of King Bohun. *Tarzan, Lord of the Jungle*

Wilson: One of three sailors on a lifeboat from Lord Tennington's wrecked yacht, the *Lady Alice*, along with Jane Porter, William Cecil Clayton and M. Thuran (Nikolas Rokoff). Wilson was the first person to suggest that they eat one among them in order to survive. The others were revolted and refused. Later the hunger-crazed Wilson threw himself overboard and drowned. *The Return of Tarzan*

Witch Doctor of the Mbonga: Even though Tarzan saved him from a lion, this witch doctor was still mortally wounded by the beast. He recognized Tarzan as Munango-Keewati, the forest devil, who had terrorized the village of Mbonga years earlier, and thought he would kill him. The Jungle Lord assured him he would not. The witch doctor then offered Tarzan a prophecy of evil and misfortune, and died.

Although no name was given him, this witch doctor told Tarzan that he had practiced in the village of Mbonga when the Jungle Lord first started terrorizing them in his youth. According to *The Jungle Tales of Tarzan*, the actual witch doctor at that time was Rabba Kega, but he was put in a lion trap by Tarzan and killed. However, he had an apprentice by the name of Tubuto training with him at the time. It is distinctly possible that Tubuto and the Witch Doctor of the Mbonga were one and

J. Allen St. John illustration from *Jungle Tales of Tarzan* (© 1919 Edgar Rice Burroughs, Inc.).

same. *Tarzan and the Jewels of Opar* and (possibly) *Jungle Tales of Tarzan*

Witch Doctor of Tippoo Tib's grandfather: Tarzan explained that while still young he had saved this witch doctor from an attack by a lion. The witch doctor claimed to be very old even though he looked in his twenties. As a reward for saving his life, he gave Tarzan a perpetual youth concoction that took a whole month of brewing, and also required the transfusing of several quarts of the witch doctor's blood into Tarzan's veins. *Tarzan and the Foreign Legion*

Wlala: The widowed pygmy woman from the cannibal Betetes village who was assigned the task of housing and caring for the white woman,

Kali Bwana, while they watched her for the neighboring chief, Bobolo. Wlala was cruel to her. When the village decided to eat Kali, Wlala attempted to kill her, but was shot dead by Tarzan's arrow. *Tarzan and the Leopard Men*

Wolff: Already a spy for Atan Thome, Wolff became the hired hunter for the Gregory safari and purposely led them off the trail. He then stole the map to the Forbidden City from the Gregorys so he could get more money from Thome. On the safari he disliked Tarzan and called him a monkey-man. At one point, he actually knocked the Jungle Lord down and attempted to shoot him. Wolff began to desire Magra, and after deserting the Gregorys, he forced her to go along with him. Magra killed him with his own pistol when he tried to rape her. *Tarzan and the Forbidden City*

Wolsey, Thomas: An English speaking gorilla who was a cardinal and part of the council to King Henry the Eighth in the city of London on the Thames in the Valley of Diamonds. Wolsey was loyal to the half-man, half-gorilla they considered God and led God's revolt against the king. Wolsey was the one who took Rhonda Terry to God. *Tarzan and the Lion Man*

Wood, Stanley: An American travel writer who was found by Tarzan almost starved to death, attempting to escape the Kaji country. While nourishing Wood back to health the Jungle Lord learned that Wood and his safari of friends had been captured by the Kaji women and their mind-controlling witch doctor ruler. While Wood was with them, Gonfala, the queen of the Kaji, fell in love with the man she called "Stanlee," and helped him escape. After

Tarzan told Wood that his name was Clayton, Wood thought him very Tarzan-like. He and the Ape-man then went back into the Kaji country and brought Gonfala and Wood's friends out.

While leaving for Railhead, Gonfala was taken by Spike and Troll. Wood wanted to pursue them and succeeded in getting a safari of Waziri warriors from the Greystokes to help search for her. After a while he separated from the Waziri and went alone to Athne, the City of Ivory, where he was made a prisoner. There Wood was willingly married to Gonfala by order of Menofra, the jealous wife of the dictator of Athne. Menofra hoped that her unfaithful husband would not break Wood and Gonfala's wedding vows and try to seduce the former queen of the Kaji. After Tarzan rescued the newlyweds from Athne, he planned to give them one or possibly both of the large and mystic jewels of the Zuli and Kaji, so they could sell them in civilization and become wealthy.

Wood was one of the few men Tarzan called friend. *Tarzan the Magnificent*

Woora: The old and shriveled Columbian magician–witch doctor of the Zuli warrior women. Woora had a falling out with his identical twin brother, Mafka (ruler of the Kaji), and made his own society to rule. To mentally control his people and bend them to his will, Woora used the Great Emerald of the Zuli. When he captured Tarzan and attempted to burn the Ape-man's eyes out, the old magician was killed by Lord, a male slave Tarzan had helped escape earlier. *Tarzan the Magnificent*

Wright-Smith, Algernon (Algy): A brave young Englishman who wore flannels while on the pirated yacht *Naiad*. Algernon was to marry Patricia Leigh-Burden. *Tarzan and the Castaways*

Xanila: The old blue-eyed Englishwoman who had been captured 60 years before while a young missionary and made queen of Xuja by King Ago XXV. Even though she was the queen, Xanila was a prisoner and forbidden to see or be seen by other women. Although the captive queen of many kings, her husband at the time of Tarzan was King Herog XVI. When Bertha Kircher was brought to her to be dressed and prepared to become the new queen, Xanila was courteous to her. *Tarzan the Untamed*

Xarator: The volcano in the land of Onthar where the inhabitants of Cathne, the City of Gold, sacrificed people to Thoos, their lion god. *Tarzan and the City of Gold*

Xerstle: The narrow faced rat-like friend of Erot, Queen Nemone's favorite in Cathne, the City of Gold. Xerstle was made a noble because of his relationship with Erot, and became Gemnon's roommate. When Tarzan came under Gemnon's care and supervision, Xerstle was evicted to allow the two to stay close to each other. Xerstle plotted with Erot to kill Tarzan in a manhunt with lions. The plot failed. *Tarzan and the City of Gold*

Ydeni: A Kavuru warrior priest who Tarzan saved from an attacking lion. After Ydeni captured Naika, the daughter of the witch doctor in the Bukena village, Tarzan took her from him and returned her to the village. Ydeni then captured Annette, the French maid of Princess Sborov, and took her to the Kavuru village. He later found the mentally unstable Prince Sborov, too, and

took him back to his village to use as one of their maniac servants. In return for saving his life earlier Ydendi showed Tarzan the secret tunnel exit from the temple of the Kavuru. *Tarzan's Quest*

Yip Xiu, Chal: The *ah kin mai* (high priest) of the Mayan city Chichen Itza upon the lost island of Uxmal. When Tarzan was presented to Chal Yip Xiu as a god, the *ah kin mai* was suspicious of the veracity of this claim and wanted to sacrifice the Ape-man. *Tarzan and the Castaways*

Za: A female dog which had lost its pups and which Tarzan acquired as a gift from the Umanga native village to suckle the young and recently orphaned Jad-bal-ja. *Tarzan and the Golden Lion*

Zek, Achmet: An Arab slave raider who hated all Europeans. He did, however, allow Albert Werper to join his group because the Belgian was an outlaw with military training. Zek ended up trusting Werper and made him a lieutenant in his camp. Together they plotted to get revenge on Tarzan. In accordance with the plan, Zek took Jane captive after razing the Greystoke estate while Tarzan was away at Opar. When Werper returned from Opar, Zek desired the gold the Waziri accompanying the Belgian had brought from the lost city. He also wanted the pouch of jewels Werper attempted to hide from him. After Werper escaped him, Zek went to the Greystoke estate to get the Waziri's buried Oparian gold. There he found the Belgian again and they fought a running battle until Werper killed Zek during a shootout in the jungle. *Tarzan and the Jewels of Opar*

Zeyd: A young Arab in the raiding party of Sheik Ibn Jad when they were searching for the fabled lost treasure city of Nimmr. Zeyd was in love with Ibn Jad's daughter, Ateja, and she loved him. A fellow raider, Fahd, also desired Ateja and framed Zeyd to be rid of his rival. Zeyd escaped the false accusation by fleeing into the jungle. There he met Tarzan who took a liking to the young Arab and had his Waziri guide him around. When Fahd met up with Zeyd again, he informed him that Ateja had been raped and murdered. Enraged, Zeyd killed Fahd with his khusa knife. Ateja was not, however, dead and the two were happily reunited. *Tarzan, Lord of the Jungle*

Zoanthrohago: The *zertol* (prince or noble) and *walmak* (wizard or scientist) in the city of Veltopismakus who was considered to be the greatest mind in all of Minuni. Zoanthrohago invented the device that he used to shrink Tarzan to the 18 inch size of the Minuni. He was also the one that first captured Tarzan in battle thereby legally making the Apeman his slave. King Elkomoelhago was jealous of the *walmak's* scientific achievements and had him imprisoned. Zoanthrohago loved the king's beautiful daughter, Janzara (who eventually returned his love), and escaped with her, and with Tarzan, Komodoflorensal, and a few others to the city of Trohanadalmakus. *Tarzan and the Ant Men*

Zopinga: A Mugalla cannibal from the Bagalla tribe in Ugalla. When he captured the Tarzan Twins, Dick and Doc, Zopinga wore many ornaments and had filed teeth. *Tarzan and the Tarzan Twins*

Zuanthrol: "The giant" in the language of the Minuni. When Tarzan was overcome and captured by the warriors of the city of Veltopismakus he was shrunk to a quarter of his size (which is the size of the Minuni) by

the *walmak* Zoanthrohago. Afterwards Tarzan pretended not to speak their language and, because they could not discover his real name, they were forced to call him Zuanthrol, the Giant. *Tarzan and the Ant Men*

Zubanev, Nikolai: A Russian exile, and the mysterious little man who made friends with Joseph "Joe the Pooch" Campbell while boarding in London. After stealing some invention plans Zubanev tried to sell them to the Italians. The plans were then taken from him, and he and Campbell followed the thief to Africa by plane where they all shot each other down. Lost in the jungle they came upon the Ramsgate safari, and with them Zubanev used the alias, Peterson. Zubanev was later found stabbed through the heart in the tent he shared with Campbell. It was ultimately revealed that Campbell had killed him. *Tarzan and the Jungle Murders* in *Tarzan and the Castaways*

Zugash: "Big tooth/fang." The fierce king of the Tongani (baboons). *Tarzan Triumphant*

Zuppner: The captain of the dirigible O-220 that, with Tarzan and Jason Gridley aboard, was taken through the polar opening in the Earth's crust and into the land of Pellucidar. *Tarzan at the Earth's Core*

Zu-tag: "Big neck." A larger, more powerful and intelligent Mangani bull of the tribe of Go-lat. The curious Zu-tag liked to watch the Wamabo Gomangani cannibal tribe from a tree. Doing this on one occasion, he observed Tarzan — who his tribe had recently befriended — fall from a broken branch and into the center of the cannibal village. As Zu-tag watched, the Ape-man just lay there in an unconscious heap among the Gomangani. With a sense of duty, he rushed back to the tribe and enlisted several bull Mangani and the Tarmangani-she, Fräulein Bertha Kircher (who he had trouble explaining his plan to), to go with him in an attempt to rescue Tarzan. The rescue worked and the Mangani saved not only Tarzan, but another Tarmangani, Lt. Harold Percy Smith-Oldwick, who they did not know was there. *Tarzan the Untamed*

Zutho (or Zu-tho): A Mangani bull from the tribe of Toyat and later the tribe of Ungo. Zutho was a friend of Tarzan's because the Jungle Lord had nursed him back to health when he was sick and the other Mangani had abandoned him. In *Tarzan and the Lost Empire* Zutho was captured along with a few other members of the tribe for the gladiator games in the Colosseum of the lost Roman city of Castra Sanguinarius. When they were sent out to attack Tarzan, he recognized them and renewed their friendship. He then used them to help him start a revolt and escape the Colosseum.

In *Tarzan and the Leopard Men* , it was revealed that Zutho often argued with Toyat. When they both desired the same female Mangani, Zutho succeeded in luring her away, along with several other disgruntled bulls and their mates, to form his own tribe.

In *Tarzan and the Forbidden City*, Zutho was a member of the tribe of Ungo when they entered the forbidden volcano land of Tuen-Baka at Tarzan's behest. There Zutho seized the Tarmangani female, Magra, from the priests of Chon, the True God, and dragged her away by the hair. Afterward he feared being killed or punished by Tarzan and attempted to murder Magra. But she thwarted him by jumping from a cliff into the lake Horus, together with Helen Gregory, who was also a captive. *Tarzan and the Forbidden City, Tarzan, Lord of the Jungle, Tarzan and the Lost Empire, Tarzan the Invincible, Tarzan and the Leopard Men*, and *Tarzan and the Madman*

Zu-yad: "Big-ear." The king of the Mangani tribe who came upon the Tarmangani-she, Jean Hanson, and her father, Eugene, in the jungle. Zu-yad and Go-lot, a young insubordinate bull, both desired Jean, and after fighting over her, Go-lot killed Zu-yad. *Tarzan: The Lost Adventure*

Zveri, Peter: The large Russian who was the leader of a communist treasure raiding expedition to Opar. Zveri sought the peace of Europe and control of a large section of North Africa. He became a little power mad, however, and had delusions of becoming the Emperor of Africa. Because of his brutality, he was deserted by his native porters and was finally shot in the back and killed by Zora Drinov, a fellow communist who had accompanied him to Africa, and the woman he loved. *Tarzan the Invincible*

Zygo: The king of Athne who went into hiding in the mountains after Phoros usurped the throne. Zygo was returned to the throne after Tarzan started a successful revolt. *Tarzan the Magnificent*

Zytheb: The keeper of the keys and a priest in the temple of Brulor, the Father of Diamonds, in Ashair, the Forbidden City. Zytheb was given Helen Gregory as a servant by Brulor. This meant that she also became his mate. After they were officially married by Ashairian standards and alone in Zytheb's chambers, Helen killed him by hitting him over the head with a vase. *Tarzan and the Forbidden City*

NUMBERS AND SYMBOLS

800³ + 19: See **Aoponato**
800³ + 21: See **Aopontando**

 : See **Aoponato**

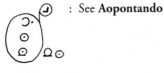 : See **Aopontando**

SECTION FIVE

Book Summaries

(In chronological order)

1. Tarzan of the Apes

First published in *All-Story* magazine, October 1912, as *Tarzan of the Apes*. Book published 1914, A.C. McClurg & Co.

Cast: Alice (Rutherford) Clayton; Lady Greystoke; Ancient Mariner; Archimedes Q. Porter; (Capt.) Billings; Black Michael; (Lt.) Charpentier; (Capt.) Dufranne; Esmeralda; Father Constantine; Gunto; Jane Porter; John Clayton; Lord Greystoke; Kala; Kerchak; King; Kulonga; Mirando; Mungo; Neeta; Paul d'Arnot; Robert Canler; Samuel T. Philander; Snipes; Tana; Tarrant; Tarzan; Terkoz; Thaka; Tublat; William Cecil Clayton

Summary: Tarzan's biological parents, John and Alice Clayton, Lord and Lady Greystoke of England, are marooned by mutinous sailors in an uncharted jungle on the West Coast of Africa. They build a cabin and Lady Alice gives birth to a son they name John. A year later she dies and her husband is killed in his cabin the same day by Kerchak the king of the local tribe of "Mangani," or great apes. Before the

year old toddler is killed too, he is taken and adopted by a bereaved female ape named Kala who has recently lost her little one. She takes the human baby from the crib and deposits her dead baby in its place. The human baby boy is dubbed "Tarzan" which means "white skin" in the language of the Mangani and is raised and nurtured as one of the tribe.

Tarzan grows and develops as a Mangani without any memory of his former parents or knowledge that he is anything but a hairless ape. Eventually he stumbles upon his parents' time-worn cabin and discovers their remains along with his father's hunting knife. This weapon gives him the "edge," literally, over the other denizens of the jungle. Being filled with curiosity Tarzan studies the various books and children's primers in the cabin and teaches himself to read and write English. Through this self-education the young Ape-man realizes that he is different from his ape brothers because he is a "M-A-N." He also acquires his father's diary and mother's locket which has, unbeknownst to him, graven images of his parents in it.

Kala is soon killed by a black native, Kulonga, of a newly relocated tribe of cannibals. Tarzan hunts and kills Kulonga in revenge even though the native is the first human being Tarzan has ever seen. Thus begins Tarzan's periodic terrorization of the native village. Through observation he learns to shoot with their bow and poison tipped arrows and to use their spear. With these, along with his father's knife and a grass lasso he stumbled upon as a youth, he becomes a formidable fighter. And eventually, through battle, Tarzan becomes the king of his tribe of apes.

In a challenge to his kingship a large ape named Terkoz, his foster brother, attacks the Jungle Lord. During the battle Tarzan receives a large cut to his forehead. The resulting scar becomes an identifying feature that stands out as a crimson band across his forehead whenever he is angered. During this same battle Tarzan accidentally discovers the wrestler's hold — the full Nelson. He uses it to subdue Terkoz, and make him surrender, without killing him.

Around Tarzan's nineteenth birthday another ship of mutinous sailors strikes land near the cabin and maroons Jane Porter, her father, his assistant, a black maid and, ironically, Tarzan's biological cousin, William Cecil Clayton. While attempting to keep his distance, the Jungle Lord helps and rescues all the members of the marooned party from man and beast. He also quickly falls in love with Jane who is the first white woman he has ever seen. When Jane is abducted by the still living and bitter Terkoz, Tarzan is forced to battle him again; but this time he kills the great ape. This is the first time Jane sets eyes on Tarzan, and during the few days that they spend together in the jungle, she falls in love with him.

The French Navy eventually appears on the scene and during a search for Tarzan and Jane, they are attacked by the local tribe of cannibals. One of the French officers, Lt. Paul d'Arnot, is captured and taken back to the village and tortured in preparation for being killed and eaten. Tarzan, having just returned Jane to her party, goes to the village and saves d'Arnot before he can be killed. The Ape-man spends a lot of time in the jungle nursing d'Arnot back to health before returning him to the others. During this time d'Arnot mistakenly teaches Tarzan to speak the French language instead of English which Tarzan can already read and write. He then teaches Tarzan to speak English as well.

While d'Arnot is healing the rest of the Porter party leave the continent with the navy. Tarzan and d'Arnot finally return and discover them gone. At Tarzan's request, the two then begin the long trek into civilization so that the Lord of the Jungle can be with Jane and other humans. During their travels d'Arnot reads Lord Greystoke's diary and suspects Tarzan's true origin. The pair eventually reach America. Then, finally reunited with Jane, Tarzan rescues her from a forest fire. In the end, Paul d'Arnot tells Tarzan about his true origins, and uses his dead father's diary as proof. But the Ape-man denounces his real identity and birthright even though they mean wealth and possibly marriage to Jane.

2. The Return of Tarzan

Published in *New Story* magazine, June to May 1913, as *The Return of Tarzan*.

Book published 1915, A.C. McClurg & Co.

Cast: Abdul; Alexis Paulvitch; Ali-ben-Ahmed; Archimedes Q. Porter; Busuli; el adrea; Esmeralda; Flaubert; (Capt.) Gerard; (Lt.) Gernois; Hazel Strong; Jane Porter; Jean C. Tarzan; John Caldwell (London); Kadour ben Saden; Karnath; La, of Opar; Nikolas Rokoff; Olga de Coude; Ouled-Nail; Paul d'Arnot; Raoul de Coude; Samuel T. Philander; Spider; Tarzan; (Lord) Tennington; Tha; Thompkins; Thuran; Waziri; William Cecil Clayton; Wilson

Summary: A Jane-less Tarzan returns to Europe from America on an ocean liner. During the voyage, he foils several attempts by the Russians, Nikolas Rokoff and his cohort, Alexis Paulvitch, to blackmail Count Raoul de Coude and his wife Olga, who happens to be Rokoff's sister. The Russians swear vengeance on the Ape-man, while the young and beautiful countess develops a crush on him.

In Europe, Rokoff and Paulvitch maneuver Tarzan and Olga into a compromising situation that is discovered by the count. For the sake of his honor, the count challenges Tarzan to a duel with pistols. In recompense for the wrong he has caused the de Coudes, the Jungle Lord allows the count to shoot him without returning fire. Touched by the Ape-man's bravery and humility, the count forgives him, and the two men become trusted friends.

The count gets Tarzan his first job, as a secret agent in the French ministry of war. His initial assignment is to watch a Lt. Gernois in desert communities in Algiers. Rokoff and Paulvitch follow Tarzan into the desert where they attempt to have him captured and killed. Again they fail.

Tarzan is assisted and aided in a few escapes by a young *Ouled-Nail* (see Section Four). She develops a crush on him. He returns the *Ouled-Nail* to her father, a sheik, and is greatly honored and welcomed in their community. The Ape-man loves the life of the nomadic Arabs and is tempted to stay with them indefinitely.

Tarzan is reassigned as a secret agent, and on the boat back to Europe he meets and makes friends with Hazel Strong, Jane's best friend. He also discovers a shaved Nikolas Rokoff using the alias of M. Thuran. During the cruise Rokoff and Paulvitch throw the Ape-man overboard. Tarzan makes it to the African shore at, coincidentally, the very beach of his parents' cabin in the jungle where he was raised among the great apes.

Here Tarzan stumbles upon the Waziri tribe. After living with them, he is elected their new chief and given the name of their dead chief, also Waziri. Tarzan learns of Opar from his new people and leads them on a raiding party to the fabled lost city. In Opar, Tarzan is captured by its savage priests and placed upon the altar of their Flaming God to be offered as a sacrifice by the beautiful High Priestess La. After escaping the altar, the Jungle Lord discovers Opar's ancient and forgotten treasure vaults. With his Waziri, he takes a load of gold, and buries it in the dum-dum amphitheater.

Meanwhile, Jane Porter becomes engaged to William Cecil Clayton (Tarzan's cousin), and together with Professor Porter, Mr. Philander, Esmeralda, and a Lord Tennington they take a cruise on Tennington's yacht. On the way they meet up with Hazel Strong and M. Thuran (Rokoff) at a port, and they all decide to travel together back to Europe. Paulvitch parts with Rokoff who falls in love with Hazel Strong and starts courting her. Unfortunately, Tennington's yacht hits a derelict and sinks, but everyone escapes into lifeboats. Jane's boat, which also contains Rokoff, Clayton and three sailors, has no provisions, and after getting separated from the others during the night, they lose their oars. The little boat drifts aimlessly, and one by one the sailors die off. But luckily, before the three others succumb, they wash ashore near Tarzan's cabin.

Here they make a tree fort and forage for food, and Jane finally tells Clayton that she loves only Tarzan and calls off their engagement. She is then abducted by 50 frightful priests of Opar who are searching for the escaped Tarzan. Clayton contracts a fever, but Rokoff abandons him anyway, and meets up with the rest of the survivors of Tennington's yacht who have landed further up the coast, even nearer Tarzan's cabin. Rokoff tells them that Jane and Clayton are dead. They then wait for rescue.

The Ape-man is informed by a Mangani that a white woman Tarzan suspects to be Jane has been taken captive by the 50 priests of Opar. He immediately goes in pursuit, and ends up back in Opar right before La plunges the ceremonial knife into Jane's heart. He violently interrupts the ceremony and flees with an unconscious Jane, after informing La — who is lovesick for him — that Jane is his woman. La is crushed. Jane regains consciousness and is overjoyed at being again with her Tarzan, and they profess their love for each other. On the way back, Tarzan and Jane meet up with some of his Waziri warriors. All together they return to the nearly dead William Cecil Clayton and witness his last breath. Before he dies, he informs Jane that Tarzan is the rightful heir to the Greystoke estate and title.

They then find the rest of the party, which has also been discovered by Paul d'Arnot and a navy cruiser. At the sight of Tarzan, Rokoff takes a shot at him, but is overcome by the Ape-man. The Russian is put under arrest, and William Cecil Clayton is buried next to Tarzan's parents' graves near the cabin. Tarzan and Jane, along with Lord Tennington and Hazel Strong, decide to get married in a double ceremony that is performed by Jane's father, Archimedes Q. Porter, next to the cabin.

3. *The Beasts of Tarzan*

Published in *All-Story Cavalier* magazine, May 16 to June 13, 1914, as *The Beasts of Tarzan*. Book published 1916, A.C. McClurg & Co.

Cast: Akut; Alexis Paulvitch; Buulaoo; Carl; Esmerelda; Gust, the Swede; Jack Clayton; Jane Clayton; Jones; Kai Shang; Kaviri; Schmidt; Schneider; M'ganwazam; Molak; Momulla, the Maori; Mosula woman; Mugambi; Nikolas Rokoff; Paul d'Arnot; Sheeta the Terrible; Sullivan; Sven Anderssen; Tambudza; Tarzan

Summary: Nikolas Rokoff and Alexis Paulvitch attempt to get revenge on Tarzan by kidnapping his infant son, Jack, and demanding a reward. The Ape-man agrees to meet them, and Jane secretly follows, but both are separately taken captive and put on the ship the *Kincaid*. After it sails to Africa, Tarzan is stripped and put ashore on an isolated jungle island as his punishment for incurring the wrath of Rokoff and Paulvitch.

Aboard ship Jane befriends the Swedish cook, Sven Anderssen, who helps her and the baby escape by going ashore with them into the African jungle to some native villages. Rokoff and Paulvitch pursue them, and Sven

J. Allen St. John illustration from *The Beasts of Tarzan* (© 1916 Edgar Rice Burroughs, Inc.).

Anderssen tries to defend Jane but is killed in the attempt. Jane also discovers that the baby she has is not her son, Jack, but another. The infant dies in the jungle and she buries it.

On the island Tarzan wins the respect of the Mangani tribe of Akut and joins them. He also decides to save a trapped Sheeta, the panther, and the grateful feline remains faithful to the

Jungle Lord. He then has the Mangani and Sheeta get to know and associate with each other. When some natives canoe to the jungle island, Tarzan and his Mangani attack them and take one of their warriors, Mugambi, captive. Although terrified, Mugambi obediently helps Tarzan teach the apes how to paddle the canoe. The men and apes leave the island together, taking Sheeta with them, and make the mainland. There Tarzan takes up the trail of Rokoff and Paulvitch to regain his son. He also learns that Jane is there. Sheeta and the apes of Akut follow Tarzan faithfully and respond to his call and save him a few times. Mugambi also learns to respect and follow Tarzan, and the beasts follow and obey the brave native as well.

After finally meeting up with Rokoff on the *Kincaid* Tarzan gets Jane back, and Sheeta the Terrible gets the honor of killing the Russian. Paulvitch is left a captive of a cannibal tribe of natives and Akut and his fellow Mangani return to their island.

An attempt to kidnap Jane by another group of sailors is thwarted and the Greystokes return safely to Europe where Jack is actually in the keeping of the faithful Esmeralda.

4. The Son of Tarzan

Published in *All-Story Cavalier* magazine, December 4 to 25, 1915, as *The Son of Tarzan*. Book published 1917, A.C. McClurg & Co.

Cast: Abdul Kamak; Achmet ben Houdin; A'ht; Ajax; Akut; Alexis Paulvitch; Ali ben Kadin; Amor ben Khatour; Armand "The Hawk" Jacot; Bwana; Carl Jenssen; Condon; Geeka; Goob; Harold Moore; Herr Skopf; Jack Clayton; Jane Clayton; Jeanne

Jacot; Jervis; Kovudoo; Mabunu; Mbeeda; Meriem; Michael Sabrov; Morison Baynes; Mr. Hanson; Mrs. Billings; Muviri; My Dear; Simpson; Sven Malbihn; Tarzan; The Sheik

Summary: It is ten years since Tarzan left Jungle Island and Paulvitch is still a captive of the cannibals and has been cruelly beaten, abused and mutilated. When a passing ship comes ashore Paulvitch is rescued, and he uses the alias of Michael Sabrov. The ship stops at the jungle island where Akut, the intelligent Mangani friend of Tarzan lives, and is waiting for Tarzan to return. The curious ape approaches Paulvitch and the sailors, hoping to find Tarzan amongst them. The Russian, seeing the timidity of the great ape, decides to capitalize upon it and takes Akut with him. Paulvitch names him Ajax and becomes his trainer. Together they join a traveling show and perform for the public.

The show stops in Europe where the Greystokes are living. Their now older and physically well-built son, Jack, hears about the ape and sneaks out to see him. As part of the usual show, Akut enters the audience and encounters Jack. After sensing something about the youth, the Mangani stays with him. Tarzan arrives to take Jack home and is reunited with Akut. Jack is delighted to learn about his father's past because, until now, it has been withheld from him on Jane's insistence. Tarzan tries to purchase Akut, but he is turned down by Paulvitch who the Jungle Lord does not recognize.

Once more the Russian begins to scheme to get his revenge upon Tarzan, and decides again to use Jack. After letting the younger Greystoke visit Ajax at will, Paulvitch attempts to kill Jack. But in defense of the youngster, Akut attacks and kills the Russian. Jack then secretly goes to Africa to return Akut to the jungle. On the way they disguise Akut as his invalid grandmother, Mrs. Billings. When a burglar breaks into their room, the apparent old lady surprises the would-be robber and kills him. Terrified of prosecution Jack enters the jungle to live with Akut. There the ape takes him under his wing and instructs the youth in all the jungle lore of his father. He calls the son of Tarzan Korak, because that is as close as he can get to saying "Jack." In the language of the Mangani, Korak means "the Killer." From his experiences in the jungle, Korak ultimately becomes almost identical to his father in all respects except that his victory cry is silent.

While living in the jungle, Korak comes upon some Arabs and sees an abused girl about his own age amongst them. It is Meriem who was abducted by the Sheik, Amor ben Khatour, in an act of revenge against her father, Capt. Armand Jacot of the French Foreign Legion and the Prince de Cadrenet, for executing his nephew. Meriem has lived with the Arabs for about three years and has almost completely forgotten her past life as a French princess. Korak defends her and takes her with him into the jungle. There the three live together platonically, and Meriem learns the Mangani language and her share of jungle lore and woodcraft. Jack then begins to fall in love with Meriem, but she sees him only as a brother and protector.

After Meriem is taken by natives and sold to two Swedish bounty hunters, she is almost raped by one of them. Tarzan arrives and saves her, then takes her to his wife, Jane, at their bungalow. There Jane teaches Meriem to speak English and French, and instructs her in proper etiquette and customs. Meriem is also courted by an English visitor to the Greystokes'

named Morison Baynes, and almost forgets about Korak who she believes is dead. Another visitor then comes to the Greystokes'. It is the Swedish bounty hunter, Sven Malbihn, who attempted to rape Meriem earlier. He is in disguise as Mr. Hanson, and collaborates with Baynes to abduct Meriem.

After succeeding in their abduction Hanson betrays Baynes, and Meriem ends up a prisoner again of the same Arabs that Korak rescued her from years earlier. Korak is taken prisoner by them too. But Tantor, the elephant, is called to the rescue. The enraged pachyderm kills the Sheik and Mr. Hanson, and takes Korak away. Then Tantor almost kills Meriem, but Tarzan arrives and saves her.

Meriem and Jack are married. The new Mrs. Clayton is reunited with her father and finally learns her true identity.

5. Tarzan and the Jewels of Opar

Published in *All-Story Cavalier* magazine, November 18 to December 16, 1916, as *Tarzan and the Jewels of Opar*. Book published 1918, A.C. McClurg & Co.

Cast: Abdul Mourak; Achmet Zek; Albert Werper; Basuli; Cadj; Chulk; Jane; Jules Frecoult; La; Lady; Mohammed Beyd; Mugambi; Munango-Keewati; Taglat; Tarzan; Tha; Witch-Doctor of Mbonga village

Summary: Albert Werper is a murdering traitorous exile from the Belgian army who joins Achmet Zek's slave raiders. He gets along well with Zek and becomes the Arab's lieutenant. Zek and Werper then plot to extort money from Tarzan. As part of the plan Werper goes to the Greystoke estate under the alias of M. Jules Frecoult and gets in their good graces. Soon afterward, Tarzan learns that he is bankrupt due to the possible mishandling of funds they had in a company. Consequently, he must return to the treasure vaults of the fabled lost city of Opar to get more money. He sets out with 50 Waziri warriors. Werper, who overheard the details of the expedition, secretly follows.

At Opar Tarzan and the Waziri take a hundred pieces of gold from the treasure vault. Then an earthquake strikes and knocks Tarzan out. At the same time it blocks the exit out from the treasure room where Werper was hiding and is also trapped. The Belgian is unharmed and manages to get out of the room by a back way. But it leads into the heart of Opar, and he is taken captive there and put on the altar to be sacrificed by La, the high priestess of the Flaming God.

In the meantime Tarzan regains consciousness, but is suffering from amnesia due to the blow on the head. This causes him to revert to his primate mentality. Finding his way out of the treasure room, he passes through a room filled with buckets of jewels. He takes a fancy to the shiny stones and fills a pouch for himself. He then heads to the altar room where Werper is about to be sacrificed. He rescues the Belgian from the altar and together they head back in the direction of the Greystoke bungalow. For this sacrilege, La and some priests go after Tarzan to find and punish him.

Back at the Greystoke bungalow, Achmet Zek arrives and, after razing the estate, takes Jane captive and leaves the others for dead. The huge Mugambi, however, is not dead. He survives and tracks the Arabs. The Waziri who were with Tarzan in Opar then arrive and bury the gold near the remains of the bungalow. The Ape-man observes them from a tree, but does not recognize his friends.

Werper steals the pouch of jewels from a sleeping Tarzan and runs back to Achmet Zek. After putting the buried gold elsewhere, the Lord of the Jungle discovers the jewel pouch missing and pursues Werper.

La catches up to Tarzan and takes him prisoner. The high priestess offers the Ape-man his freedom in return for his love. He refuses and is prepared to be sacrificed right there in the jungle. At that moment an enraged Tantor arrives and scatters La and her priests. After saving her, Tarzan continues on the trail of Werper. On the way he befriends some Mangani and takes two with him: Chulk and Tag-lat. He disguises them as Arabs and enters Zek's camp.

By this time Jane has escaped on her own, and Werper informs Achmet Zek of the buried gold. Zek then sees the pouch of jewels and realizes that Werper was not going to share them with him. But the Belgian has seen Zek spying on him and escapes, but is soon caught by some Abyssinian soldiers. They also capture Mugambi. Werper tells the Absyssinians of the buried gold to bribe them into letting him go, but they take him with them to the Greystokes'.

During this time Mugambi sees the pouch of jewels and recognizes it as Tarzan's. After the faithful native steals the precious stones and replaces them with pebbles he escapes. Then the curious and intelligent Chulk discovers Mugambi and takes the pouch of jewels from him while the giant native sleeps. Mugambi awakens mystified at the loss.

At the bungalow both the Arabs and the Abyssinians meet and battle each other. Zek sees Werper and chases him into the jungle where the Belgian kills the Arab. From the safety of a tree Jane witnesses the struggle and, still believing Werper to be Jules Frecoult, she comes out of hiding to be with him. He desires her and convinces her to go with him. During their journey they are taken by the Congo Free State military.

Tarzan finally regains his senses and goes to the Congo Free State military camp as it is being attacked by lions. Under the Ape-man's command, Chulk carries Werper off while he saves Jane. During the rescue Chulk is mortally wounded and dies with the Belgian in his arms. Werper discovers the missing jewel pouch on Chulk and, after snatching it, runs off alone into the jungle.

Mugambi is then reunited with Tarzan and Jane and they all return to the bungalow and have it repaired. The gold is also retrieved. The whereabouts of the jewels is still an unsolved mystery to all of them until they discover Werper's remains in the jungle with the pouch nearby. How he obtained them again becomes the new mystery for them.

6. Jungle Tales of Tarzan

Published in *Blue Book* magazine, September 1916 to August 1917, as *The New Stories of Tarzan*. Book published 1919, A.C. McClurg & Co.

This book is a collection of short stories set in Tarzan's youth before he met Jane, but after he met the tribe of Mbonga. Each story is listed below in the order in which it is presented in Burroughs' book, and each has its own individual summary.

Cast: Bukawai; Bulabantu; bumude-mutomuro; Devil-god; Gazan; Go-bu-Balu; Gozan; Gunto; Histah; Ibeto; Kama; Mamka; Manu; Mbonga; Momaya; Mumga; Mweeza; Numgo; Rabba Kega; Tantor; Tarzan; Taug; Teeka; Thaka; Tibo; Toog; Tubuto; White God of the Jungle

SUMMARIES

I   Tarzan's First Love: As Tarzan matures he falls in love with a beautiful she–Mangani named Teeka who used to be one of his childhood playmates. Taug, who also used to be one of Tarzan's childhood playfellows, is now a large and surly bull, and he desires Teeka as well. Taug and Tarzan both vie for Teeka's love, and at first Tarzan wins out because of his human cunning. But while the Ape-man is away, Teeka chooses Taug for her mate. Tarzan is hurt, and when Taug gets caught in a native trap, he is happy, because he feels that he will no longer have a rival for Teeka. He leaves Taug in the trap and returns to tell Teeka. The young she-ape shows concern for Taug and the compassionate Tarzan returns and lets Taug loose. Tarzan remembers that he is different from the rest of the tribe and understands that every creature should have a mate of its own species.

II   The Capture of Tarzan: Tarzan observes the warriors of Mbonga digging an elephant pit with upward-pointing stakes at the bottom. Figuring out the nature of the trap he warns Tantor off, but falls into the pit himself. The young Jungle Lord is taken back to the village unconscious. There he breaks free and fights for his life, but is almost overpowered and killed by the warriors when Tantor comes to his rescue.

III   The Fight for the Balu: Taug and Teeka's union produces a

J. Allen St. John illustration from *Jungle Tales of Tarzan* (© 1919 Edgar Rice Burroughs, Inc.).

small reddish *balu* they appropriately named Gazan, which means red-skin. Teeka is very protective of her baby and will not let anyone near it — not even Tarzan. Taug sides with his mate and helps to keep Tarzan away. During one careless moment, however, Teeka forgets about her *balu* and turns away from it. Sheeta, the panther, takes advantage of this lapse and moves in for an easy meal, but Tarzan leaps to the rescue. A battle between Tarzan and Sheeta ensues. Gazan is taken up by Teeka, and Taug joins Tarzan in the fight. Together the two males kill the hungry feline. Thereafter Teeka permits Tarzan to play with her *balu*.

IV   The God of Tarzan: Tarzan learns something about deity from the books in his biological parents' cabin. The young Jungle Lord questions the apes of his tribe about the nature and identity of God, but does not receive any satisfactory answers. At one point he thinks that Goro, the moon, is God and questions the silent satellite. Receiving no answer, he goes to the village of Mbonga to seek illumination. There a ceremony with the witch doctor is taking place. Tarzan, thinking that maybe the witch doctor is God, boldly enters the village and confronts the terrified medicine man. Not being God, he runs in fear, and the impatient Tarzan becomes angry. While the Apeman is facing away from Chief Mbonga, the old native attempts to put a spear in his back. Tarzan senses it, wheels about, and captures Mbonga. But something mysteriously stays his hand from killing the old man. Tarzan then leaves the village.

Back near the tribe of Kerchak, Gazan is captured in the coils of Histah the snake. Tarzan observes Teeka as she throws herself against this hated and repulsive enemy of the tribe. He goes to her assistance and is surprised at Teeka's lack of fear when her baby is in danger: under normal circumstances she would run in fear from Histah. After the great snake is defeated, Tarzan realizes that it must have been God that stayed his hand from killing Chief Mbonga, and that it must have been He who caused Teeka to do something so against her nature like attacking Histah to save her balu. Tarzan decides

that all good things come from God, whatever or whoever God may be.

V   Tarzan and the Black Boy: Tarzan, feeling maternal, decides that he wants to care for something. So he goes to the village of Mbonga and abducts a young boy named Tibo. The terrified boy is never happy living with Tarzan and the tribe of Kerchak although he does pick up some of the Mangani language.

Back in the village, Momaya, Tibo's mother, is grief stricken at the loss of her son, and seeks out the village witch doctor for help. After gaining no assistance from him, she remembers the leprous witch doctor, Bukawai, who lives in a cave and entertains devils in the form of two hyenas. Bravely she makes her way to the cave of the unclean one. Bukawai informs her that he can restore Tibo if he is paid in advance. Unable to do so, she leaves.

The Jungle Lord finally feels sorry for his poor motherless foster child. While Tarzan is away, Tibo comes upon his mother on her way back from Bukawai, and their reunion is joyous. After Tarzan arrives and saves them from an attacking lion, Tibo pleads with him not to take him away from his mother again. Tarzan agrees and escorts them back to the village. Bukawai observes all of this from the shadows.

VI   The Witch-Doctor Seeks Vengeance: Bukawai attempts to extort money from Momaya claiming that it was his power that brought little Tibo back to her. She refuses to pay and ends up hating all witch doctors. Bukawai then decides to abduct Tibo, to force her to pay him even more in ransom.

Tarzan recognizes Tibo's footprints and follows them to Bukawai's cave. There the boy is being held prisoner behind a wooden lattice that is barely able to keep the hungry pet hyenas away from his soft flesh. The Jungle Lord enters, fends off the beasts, and rescues Tibo. He then returns the boy to the village and his mother. Momaya is overjoyed and knows that Tarzan's magic is more powerful than that of her village witch doctor and of Bukawai.

VII   The End of Bukawai: Bukawai comes upon an unconscious Tarzan who has been knocked out in a rainstorm. The unclean witch doctor binds the Ape-man and takes him to his cave where he ties him to a tree inside. Bukawai has to beat his hyenas to prevent them from attacking the defenseless Tarzan. The leprous witch doctor finally leaves the man and the animals alone to let whatever will happen happen.

The ingenious Tarzan is not helpless, though, and begins using friction to wear his bonds away. Just as he finally breaks free, the hyenas attack. He fends them off, then captures Bukawai and ties him to the same tree. The Jungle Lord leaves and lets the hyenas do what they will. And they do.

VIII   The Lion: Numa, the lion, kills one of the Mangani and the young Jungle Lord is for not letting the great cat get away with it. With this in mind, he leads the rest of the tribe in tormenting Numa in such a way that the lion cannot eat his ape meal. Tarzan even goes so far as to snatch the corpse of the dead Mangani from the clutches of the harassed feline.

The Lord of the Jungle advises the tribe to place sentries around their feeding grounds to ward off and warn of any other would-be attacker. The Mangani eventually see the wisdom of this advice and do so. But Tarzan knows how lazy his primate brothers are, and what short attention spans and memories they have. So he decides to play a joke on them as an object lesson. He dons an old lion hide with head intact that he stole from the tribe of Mbonga, then approaches the tribe of Kerchak on all fours and imitating a lion in every respect. His ruse works better than he expects. Unfortunately for him, the Mangani have exceeded his expectations for them: they still have sentries posted. And the tribe attacks him.

Tarzan is knocked out by a rock and would be killed by the bulls of the tribe but for a gray-whiskered Manu, the monkey, that races to his rescue. Even after Manu withdraws the lion skin from the unconscious body beneath and reveals that it was Tarzan all along, several older members of the tribe still wish to finish him off. But Taug and Teeka do not, and they stand up for their Tarmangani friend. Others follow their example, and Tarzan is saved. Albeit sore, he is gladdened that the tribe listened to his advice and posted sentries for protection.

IX   The Nightmare: A very hungry Tarzan decides to steal cooked elephant meat from the pots of the tribe of Mbonga after one of their late night food orgies. It tastes disgusting to the primitive Jungle Lord, but he eats it anyway. He then goes to sleep in a tree where he has nightmares induced by the strange fare he has eaten.

When he goes to his cabin, he is attacked inside by a trespassing gorilla Bolgani. But believing it all another dream, he allows himself to be carried off by the large anthropoid ape. Finally, after Tarzan has tried to wriggle free, the gorilla bites him on the shoulder, and it is then that he realizes this is not a dream. They fight, and Tarzan kills Bolgani with his knife. The confused Jungle Lord decides never to eat the flesh of Tantor again.

X   The Battle for Teeka: Tarzan

discovers some shiny rifle cartridges in his father's cabin. Not knowing what they are he takes some with him, putting them in his pouch. Near the tribe, Teeka is on sentry duty and is abducted by Toog, a rogue Mangani bull from another tribe, to be his mate, and Gazan is left for dead. When Tarzan learns of all this, he rallies Taug and the two go after the impetuous Mangani to rescue Teeka.

They overtake the captor and captive near Toog's tribe, and a battle ensues. Being so near them, Toog alerts his brothers to come to his rescue. Tarzan and Taug are then outnumbered and it looks like the end, but Teeka tries to help by throwing things. Some of the things she throws are the rifle cartridges from Tarzan's pouch which hit a rock outcrop and discharge. The sound scares off Toog and his rescuing tribe.

XI   A Jungle Joke: A bored Tarzan finds some warriors of the tribe of Mbonga setting and baiting a trap for Numa, the lion. He decides to play a joke on them and carries off their witch doctor, Rabba Kega, replacing the bait in the trap with him. The members of the hunting party, finally missing the witch doctor some distance off, return looking for him, only to discover his body being eaten in the trap by a large lion. Although horror-struck, they take the lion alive back to their village anyway. Tarzan, still observing, feels sorry for Numa, and decides to play another joke upon the tribe. Retrieving the same lion head and hide that he used to trick the tribe of Kerchak, he enters the village at night with the costume on.

Just when the dancing villagers are at a frenzied peak in a ceremony and are ready to bring out the caged lion to torture and eat him, Tarzan walks into view imitating the beast at liberty. The villagers begin to flee in terror. Then Tarzan stands and takes off the costume to let them see that it is him. The astonished natives decide to attack this evil forest god and rid themselves of it. After easily eluding them, Tarzan returns to the real caged lion and releases it. When the villagers see the real lion they think it's Tarzan and attack it. But when the angry beast returns the fight, they are terrified. After this, they believe Tarzan is a shape changer.

XII   Tarzan Rescues the Moon: Tarzan explores the jungle at night and discovers a camp of warriors from the tribe of Mbonga. All but one of the warriors fear the glowing eyes outside the ring of their campfire light. This one is Bulabantu the underchief of the tribe. He bravely faces the glowing eyes and throws fire brands at them. Tarzan sees the campfire as Goro, the moon, at night, and the stars as the eyes of predators wanting to pounce upon Goro and kill him. Pondering this, the Ape-man returns to his tribe of Mangani and tries to explain his thoughts to them. They do not understand him at all. And after he leaves, they talk about him and conclude that he is more peculiar than ever. They want to kill him. But Taug and Teeka stand up for him once again.

When Bulabantu accidentally crosses the boundaries of the tribe of Kerchak and is spied by one of the sentries, the apes prepare to attack and kill him. When Tarzan sees who it is he goes to the courageous native's side to try and protect him from the menacing Mangani. When the worked-up tribe decides to attack and kill both the humans, Taug steps to Tarzan's side to defend his friend. The three are vastly outnumbered, but just at this point, Tantor comes to the rescue.

Tarzan is disgusted with the tribe and leaves them for his parents' cabin.

He tells them that among their whole number only Taug and Teeka are not foolish, and that these two alone may come to visit him in the future. A month passes and Tarzan still has not come back to the tribe. One night while Taug is watching the moon and the stars, he thinks about the things Tarzan has told them. Just then an eclipse occurs, and Taug believes that Goro is being eaten by Numa of the stars. The excited ape awakens the tribe and tells them that Tarzan was right all along. Terrified and confused, they send Taug to the cabin to see if Tarzan will come and rescue the moon. Tarzan duly shoots arrows into the sky. The eclipse ends and Goro emerges from the shadow of the Earth. The tribe is ecstatic and welcomes the young Tarmangani back into the tribe.

The only one skeptical of this rescuing of the moon is Tarzan himself.

7. *Tarzan the Untamed*

Published in *Red Book* magazine, March 1919, as *Tarzan the Untamed*. Book published 1920, A.C. McClurg & Co.

Cast: Bertha Kircher; (Colonel) Capell; Fritz Schneider; Go-lat; Harold Percy Smith-Oldwick; Herog XVI; (General) Kraut; Metak; Naratu; Numa of the Gulch; Numa of the Pit; Numabo; Otobu; Patricia Canby; (Major) Preswick; (Major) Schneider; (General) Smuts; Tarzan; Thompson; Usanga; Vesa; von Goss; Wasimbu; Xanila; Zu-tag

Summary: A company of German troops pillage and burn the Greystoke bungalow in British East Africa while Tarzan is away. He arrives home to sort through the wreckage and the corpses of his comrades, and discovers what he believes to be Jane's body. A native askari gives the Jungle Lord the names of the men who led the company, and he swears an undying vengeance upon them, and upon all Germans. He immediately heads for enemy lines looking for the company's commanders. On the way there he seeks shelter in a cave that leads to an enclosed gulch. The gulch is the dwelling place of Numa, the lion. When Numa returns to the gulch, Tarzan blocks the cave entrance to it, trapping Numa within. He then continues on to the battle front where the British and the Germans are fighting.

The Jungle Lord boldly enters a German headquarters and mistakenly captures the brother of Hauptmann Fritz Schneider, the officer commanding the company that destroyed his wife, his friends and his property. Tarzan takes his captive back where a very hungry and angry Numa is still a prisoner, and forces the German down a cliff into the gulch.

Tarzan also enters the British headquarters of the Second Rhodesian Regiment and notices a girl who looks just like one he saw behind German lines. She is Bertha Kircher and he deduces that she is a German spy.

Deciding to help the British, Tarzan kills an enemy sniper and turns the rifle on the Germans, taking a deadly toll on them. He then concocts a plan to give the British an even greater advantage, and returns to the gulch where Numa is still trapped. He forces the lion to go with him and lets it loose in a German machine-gun trench. The great cat wreaks havoc with its fangs and claws. The Jungle Lord then commandeers the machine gun and turns it upon the German troops. As he's firing, a soldier sneaks up behind him and attempts to bayonet him. Tarzan turns in time to defend himself, and recognizes the insignia on the German's blouse as those of the troops he was searching for with such vengeful rage. The soldier is helpless in his hands, and the Jungle Lord easily breaks his spine. It is von Goss, the under-lieutenant to Hauptmann Fritz Schneider.

Tarzan then tracks Bertha Kircher. After Numa of the gulch attacks her horse, the Ape-man drives the cat away and saves the German spy, but only because she is a female. He discovers that she is wearing his mother's locket. Jane was wearing it when the Germans raided their estate, but it was not on her burned corpse when he found it. He takes the locket from Bertha and escorts her through the jungle with the plan of turning her over to the British as a spy. As they are walking together, she knocks Tarzan out and retrieves the locket. She then heads to her rendezvous point and meets up with Hauptmann Fritz Schneider. Bertha uses the locket as the agreed friendly sign. The Prussian desires Bertha and forces himself upon her. Tarzan, disguised as a German officer, enters the room and stops him. The Jungle Lord then announces who he is, and attacks and kills Schneider. He again lets Bertha Kircher live and, after obtaining his locket, leaves.

He heads out into the jungle promising to himself to avoid mankind for good, and asks Manu, the monkey, where the closest tribe of Mangani can be found. Manu tells him that they are located in a rich country on the other side of the desert before him. Tarzan heads out across the desert, and begins to suffer from hunger and thirst, but he eventually makes it to the plentiful country on the other side of the desert, where he eats and regains his strength and health.

While there he observes a runaway troop of native German recruits who have Bertha Kircher as a prisoner. The troops are under the leadership of a big black sergeant, Usanga, who desires Bertha, but fears the wrath of his jealous wife, Naratu, if he touches the white woman. After befriending the local tribe of cannibals, the Wamabos, Usanga sets up camp in their village. Bertha escapes and stumbles into the Mangani tribe of Go-lat where Tarzan is living. The Ape-man protects her and builds her a shelter.

Meanwhile British army lieutenant, Harold Percy Smith-Oldwick, who is flying solo, is forced down in the jungle for repairs. While working on his plane he is captured by the Wamabo and the tribe prepares to eat him. Tarzan discovers these preparations, and while spying on the village, falls from a broken branch and is knocked unconscious when he hits the ground. The Wamabo add the Jungle Lord to their evening's menu, and he is held captive in the same hut as Smith-Oldwick. After being informed that Tarzan is a prisoner of the Wamabos, Bertha Kircher leads the apes into the village, where they charge the natives. The two men are freed.

Smith-Oldwick falls in love with Bertha. While Tarzan is away, they decide to make a break for his airplane. There they are captured by Usanga who forces Smith-Oldwick to teach him to pilot the craft. On his first solo flight, Usanga takes Bertha and plans never to return. While the plane is taking off, however, Tarzan arrives and lassoes it. As the machine ascends, Tarzan climbs into it. He and Usanga struggle until he succeeds in throwing the sergeant out of the plane.

Bertha takes the controls and they return for Smith-Oldwick. After letting Tarzan out, the two lovers fly away together. From a tree, the Jungle Lord watches them fly over the desert. Then

Fazekas Attila illustration for *Tarzan the Untamed* (© 1988 Edgar Rice Burroughs, Inc.).

he sees the plane take a dive and vanish into the horizon. Feeling obligated to them, he heads out to see if they need his assistance. On his way he comes upon a great black lion caught in a Wamabo pit. He feeds it, then frees it, and continues on his way, chiding himself for how soft he has become, aiding a German female, an Englishman, and a lion.

Smith-Oldwick brings the plane down in the desert in a forced landing. He and Bertha find themselves in a canyon and come across a skeleton there. Tarzan was in the canyon too when he was traveling to the land of the Mangani, and he came across the same skeleton. After a while a lion approaches them. It is the beast that Tarzan rescued from the pit. When the Jungle Lord reaches them, the big cat is friendly to him, and the four head down the canyon together. The lion's presence suggests a source of water nearby. As they travel they realize they are being followed. They are then attacked at night by black-maned lions and their human masters. Tarzan is left unconscious, and Bertha and Smith-Oldwick are taken prisoner to a hidden valley wherein lies the walled city of Xuja. The Xujans are maniacs and use lions as pets and food. The people also talk to and worship parrots and monkeys.

There Bertha is set to become the bride of the king, but instead is abducted by the crazed prince. As for Smith-Oldwick, after he escapes a lion den, he has a beautifully shaped maniac woman make advances toward him. Tarzan finally enters the city and finds both Smith-Oldwick and Bertha. They all make their escape and are pursued up the canyon by the warriors and lions. A battle ensues. Tarzan and company make a good stand, but the odds are overwhelming. At the last moment,

a search and rescue group from Smith-Oldwick's military unit comes to their aid, and the day is saved.

When they are all safe, Tarzan and Smith-Oldwick learn that Bertha is a double agent ultimately working for the English. Tarzan also learns from the diary of Fritz Schneider that Jane could still be alive.

8. Tarzan the Terrible

Published in *All-Story* magazine, February 12 to March 27, 1921, as *Tarzan the Terrible*. Book published 1921, A.C. McClurg & Co.

Cast: A-lur; An-un; Bu-lot; Dak-lot; Dor-ul-Otho; Erich Obergatz; Es-sat; Gryf; Ho-don; Id-an; In-sad; In-tan; Jad-ben-Otho; Ja-don; Jane; Korak; Ko-tan; Lu-don; Mo-sar; O-dan; O-lo-a; Om-at; Pal-ul-don; Pan-at-lee; Pan-sat; Ta-den; Tarzan-jad-guru; Tor-o-don; Waz-don; Waz-ho-don

Summary: While searching for Jane, Tarzan wanders into an isolated land with mountains on three sides and a swamp on the other. It is the semi-primeval land of Pal-ul-don where two main groups of people live. One group, the Ho-don, are Caucasian. They do not have hair on their bodies, but they do have a prehensile tail. The other group, the rival Waz-don, are covered with dark fur and also have the prehensile tail. The Jungle Lord meets one of the Ho-don named Ta-den and befriends him. As they travel, Ta-den is attacked by a Waz-don named Om-at, but Tarzan intervenes. He persuades Om-at and Ta-den to forget their differences and enter into a tripartite pact with himself. Then they all travel on together. Ta-den and Om-at teach Tarzan the language and customs of Pal-ul-don.

They go to the Waz-don's cave village so that he can claim the kingship of his people. This is also where the beautiful Pan-at-lee, the woman he wants to marry, is living. Just before they arrive, however, the current king makes advances toward Pan-at-lee and she runs away. When Om-at gets there, he attacks the king and kills him. While searching for Pan-at-lee, the Jungle Lord is captured by a rival tribe. But he escapes after cutting off the tail of the guard and beheading him. This helps earn the Ape-man the notorious title of Tarzan-jad-guru, Tarzan the terrible.

The Jungle Lord continues on Pan-at-lee's trail and finds her in an abandoned cave being attacked by a rare and lower breed of man called a Tor-o-don. Tarzan kills the Tor-o-don and makes friends with Pan-at-lee. While heading back to Om-at's cave city they are treed by the Triceratops-like *gryf*. This ferocious and carnivorous animal will not let them down, but Tarzan figures a way to let Pan-at-lee escape anyway. He then learns how the Tor-o-don tame and ride the *gryfs*. He masters the skill and rides one to the Ho-don city of A-lur.

In A-lur Tarzan claims to be Dor-ul-Otho, the son of their god, Jad-ben-Otho, and befriends O-lo-a who loves Om-at. O-lo-a's new personal servant is none other than Pan-at-lee who was captured after leaving Tarzan. The Ape-man also incurs the wrath of the high priest, Lu-don, who is suspicious of the stranger's godhood. Tarzan then discovers that Jane is a prisoner in the city and is desired by both the king and Lu-don. While attempting to rescue his wife, he is captured, but gets away.

After being abducted by a rival king, Jane escapes and lives on her own in the forest, using the many survival skills she has learned from her husband. At this time Lt. Erich Obergatz,

one of the Germans responsible for her capture and supposed death, finds her and tries to befriend her. Jane rejects his approaches and threatens him. When Obergatz tries to force his way into her tree fort, she stabs him with a spear. Wounded, he wanders away half-crazy and heads toward A-lur. There he puts flowers in his hair, and, totally naked, pretends to be Jad-ben-Otho, the tailless god of Pal-ul-don. Most believe him. The crafty Lu-don does not, but he decides to use him as his puppet to gain the favor of the people and assume complete religious and political control.

Jane and Tarzan are both recaptured after a civil war breaks out, and the Ape-man is placed on an altar to be sacrificed alive by Obergatz. Just as Obergatz raises the knife, he is shot by the rifle of Korak who, while searching for Tarzan, met Ta-den and was taken to the city. Korak also shoots Lu-don and a few others, and is proclaimed the Messenger of Death of the Great God. Pan-at-lee and Om-at are finally married, as are Ta-den and O-lo-a.

9. *Tarzan and the Golden Lion*

Published in *All-Story* magazine, December 9, 1922, to January 20, 1923, as *Tarzan and the Golden Lion*. Book published 1923, A.C. McClurg & Co.

Cast: Adolf Bluber; Blagh; Bolgani; Cadj; Carl Kraski; Dick Throck; Dooth; Esteban Miranda; Flora Hawkes; Gobu; Gomangani; Jad-balja; Jane; Jervis; John Peebles; Keewazi; Korak; La; Luvini; Numa, King of Beasts, Emperor of All Created Things; Oah; Obebe; Old Man from the Valley of the Palace of Diamonds; Owaza; Pagth; Tarzan; Usula; Za

Summary: While Tarzan, Jane, and Korak travel back from the land of Pal-ul-don they come upon an orphaned lion cub. Tarzan decides to befriend it and raise it as a pet. He names it Jad-bal-ja, which in the language of Pal-ul-don means the Golden Lion. Jad-bal-ja's training goes wonderfully. The Golden Lion learns to obey Tarzan, to fetch, and not to kill unless ordered to.

In the meantime a former maid of the Greystokes, Flora Hawkes, along with some co-conspirators, hires a Tarzan look-alike named Esteban Miranda and form a safari to steal treasure from Opar. On the way Miranda plays his part well and is seen by natives who mistake him for the true Jungle Lord. He does, however, kill animals indiscriminately with his primitive weapons and is not friendly to those he meets. After finding Opar with Flora's directions, Miranda enters through Tarzan's secret granite boulder passage and carries out a load of gold.

By this time Tarzan has heard rumors of a possible Tarzan impersonator and goes off with some of his Waziri to investigate. After discovering Flora's safari, he boldly enters it alone. His former maid recognizes him as the real Jungle Lord, while her cohorts think he is Esteban. At Flora's word Tarzan is drugged and left behind.

While still in the jungle, Esteban stumbles into the Waziri warriors who accompanied Tarzan. They believe him to be the real Jungle Lord, their master. Esteban uses them to steal all the Oparian gold from his own safari so that he can come back for it later with Flora who he has fallen in love with.

From the walls of Opar, Esteban's closeness to the ancient city is observed, and he is thought to be the real Tarzan who committed sacrilege and desecrated the temple of the Flaming God. Cadj, the traitorous high priest, is informed and decides to go after the Jungle Lord without informing La. After Cadj sets out he discovers Tarzan's still unconscious body in the abandoned camp of Flora Hawkes. There the high priest attempts to sacrifice him but is stopped by La who has followed him after being informed of his plans. Tarzan is taken back to Opar and thrown in prison.

After a while, La comes to Tarzan's cell and leads him from Opar through a narrow pass in the back mountains, because her love for him is still strong. They continue on into the strange land behind Opar called the Valley of the Palace of Diamonds. There in the forest they discover a tribe of a lower order known as Gomangani who are ruled by a cruel and more advanced tribe called Bolgani. The Bolgani wear jewelry, use weapons and walk upright. In defense of the Gomangani, Tarzan kills one of the Bolgani. They are then fearful of the revenge of the Bolgani, so the Jungle Lord takes the body of the Bolgani to the outside of its own city, and leaves it there. It is discovered and the Bolgani attack the Gomangani village anyway, and take La prisoner.

Tarzan enters the city of the Bolgani and discovers that they worship a lion and use the Gomangani as slaves to mine diamonds. He also discovers an old white man who has been a prisoner of the Bolgani since his youth. Over the years the Bolgani have used this white man's outside knowledge to build and do other advanced things.

After sending a messenger to gather all the oppressed tribes of Gomangani, Tarzan rescues La and kills the Bolgani ruler, Numa, King of Beasts, Emperor of All Created Thing. Jad-bal-ja, who escaped to follow his master, arrives and the Jungle Lord places the Golden Lion on the throne. Finally the tribes of Gomangani arrive and help take over, and the old white man is ultimately made the new ruler. Tarzan, with a bag of diamonds from the vaults of the Bolgani city, then leads an army back to Opar to place the exiled La back on the throne. The coup succeeds, then Tarzan and Jad-bal-ja leave. Back in the jungle Esteban begins to believe that he really is Tarzan. He abducts Jane after abandoning Flora who now hates him. Tarzan and Jad-bal-ja arrive and rescue Jane, and the Golden Lion pursues Miranda. After the Tarzan impersonator jumps into a river, they assume he is dead. In reality he has been captured by the Obebe cannibals who fear and hate the real Tarzan. They hold Miranda a chained prisoner until they can decide if he is the Ape-man or a devil.

10. Tarzan and the Ant Men

Published in *All-Story* magazine, February 2 to March 17, 1924, as *Tarzan and the Ant Men*. Book published 1924, A.C. McClurg & Co.

Cast: Adendrohahkis; Alalus; Andua; Aoponato; Caraftap; "Dackie" (Jack Clayton); Dalfastmalo; Eight Hundred Cubed Plus Nineteen; Eight Hundred Cubed Plus Twenty-one; Elkomoelhago; Esteban Miranda; Flora Hawkes; Gefasto; Gofoloso; Jane; Janzara; Kalfastoban; Khamis; Komodoflorensal; Korak; Makahago; Meriem; Minuni; Obebe; Oratharc; Son of The First Woman; Talaskar; Tarzan; The First Woman; The Giant; The Second Woman; The Third Woman; Throwaldo; Torndali; Uhha; Usula; Vestako; Zertalacolols; Zoanthrohago; Zuanthrol

Summary: Esteban Miranda escapes the Obebe with the aid of the superstitious daughter of the witch doctor. After some time in the forest with him, she realizes that he is neither a demon nor Tarzan of the Apes. She knocks him over the head and runs away. This blow to the skull pushes the almost insane Miranda over the edge completely and he wanders about the jungle aimlessly.

At the Greystoke bungalow, and against his son's protests, Tarzan decides to take his first solo airplane flight after being taught how to fly by Korak. Over the Great Thorn Forest, his plane crash-lands and Tarzan is knocked out. Unconscious, he is discovered and carried off by a large muscular primitive female and taken to her cave village to be her mate. She places him in a walled structure which is a prison and nursery for her children. He regains consciousness inside it, then escapes with a youthful son of the female. In the jungle, Tarzan teaches the boy how to use and make weapons and stand up for himself against the larger domineering women in his society. From the youth, Tarzan learns the rudimentary sign language of his people.

While hunting alone, the Lord of the Jungle discovers an 18 inch tall man held captive by one of the large women. She is actually being attacked by the man's compatriots, who are just as small. Tarzan kills the woman and saves the little man who happens to be Komodoflorensal, the son of the Minuni king of Trohanadalmakus, and the greatest swordsman of his people. The Minuni are indebted to Tarzan and befriend him, and he travels with them to their city. There he is well received and learns their language and customs.

In the meantime the Son of The First Woman has gathered a great following of his fellow submissive and passive males, and is training them all in fighting and warfare. Now the tables are turned and they capture the larger women for their mates.

When the city of Trohanadalmakus is attacked by the rival city of Veltopismakus, Tarzan goes with his friends to fight. He believes he can easily subdue these diminutive men with a large tree branch. He is sorely mistaken, and is soon overwhelmed. When he comes to, he finds himself a prisoner and only as tall as the Minuni. He thinks that the entire people and the city have increased their size, but the opposite is true — he has been shrunk to their 18 inch size by a wizard. In addition, he is informed that he is a slave. In the slave quarters, he makes friends with a pretty slave girl named Talaskar. He also makes an enemy of another prisoner who likes Talaskar. He then discovers that Komodoflorensal is a prisoner as well, but is keeping his royal identity a secret.

When Tarzan meets the royal family of Veltopismakus, the beautiful princess, Janzara, desires him. But he does not return the feeling, and she is offended and angered. After Tarzan and Komodoflorensal make an escape, they rescue Talaskar who has been taken to be the wife of the guard of the slaves. The escapees then get involved with Janzara who has changed her ways: she wants to go with them and aid them in their escape. They all get out of the city and make a run for it, but are pursued. Just when it seems they will be overtaken, a group of the large Alali men and women come out of the woods and snatch them up. Tarzan recognizes the youth he helped and signs to him. The group's leader sees Tarzan doing this, and, after chasing away their pursuers, stops his people from harming any of the little people. In the city of Trohanadalmakus, Jan-

zara is given her freedom and Komodoflorensal and Talaskar are married.

Tarzan leaves. He makes it through the barrier of the Great Thorn Forest and changes back to his normal size, but is rendered unconscious by the transformation. In this state he is discovered by the Obebe witch doctor who takes him a prisoner and back to his village. The villagers attempt to torture him, but he escapes and heads home.

In the meantime, the crazed Esteban Miranda has been discovered by a Waziri warrior searching for his bwana. The warrior believes him to be Tarzan and escorts him back to Jane at the bungalow. She believes this mad man is her lost mate, and calls in a specialist to work on his mental disorder. Miranda is cured and, grasping the opportunity before him, decides to really play the part of Tarzan, to gain all that the Jungle Lord possesses including his wife. At this point, Flora Hawkes, who has returned to the Greystokes as a servant in good standing, recognizes Esteban Miranda and proclaims his imposture. The actor tries to deny what Flora has said and continue his charade. But then the real Tarzan, John Clayton, Lord Greystoke, enters and decides the matter once and for all.

11. Tarzan, Lord of the Jungle

Published in *Blue Book* magazine, December 1927 to May 1928, as *Tarzan, Lord of the Jungle*. Book published 1928, A.C. McClurg & Co.

Cast: Abd el-Aziz; Ateja; Batando; Bertram; (King) Bohun; Bolgani; (Princess) Brynilda; Bulland; Edward; el-fil; Fahd; Fejjuan; Galahad;

Gayat; (Prince) Gobred; Go-yad; (Princess) Guinalda; Guy; Hirfa; Jadbal-ja; James Hunter Blake; Malud; Michel; Morley; Motlog; M'walot; Naliny; Paul Bodkin; Peter Wiggs; Richard Montmorency; Sheik Ibn Jad; Simba; Tabo; Tarzan; Tollog; Toyat; Wilbur Stimbol; Willard; Zeyd; Zutho

Summary: A group of Arabs led by Sheik Ibn Jad search for a lost valley full of treasure and beautiful women. On the way they capture Tarzan, but the Jungle Lord is saved by Tantor. In the Arab camp the daughter of the Sheik, Ateja, is in love with the young Bedouin Zeyd, but a rival suitor, Fahd, attempts to get Zeyd out of the way by framing him for an attempted murder. Zeyd flees in fear of wrongful prosecution.

In a nearby part of the jungle, James Hunter Blake is on a safari with an older man named Wilbur Stimbol. While Blake is kind to the porters, Stimbol is abusive. He ultimately has a falling out with the younger man. With Tarzan's intervention they split the safari and go their separate ways. In no time, Stimbol's porters desert him and he wanders into the Arab camp. There he becomes an ally of the Arabs and helps plot to kill Tarzan. Blake, on the other hand, is almost struck by lightning and becomes lost. He eventually wanders to the entrance of the medieval Valley of the Sepulcher and is taken captive.

In the valley are castles, knights and princesses, and the population is divided into two rival groups. Despite Blake's peculiar outside ways, he makes friends among the people. He is accepted into their society and becomes a knight. He also wins the favor of the beautiful Princess Guinalda as well as the enmity of Sir Malud who challenges him to a duel. After winning the bout with his fencing ability and horse

riding skills, Blake does not kill Malud. This peculiar compassion and sportsmanship, which he displays on several other occasions, wins him praise and honor.

Tarzan is again captured by the Arabs, but escapes before Stimbol can kill him. He then tracks Blake down to the Valley of the Sepulcher, and is accepted eagerly into the medieval society because he is an English viscount. They dress Tarzan in the finery of the Middle Ages and escort him to where the great tournament is just ending between the two rival peoples of the valley. At the tournament, Guinalda is forcibly abducted by the knights from the other city who were just fighting in the tournament. Blake goes after them, and Tarzan follows.

About this time the Arabs find their way into the valley and easily take over one castle with their rifles while everyone is at the Great Tourney. Emboldened, they sweep further into the valley, but Tarzan and Blake help overthrow them. Some escape, though, and seize Princess Guinalda. They take her out of the valley, and both Blake and Tarzan pursue them.

Outside the valley, Fahd is killed by Zeyd and Guinalda is abducted by some Mangani who fight over her. Jadbal-ja, and then Tarzan, save her and take her back to the valley. Finally, Zeyd and Ateja are reunited, and Blake returns to the Valley of the Sepulcher to be with Guinalda.

12. Tarzan and the Lost Empire

Published in *Blue Book* magazine, October 1928 to February 1928, as *Tarzan and the Lost Empire*. Book published 1929, Metropolitan Books, Inc.

Cast: Appius Applosus; Axuch; Caecilius Metellus; Cassius Hasta; Claudius Taurus; Dilecta; Dion Splendidus; Dr. von Harben; Erich von Harben; Fastus; Favonia; Festivitas; Fulvus Fupus; Gabula; Go-yad; Goyat; Lukedi; Mallius Lepus; Maximus Praeclarus; Mpingu; Mulungu; Muviro; Nkima; Nyuto; Ogonyo; Rufinus; Sarus; Septimus Favonius; Son of Tabernarius; Sublatus Imperator; Tarzan; Zutho

Summary: The medical missionary Dr. von Harben enlists Tarzan's help in finding his son Erich who has gone to look for a lost civilization.

While exploring, Erich actually succeeds in finding a hidden valley that contains two rival cities both fashioned after ancient Rome. In the eastern city of Castra Mare he wins favor and is used as a scholar. There he meets Favonia, the beautiful daughter of his new patron, Septimus Favonius. They fall in love with each other, but Favonia has an unwelcome suitor by the name of Fulvus Fupus who is a dark, greasy conniving man. Fupus is jealous of Erich and wants him removed, and begins to spread rumors about him.

Searching for Erich, Tarzan, along with Nkima, enters the valley from the west end and is taken a prisoner in Castra Sanguinarius. There he is presented to Caesar and, after offending him, escapes the palace. The Jungle Lord swings through the trees of the city until he comes to a garden where a rat-faced man named Fastus is forcing himself upon the beautiful Dilecta. He repels Fastus and wins Dilecta's friendship. It is then that the officer, Maximus Praeclarus, arrives searching for the escaped Tarzan. Dilecta and Maximus are in love with each other. She explains how Tarzan protected her and says that she does not want him arrested. A grateful Maximus readily

complies and offers the Lord of the Jungle asylum in his house.

Tarzan enjoys himself there. Among other things, he learns to speak Latin from the mother of his host. But word leaks out about where he is, and Tarzan, Maximus Praeclarus and the whole of his household are arrested. Tarzan is put in a prison cell with Cassius Hasta, the heir to the throne of Castra Mare and a man liked by the citizens of both cities. From there the Ape-man is put in the Colosseum games, and wins them all. He then enlists the aid of six Mangani and makes an escape with Cassius Hasta and the remaining prisoners. They attack the palace where Dilecta is being blackmailed into marrying Fastus. Tarzan and his followers are nearly defeated, but the Waziri arrive after having been brought by Nkima.

Tarzan, Cassius and an army march on Castra Mare to find Erich von Harben. They meet little opposition and get Erich out of prison where he has recently been put as a result of Fupus's doing. After they unite the two cities, Cassius is made the ruler of both.

13. Tarzan at the Earth's Core

Published in *Blue Book* magazine, September 1929 to March 1930, as *Tarzan and the Earth's Core*. Book published 1930, Metropolitan Books, Inc.

Cast: Abner Perry; Avan; Carb; David Innes; Dorf; Gluf; (Lt.) Hines; Ja; Jana, the Red Flower of Zoram; Jason Gridley; Lajo; Lana; Maral; Muviro; M'wa-lot; Ovan; Rela; Robert Jones; Skruk; Tanar; Tar-gash; Tarzan; Thoar; Tomar; To-yad; Ulan; Victor; von Horst; (Capt.) Zuppner

Summary: The inventor of the Gridley Wave, Jason Gridley, comes to Tarzan to enlist his aid in going into the Earth's core to the primitive land of Pellucidar. He wants to rescue David Innes, the first Emperor of Pellucidar, from pirates. Tarzan agrees to go. A dirigible, the O-220, is constructed from a light but strong metal dubbed *Harbenite*, mined in the Roman land where Erich von Harben occasionally resides. Taking provisions, rifles, ten Waziri and several crew members, Gridley and Tarzan head to the north polar icecap and find a hidden entrance to Pellucidar.

Once in Pellucidar, they begin exploring, and Tarzan is in heaven. While exploring alone, though, he becomes lost, and is eventually captured by a tribe of ape-like men who speak the Mangani language. Tar-gash, one of the members of the tribe, aids Tarzan and they are both forced to flee. They travel together and meet up with a human named Thoar. All three journey together and help each other by sharing their skills, until Tarzan is carried away by a pteranodon.

After a while Jason Gridley goes with the Waziri and the crew member, von Horst, to look for the Ape-man. Gridley is separated from the others, then von Horst becomes lost. Despite the eternal noonday sun of Pellucidar — which makes it almost impossible to know directions — Gridley somehow makes it back to the O-220, then sets out in a small plane to search the area. While flying he is attacked by a pteranodon and has to parachute out of his wrecked craft. He reaches the ground just in time to save Jana, the beautiful Red Flower of Zoram, and sister of Thoar, from some attacking prehistoric men. Gridley and Jana travel together and fall in love. But due to his lack of knowledge of Pellucidarian courting habits and rituals, Jana is offended and runs away from him.

Tarzan succeeds in killing the giant flying reptile, the pteranodon, and escapes its high mountain nest. He then comes upon a cave dwelling youth and saves him from a giant bear. The youth, Ovan, befriends Tarzan and takes him to his village where he hopes his people will accept the Jungle Lord as a friend and ally. He is voted an enemy, however, and sentenced to be killed. He is imprisoned in a cave with Jana, the Red Flower of Zoram, who was captured after running away from Gridley. Tarzan and Jana escape together.

Gridley comes upon Thoar being attacked by a dinosaur, and uses his pistols to save him. He believes Thoar is Jana's lover, but despite this they become friends and travel together, and follow Jana's trail until they are captured by the Korsar pirates. The Korsars are then attacked and taken captive by the snake-men, the Horibs, and placed in an underground prison cavern until they are ready to be eaten. Not about to give up, Gridley and his fellows begin to dig their way toward freedom.

Coincidentally, Tarzan and Jana are also taken prisoner by a party of Horibs, and while being escorted back to the main village, Tarzan easily escapes into the trees. And after he finds his lost Waziri nearby, they all return and attack the Horibs with their guns, and save Jana. At this juncture, Gridley is discovered emerging from the ground, having escaped from his prison.

With the few pirates who are left, they decide to get on a boat and head to Korsar. On the way, they are overtaken by a fleet of ships manned by friends of David Innes who are going to attempt their own rescue. The two groups join forces and continue on.

When the searching O-220 arrives, the Emperor of Pellucidar is finally and successfully rescued, and without a single death. Gridley then decides to stay and search for the still missing von Horst. At this point, he learns that Thoar is actually Jana's brother. Gridley and the Red Flower of Zoram then announce their love for each other.

14. Tarzan the Invincible

Published in *Blue Book* magazine, October 1930 to April 1931, as *Tarzan, Guard of the Jungle*. Book published 1931, Edgar Rice Burroughs, Inc.

Cast: (Sheik) Abu Batn; Antonio (Tony) Mori; Bukula; Dareyem; Darus; Dogman; Dooth; Firg; Fodil; Ga-yat; Hajellan; Ibn Dammuk; Jadbal-ja; Kahiya; Kitembo ; La; Michael Dorsky; Miguel Romero; Nao; Nkima; Oah; Paul Ivitch; Peter Zveri; Raghunath Jafar; Tarzan; To-yat; Wamala; Wayne Colt; Zora Drinov; Zu-tho

Summary: A group of communists from various countries travels through Africa to seek the treasures of Opar with Arabs as their guides and guards. They are led by the Russian Peter Zveri and the beautiful Zora Drinov. When the American communist, Wayne Colt, arrives he saves Zora from rape at the hands of one of the party. Colt and Zora then develop feelings for each other.

Once they reach Opar a small party enters, but gets scared off. Wayne Colt, however, is captured and put in prison to be sacrificed. A young priestess named Nao falls in love with him and sets him free after giving him a knife.

Tarzan enters Opar and finds that La has been usurped and imprisoned by the high priest Dooth and the priestess Oah. The Jungle Lord finds La and they attempt to take back the throne, but fail. La still loves Tarzan and together they escape Opar. At one point, after going off to hunt, Tarzan does not return right away, and La feels he has abandoned her. She then disappears into the jungle alone and wanders into one of Peter Zveri's camps. There she and Zora become acquainted and Zora teaches her English.

The Arabs take a special interest in La, and when their leader, Sheik Abu Batn, has a falling out with Zveri, he deserts and takes La and Zora as prisoners. One of Abu Batn's men, Ibn Dammuk, also desires La and after getting a few faithful followers to go with him, he deserts Batn and takes La with him. Dammuk then attempts to rape La, but she kills him with his own dagger. Alone in the jungle, she runs into Jad-bal-ja who remembers her as an ally of his master and accompanies her.

After leaving Opar, Wayne Colt wanders near a camp and finds Abu Batn chasing Zora through the jungle. He kills the Arab with the Oparian knife, but he and Zora become lost in the jungle. When the two of them are on the brink of starvation, Colt goes off to hunt, and they become separated. Zora is then found and carried off by the Mangani king, To-yat. Tarzan arrives with Tantor and To-yat is scared off by the great pachyderm. Tarzan and Zora travel together and she develops feelings for the Jungle Lord. When he returns her to the camp of her communist friends, he is shot at and knocked out by a bullet grazing his head. The communists make him their prisoner, but he escapes with the help of Tantor and then Nkima, who has just returned from alerting the Waziri. The Lord of the Jungle then goes back to torment and harass the Russians.

La and Jad-bal-ja find Colt. The

American develops a fever, but La nurses him back to health. They become friends, and after she returns him to his camp, she heads back to Opar with Jad-bal-ja. In camp, Zora kills Zveri and denounces communism and says that she never really embraced it, but had been blackmailed into saying she had by Zveri. She and Colt, who it is revealed is also not a true communist, then announce their love for each other. Tarzan and his Waziri overtake La and Jad-bal-ja near Opar, and restore the high priestess to the throne.

15. Tarzan Triumphant

Published in *Blue Book* magazine, October 1931 to March 1932, as *The Triumph of Tarzan*. Book published 1932, Edgar Rice Burroughs, Inc.

Cast: Abraham, the Son of Abraham; (Lady) Barbara Collis; Danny "Gunner" Patrick; Dominic Capietro; Dongo; Elija, the Son of Noah; Eshbaal; Goloba; Isaza; Jobab; Jezebel; Kabariga; Joseph Stalin; Lafayette Smith, A.M., Ph.D., Sc.D.; Lamech; Leon Stabutch; Martha; Muviro; Ntale; Obambi; Ogonyo; (Lord) Passmore; Tarzan; Timothy; Zugash

Summary: Lady Barbara Collis flies solo over Africa and runs out of gas. She parachutes out and lands in the isolated land of Midian where fanatically religious epileptic people dwell. By the method of her arrival she is accepted as a messenger of deity, although some are skeptical. Barbara is immediately championed by the golden haired Jezebel, an unusually beautiful girl compared to the rest of the citizens. Barbara and Jezebel teach one another their languages. And Barbara learns that there is no known way out of the valley.

A young geologist from America, Lafayette Smith, decides to go on an expedition to Africa to look for rocks and study land formations. On the boat ride over he makes friends with a Chicago gangster named Danny "Gunner" Patrick who is in self-imposed exile. They decide to travel together. Gunner has a Thompson submachine gun with him, is uneducated and rough around the edges, but has a good heart.

Tarzan has been enlisted to help some distant natives fend off a slave-raiding band of *shiftas*. The *shiftas* are led by a communist Italian named Domini Capietro. He has recently been joined by the Russian communist Leon Stabutch who was sent to Africa by Joseph Stalin to wreak revenge on Tarzan for Peter Zveri's death and failure.

In Midian, Collis begins to have trouble as the people cease to believe she is a messenger of deity. And she and Jezebel are almost put to death several times by these religious fanatics. Smith, after meeting Tarzan, is studying the geology of the area alone, and accidentally finds an entrance to the land of Midian. He is forced to rescue Collis and Jezebel. They escape the South Midians, but are taken captive by the rival North Midians.

Tarzan is captured by Stabutch and Capietro, but is rescued by Gunner Patrick and his machine gun. Then Gunner is captured by the two communists, and Tarzan returns the favor and saves him. Tarzan and Gunner then follow Smith's trail and enter the land of Midian. The Ape-man goes on ahead and helps Smith and Collis escape after they become separated from Jezebel. Jezebel and Gunner meet up and fall in love, and Collis and Smith also fall in love. Tarzan takes Collis and Smith to his camp of Waziri where he is posing as a big hunter named Lord Passmore.

©1918 Edgar Rice Burroughs, Inc.

J. Allen St. John illustration for the *Tarzan and the Jewels of Opar* newspaper serialization (© 1918 Edgar Rice Burroughs, Inc.).

Jezebel is taken by the *shiftas*, and Stabutch and Capietro both desire her. They gamble for her and Stabutch loses, but kills Capietro to obtain the young girl. He then leaves the camp with her, but she escapes. Tarzan soon tracks Stabutch down and kills him. The Lord of the Jungle then goes off to search for Jezebel, but Gunner finds her. Tarzan is cornered by the remaining *shiftas* and taken captive, then Jezebel and Gunner are taken captive as well. Tarzan easily escapes from them, and goes to fetch his Waziri. Gunner and Jezebel free themselves from their bonds, and he discovers his machine gun hidden in the tent where they are being held captive. The Waziri then attack from without, and Gunner attacks from within. After a brief battle, the *shiftas* are defeated and the heroes are safely reunited.

16. Tarzan and the City of Gold

Published in *Argosy* magazine, March 12 to April 16, 1932, as *Tarzan and the City of Gold*. Book published 1933, Edgar Rice Burroughs, Inc.

Cast: Alextar; Althides; Belthar; Doria; Erot; Gemba; Gemnon; Hafimi; Jad-bal-ja; Maluma; M'duze; Nemone; Niaka; Phobeg; Phordos; Pindes; Tarzan; Thoos; Thudos; Tomos; Valthor; Xerstle

Summary: Tarzan saves a strangely dressed warrior from some *shiftas*. The warrior is named Valthor and he is from the lost city of Athne, the City of Ivory. They become friends, respecting each other's prowess. Tarzan travels with Valthor to the land of Athne and learns his language. Once in the valley they become separated during a storm and Tarzan is swept down a river until he is able to gain the shore. He is captured by warriors of Athne's rival, Cathne, the City of Gold, and put in a cell there.

Tarzan is then presented to Nemone, the beautiful but jealous queen of Cathne. She desires Tarzan and her beauty is intoxicating to the Jungle Lord. Nemone has a large lion named Belthar as a guard and pet which she feels she is spiritually linked to. Belthar does not like Tarzan. The queen also has around her an old black woman named M'duze who controls her almost completely. M'duze does not like Tarzan either — him, his presence or his influence.

Tarzan is put into some gladiator-like games and easily wins. He then gains favor with the queen and is given certain freedoms. In addition, he makes friends with a young noble named Gemnon who is assigned to be his roommate. The Jungle Lord makes a few enemies, too, who plot to kill him. Some of these enemies also plot against Gemnon, telling Nemone about his beautiful girlfriend, Doria. The vain and jealous queen puts Doria in prison to be sacrificed, because none in the realm may be more beautiful than she. Tarzan rescues Doria and hides her with some allies.

He then incurs Nemone's animosity and she sentences him to death in a lion manhunt. Belthar is sent after him, and the Jungle Lord is about to be caught and killed when Jad-bal-ja, who has tracked Tarzan to the valley, arrives and kills the royal lion. Nemone then commits suicide because of the link she believed she had with Belthar. Nemone's imprisoned brother, Alextar, is released and put on the throne.

17. Tarzan and the Lion Man

Published in *Liberty* magazine, November 1933 to January 1934, as *Tarzan and the Lion-Man*. Book published 1934, Edgar Rice Burroughs, Inc.

Cast: Ab el-Ghrennem; Abe Potkin; Anne Boleyn; Atewy; Balza; Benny Goldeen; Bill West; Billy Bourke; Catherine of Aragon; Catherine Parr; Clarence Noice; Cranmer; Cyril Wayne; Dan Puant; Duke of Buckingham; Eyad; Freeman Lang; God; Gordon Z. Marcus; Henry the Eighth; Howard; Jad-bal-ja; Jerrold Baine; Jimmy Stone; Joe; Kwamudi;

Major White; Malb'yat; Maya; Milton Smith; Mpugu; Naomi Madison; Pat O'Grady; Prince of Wales; Reece; Rhonda Terry; Rungula; Shorty; Stanley Obroski; Suffolk; Tarzan; Thomas Wolsey; Thomas Orman; (Father) Tobin; Walumbe

Summary: The cast and crew of a Tarzanlike picture are trying to shoot on location in Africa, while wading through the jungle in cannibal country. As guides and for security, the outfit has with them a band of Arabs led by Sheik Ab el-Ghrennem who thinks the foreigners are actually on a treasure hunt rather than creating make-believe for the screen.

The movie's director is Thomas Orman who drinks a lot and abuses the native porters. The pampered star of the show is Naomi Madison. Her look-alike stunt double is Rhonda Terry who is very athletic and likable. The Tarzanesque principal character in the *Lion Man* is to be played by marathoner Stanley Obroski whose resemblance to the Jungle Lord is uncanny, although Obroski is a coward and lazy.

The movie outfit's safari is set upon by cannibals several times. After many of the cast and crew are killed and the porters desert them, the survivors are separated from one another. During an ambush, Obroski runs off in fear and is taken captive by the cannibals.

Finally, because they cannot tell the two girls apart, the Arabs abduct both Naomi and Rhonda for the prop treasure map. The map turns out to be authentic, and after the Arabs get close to the treasure valley depicted on it, the women escape. Naomi is recaptured by the Arabs. But Rhonda goes on alone and is captured by English speaking gorillas and taken to their gorilla king, Henry the Eighth, in the Valley of Diamonds. Henry desires Rhonda for a wife even though he already has six. She is then presented to "God," originally a human but now half-man, half-gorilla because of the genetic longevity experiments he has conducted on himself. God desires Rhonda as well.

Tarzan rescues Obroski from the natives, but his look-alike gets a fever and eventually dies. The Jungle Lord also searches for the rest of the scattered movie outfit, and all who see him think he is Obroski. He lets them believe he is, so as not to taint the memory of their friend.

The Arabs attempt to enter the Valley of Diamonds but are killed outside it. But Naomi is captured and desired by Buckingham, one of the gorillas, who takes her to a nearby cave for himself. Tarzan arrives and saves her, though, and returns the actress to her movie friends who have tracked their missing colleagues to the base of the cliff outside of the valley. The Jungle Lord then finds his way into the Valley of Diamonds itself, and is captured and placed in a cell with Rhonda. They attempt an escape and are on the point of success when a fire breaks out.

During the fire, Rhonda is spirited out of the city by Henry the Eighth and taken across a plain. There he abandons her, and is attacked and killed by a lion. She is then taken by human, ape half-bloods with wild-gorilla minds. When Tarzan arrives he defeats their leader, Malb'yat, and rescues Rhonda. Balza, the beautiful English speaking mate of Malb'yat, believes she now belongs to Tarzan, and she doggedly accompanies him and Rhonda as they escape the rest of the tribe.

Tarzan takes both women to the movie company. He introduces Balza to the cast and crew and she easily makes friends among them and is taken in by them. The Jungle Lord continues to pretend that he is Obroski and makes the motion picture with them. Some time later Tarzan visits Hollywood and finds out what has happened to all those he knew and met on the *Lion Man* picture.

18. Tarzan and the Leopard Men

Published in *Blue Book* magazine, August 1932 to January 1933, as *Tarzan and the Leopard Men*. Book published 1935, Edgar Rice Burroughs, Inc.

Cast: Andereya; Bobolo; Gato Mgungu; Golato; Go-yat; Hiram "Hi"; Imba; Imigeg; Jerry Jerome; Jessie Jerome; Kali Bwana; Kapopa; Kid; Lobongo; Lulimi; Lupingu; Mumga; *muzimo*; Nkima; Nsenene; Nyalwa; Nyamwegi; Old Timer; Orando; Rebega; Sobito; Tarzan; The Spirit of Nyamwegi; Ubooga; Wlala; Zu; Zutho

Summary: Kali Bwana is in Africa searching for her brother when her safari enters the territory where the Secret Order of the Leopard Men are strongest. Kali's safari deserts her and she is left alone.

Nearby Tarzan is knocked out in a storm and pinned under a tree. He is discovered by a native warrior named Orando who at first wants to kill him, but then decides not to. The Jungle Lord awakens with amnesia, and Orando believes him to be his *muzimo*, or the guardian spirit of a dead ancestor. Tarzan, accepting this to be true, duly plays the part of the *muzimo*. Later, when his friend, Nyamwegi, is discovered slain by the Leopard Men, Orando also believes that Nkima, the Jungle Lord's little monkey companion, is Nyamwegi's *muzimo*. Orando swears vengeance upon the Leopard

Men. With the help of Tarzan, he organizes a strong force to go against them, and with the Ape-man by their side, they are confident. The only obstacle is the village witch doctor, Sobito, who is secretly a member of the Leopard Men. Sobito plots to foil their raid against his secret society especially after Tarzan affronts him.

Kali Bwana is eventually discovered by the elephant hunter, Old Timer, who is hunting away from his younger partner, Kid. Old Timer falls in love with Kali, and she with him, although they are not able to admit it completely to each other. She is then abducted by the Leopard Men, and Old Timer gives chase. In the Leopard Men's secret village and temple, Kali is prepared by the other priestesses to become their high priestess. A ceremony takes place, and during it, Old Timer is captured. He is aided in escaping, along with Kali, by a native chief named Bobolo, but Bobolo desires the girl for himself. During their escape, they are attacked by the Leopard Men and Old Timer is recaptured. This time Tarzan saves him from the temple, while Kali is taken by Bobolo and hidden in a pygmy village. Old Timer tracks her there.

Orando and Tarzan's native army win a battle against the Leopard Men and Tarzan regains his memory. He then makes his way to the pygmy village and secretly helps Old Timer rescue Kali Bwana. The Jungle Lord, however, is taken prisoner by the pygmies. But he is soon rescued by the Mangani.

Kali and Old Timer finally announce their love for each other. And when his younger companion, Kid, catches up with him, it is revealed that he is in fact the brother Kali Bwana has been searching for. His name is Jerry Jerome and hers is Jessie Jerome.

19. Tarzan's Quest:

Published in *Blue Book* magazine, October 1935 to March 1936, as *Tarzan and the Immortal Men*. Book published 1936, Edgar Rice Burroughs, Inc.

Cast: Alexis Sborov; Annette; Balando; Buira; Gupingu; Hazel (Strong) Tennington; Jane; Kavandavanda; Kavuru; Kitty (Krause) Sborov; Medek; Mem-sahib; Muviro; Naika; Neal "Chi" Brown; Nkima; Ogdli; Tarzan; Tibbs; Udalo; Ydeni

Summary: Jane and her friend Kitty who has married the Russian, Prince Sborov, are on a small plane that crash-lands in the jungle. The purpose of the flight was to take the Sborovs in search of a fountain of youth. With them are the Sborovs' two servants, Tibbs, the valet, and Annette, the French maid. Their pilot is the American, Neal Brown. Together the survivors forage through the jungle with the aid of the jungle craft Jane acquired from her husband.

In another part of the jungle, Tarzan, along with Muviro and several other Waziri, are hunting for Muviro's missing daughter. On the way they begin to hear stories about a tribe of white natives called the Kavuru who kidnap young girls. Alone Tarzan runs into a Kavuru warrior and saves him from a lion.

In Jane's camp dissension and disputations arise because of the pride and selfishness of Prince Sborov, and the fact that he begins to desire Jane and makes a play for her. Sborov then murders his complaining wife and tries to blame the pilot, Neal Brown, for it. Brown and Annette develop feelings for each other, and Tibbs becomes disgruntled. Jane and Annette are then both captured by a Kavuru, and are taken separately to his village. There Jane learns that the Kavuru

are all males who have eternal youth. They are led by a very good-looking man named Kavandavanda who believes he is godlike because of his perpetual life. The longevity elixir pills the Kavuru use are made from certain parts of the bodies of the young girls they capture and sacrifice, mixed with other things. Instead of sacrificing Jane, though, Kavandavanda desires her to be his mate and high priestess, and offers her eternal youth if she will acquiesce.

Tarzan meets up with those who remain from Jane's safari. Sborov runs off in fear and eventually goes crazy. He is then captured by the Kavuru, but eventually kills himself. Tarzan and the rest continue on to the Kavuru village, where the Waziri have already arrived and met with defeat. Neal Brown and Tarzan successfully start an abandoned airplane, fly it over the Kavuru village, and parachute out. The plane crashes and sets the village on fire. The Jungle Lord finds and kills Kavandavanda just before the Kavuru can kill Jane.

All the survivors escape and take with them a large number of the eternal youth elixir pills which they distribute equally among themselves, Nkima included.

20. Tarzan and the Forbidden City

Published in *Argosy* magazine, March 19 to April 23, 1938, as *The Red Star of Tarzan*. Book published 1938, Edgar Rice Burroughs, Inc.

Cast: Akamen; Atan Thome; (Queen) Atka; Brian Gregory; Brulor; Chemungo; Chon; Ga-un; (Mr.) Gregory; Helen Gregory; (King) Herat; Herkuf; Jacques Lavac; Lal Taask; Magra; Mbuli; Mentheb; Mesnek;

Mpingu; Ogabi; Paul d'Arnot; Tarzan; Thetan; Ungo; Wolff; Wong Feng; Zutho; Zytheb

Summary: Paul d'Arnot enlists Tarzan to head a safari for Helen Gregory and her father to search for her brother and his son, Brian Gregory. Brian and Tarzan, coincidentally, look a lot alike. This resemblance mistakenly causes some old and sinister acquaintances of Brian's to attempt to take the life of the Jungle Lord. These villains are after a map Brian left his sister which shows the way to Ashair, the Forbidden City, where a large diamond is to be found. Their leader is Atan Thome who has a beautiful female cohort named Magra who used to be in love with Brian.

Helen Gregory is kidnaped by Thome's men, and then the map is stolen by Wolff, one of Thome's spies among the Gregorys. Wolff also happens to be the Gregorys' hired hunter. With the map in hand, Atan Thome leads his safari toward the lost city. Tarzan and the Gregory safari — which has been infiltrated by the beautiful Magra as part of her cohort's sinister plan — take a plane to try and make up the distance Thome has gained. But the plane is forced down in the jungle where Tarzan has to provide for them all. When he saves Magra from a lion, she realizes that he is not Brian Gregory, and she starts to fall in love with him. And he soon realizes that Wolff is working against them.

Thome begins to like Helen Gregory, but she escapes and is captured by cannibals and tied to a stake. Tarzan saves her and returns her to her father and his safari, while Thome pushes on to Ashair. All of Thome's porters run away out of fear, and only he and his manservant, Lal Taask, remain. They are quickly taken prisoner by the Ashairians.

D'Arnot and Helen soon fall in love, but are taken prisoner by the Ashairians as well. D'Arnot is placed in a cage in the underwater temple of Brulor with a bearded and emaciated man. It is Brian Gregory and he is still alive. The temple is where the great diamond called the Father of Diamonds is supposed to be kept. Helen is forced into becoming the slave-mate of the key-master. But she kills him, takes his keys and releases the prisoners. But unfortunately, she is quickly recaptured.

Tarzan and the rest of the Gregory safari reach the valley of Tuen-Baka where the Forbidden City of Ashair is located. There Tarzan saves Thetan, a warrior of Thobos, the rival city of Ashair, from a small T-Rex. They make friends and Thetan takes them all to his city. But there, they are made prisoners. Tarzan wins his freedom and heads to Ashair.

In Ashair, Tarzan is taken prisoner. But he joins up with Helen and the two escape with the help of Herkuf, a captive high priest, who takes them into the lake in scuba suits. Along the lake bottom Herkuf finds the actual Father of Diamonds in a sunken ship. And Helen is taken by Chon, the true god, who has been in hiding with several of his followers.

In the meantime, Thetan helps Magra and Mr. Gregory leave Thobos, then organizes a naval attack against Ashair. But, close to Ashair, Magra and Gregory are taken by followers of Chon.

Atan Thome, looking after his own interests, throws Lal Taask to the wolves to get what he wants. He has his trusty servant attempt to assassinate the queen of Ashair so that he, Thome, can be thrown into the prison which he believes is next to where the Father of Diamonds is kept. He escapes from the prison, finds the chest containing the diamond, and takes it with him. Lal Taask escapes, too. He follows Thome and tries to kill him for his treachery. But Thome, who is now slightly insane, kills Taask instead. He then opens the chest and finds, not the Father of Diamonds, but a piece of ordinary coal. He promptly has a heart attack and dies.

Thetan arrives with the Thobotian navy, and with Tarzan's aid they are victorious over the Ashairians. Chon is then reinstated as the true god, and all the members of the Gregory safari are released.

21. Tarzan the Magnificent

Published as two separate stories: *Tarzan and the Magic Men* in *Argosy* magazine, September 19 to October 3, 1936, and *Tarzan and the Elephant Men* in *Blue Book* magazine, November 1937 to January 1938. Published together as *Tarzan the Magnificent* in 1939, Edgar Rice Burroughs, Inc.

Cast: Alextar; Daimon; Dyaus; Gemba; Gemnon; Gonfala; Hyark; Jane; Kamudi; Kandos; Lord; Lorro; Mafka; Menofra; (Lady) Mountford; (Lord) Mountford; Muviro; Phobeg; Phoros; Robert van Eyk; Spike; Stanley Wood; Tarzan; Thudos; Tomos; Troll; Valthor; Waranji; Woora; Zygo

Summary: Tarzan meets the American travel writer Stanley Wood wandering and starving in the jungle. The Jungle Lord saves Wood from a lion, then feeds him. He tells Tarzan of the Kaji warrior women village that is ruled by the tyrannical wizard Mafka who uses a large diamond called the Gonfal to control the minds and will of people. He also tells him about the beautiful queen of the Kaji named

Gonfala who he is in love with. Gonfala loves him, too, Wood says, but she has a dual personality.

After Wood is drawn back to the Kaji, Tarzan is taken prisoner by the Zuli, the rivals of the Kaji. The Zuli are also warrior women, and are ruled by Woora, the twin brother of Mafka. Rather than a diamond, Woora uses a giant emerald to control the minds and will of his people. But he is frustrated that his mind-controlling emerald does not work on Tarzan. While attempting to torture the Ape-man, Woora is killed by a prisoner named Lord who is an ally of Tarzan's. The Ape-man escapes and takes the Great Emerald of the Zuli with him. He soon discovers that he also can use it to control the minds of others.

Lord steals the emerald from him, though, and Tarzan is caught by the Kaji and taken prisoner. In their village, he meets Gonfala and Mafka, as well as Stanley Wood and his friends. At this point it is revealed that Lord was taken prisoner by Mafka and beheaded. Now Mafka has possession of both mystic jewels. Despite this Tarzan succeeds in overthrowing Mafka and taking possession of the Gonfal diamond and the Great Emerald of the Zuli. All the prisoners escape, including the members of Stanley Wood's safari and Gonfala who is in love with Wood.

But two of Wood's safari, Troll and Spike, take the jewels from Tarzan while he is asleep. Tarzan then takes Wood and Gonfala to his estate to live with him, but while out hunting Gonfala is captured by Spike and Troll who have lost one of the jewels. They have a dream of being rulers in their own land with Gonfala as their queen, but become jealous of each other and fight over Gonfala and the remaining jewel. Spike hits Troll so hard in the head that he is literally knocked silly. All three are then taken prisoner to Athne, the city of Ivory.

Tarzan follows them. He expects a friendly reception from the people of Cathne, who he once aided and befriended, but he is disappointed and they take him prisoner. He still has friends, however. With their help, he sets things right politically and goes on to Athne in the hope of a friendly reception there. But the City of Ivory is now ruled by usurpers, and Tarzan is again taken prisoner. Stanley Wood is also a prisoner in Athne, and he ends up getting married to Gonfala while there. Tarzan starts a revolt, and with the help of the Cathneans, he escapes and returns the ruling of the city to friendly hands.

22. Tarzan and the Foreign Legion

Book published 1947, Edgar Rice Burroughs, Inc., as *Tarzan and "The Foreign Legion."*
Cast: Alam; Alauddin Shah; Amat; Bill Davis; (Lt. Commander) Bolton; Carter Douglas; Corrie van der Meer; de Lettenhove; Dr. Reyd; Elsje van der Meer; Grotius; Hendrik van der Meer; Hideo Sokabe; Hoesin; Hooft; Hugo; Iskandar; Jerry Lucas; Joe "Datbum" Bubonovitch; John Clayton; Kanji Tajiri; Kenzo Kaneko; Kervyn van Prins; Keta; Kumajiro Tada; Lara; Lum Kam; Melrose; Oju; Sarina; Sing Tai; Tak van der Bos; Taku Muda; Tarzan; Tiang Umar; Tokujo Matsuo; Tony "Shrimp" Rosetti; Uglo; Vanda; Whale
Summary: The van der Meer family is pursued by the invading Japanese army in Sumatra in the Dutch East Indies. After much running, the only surviving family member is the 16-year-old daughter, Corrie. She is taken and protected by Sing Tai, the van der Meers' Chinese servant. Corrie and Sing Tai hide safely for two years until betrayed to the Japanese. She is taken captive, and Sing Tai is wounded and left for dead.

Tarzan, under the name of Col. John Clayton of the Royal Air Force, is accompanying an American B-24 bomber crew on a photographic mission over Sumatra when they are shot down into the jungle. Most parachute safely into the jungle. There Tarzan quickly changes into a G-string made from his silk parachute and takes control of the remaining men as they attempt to get through to the coast. On the way, Tarzan discovers Corrie, a prisoner of the Japanese. He rescues her and takes her back to his group. As they travel on, she and Captain Jerry Lucas of the B-24 fall in love.

Under Tarzan's direction all the members of his party learn to make primitive weapons to survive. Along the way, they encounter two separate bands of Dutch guerrillas: one friendly, the other not. The Ape-man's group takes in a girl named Sarina who has decided to break away from the bad guerrillas. She and Rosetti, another crew member, fall in love. As this mixture of people push on together, they fight the Japanese and successfully rescue two other survivors from their plane who were being held as prisoners of war. Once they make the coast, they are taken aboard a ship and head out to sea. On the water, they are shelled by a Japanese merchantman. At the last moment before annihilation, they are saved by a British submarine.

Tim Gaydos illustration for *Tarzan of the Apes* (© 1982 Edgar Rice Burroughs, Inc.).

23. Tarzan and the Mad Man

Book published 1964, Canaveral Press, Inc., as *Tarzan and the Madman*.
Cast: Alemtejo; Ali; Bill Gantry; Colin T. Randolph, Jr.; Cristoforo da Gama; Fernando; Francis Bolton-Chilton; Ga-un; God; Ivan Minsky; Kyomya; Mal-gash; Mutimbwa; Osorio da Serra; Pedro Ruiz; Pelham Dutton; Quesada; Rateng; Sancho; Sandra

Pickerall; Tarzan; The Man Who Thought He Was Tarzan; Tom Crump; Ungo; Zutho

Summary: A man who looks and acts like Tarzan, and claims to be him, has captured an Englishwoman named Sandra Pickerall. He is also known to have carried off women and children from the tribes friendly to the Ape-man. A safari led by Pelham Dutton — the man in love with Sandra — is searching for the Englishwoman. At the same time, the real Tarzan has set out to find the person who has claimed his identity, so that he may kill the impostor. Sandra escapes from the Man Who Thought He Was Tarzan, but is captured by cannibals. The real Tarzan saves her and escorts her to the Dutton safari. She is then taken from them by the false Tarzan. And the real Jungle Lord saves Dutton from a lion. The Englishman believes that Tarzan is the impostor, though, and considers him mentally unstable. Dutton gets away from the Ape-man and is also taken by cannibals. Tarzan saves him again.

The Man Who Thought He Was Tarzan takes Sandra to the lost Portuguese city of Alemtejo where he is considered to be God. Sandra is to be his mate and a goddess, and for her own safety she plays along. She then begins to be attracted to God and talks to him. God, for his part, regrets abducting her and, in restitution, helps her escape. He also begins to fall in love with her. As they leave they are taken captive by a rival city of Moslems.

Tarzan and Dutton follow Sandra to Alemtejo but are separated there. Dutton is taken captive by the Moslems as well. But he escapes from them, with God and Sandra. As the trio travels through the jungle, they are attacked by great apes and Dutton is killed.

With the help of the favorite son

of Alemtejo, the nobleman, Osorio da Serra, Tarzan pretends to be their true god. He backs da Serra in a revolution against the current rulers of Alemtejo, at the successful conclusion of which, the nobleman becomes king. Tarzan, as the true god, takes Francis Bolton-Chilton, an English prisoner, as his slave and leaves Alemtejo. With Bolton-Chilton, he continues tracking Dutton, Sandra, and the Man Who Thought He Was Tarzan, alias God.

After Sandra and God realize they are in love with each other, the real Tarzan arrives ahead of Bolton-Chilton and prepares to kill the man who was impersonating him. But Sandra talks him out of it. And when Bolton-Chilton arrives soon after, he recognizes the Man Who Thought He Was Tarzan as a lost friend. His real name is Colin T. "Rand" Randolph, Jr., and he lost his memory in a parachuting accident.

It is then explained that Rand was obsessed with the Tarzan character and bet Bolton-Chilton that he could live like his idol for a month in Africa. Bolton-Chilton took the bet. While the two were flying over Africa, they developed problems with their plane and were forced to bail out. Rand landed in the city of Alemtejo, but he hit the castle wall on the way down, which caused the amnesia. When he awoke, he could remember nothing but the concept of Tarzan, and so thought he was the Jungle Lord. The Alemtejos made him God because of his ostensibly divine descent into their land.

Sandra, Rand, Bolton-Chilton and Tarzan search for the plane. When they find it still intact, they take off in it and fly away.

24. *Tarzan and the Castaways*

Published as three separate stories: *Tarzan and the Jungle Murders* in *Thrilling Adventures* magazine, June 1940; *Tarzan and the Champion*, in *Blue Book* magazine, April 1940; and *The Quest of Tarzan* in *Argosy* magazine, August 23 to September 6, 1941. Published together as *Tarzan and the Castaways* in 1964, Canaveral Press.

I   Tarzan and the Castaways
Cast: Abdullah Abu Néjm; Algernon "Algy" Wright-Smith; Asoka; (Capt.) Bolton; Chal Yip; Chand; Che, Lord Forest; Chuldrup; Cit Coh Xiu; (Dr.) Crouch; Fritz Krause; Hans de Groote; Itzl Cha; Jabu Singh; Janette Laon; Larsen; Lum Kip; Oubanovitch; Patricia Leigh-Burden; Penelope Leigh; Tarzan; Thak Chan; Tibbet; Wilhelm Schmidt; William Leigh; Xatl Din

Summary: After a brain lesion leads to aphasia and a loss of his ability to speak or understand language, Tarzan is caught by Abdullah Abu Néjm and sold to Fritz Krause to be put in a traveling wild animal show. The Jungle Lord is placed in a cage aboard Krause's ship which immediately sets sail on the Pacific. Most of the crew is cruel to Tarzan except for the first mate, Hans de Groote, and the only female on board, Janette Laon. Janette wants the Ape-man's bonds cut. As a mean-spirited joke, she is made to do it herself, despite her fears of this "wild man."

The second mate, Wilhelm Schmidt, leads a successful mutiny and puts de Groote in a cage. After Janette spurns Schmidt's advances, she is put into the cage with the Ape-man, who is kind to her. He then recovers from the aphasia and communicates with her.

Schmidt pirates a yacht with the Leigh family on it. The whole family and crew are brought on board the larger ship and put into cages. When the vessel is hit by a hurricane Tarzan escapes, and, with the help of de Groote, succeeds in retaking the ship. He puts the yacht's captain and de Groote in charge of the sailing, and has Krause, Schmidt, and Néjm put into cages along with the rest of their followers. The fury of the storm breaks the ship's rudder and they drift near a corral reef surrounding an island. While attempting a landing, they get stuck on the reef and the vessel is shivered. The Jungle Lord releases all the caged animals including a lion and some elephants. Then they abandon ship and make the beach.

On the beach Tarzan separates the humans into two groups. He makes Schmidt, Krause, Néjm and their wicked followers go a safe distance off without weapons, to make their camp. The Leigh family, Janette, de Groote and other faithful crew members make up Tarzan's camp with him.

When Tarzan goes exploring, he comes upon a native Mayan hunter. After the Ape-man saves him from a lion, the Mayan thinks he is one of his gods named Che, Lord Forest. He takes Tarzan to his city, Chichen Itza, which is ancient Mayan in design and culture. Even though he cannot speak their language, the Jungle Lord is escorted in and presented to their leaders. He saves a young maiden, Itzl Cha, from sacrifice and takes her back to his camp for safety.

The care and education of Itzl Cha are entrusted to Patricia Leigh-Burden. Itzl Cha teaches both Tarzan and Patricia the Mayan language while she learns English. During this time Itzl Cha falls in love with Tarzan, and is jealous of Patricia who has fallen in love with him as well. When he goes into the jungle to explore, Patricia stubbornly follows. She is taken captive by the Mayans and desired by their king.

Back at the camp, Krause, Schmidt, and Néjm decide to steal supplies and weapons from Tarzan's camp. They succeed because the men of Tarzan's camp are in the jungle looking for Patricia. They also abduct Janette. When de Groote and the other men return, they follow the thieves back to their camp. But Tarzan arrives first and kills Schmidt and Krause with his arrows and rescues Janette. De Groote and his men soon get there and kill Néjm and some others.

The Jungle Lord then goes looking for Patricia. In her jealousy, Itzl Cha runs to Uxmal to warn them that Tarzan is coming for the captive white girl. Tarzan is consequently captured. Patricia plays up the belief that Tarzan is a god to try and save them both. He is put to the test: in order to prove his godliness, he must survive in a crater of water for a whole morning. This he easily does, and they are satisfied as to his divinity. He and Patricia ultimately make a grand exit, courtesy of Tantor, the elephant.

Back at camp, Tarzan informs Patricia that he is married and that her love for him must go unreturned. The previously pirated Leigh yacht then comes to the island, and they are rescued.

II   Tarzan and the Champion
Cast: Babangos; Joey Marks; Melton; Muviro; Nkima; "One Punch" Mullargan; Tarzan
Summary: "One Punch" Mullargan is declared the heavyweight boxing champion of the world, and the title goes to his head. He takes a break from boxing and goes on an animal hunting safari with his manager, Joey

Marks. In Africa Mullargan ruthlessly slaughters herds of beasts with a machine gun. Tarzan hears of it and goes after him. When they meet and fight, to the amazement of both Mullargan and Marks, the Jungle Lord gets the better of the champion. Before the fight can be finished, though, they are attacked by the Babangos cannibal tribe and all taken prisoner.

While being prepared for dinner, they escape, but Mullargan and Marks are retaken. Tarzan then helps them escape again, after saving them from a lion that made its way into the village. Nkima the monkey has summoned the Waziri, and when they arrive, they rout the Babangos. Tarzan tells Mullargan and Marks never to come to Africa again. At this point, Marks offers to make Tarzan the next heavyweight champion of the world and be his manager. Tarzan simply leaves them.

III   Tarzan and the Jungle Murders:
Cast: Barbara Ramsgate; Cecil Giles-Burton; Chemungo; Duncan Trent; Gerald Gault; (Col.) Gerald Giles-Burton; Horace Brown; John Ramsgate; Joseph "Joe the Pooch" Campbell; Mary Graham; Mpingu; Nikolai Zubanev; (Mr.) Petersen; Pierce; Pilot Number One; Pilot Number Two; Romanoff; Sergei Godensky; (Mr.) Smith; Tarzan; Tomlin; (Lt.) Torlini; Violet
Summary: Tarzan discovers two planes downed near each other in the jungle and follows the trails of the survivors. One plane was flown by Lt. Cecil Giles-Burton who had recovered the plans of an invention of military importance and was taking them to his father stationed in Africa. The other plane carried Nikolai Zubanev and Joseph "Joe the Pooch" Campbell who were pursuing Giles-Burton for the plans. The two craft had shot each

other down. Giles-Burton wanders through the jungle with the plans until he stumbles upon the Ramsgate photographic safari which has joined the Romanoff hunting safari. The combined safaris have also been recently joined by two other lost men named Smith and Petersen. Giles-Burton is an old friend of the Ramsgates, but gets on the bad side of several men of the safari, and one morning is found murdered in his tent. The plans are missing.

Tarzan arrives and is not treated very kindly. Then Petersen ends up murdered and Tarzan is framed for it. The Jungle Lord escapes and goes to a military headquarters and talks to Col. Giles-Burton. A force of men is sent with Tarzan back to the camp of the two safaris.

The people try to convince the military that Tarzan is the murderer, but they are silenced as he solves the murders with his jungle lore and tracking abilities. Smith is uncovered as the murderer of both men, although Petersen was his accomplice in the Giles-Burton's murder. It is also revealed that Smith is really "Joe the Pooch" Campbell and Petersen was Nikolai Zubanev. Campbell is found to have the missing plans with him.

Tarzan and the Tarzan Twins

This is the title of the 1963 Canaveral Press edition that combined the two short stories *The Tarzan Twins* and *Tarzan and the Tarzan Twins with Jad-bal-ja the Golden Lion*. *The Tarzan Twins* was published in 1927 (P.F. Volland Co.) and fell between *Tarzan and the Ant Men* and *Tarzan the Invincible*. *Tarzan and the Tarzan Twins with Jad-*

bal-ja the Golden Lion was printed in 1936 (Whitman Publishing Co.) and fell between *Tarzan the Invincible* and *Tarzan and the Lost Empire*. These are the only stories Burroughs wrote expressly for a juvenile audience, and they are not usually included in or considered a part of the Tarzan series.

Cast: Blk; Bulala; Dick; Doc; Galla Galla; Gretchen von Harben; Gulm; Intamo; Jad-bal-ja; (Dr.) Karl von Harben; Kla; Muviro; Natando; Paabu; Tarzan; The Man; Ukundo; Ulp; Zopinga

Summary: Dick is born in England on the same day that Doc is born in America. Their mothers are identical twins and consequently the cousins, Dick and Doc, look very much alike except Dick has black hair and Doc blond. Regardless, once their classmates learn that Dick's English father is a cousin of Tarzan of the Apes, the two boys are dubbed the Tarzan Twins. Desiring to live up to their nickname Dick and Doc exercise and practice tree climbing.

At the age of 14 they are invited to spend a few months at Tarzan's African estate. During the train ride through the dark continent, the train is derailed. The two curious boys wander off into the jungle and become lost. There they hone their tree climbing skills to avoid the larger carnivores, but are captured by cannibals.

In the cannibal village the Twins befriend two native prisoners and learn to speak the cannibal dialect from them. In front of the chief Doc performs some magic tricks and impresses the superstitious natives with his big medicine. The Twins are still kept as prisoners to be fattened up for the pot, but they are given an unusual amount of freedom because of the respect and fear the natives have for Doc's magic. This makes the village witch doctor,

Intamo, jealous and he tries to disprove Doc's abilities. Intamo then attempts to poison the boys, but a native youth warns them. All four prisoners escape together, but are pursued by the cannibals. Luckily, Tarzan and 50 Waziri arrive and save the Twins from recapture.

While at the Greystoke estate awaiting their luggage, the boys — armed and dressed as primitively as Tarzan — meet Jad-bal-ja, and go exploring in the jungle with the Ape-man and the Golden Lion. At one point Tarzan goes ahead to investigate something and leaves the boys in Jad-bal-ja's care. The boys get nervous around the lion and climb a tree. While waiting for Tarzan to return a violent storm breaks out and Jad-bal-ja wanders away. Dick and Doc then attempt to head back to the Greystoke bungalow, but become lost again.

Along the way they come across 20 outcast priests of Opar who are heading to a new temple site with a captive 12-year-old white girl who they are forcing to be their new high priestess. The Twins decide to rescue the girl and succeed in getting her away from the priests with the unintentional help of a disgruntled priest. Unfortunately they are overtaken by the Oparians and Dick and the girl, Gretchen von Harben, are taken prisoner, but Doc avoids capture. Following the party, Doc begins systematically shooting his arrows at the priests from the trees and kills them one by one.

Before Doc can effect a rescue, the priests reach the new temple site and construct a makeshift altar where Gretchen is forced to sacrifice Dick to the Flaming God. Unable to go through with the sacrifice, Gretchen swoons and the reigning high priest of the group, Gulm, continues the ceremony. But the Golden Lion and Tarzan arrive — having picked up the boys' spoor and followed it to the spot — and Jad-bal-ja attacks the high priest and kills him before any harm can befall Dick. Gretchen is then reunited with her father, Dr. Karl von Harben, who is a missionary and has been relentlessly searching for his missing daughter.

Tarzan: The Lost Adventure

This work started as an incomplete manuscript found in Edgar Rice Burroughs' safe after his death. It was finished by Joe R. Lansdale and first published by *Dark Horse Comics* in a four-part illustrated pulp magazine-like series in January–April 1995. It finally made book form in 1996.

Cast: Billy; Cannon; Charles Talent; Ebopa, the Stick That Walks, and the Undying God of Ur; Elbert Small; Eugene Hanson; Gerooma; Go-lot; Gromvitch; Hunt; Jad-bal-ja; Jean Hanson; Jeda; Kurvandi; Meredonleni; Miltoon; Nkima; Nyama; Tarzan; Wilson Jones; Zu-yad

Summary: A group of evil men led by Wilson Jones are on safari in Africa. They take over the safari of Eugene Hanson and his daughter, Jean, who are searching for the Mangani and the fabled lost city of Ur. Tarzan discovers the Hansons alone, and after saving them from some Mangani, he pursues Wilson Jones and his cohorts. Tarzan fights Jones and his men and handily wins. He then returns the safari to the Hansons.

Jones' group comes upon a safari that is searching for the Hansons and takes it over. They capture Tarzan and tie him to a tree to die a slow death. He escapes, though, and meets up with one of the escaped friends of the Hansons' named Hunt. Tarzan and Jad-bal-ja take Hunt to a cave for safety, and the Jungle Lord leaves the Golden Lion to guard him while he searches for Hunt's friends. The cave has ancient writings on the walls and contains many artifacts.

The Hanson safari is attacked by warriors of Ur and Jean is taken captive while her father and the others are left for dead. Eugene does not die, however, and he and his faithful askari, Billy, continue on together. But they are captured and tortured by Jones and his ruthless cohort Cannon. The two then escape and take Jones and Cannon captive. Billy wreaks revenge on Cannon by killing him.

Jean's guard is a female warrior named Jeda who plays cruel jokes upon her and who Jean develops a deep hatred for. In Ur, Jean is presented to King Kurvandi. He is a very tall man who bathes in human blood and kills without conscience. Kurvandi decides to put Jean in the gladiator-like games against Jeda.

Tarzan finds his way to Ur as do Hanson, Billy, and Wilson. The Ape-man is captured and also made ready for the arena. In the games, Jeda is overconfident and Jean is able to use that to kill the female warrior. Tarzan also wins his match.

Hunt wanders around his cave and falls into a pit. At the bottom of it, he discovers many interconnecting chambers and tunnels. Jad-bal-ja follows him, and something else follows the both of them. It is a giant praying mantis known as Ebopa, the Undying God of Ur, or the Stick That Walks. It pursues them until all three are forced through a sewer opening into Kurvandi's arena box during the games. Jad-bal-ja, unable to inflict a wound on Ebopa, attacks and kills Kurvandi. But Tarzan confronts the Stick That Walks.

The creature fights with a style of martial arts that Tarzan recognizes, and he is able to defend himself against the giant insect and counterattack. For the first time in its life, Ebopa is wounded. As a consequence, the Undying God of Ur retreats and heads for the packed stands. The audience panics and flees in terror. Jean, Hunt and Jad-bal-ja escape the city, but Tarzan pursues Ebopa into the caves beneath. In all the commotion, the city catches fire and collapses into the labyrinth of tunnels Tarzan and Ebopa have just gone into. In the dark passages, Tarzan finds Ebopa in time to watch it die. He also meets Ebopa's baby. He then realizes that the one Undying God of Ur is not "undying" at all — there is merely a succession of different insects, each the offspring of the one that preceded it.

Knowing that he cannot now regain the surface, the Ape-man decides to follow the newborn Ebopa down a tunnel that may lead to Pellucidar.

The Eternal Savage (Lover)

Although not a true Tarzan story, this book has John Clayton, Lord Greystoke (Tarzan), and his family at their African estate entertaining Barney Custer and his sister, Victoria. Barney Custer is a character from Burroughs' non–Tarzan adventure, *The Mad King*. *The Eternal Savage* is set in the time between *The Return of Tarzan* and *The Beasts of Tarzan*, and contains the first appearance of Tarzan and Jane's son, Jack.

Published in *All-Story* magazine, March 7, 1914, as *The Eternal Lover*. Book published 1925, A.C. McClurg & Co.

Cast: Abdul Mukarram; Aht;

Frank Hoban illustration for *Tarzan the Invincible* (© 1930 Edgar Rice Burroughs, Inc.).

Barney Custer; Brown; (Lt.) Butzow; Dag; Esmeralda; Gron; Hud; Ibn Aswad; Jack Clayton; Jane Clayton, Lady Greystoke; John Clayton, Lord Greystoke; Lu-tan; Nat-ul; Nu; Nu, the son of Nu; Old Raffles; Ra-el; Scrab; Terkoz; Tha; Throk; Tur; Una; Victoria Custer; William Curtis

Summary: Nu, the son of Nu, a troglodyte of the Niocene period of Earth's history, hunts a saber-toothed tiger to prove he is worthy of Nat-ul, the cavewoman he loves and desires. Nat-ul loves and desires Nu in return. Nu, the son of Nu has a successful hunt, and kills and decapitates the eater of men, Oo, the saber-toothed tiger. While in a cave, however, an earthquake strikes and knocks Nu out.

In the present day period, Victoria Custer and her brother Barney are

visiting the Greystokes' African estate. Victoria has a phobia for mice and anything to do with earthquakes. Every time she is near or caught in an earthquake, she has dreams about a large caveman from another long ago age. After she wakes, she feels a hopeless longing and loss for this unknown primitive. Because of this haunting feeling, she has never married, even though she is young, healthy and beautiful. Just then at the Greystokes', an earthquake strikes, and Victoria passes out.

She awakens a short time later and is inexplicably drawn to a nearby cave. There she discovers Nu, the son of Nu, unconscious but intact after being hermetically sealed for the past 100,000 years. While tending to him she goes to retrieve water from a nearby stream and is abducted by Arabs. Nu, the son of Nu, regains full consciousness and emerges from his cave into a strange and tamer time. But he remembers Victoria nursing him. While searching for Victoria, who he thinks is his Nat-ul of the Niocene, Nu looks around the Greystoke estate where he is shot by a rifle. He is then taken in and cared for by the Greystokes.

Barney believes Nu is the man from his sister's dreams, and they all believe he is linked to Victoria's disappearance. Once Nu recovers from his wounds and learns the English language, he goes after Victoria, and Tarzan, Barney and a few others follow a little later. Nu overtakes Victoria and rescues her from an Arab. Then, somehow, surreally, she becomes Nat-ul and the two of them are together back in the Niocene period of the Earth's history.

In the Niocene, Nat-ul is abducted by a rival caveman, but she kills him and escapes. While she is gone, Nu, the son of Nu, goes after her and is always just a step behind her. When Nat-ul is chased by a Boat Builder, she is taken to an island by a Pterodactyl, but Nu follows. After several captures, rescues, and escapes Nu and Nat-ul are reunited and living safely back in their village. Nu again goes out to kill Oo, the eater of men, to prove his love for Nat-ul and that he is worthy of her. She tries to dissuade him, but he insists. While he is gone, there is another earthquake.

Back in the present time, it is just moments after Victoria passed out from the initial earthquake at the Greystoke estate. Upon awakening, a curious Victoria goes unerringly to the cave Nu was originally knocked out in, which is not far from the Greystoke estate. There she and her brother find the skeleton of a large caveman with the skull of a saber-toothed tiger nearby.

Index